THE YEARS OF HOPE

THE YEARS OF HOPE
Cambridge, Colonial Administration in the South Seas and Cricket

Philip Snow

The Radcliffe Press
London · New York

Published in 1997 by
The Radcliffe Press
An imprint of I.B.Tauris & Co Ltd
Victoria House
Bloomsbury Square
London WC1B 4DZ

175 Fifth Avenue
New York
NY 10010

In the United States of America
and Canada distributed by
St Martin's Press
175 Fifth Avenue
New York
NY 10010

A full CIP record for this book is available from the British Library

A full CIP record for this book is available from the Library of Congress

ISBN 1–86064–147–4
Library of Congress Catalog card number: available

Copy-edited and laser-set by Oxford Publishing Services, Oxford
Printed and bound in Great Britain by WBC Ltd, Bridgend, Mid Glamorgan

For
the chiefs and the variety of people of the islands,
returning affection,
and for
Anne
who shared much of what is told here.

Contents

Illustrations

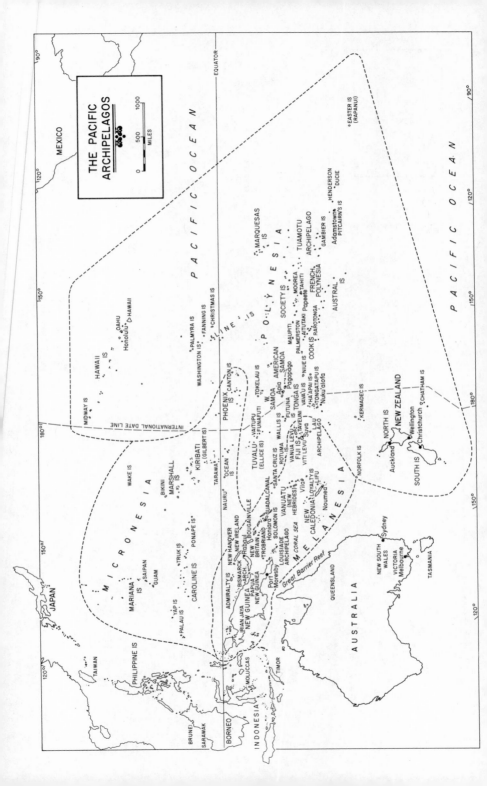

THE PACIFIC ARCHIPELAGOS

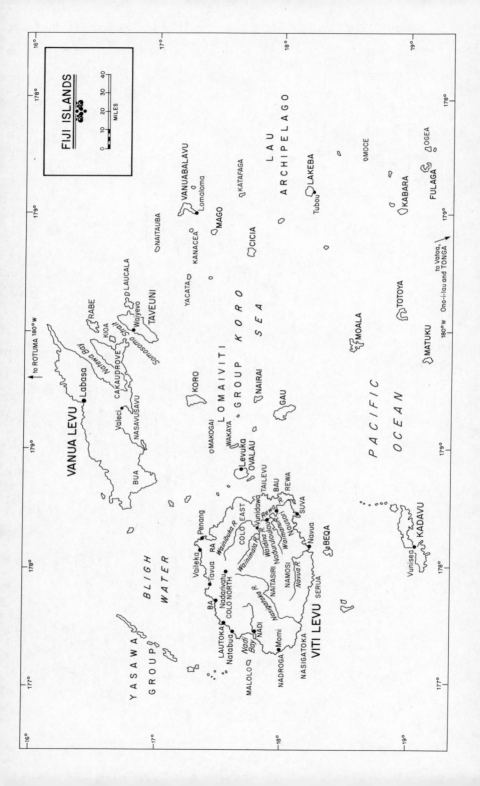

Abbreviations

ACS	Assistant Colonial Secretary
ADC	Aide-de-Camp
AM	Member of the Order of Australia
ANA	Adviser on Native Affairs
ARP	Air-Raid Precautions
BA	Bachelor of Arts
BG	Bridge Guard
BP	Burns, Philp (South Sea) Company Ltd
CBE	Commander of the Order of the British Empire
CC	Cricket Club
CCU	Civil Construction Unit
CH	Companion of Honour
CID	Criminal Investigation Department
CJ	Chief Justice
CMG	Companion of the Order of St Michael and St George
CMS	Central Medical School
CPM	Colonial Police Medal
CS	Colonial Secretary
CSO	Colonial Secretary's Office
CSR	Colonial Sugar Refining Company
CVO	Commander of the Royal Victorian Order
CWMH	Colonial War Memorial Hospital
DC	District Commissioner
DCMG	Dame Commander of the Order of St Michael and St George
DDT	dichlorodiphenyltrichloroethane
DFC	Distinguished Flying Cross
DMS	Director of Medical Services
DO	District Officer

DPW	Director of Public Works
DSO	Distinguished Service Order
FRCO	Fellow of the Royal College of Organists
FRS	Fellow of the Royal Society
FS	Financial Secretary
GBE	Knight *or* Dame Grand Cross of the Order of the British Empire
GCMG	Knight *or* Dame Grand Cross of the Order of St Michael and St George
GCVO	Knight *or* Dame Grand Cross of the Royal Victorian Order
GH	Government House
GM	George Medal
GPH	Grand Pacific Hotel
HE	His Excellency
HMNZS	His (*or* Her) Majesty's New Zealand Ship
JP	Justice of the Peace
KBE	Knight Commander of the Order of the British Empire
KCB	Knight Commander of the Order of the Bath
KCMG	Knight Commander of the Order of St Michael and St George
KCVO	Knight Commander of the Royal Victorian Order
l.b.w.	leg before wicket
LVO	Lieutenant of the Royal Victorian Order
MA	Master of Arts
MB	Bachelor of Medicine
MBE	Member of the Order of the British Empire
MC	Military Cross
MCC	Marylebone Cricket Club
MH	Morris Hedstrom Ltd
MOF	mattress on floor
MRCS	Member of the Royal College of Surgeons
MVO	Member of the Royal Victorian Order
NMP	Native Medical Practitioner
NSM	Native Stipendiary Magistrate
OBE	Officer of the Order of the British Empire
P & O	Peninsular and Oriental Shipping Company
PC	Provincial Commissioner
Ph.D.	Doctor of Philosophy
p.p.c.	*pour prendre congé*

Abbreviations

PRAI	President of the Royal Anthropological Institute
PWD	Public Works Department
QVS	Queen Victoria School
RAF	Royal Air Force
RMA	Royal Military Academy
RNZAF	Royal New Zealand Air Force
RSPCA	Royal Society for the Prevention of Cruelty to Animals
VC	Victoria Cross

Glossary of Fijian Words (and other languages where indicated)

Adi	title of rank for a woman, Lady
agora	marketplace (Greek)
bilo	coconut cup
bulamakau	bull or cow, meat
Buli	district head
bure	house totally made of thatch
cakau	reef
cavuikelekele	ceremony of going to meet a chief, inviting him to take up his anchors and come closer to shore
cere	custom of racing after long ribands of *tapa*
dalo	root vegetable (taro)
dhoti	white cloth pulled up between the legs by Indians (Hindi)
draunikau	witchcraft
duo-o-o	formal acclamation of thanks in ceremony for a chief
Hakim sahib	Doctor, sir, administrator (Hindi)
i luva ni tawake	whale's tooth offered as a request for the war flag on a chief's craft to be lowered (only in Lau)
i sosomi	representative or successor
i Taukei ni Waluvu	Owner of the Floods
i vono	ceremony in which a man waddles on his knees to place two green coconuts before a chief guest (only in Lau)
kai loma	Euronesian, part-European
kava	drink prepared from *yaqona* roots (Polynesian)
khubutar sahib	pigeon gentleman (Hindi)
Kovana	Governor

Glossary of Fijian Words

lali	hollowed-out wooden drum
magimagi	thinned-out coconut fibre used for tying and decorating house rafters and canoe decks
magiti	presentation of food
mana	prestige, ritual authority
matanivanua	eyes of the land, herald
megass	waste from the refining of sugar (derivation unknown)
meke	Fijian dance
mimimata	member of the giant praying mantis family
pikeu	zigzag
poi	kind of dance in flax skirts using twisted, suspended balls of flax (Maori)
pugree	turban (Hindi)
punkah	wide stretch of canvas suspended from a roof (Hindi)
punkah-walla	person who swings a *punkah* to generate cool air (Hindi)
qaloqalovi	ceremony offering a whale's tooth taken to a vessel as a welcome for going ashore (sometimes performed on land)
qiri kapa	beating the tins
raikoro	village inspection
Ranadi	Queen
rara	village green
Ratu	chief, Sir
reguregu	ceremony in which a whale's tooth is presented to a mourning family
Roko Tui	Government head of a province
roqo tabakau	presentation by two crawling men of strips of mats made of coconut palm leaves (only in Lau)
sevusevu	presentation of *yaqona*
sulu	skirt
tapa	decorative cloth handmade from tree bark
taralala	form of dance
taro	root vegetable
tauvu	ancestral founders
topee	sun helmet (Hindi)
Tui	king
Tui Cakau	King of the Reefs
Tui Lau	King of Lau

turaga ni koro	village head
vakamamaca	presentation of folds of mats representing a change into dry clothes after nautical discomforts
vakatunaloa	temporary structure of palm leaves ornamented with hibiscus and crotons
vakaturaga	chiefly
vale ni mate	house of death
vale ni veivakabulai	house of health, hospital
vale ni vo	house of the po, lavatory
Vunivalu	title of high rank
yaqona	shrub of the pepper family, the roots of which when powdered are strained and mixed with water to form the ceremonial and social drink, *kava*
yaqona vakaturaga	chiefly ceremony accompanied by archaic chanting in which *kava* is mixed and chief guests and *matanivanua* are handed cups from which to drink
yavu	mound of stones as site for house

Preface and Acknowledgements

E arly on, somewhere I read or someone told me, 'Never forget a name. Never forget a face. And never forget which goes with which.' In the course of life, remembering these words of wisdom has caused me to forget where I read the advice or who told it to me. It's like the start that an octogenarian can make to a speech on his eightieth birthday: 'There are three things that fade as age advances. The first is memory. The second and third are ... [long pause] I'm awfully sorry, I can't remember them.' Of course it's not uncommon advice, but I must say that I took the precept to heart. Not only has it been of paramount value in my professional careers but it has also had its place in my amateur and often trivial pursuits. The sagacity of the advice which I trained myself to adopt has helped me in these random reflections and off-the-cuff observations.

There being two sides of a coin, I have tried to be as candid as diplomacy allows to give all-round thoughts and views. For instance, in the major part of this volume dealing with Colonial Service life, I have sought to show both its rigidities — for it was after all a Service with discipline its main buttress — and unstuffy sides of officialdom. The aim has been not only to supply information, always meanwhile recalling that there are specks of dust floating in every sunbeam, but, to make it the more palatable and avoid imposing a lecture, to offer here and there light entertainment. It is hoped that if paternalism shows through it was not patronizing.

As a historian, I would like to have included more history, but lack of space has precluded it. After all, the work already runs to two volumes, with a third having had to rest on the cutting floor. While the corpus of this volume reflects and observes colonial administration in the South Seas, the subtitle includes cricket. Here I have resolved to offer nothing but the less usual, steering right away from the hackneyed material now monopolizing publications on the game. I feel, however, that I have to justify the inclusion of what some might regard as a philistine section of the subtitle. Apart from its being an inseparable part of my leisure activity, cricket had an important place in the lives of three of the four most important Fijian figures from the end of the 1940s. The high chiefs, Ratu Sir Edward Cakobau (for Auckland as well as Fiji), Ratu Sir George Cakobau (the first Fijian Governor-General) and Ratu Sir Kamisese Mara (the current President of Fiji) were all officially and internationally graded as first-class cricketers. And the pre-eminent Ratu Sir Lala Sukuna of a slightly earlier generation told me more than once in his endearingly modest fashion (when he could have had higher ambitions such as the governorship of the islands) that his greatest unfulfilled wish for which he would have given much was to have played cricket at first-class level. So the game and colonial administration in Fiji, willow and palm, are not too far apart. Parenthetically, there is a summary here of what is generally regarded as one of the more unusual cricket tours of any length, aiming to be of interest to those who know the game and to those who don't or may not be inclined to care for it. A fuller account of this was in my *Cricket in the Fiji Islands* (1949), now so rare that the copy in the MCC library at Lord's has gone missing.

The first subject in the subtitle, Cambridge, gives a first glimpse in early days of my brother C. P. Snow, about whom I have written separately in *Stranger and Brother: A Portrait of C. P. Snow* (1982 and 1983): there will be more about him in the companion to this first volume, which ranges from 1915 to 1951. What is assembled here is not an autobiography or memoirs, terms which should be reserved — but too often aren't — for the eminent. With pathos and bathos there are some, if not of course all, of the human and less than human conditions — naïveté and irony, trauma and farce, ambition and absolute lack of it. Everyone has his or her own eccentricity. Some people naturally have more of it than others to make the variety of men and women, which enthralls an observer like myself. Studying them is one of my own eccentricities. This is, however, not a recital merely of idiosyncrasies: if it were, I might emerge as having more than my fair share of them. But eccentricities are turned up in dusty corners of colonial service in the South Seas, which has been only rarely described and for which this might, by the laws of mortality, be a last-chance record. Parts of this account, if they do no more, may serve as such a register not so much for contemporaries, who are dwindling, as for generations younger than mine, including that of my granddaughter. They may consider it too old hat (or, in their phraseology of which I have imperfect knowledge, less than cool). I run that risk, but what is certain is that phases of a chunk of my career can (sadly, at least to my mind) never any more be theirs to experience. India has recently been graphically covered in writing or on films and television. The colonies and the Colonial Service, so different from India and its Service, are, provocatively speaking, less ostentatious and certainly less publicized. Some curiosity may lie, and some perspective may be restored, in the fact that what is told in part here relates to the remotest segment of the largest empire in the world's history.

I have tried not to overlook, or be forgetful about, the sentiments I can admit naturally enough, if frankness predominates, to have experienced. In that sense they observe and reflect, without the need to invent for a single moment, the truth in the life of my time. Very personal impressions are offered. Some of the profiles of people and places are encapsulated in intermittently kept diaries. But for the most part they are in the memory which, as we know, can play tricks. Many are the times when I could swear as a witness in court that I had or had not met such and such a person or had or had not visited such and such a place — only to be disproved shockingly by a diary. It is hoped that this chronicle will strike a chord here and there, however unusual the setting. At least, unusual it seems to me on long reflection.

The second volume, appearing almost simultaneously, deals from 1951 to 1995 with a different ambience except for cricket running through as a background theme and for ineluctable South Seas links. These are my last books. No one can any longer read my speedy but perplexing script; and shorthand is regrettably a dying art. My almost infinite patience doesn't run to being able to type. I refuse to entangle myself again with dictated-to tapes. Computers will forever be beyond my very circumscribed understanding of things mechanical. There is a limit and I have reached it in that context.

As for acknowledgements, since splitting the original, quite huge book into two, I have now had to put these where they belong in the respective volumes, although some are of course applicable to both. I only hope that none of those who have helped eliminate or reduce my shortcomings with advice, perspective and wisdom from various parts of the world have fallen unacknowledged between the two pro-ductions. Magnanimity is the word I want to use in acknowledging my debt, for those who have shown it, including those who have often graciously provided the heterogeneous material without which this work could not have been envisaged. (Of course, remaining defects are mine and I apologize for them in advance.) My thanks (I steer clear of the redundancy in the phrase 'grateful thanks' so often seen in acknowledgements as, for the life of me, I can't see how thanks can be other than grateful) therefore to my daughter Stefanie and her husband Peter Waine, who believed that I should go on record with this and were instrumental in discovering the right publisher; my granddaughter Philippa for her inspiring curiosity; my wife Anne (her diary was an invaluable aide-mémoire) who typed unselfishly seemingly ceaseless drafts in my execrable script of all my previous seven books but was pressed to take hard-earned, reluctant but absolutely deserved retirement before the current book and then became a diligent, tireless critic and proofreader; Joe and Lindsay Buzaglo for generous help; Lindsay again and Linda Mitchell for the practicality of extracting this so patiently from a tangled manuscript and recalcitrant, occasionally quite crazy tapes; over many years the staff of West Sussex County Council's superb library service, notably those of Rustington and Angmering libraries, and particularly Debra Wilson, ALA, Sandra Seddigh and Margaret Smart; Beverley Barrett, Dorothy Sterling and Janet Plomer; all who contributed consciously or unconsciously to the material such as Charles, Lord Snow of Leicester, CBE, Ph.D.; Lady Snow (née Pamela Hansford Johnson), CBE; Eric E. Snow, FIHVE; Humphrey S. Evans, MRCS, LRCP, BA; Christopher C. Legge, BA; Reginald and Gillian Caten; Noel and Alison McEvoy; Martin and Diane Daly (née Carrick); Pamela Hampton (née Langford); Thomas Pickering, MA; Donald Gould; John Whall; Anne Lenner-Little; Martin Clemens, CBE, AM, MC, MA; Wilfred Wooller, JP, BA; Paul A. C. V. Geraghty, Ph.D., MA; William Warden; Jane F. V. Roth; Adi Sofia Veisa Mara Pennington-Richards (née Hennings); Editha Pease (née Le Hunte); Pearl Chamberlain; Andrew Hunter-Rodwell; Iris Johnston (née May); Professor E. John H. Corner, CBE, FRS, MA; Enid Wise (née Thomson); Raymond Burr; Reginald, Lord Paget of Northampton, QC; Sir David F. Attenborough, CH, CVO, CBE, FRS, MA; Ratu Sir Lala Sukuna, KCMG, KBE, BA, *Méd. mil.*; Ratu Sir Edward Cakobau, KBE, MC; Ratu Sir George Cakobau, GCMG, GCVO, OBE, JP, Royal Victorian Chain; Ratu Sir Penaia Ganilau, GCMG, KCVO, KBE, DSO; Ratu Sir Kamisese Mara, GCMG, KBE, MA, PC; Walter A. Hadlee, CBE; Kenneth A. Stuart, OBE, LL B; Sir Robert L. Munro, CBE, LL B;

Colonel Derek G. M. Fletcher, DSO; Henry G. Button, MA; E. James Coode, OBE, MA; Katherine Belgrave (née Berkeley); John A. Lourie, MA, BM, Ph.D., B.Ch., FRCS; Professor Harry E. Maude, OBE, MA; Charles R. H. Nott, CMG, OBE, MA; Dorothy Kearsley; Dianne Beattie (née St Aubyn); Anne Gittins; June Knox-Mawer; Ronald W. Paine, BA; Estelle Fuller; Ngaire Williams; Jean Brown; Marjorie Anderson; June Wilkinson; Adi Losalini Cakobau Browne; Joseph D. Gibson, CBE; Ratu Josua Brown Toganivalu, CBE, JP; Rt Hon George, 2nd Earl Jellicoe, KBE, DSO, MC, JP, PC; Rt Hon Malcolm MacDonald, OM, PC; Paul, Colonel 2nd Lord Freyberg, OBE, MC; John, Professor 2nd Lord Tedder, MA, Ph.D., D.Sc., FRSE, FRSC; Kenneth Rose, CBE, FRSL; Hugh Massingberd; Colonel Heinrich R. Amstütz, Swiss Cavalry; Cyril C. Goodway; C. Guy O. T. Parr; Charles Vesely; Brian V. Davies, MA; Edward A. Jones, BA; Donald H. W. Dickson, Ph.D., FRIC; Professor Albert J. Schütz; Sheila Lochhead (née MacDonald); Professor Joseph F. Maloney; Gordon A. Hutchinson, MA; Daryl Tarte; Richard D. H. Roberts; Margaret Wearn; Fergus G. A. U. Clunie, B.Sc.; Cherie Whiteside (née Wright); Gavin Snow; Baron Vaea of Houma; Alec R. Waugh; Sir Rex de Charembac Nan Kivell, CMG; Howard L. Tripp; Sylvia Legge; Captain Michael H. S. Howard, MA; Anne Griffiths, LVO; Catherine Aldington Guillaume; Patricia K. G. Lewis (née Allberry); Joanne Gordon; Lieutenant Colonel Desmond B. Pease; Commander Andrew C. F. David; John Goepel, MBE, MA; N. John Bradley, BA; Arthur L. Baker, MBE; W. C. V. C. Baker, MA; Robertson R. Wright, MBE; T. L. I. S. V. Iremonger, MP, BA; Viti Mabbutt (née Allardyce); Peter A. C. Luke, MC; Fabio y Valls (E. G. Fabio Barraclough); Jack Trotman, CPM; Douglas Ettridge; John and Margaret Goulding; Setareki Tuinaceva, Principal Archivist, and Margaret Patel, Senior Archivist, National Archives of Fiji; Major-General B. Meldrum, OBE, Chief of General Staff, New Zealand Army General Staff, Defence Headquarters, Wellington; Wing-Commander G. T. Clarke, Air Staff, Ministry of Defence, Defence Headquarters, Wellington; Captain Joseph R. McCleary, Defence and Naval Attaché, US Embassy, London; Captain William C. Heindahl, Chief, Historical Services Branch, Office of Air Force History Headquarters, United States Air Force, Washington; Captain A. J. Booth, Deputy Director of Naval History, Office of Chief of Naval Operations, Washington; HE Brigadier Ratu Epeli Nailatikau, CBE, LVO; and Adi Koila Nailatikau; T. W. Collins; John F. Hughes; Public Relations Office, Suva; *Leicester Mercury*; *Leicester Evening Mail*; *Coventry Evening Telegraph*; *The*

Preface and Acknowledgements

Dominion, Wellington; *Christchurch Star-Sun*; Iradj Bagherzade, chairman of I.B.Tauris & Company Ltd; Selina Cohen, the copy-editor coping specially admirably with the abundance of last-minute adjustments, remoulding elegantly here and keeping me to the straight and narrow there; John Crabb, production manager, for skilful arrangement of illustrations and much other prompt help kindly given; Maysoon Hamdiyyah and Catherine Rogers in connection with the jacket; and Lester Crook, Ph.D., the Radcliffe Press's publisher whose encouragement was vital and whose willingness to edit a huge manuscript, giving it sharpness and shape so expertly, went far beyond any bounds of duty; and finally those who by simply genial and general enquiry about progress in the project have kept me well and truly at it. Every effort has been made to trace any copyright holders. Any omissions are regretted and would be corrected in a following edition. Permission from the *British Medical Journal* and *The Press*, Christchurch, New Zealand, to reproduce extracts and from George P. Darwin to quote the letter from Sir Charles Darwin is gratefully acknowledged.

Angmering
Sussex, England
7 November 1988–1 July 1997

1

Moustaches, Clean Shaves and University Vignettes

I have summarized what I most clearly remember of my very happy early family life in *Stranger and Brother: A Portrait of C. P. Snow*. What follows is an epitome of background reflected upon, with a little filling in of lacunae in that publication as possibly having some relevance in this narrative.

My father, William Edward, and mother, Ada Sophia, were living at 40 Richmond Road, Aylestone Park, Leicester (since demolished: the site is marked by Leicester City Council with a blue plaque recording that Lord Snow of Leicester, author and scientist, was born there as C. P. Snow in 1905) when all their family were born. Four sons, Harold, Percy (until 1950 and thereafter Charles), Eric and myself. It suited Charles to underline his successful overcoming of social obstacles by inferring that we were upper working class, whereas lower middle class seemed more accurate. Richmond Road is characterized by unbroken terraces of houses. Numbers 40 and 42, the first to be constructed, alone formed a semidetached, three-storeyed structure. In our time neighbours included bricklayers, a cobbler, a tram conductor, a painter, stokers, hosiery trimmers, a railway signalman, a plumber and gas workers. Father did seem to represent a break in this worthy assembly of artisans. By day he was a traveller in boots and shoes within the County of Leicestershire, but after bankruptcy twice in attempts to go on his own he finally became the cashier in a boot and shoe manufacturers' firm. The brass plate outside the house proclaimed another personality at night: 'W. E. SNOW, FRCO, TEACHER OF MUSIC'. In addition, he was organist at three churches in sequence, practically stipendless. Fortunately for the four sons' predisposition to cricket, we had more garden space than our neighbours, but probably shared all other deprivations and defects — outside lavatories, no carpets but linoleum, no running hot water, no electricity, and no telephone of course.

To differentiate us further socially, all the sons from ages five to eleven went to a tiny mixed private school on the next road (where incidentally Anne Lenner lived. Her fine voice is regularly heard on records with Carroll Gibbons and his Savoy Hotel Orpheans and the bands of Joe Loss and Charlie Kunz. She told me recently that a cricketer at Lord's with a name unknown to her then in the mid-1930s asked her 'to run off with him'. It was Walter Hammond). Consisting of three rooms in a terrace, Beaumanor Villas, it had the grandiose name of Beaumanor School. Mother thought the alternative, on the same road, a board or elementary school, attended by most of the neighbours' children, 'rather rough'. She was a semi-invalid as a legacy of rheumatic fever and had a daily help. When I was 15 this was Naomi.

Then I encountered love for the first time. She was about 30, with pale violet eyes. Not only these, which I never saw as anything but indicating come hither, but there was golden hair and a shapely slimness, a quiet caressing voice and elegance of movement. Very soon I found that I was encouraged to be amorous and she would take me into the city to cinemas. When my mother decided to dispense with Naomi's help I knew that it was, at least for me, love because parting broke my heart. I would wake up afterwards in the mornings no longer jaunty in step but with despondent, frustrated longing and a vague dragging of feet. From every aspect, except the heartbreak at the end, I can recommend my relationship with Naomi for an inspiring tutorial start to one's love life. Naomi also gave me a badly needed increase of ease in talking with women.

Richmond Road was (and still is) endowed with a library. I was early very conscious of our being a four-son family with no sisters and always, in consequence I think, I have been highly susceptible to feminine attractiveness. I would go to the library nightly and lounge about chatting with young women. A gaminesque Claudette Colbert-like brunette, wearing a saucy angled beret, invited me to her house where there were two other sisters. One was slim, tall and statuesque; the other, four years older than me, had vivacious brown eyes that flashed even more than her sisters'. They were all taken for walks (and more) separately and clandestinely — an intricate triple involvement.

At 11, all the brothers, none of us overlapping because of the age gaps, went to Alderman Newton's Boys' School, a tram ride away in the city. It was the second most expensive grammar school. How Father managed to pay for the fees, modest enough, as for the preparatory school's, and our tram fares four times a day (the school did not provide lunches), cannot be conjectured. His monetary range from precious little to less than nothing — bankruptcies — must have been a source of Mother's anxiety neuroses, transmitted to her sons for life.

With the exception of the cherubic-looking but far from cherubic-acting H. E. Howard, described in my *Stranger and Brother* as Charles's first patron, stupefyingly histrionic and the pivotal propeller of myself to Cambridge, Alderman Newton's School had most likely no more outstanding staff than any other school of the period. Moustaches were varied but authoritarian. There were eccentrics among Newton's staff of my time (1927–34). The bland, phlegmatic headmaster, R. L. S. Ager, who had been a boy at Rugby, was, however, the acme of normality. Clean-shaven, liberal, he gave his disparate staff full rein. Just as well for Bert Howard and therefore myself, a protégé of Howard's. I was the first to be allowed to circumvent lessons in my last two years. Theoretically, I could concentrate on reading books recommended by Howard for the Cambridge scholarship. It was an enormous risk, with all my contemporaries steadily ploughing ahead on conventional supervised courses, and so easily I could have finished at school with no scholarship and two years behind all the others.

Most of the staff I had a liking for. Bert Chatwin, a gentle, dignified teacher behind a ginger moustache, alone made out of the incomprehensible maths some sort of sense for me. A benevolent white-moustached Belgian, Josef Legros, radiated to me a liking for French and gave me a Francophile attitude that I have never lost. Another, J. E. Ellis, a mild, pink and bare-cheeked teacher of French and notoriously absent-minded, caused hilarity when, as the headmaster's secretary made the rounds of the classrooms to note who was not present, he once solemnly commanded, 'Stand up the absentees.' Two or three I disliked or even hated, such as the clean-shaven, bad-tempered, blatant sadist, Kenneth Starkie Topping. A dislike rather than a hate was J. L. Broderick, a Catholic teacher of Latin. He made himself librarian and crudely covered with thick strips of paint the sensitive parts of nudes in books containing them. He was so inanimate a figure that it is a wonder that he knew where to paint.

Newton's was a subfusc grammar school typical of its time, made only exceptional by the odd brilliant individual such as Howard and the long-suffering, taciturn, liberal idealist in Ager, whose driving faith, transmitted to me, was in the League of Nations at Geneva. I came to know Ager again when he was, at close on 90, the oldest alumnus able to attend Rugby School's four-hundredth anniversary celebrations, which I organized. I had once seen him, after his retirement, queuing up as inconspicuously as possible (he did not see me passing by) for that vortex of pulchritude, the Windmill Theatre in London, to open. I like to think that that predilection contributed to his longevity.

The huge risk I took in confining myself to trying for a Cambridge scholarship came off. I squeezed exceedingly narrowly into Christ's with an open exhibition in history. My knowledge was shallow, but I had been advised by Howard to answer the examination questions not with a recital of facts (which I couldn't anyway muster) but as provocatively and as originally as possible. It had been a very close shave. Indeed, while staying in Charles's rooms, I had cut my index finger deeply on a razor blade and could scarcely put any pressure on it for writing.

I had been appointed a prefect. Then Ager made me head prefect and captain of the school, a post that Charles had held. The confidence primarily induced by Naomi had paid off. It had been when

4

studying European history from 1485 to 1914 for the scholarship that, drawing breath and looking out from the school hall window on to the playground, I noticed a most attractive girl — I judged about four years younger than me — among the netball players from Alderman Newton's girls' school, which regularly used our asphalt surface for the game. They came from the opposite end of Peacock Lane to the boys' school. It was the largest of windows, so I was visible if any of the girls diverted their attention from their game. When I made contact with Mary (later to use her second name, Anne) Harris, outside her school, rapport was apparent — instant and lasting.

My brother, Charles, envied me only rarely. The casual way in which I reached Cambridge compared with his frenetic struggle was one rightful source of envy. He used to mention that frequently, but most of all my adventitious luck with the opposite sex at my early age, compared with his very slow start — not really before his first 35 or so years — was what he envied in me most. This apart, he could guess, without my needing to tell him, how much and in what respects I admired his life — but with a fraternal lack of jealousy at all times. He had succeeded Harold, who died in 1926 from pneumonia-cum-diabetes at 28, as the eldest brother.

Eric used to take me to the fine, grassless nets on the county ground where Frank Bale, a gnarled, retired Leicestershire professional whose flighted left-hand bowling Hobbs used to respect, voluntarily dispensed wisdom of distinctive quality in a gruff voice and with grizzled, weather-beaten Mephistophelean amusement. He would let me bat against him: I recall his saying to me that the way I shaped resembled Ernest Tyldesley, whom I hardly knew of but who played with success for England and Lancashire. It was in the 1930s that I first heard the term 'Chinaman'. Bale could not bowl the left-hander's googly but, as a man given to originality and a much-underestimated character in cricket, applied that term to Leslie O'Brien Fleetwood-Smith, the Australian bowler of wayward genius who died as a tramp, and to another Australian, Jack Walsh, later a friend of mine, who were among the first exponents of that rare delivery from out of the back of the hand to be seen on the Aylestone Road ground. The term has since been non-sensically and generally misapplied to a left-hander's leg break: nothing of the Oriental unorthodox about that. Bale had the same flair for drawing out a player as his colleague, Geary, in the county team. While the phrase 'dropping a ball on a sixpence' is pure hyperbole, he could bowl one on to a coin twice in every dozen. That is all, I am sure, that Wilfred Rhodes could do.

Once I had entered the school team I confined my visits to watching the county. I was keen now to see if I could make the grade myself. As an amateur, I had really no chance since Newton's possessed no standing. But unabashed, attending the winter evening indoor school at the ground, I was offered by George Geary, the inestimable England and Leicestershire all-rounder in charge of the nets, engagement as a professional. By this time, however, I was expecting to enter Cambridge: George, who was to become a friend for life, understood my declining. I was to be near to joining him in the county team (in fact I did participate under his captaincy) and by the end of my time at school I was taking the game very seriously. It was to be only a year before I was selected for the County 2nd XI: at this stage emergence from a school of loftier status and truer pitches than Newton's would have been important, indeed crucial to advancement. A tinge of envy for the rival Wyggeston School's splendid ground and kindly ex-county professional, Bill Berridge, when Newton's had neither, could not be denied. It may have cost me county appearances. Despite the atrocious wickets at Newton's, Maurice Tompkin, my opening partner, went straight into the county team, scoring 91 (run out) in his first match. Judged early by Sir Pelham Warner to have England potential, he toured Pakistan with the MCC team and died of cancer later that season. By appointment as captain of the County 2nd XI from 1935 to 1938, I was given hopes that I might have a chance for the 1st XI. All my team, entirely professional except J. A. T. Sharp, referred to in the next volume, such as George Dawkes, Laurie Thursting, Fred Bowley, Gerry Lester, Harry Graham and Jim Sperry graduated during my captaincy to the county team. In fact, it must be confessed, all but me.

In all my time at Newton's I saw little of Charles. Soon to

become the greatest influence in my life, he had moved from Richmond Road after leaving Newton's to lodgings while he was at Leicester University College and very seldom came home — and then always looking pallid and gaunt. He was working intensely for a national scholarship, which alone could enable him to get to Cambridge. It was realized later that he was seriously, life-threateningly, overdoing it. Eric was to leave in 1933 when he married: 40 Richmond Road was emptying. I was only to spend vacations from Cambridge there. After its once having held as many as four or five (three or four of them constantly active sons) in addition to Mother and Father, only they were left. I have since imagined the echoes and Mother's pangs, not insulated as for Father by the opium of his music.

It was in my four years at Cambridge, 1934–8, that I first saw a good deal of Charles. We became very close for ever after. For half of those years we lived in rooms obliquely opposite each other in the First Court at Christ's College. He was in Charles Darwin's, twice the size of mine as befitted a Fellow and tutor. I in the putative ones of Milton, formerly a Fellow's rooms (Charles had earlier occupied them in that capacity). Mine were, even so, impressively oak-panelled for a mere undergraduate to whom they had been inexplicably downgraded. In this environment I made as much as I possibly could of the great wide world now piquantly opened up to me — at least as represented by the three courts of Christ's and courts of other colleges, the multiplicity of the cricket grounds, the University buildings, the lodgings of undergraduates and the homes of experts in different subjects.

I believed that if one were lucky enough to get into a University one should mix socially to the utmost of one's meagre finances. This was easy in cricket, but I could not make up my mind whether to steer as much as possible for a Blue or for a First in History. In the event I missed both. At cricket I was not helped by coming from an unknown grammar school; despite my having captained Leicestershire 2nd XI, I was never in four years given more than one single session of ten minutes in a net at the University ground. Outside Fenner's, watching out by University leaders for talent was lamentable — no notice was taken of college performances. It was soon clear that one had to have been at a public school — coached, and with the confidence that only their perfect pitches could import. No grammar school product made the University team before the war. At Fenner's, despite the fact that there could not have been two nicer professionals for the beginning of the season, Hendren (England and Middlesex) and Austin Matthews (Northants and Glamorgan), my ten-minute turn to bat came at the end of a long day for them. I was never given a bowl and I have never thought that nets are an accurate guide for judging the fundamental virtues of a player being able to place and keep down the ball when making his shots.

There was a plethora of cricket talent in my time, the University side being the equal of County teams and containing actual or potential Test Match players. In such contrast with the debilitated sides of the last three or more decades, which had the worst of meetings against 2nd XIs masquerading as County teams and into which I, in the company of so many others, would have walked, it can be said without too high an opinion of myself, effortlessly. I was elected to the Crusaders — the University 2nd XI — through a series of performances for Christ's, which somehow had filtered through to the top but had not been seen. I also became a member of the Hawks' Club, whose tie I unfailingly wore: it carried real cachet athletically. I found that I had been nominated for these by Norman Yardley, a quiet, genial future captain of Yorkshire and England. For his kind act I took him to lunch at Christ's, which seldom saw other colleges' contemporary celebrities.

On the academic side I was to miss narrowly a First in both parts of the modern history tripos. But I was conscious that I had not been working single-mindedly enough. Debating took up some time. It had been at school the most valuable training for the public speeches I had had to make there, as head prefect at the Old Newtonians' dinner and at speech day (shamelessly without the slightest nerves, such is the conceit of youth, to an audience of 2000).

I aimed at becoming president of the Milton Society, Christ's debating forum, and succeeded in election to that office more easily than I thought possible. On Charles's advice, however, that it would take up too much time, I eschewed speaking at the Union, although I attended it in my first year and was invited to, but declined, a place on the committee, which might have led to the presidency. It was there that I heard first hand the original throwaway remark: 'If Blues were given for wit, the Right Honourable Opponent speaking last would undoubtedly have been a half-Blue.'

My friends within Christ's were diverse. One was a colourful Sikh doing engineering and ending his career as Lieutenant-General Harkirat Singh, chief engineer in the Indian army. Despite vicissitudes and living half the world apart, I have kept up with Martin Clemens. He was a boisterous oarsman, not really *en rapport* as such, but we became firm friends and shared the general prewar *joie de vivre* with the feeling that *après moi la déluge* was not far off. Charles was his tutor. Of Clemens's epic exploits there is more later.

Intrepid in a different style was Wilfred Wooller, who brought distinction to a Christ's not richly endowed with Blues by being a Welsh rugby international three-quarter of devastating combination of weight and speed with an ungraspable, late side swerve. His nocturnal escapades embraced rocking telephone booths out of almost megalithic concrete bases (this antisocial behaviour would not be thought funny outside of a town used to University peccadilloes and restricted to one or two occasions) and pulling down all 20 cast-iron cisterns into the college's only block of lavatory basins. Samsonian feats, if also inconvenient in their consequences. Wooller was not a tutee of Charles, but of a great friend of his, Brian Downs, who was later Master. Downs was placed in the dilemma of deciding what form official non-approval should take for the telephone and sanitation chaos. This was near the end of term when Wilfred Wooller gave a party in his rooms to celebrate his Blue for cricket (he went on after the war to lead Glamorgan to its first County Championship). Adventitiously, it eclipsed his Herculean performances. I was in one room and Wooller happened to be in the next, jumping up and down with his 15 stone and the weight of his friends, when the middle of the floor collapsed and some half-dozen fell through it on top of a don grumpily attempting to sleep in the bedroom below. The official college pressure was for extreme retribution — the sending down of Wooller, particularly after he had been fined in the police court for his telephone tackles. This Charles managed to defer until after the imminent annual match with Oxford, and then arranged with Downs for this carrying to extremes of exhibition of high spirits plus phenomenal stamina to be condoned.

The chronology and details of disruption of telephones, lavatories and the sleep of a don differ as between Wooller's account and mine. Who was the more lucid or sober, the chief performer or the bemused observer, is a matter of doubt. There was a fair amount of alcoholic haze about. After marriage to the eldest daughter of the 2nd Earl of Plymouth, Wooller, fleeing from the Japanese advance on Singapore, where he had just landed, was caught in Java and lost six stone in three years' captivity. He later, by the course that nature takes to entertain us, became a firm upholder of the law as a JP for Glamorgan. He did survive — just — but the war killed many of our contemporaries.

Religion has not been one of my neuroses. (After an Anglo-Catholic upbringing I was helped to escape by Charles, bypassing agnosticism straight to atheism at the age of 14.) In my four years at Christ's I may have set some sort of record by never going into the chapel in First Court. After the war I did go into it to see the war memorial's list of names: its length caused me to shudder. Cheerful, nimble Colin Carpenter, who had rooms near mine, was with others who had been friends, as well as one or two for whom I had inexorably little time, such as a swaggering neighbour in First Court who had joined the air-force cadets, one felt as part of his bravado, while still an undergraduate. Ironically, he had been leader of the pro-Fascist persuasion in the college, but in hazard ing his life in the war he had turned full circle. It was a terrible forfeit.

Yet the clouds so inevitably forming for that year from the middle 1930s were not so oppressive as to be a daily weight on the mind. But a dashing friend, Ivor Hickman, his blond hair flying in waves after the style of Rupert Brooke, left Second Court prematurely to fight against Franco and be killed just as the International Brigade retreated from Spain. From Christ's, in successive years, I organized two college team cricket tours — almost unprecedented ventures — to the South and the Midlands. Playing success against County second teams was aided by my persuading Revd Gilbert Jessop to join us. He was the son of G. L. (England and Gloucestershire) who had also been to Christ's and became agoraphobic after his pre-eminent cricket career ended. It is astonishing that Hampshire never let Gilbert junior have more than a handful of matches and that he was never given a Blue. He was absolutely first class in technique and temperament. Opening together, in one match against Gentlemen of Leicestershire, he scored 100 in the time it took me to make 4. To be at the opposite end as his partner was to put one's life in danger. Twice I had to throw myself to the ground when a ball was struck back from those huge forearms, thicker than most peoples' calves, between me and the bowler at head height. Charles told me that he had a similar experience with Gilbert who was of an intake at Christ's senior to mine.

By extreme coincidence, I relived my fizzy experience about 20 years later on the same ground, at the opposite end to Morris Burton, who had forearms of exactly the same size as Jessop's: I think that they are more helpful a physical attribute for a batsman than any other except a good eye. We opened the innings after lunch for Rugby Town against Market Harborough. Halfway out to the pitch, Burton complained to me of feeling ill. I tried unsuccessfully to persuade him to return to the pavilion. He faced the first ball. It missed his stumps by the thinnest whisker. After that, scarcely a ball was left unpulverized by him. At the teatime declaration at 230 for 0 (Rugby's record partnership for any wicket), I had been allowed to score 47 not out while Burton had made 177 not out, more than once flattening me and the bowler with whirlwind straight return drives.

Another whom I persuaded to help Christ's on one of my tours was Desmond Rought-Rought who, with his brothers Basil and Rodney, played for Cambridge and Norfolk. Desmond and Rodney also represented the Gentlemen of England. A fond

11

memory is of a wet journey between matches. My Morris Cowley, bought for £5 in 1934, had only a collapsible hood for the front two seats: the other two in the dicky seat at the rear had no such cover. As the torrent increased, I called out to the back: 'Are you all right, Desmond?' 'Yes, thank you, Philip,' he replied, 'my eyebrows are working very well as gutters.' He was killed in a road accident after the war.

It was not often that guests from outside the college came to lunches and dinners in hall. They tended to be leading figures in sport. When I took in Yardley, then captain of the University cricket team, it created a minor stir among games followers. A disincentive for me was that I could not really afford to take in a guest. But I was determined to take Jack King, the former Leicestershire, England and Players' professional (the second oldest player at 54 to score a first-class century and the oldest at 52 to score a 200) who was now an umpire, when he was officiating in the latter capacity in a University match. I had met King a year or two earlier when he was strolling along the meadows near the canal in Leicester and joined in a knock-up that I was indulging in with a friend: his left arm bowling action was as high in his late sixties after retirement as before it. The reason for my determination was not only that he was an exceptionally pleasant person, a veritable, upright gentleman of dignified moustachioed mien, but that he would be, I was sure, the first professional to dine in a college hall. Despite the age gap he was warmly appreciated by the undergraduates: none knew of his distinguished record.

The guests whom Charles used to invite from outside the college to stay overnight in his rooms after dinner in hall were the first literary figures of eminence he knew. And because I was invited to drinks with them before or after dinner (Charles took them of course to high table), they were the first for me also to know. I have recounted in *Stranger and Brother* my being asked by Charles to meet Richard Aldington at Cambridge station and how greatly I took to him. Of all the literary figures I ever met he was the most personable. Then there was the original personality of H. G. Wells and the rather plain but appealingly modest James

12

Hilton whose books, *Lost Horizon, Random Harvest* and *Good-bye Mr Chips*, made such impacts. Charles's most regular visitor was G. H. Hardy from Trinity, so distinguished a mathematician, a reclusive genius who tried to commit suicide more than once and an eccentric of the rarest order. I have described him in *Stranger and Brother* as one of the three main male influences on Charles's life, with Bert Howard and C. R. C. Allberry. All were characters in Charles's novels: Hardy was a minor one, Howard is George Passant in the eponymous work, and Allberry, with his intriguing changes of mood reflected in the title *The Light and the Dark,* was almost wholly based on him and, in my view, the most gripping of the entire cycle of Charles's 11 novels in his *Strangers and Brothers* series. As I knew Charles Allberry during my time at Christ's better than anyone apart from my brother, I could myself devote a whole chapter of fact (as contrasted with the fiction) to this fascinatingly complex figure, but here can only refer the reader to my summary of him in the portrait of my brother, where there are also vignettes of persons behind characters in Charles's two other Cambridge novels besides *The Light and the Dark: The Affair* and *The Masters.* Sir Charles Darwin, grandson of Charles Robert Darwin who had been at Christ's, was Master in my time: in my brother Charles's words, he resembled a chief sea lion, not least as the moustachioed possessor of a booming voice. Charles was seldom nonplussed throughout his life, but from the head of high table Darwin bellowed to him (then plain Dr C. P. Snow): 'You're armigerous, aren't you, Snow?' Charles did not know how to answer. To have replied 'Yes' would inevitably have drawn a request for information. Safest to swallow hard and say 'No, Master.' The matter was closed, a mishap avoided. On return to his rooms Charles had to consult his dictionary. It was the right answer. The question was about 30 years too soon — he had to pay £400 to the College of Heralds for the grant of arms as a peer in 1964, arms which I am entitled to use except regretfully for the beautiful Siamese cat supporters.

The front windows of my room in Christ's looked straight down Petty Cury (the feminine parade helped distract me from my books), the back ones behind to the Master's Lodge in First Court.

As an undergraduate, I was honoured to receive the following note from C. G. Darwin, written to me from the Master's Lodge on 11 May 1936, just before George VI's coronation:

> My various children of all ages ought to see a local procession tomorrow which comes along Sidney Street and down Petty Cury, and obviously it is no use loosing them into the crowd. I think the view from your room would be good for this, and I write to ask whether they might come to watch it from there. I think the time is about 12 or a bit after. Would this be possible, or have you already let your Coronation seats? They would be accompanied by someone to prevent them falling out — probably Miss Darwin and myself, but in case we cannot get back in time from ceremonies there would be a nurse or nurses to keep them in order. I fear that this is much to ask, and if at all inconvenient, would you look in sometime today and tell me, since I do not want to be at all a nuisance. I shall be in probably from six thirty on and also earlier in the day.

Such courtesy of expression from the highest to the lowest in the academic hierarchy was something I tried to remember in later life, particularly in addressing those in arguably a lower station than myself.

The most entertaining of Charles's fictional characters, M. H. L. Gay, was based on John Holland Rose, Emeritus Professor of Naval History. As president of the college Historical Society, I persuaded him to give a talk to it. Others who agreed to my surprise were of double distinction as Masters of Trinity and Downing and Professors of Modern and Naval History respectively. The 25 books of the former, G. M. Trevelyan, made rousing reading, but his lectures, mumbled from his gaunt frame stooped over with his half-moon wire-rimmed spectacles never raised from his script, were the epitome of boredom. Said to be crotchety, gruff and laconic, he was nevertheless graciously our chief guest at the Historical Society's hundredth meeting, preceded by a dinner at which I proposed The Guests to which he replied, while Charles proposed The Society. The dozen or so in my room later for his talk sat at his feet, more out of reverence for his written work than through a shortage of chairs: sadly, the talk was not very stirring. Not a single epigram emerged. But his presence was a handsome gesture for a humble gathering. Admiral Sir Herbert Richmond was the first armed services career man to be a professor, but not the first to be a head of college, as Field Marshal Lord Birdwood of Anzac and Totnes, a trim figure among quite a few shambling academics, was at this time Master of Peterhouse. Alert and cultivated, the monocled Richmond was sprucer than Trevelyan: he too had no pomposity, putting his audience of a dozen or so on the level of dialectical equality.

A sublieutenant spending a year at Christ's just after the First World War was Lord Louis Mountbatten. With his equine nobility of features (a wonderful dolichocephalic example), he could have been expected to confine himself to a life as depicted in *The Tatler*. To his credit, however, he was a keen speaker at the Milton Society, but, reading between the lines of its minutes, also a thunderously dull one, maintaining among other philosophies that democracy is only to be found in heaven.

The claim of his denigrators that he never read a book in his life is no doubt far-fetched, but he did have the impregnable, astounding self-confidence of those who read precious little. Straddled with apparent disasters of judgement — the slaughter of Canadians on a seemingly pointless attack on Dieppe and the slaughter perhaps inevitably implicit in the partition of India or, rather, his speed of action (all to be argued about eternally) — he was not a figure to be ignored. As president of the Historical Society, I should have tried to get him to return for debate after all that. Gavin Ewart, most people's choice to be Poet Laureate, who succeeded me as president, told me years later that he had the same thought of inviting him but never acted on it. Mountbatten was an expansive enough figure possibly to have accepted.

When he and Charles, Prince of Wales (then, in 1970, an undergraduate) immediately followed the abstruse Professor George Steiner and my brother as principal speakers in a Cambridge Union debate on the motion that 'this House believes that technological advance threatens the individuality of man and is becoming his master,' Charles told me that it wasn't easy for anyone to follow Steiner, in particular, and even his (Charles's) special brand of 'anti-rhetoric'. I asked how Mountbatten (on Charles's side) and the Prince of Wales (neutral) had performed. Perhaps a shade patronizingly, he replied: 'They coped remarkably well.'

Jack Plumb (later Sir John, Professor of Modern History and Master of Christ's), who had been one of Bert Howard's protégés at Newton's for half of my time there and all my years at Christ's, gave a party for Howard in Charles's Darwin reception room. There I was reported by the gossip columnist in the *Varsity News* as 'not talking much but thoroughly enjoying himself'. The columnist recorded that Plumb went on to a gathering of many different political creeds 'at King's where Mr Anthony Blunt had been acting as host. ... Here Mr Charles Allberry ... '. So far as I know, I never met the egregious pair, Blunt and Burgess, though I must have been on the fringe. Attempts were made by Communist Club officers, some quite grotesquely impersonable, to inveigle me into the party. I did go to Cambridge town hall to listen to Harry Pollitt, secretary of the British communists and a captivating orator, Shapurji Saklatvala, the Parsi communist MP and an impressive speaker, and Aneurin Bevan, slightly more to the right and scintillating. And I was proud to have been ejected, narrowly avoiding being coshed, by the British Fascist black-uniformed thug-stewards of the supercilious Sir Oswald Mosley before he had got into full tirade. Charles sagely advised me to avoid implications with the Communist Party, although we were both fervently anti-Franco, as likely to blacklist me for my career. By now it was shaping up that if I obtained a final First I would be welcomed as a Fellow, probably doing international law. Or, if I didn't, I would probably try for the Sudan Political Service (the Indian Civil Service was out, as this meant a stiff written examination to which I was not disposed after two triposes). Failing everything, there seemed to be journalism. That had its own uncertainties apart from the intervention of war. One could not foresee, if the war was survived, the television possibilities in which, for instance, cricket reporting might have had a place.

Having mentioned Jack Plumb, I am reminded that in the days when there were no driving schools he taught me to drive. My bull-nosed Morris Cowley had to be put into motion with a wrist-breaking crank handle. There was an electric starter, but with batteries as they were they had to be used sparingly because (it is now easy to forget or not to know) the law required any parking in a road after dark to be with lights. There were of course no sophistications like direction signals. One's movements had to be with gestures like an orchestra's conductor. I took the first driving test of the City of Leicester on the first day when the law requiring tests came in.

The examiner told me that I was the first to be tested: he chose the city centre for the location. Perhaps not many firsts have come my way in my life, but that was one, perhaps even a national one as the test was at 10.00 a.m. I don't think Jack Plumb would claim that he was a natural motorist, but I did make it as his pupil.

The joys of Cambridge, too many to be listed, still included some offbeat ones for me to savour fully as part of the all-round man. One was to gain a half-Blue at chess, of which I had been champion at Newton's, beating there some of the Leicestershire team. I just got into the University team against Oxford at bottom table (Hoyle, later Sir Fred and professor of astronomy, was number one). Its refinements could be seen to be too Delphic by me. I retired from it for ever on a semi-high note, my last game being in a simultaneous display by the British chess (and badminton) champion, near to the world's highest class, Sir George Thomas, 7th Baronet, against 20 opponents. At number six I lost my queen in the first seven moves and of course offered to resign. Thomas smilingly declined to give himself the game and, as it progressed (for me queenlessly), I somehow surprisingly improved and was congratulated by him when I captured his castle. But still naturally when the time came for adjudication I lost. He won seventeen, drew two and lost one.

If two half-Blues ranked as a Blue, which they didn't of course, I had scored the other half at table tennis. The team chosen to represent Cambridge against Oxford consisted of an Egyptian, I. Safwat (who played Davis Cup tennis for Egypt); a Russian,

Prince S. Obolensky; a Dane, A. T. Grut; a Frenchman, F. Leduc; and myself as captain, but less successful a player than Safwat and Leduc. We each played five games: I was the only one to lose a single game, but we still won 24–1. For daily practice there was Charles, with whom Homeric struggles of whirlwind top spin and vicious back-cut from yards behind the table have been described in *Stranger and Brother*. Table tennis elicited the most strenuous athletic movement (so sudden and rapid are the reactions at such short range) I ever had to produce (next came deck tennis) in a life given to a lot of sport. Another practice opponent was Paul Gibb, batsman and wicketkeeper for Sir Julien Cahn's XI, Cambridge and Yorkshire (then England and Essex). He occupied the number one batting position for Cambridge. I like to think that I had not too dissimilar an intensity of concentration, but he had some offside shots in addition to his legside mastery, whereas my 90 per cent legside method of survival or scoring lacked counterpoise. I knew myself of course to be in a widely different class from him, but not from the number two position of a succession of varying partners: that was where my sights lay. I would like to have seen P. A. Gibb and P. A. Snow bringing poetry of initials to the opening lines of the score cards. At table tennis we would play with similar styles, but I never conceded a game to him.

So far as one could get to know Gibb, I did. Paul would have tea and toast afterwards in my room, or I in his. Of course, we always played in winter, for we were so committed to cricket in the summer. The essence of imperturbability, he was very withdrawn, laconic and stiff-lipped, but remarkably persistent and stoical. He suffered from hydrocele, water on the testicles, which of all maladies that a wicketkeeper should be relieved from that is it. He mixed with virtually no one throughout his life. I don't believe that many capers went his way. A pilot of Sunderland and Catalina flying boats in the war (I would have felt safe with him), he was the first amateur to turn professional — a step that took some mental courage — after the war, then the first amateur to become an umpire. He would take himself round the country, like a tortoise in its shell, in a motor-drawn caravan in which he lodged overnight within the county grounds. Finally, he became a bus driver. One of the most eccentric of people, he was, for a man who had appeared before crowds of thousands in his life, totally introspective and never less than a natural recluse.

Practically my last activity at Christ's was to organize, as secretary, the May Week ball. I engaged the American Marius B. Winter and his orchestra, the first to be broadcast from the BBC. He had a highly attractive singer, Paula Green. Knowing fellow undergraduates, I had arranged that there should be no dancing with the singer. I have to confess that, once having met her, I used my prerogative, broke my own rule and danced with her not once but three times, while under my rules she declined all others.

At that time, if I had obtained a First I would like to have stayed in the college. But never subsequently: I came to sense, as Charles did, its claustrophobic confines. But it was not to be Cambridge for me in any case. It was Charles who thought that the Colonial Service might suit me. So I applied for it. I was confident that imperialism, despite all the left-wing propaganda, had its benevolent side. Besides, I had found a predisposition at school, in the University and college for administering. I enjoyed the gentleness of diplomacy required for seeking and achieving one's ends and the ends of others, as well as the cross-racial friendships I had made, as with Arnold Kelshall, my distinguished-looking brown opening partner batting for Christ's, from Trinidad. With his usual perception, Charles had made a note of my temperament over quite a period of time.

After three interviews in the Colonial Office by a Northern Rhodesian administrator on leave, C. A. R. Charnaud, whom I took to on first sight, I was finally seen by the éminence grise of the Office himself, Major Sir Ralph Furse, deaf and, so far as I could assess my chances, less *simpatico*. I was told that I would be selected for the Colonial Administrative Service but that my first odd choice, Cyprus (which my history supervisor had thought, not over-imaginatively, was the locale for me) was coveted by Mussolini and would have no further civilian administrators. Asked to think hard about my next choice, which I would get, I looked at the map, thought that Fiji seemed sufficiently unknown (perhaps it might be easier to make some kind of mark there than, say, in a colony the size of Nigeria or Kenya) and that its people seemed appealing, from accounts and pictures of them in the few books that could be quickly consulted, and I told this to the Colonial Office in almost those words, though not the words about making some kind of mark. I went into it as lightly as that. Back came a letter from Mr Secretary Ormsby-Gore (later Lord Harlech), Secretary of State for the Colonies, confirming that, subject to medical examination, I had been appointed a cadet in the Colonial Administrative Service of Fiji and the Western Pacific. It was also required that there should be any necessary dental treatment: of course this was sensible and in any case it improved my appearance. The appointment gave me a fourth year in Cambridge — further opportunities to know those whom I had already met and to see fresh faces.

The Colonial Administrative Service course at Cambridge deserves mention for its eccentric versatility. First of all, it was orientated for the 40 or so Colonial Service cadets going to Africa and not at all for the eight going to the Pacific (six to Fiji and two to the Solomons, Martin Clemens, whom we have met briefly and will do so more fully later, and David Trench, who finished in the Service as Governor of Hong Kong with the concomitant knighthood). This meant that we eight had to go to lectures on Muslim law (not in the slightest applicable in the Pacific). There were also tropical medicine and hygiene (of some importance except that it concentrated on yellow and blackwater fevers, neither of them endemic in the Pacific), anthropology (there was no Pacific anthropologist lecturer), first aid (unmemorable) and typing (unmanageable). Significantly, there was no one in England to teach Fijian or the pidgin English that the two going to the Solomons would have to use. For the cadets destined for Fiji there was, however, invaluable Hindi taught in the Devanagri script. There was also a kind of tutor for our quite unexpectedly large number of eight going to the Western Pacific. This was J. H. Hutton, who was now Professor of Social Anthropology after having been a provincial commissioner in the Naga Hills of Assam. He could tell us nothing about Pacific anthropology, but would entertain us with apocalyptic tales of his life as a provincial commissioner (I was the only one of the eight to become such in name myself). Resting his feet on a dormant golden retriever, he puffed at a pipe which gave off such a delightful aroma that I too went through a phase of smoking Heath and Heather herbal mixture.

The most striking lecturer on the course was Margery (later Dame) Perham. Attractive to look at, she was sturdily independent and impressively coherent. An African expert and later biographer of Lord Lugard, she had toured Samoa and Fiji. I used to talk to her after her lectures on colonial history. As a very young don from Oxford she had early triumphed in bearing down indomitably on colonial administrators, her cogent mixture of acumen and charm drawing out a wealth of information.

Alfred Haddon, one of Christ's octogenarian Fellows, learning that I was going to make a career in Fiji, invited me to his house for tea. He thought that I was making a mistake in my choice of destination: the Gilbert and Ellice Islands were, he considered, less well known and would provide more scope for original study.

It was just as well that I did not go to those beautiful groups of mostly minuscule coral atolls, less than the height above sea level of a man with another standing on his shoulders. Sir Arthur Grimble and my friend-to-be, Harry Maude, had preceded me, the former eventually bringing out the bestseller, *A Pattern of Islands*, and the latter all the worthwhile research possible on those islands. Haddon had himself made his name in Papua with zoological and anthropological expeditions to the Torres Straits in 1889 and, among other works, had written *Head Hunters: Black, Brown and White*.

Although I was to meet many very old Fijians who looked as though they had taken part in, or at least observed as children, feasts centred round human flesh and last indulged in about 60 years before my going to the country, which was the most cannibalistic of all in the world, Haddon is the only person I have met and known positively to have been a cannibal. As a hapless devotee of his sciences, he explained that as part of his getting on with a rather truculent tribe in the closing years of the nineteenth century he had had to partake with nothing less than sang-froid in a cannibal feast. He surprised me by declaring that the best part of

21

it was the ball of a thumb, quite the most tender portion. Not at all uneupeptic. Haddon, with his leonine mane of white hair, bushy white moustache, white shaggy eyebrows and tough short build, was quite one of my favourite Cambridge persons.

A fortnight away from my departure for the great beyond and with the variegated world of Cambridge behind me, Ewart Astill, the perpetually bronzed, fair-haired, open-faced hero of my teens (for Leicestershire and England) and the complete paragon — he had retired from being the first professional captain of any county team — invited me to be twelfth man for Leicestershire against Somerset in two days' time. I had just had a typhoid inoculation and smallpox vaccination and could not bend my left arm (I was right handed). Ewart said that it would be most unlikely that I would be called upon to do more than sit outside on the balcony of the changing room at the Aylestone Road pavilion for the three days. I had never known of an amateur being twelfth man, but it was obviously a kind gesture and I had been so near to moving up from years of successful captaincy of the 2nd XI.

In the event, Somerset (Gimblett and Frank Lee) batted first and very soon George Geary, captain and the other bronzed England-playing idol of my youth (of whom I was to see much up to his death in 1981), signalled to me from the field. I ran down the steps to pass the opening bowler, Haydon (*sic*) Smith, a friend of mine over the previous four years who, with a wink, stated cheerfully that he was feeling sick. He let me stay in the field for most of the Somerset innings to enjoy the first-class experience. At mid-off I was positively peppered with shots for which I could hardly get my arm down to my feet. The force with which Lee, not known for his aggression, propelled the ball from a defensive position off his back foot made me think that this indeed was the difference between county and 2nd XI standard. I was experiencing the testimony first-hand and mighty close. Somerset happened to have the hardest hitters of all sides at that time, notably the brilliant Gimblett (of real England class who was, out of frustration, to commit suicide), Guy Earle, Wellard, Andrews and M. D. Lyon (close to England selection when on leave from the Colonial Service where later, as Chief Justice of the Seychelles, he became the subject of unprecedented questions in the House of Commons for his alleged intoxicated judgments and eccentric conduct).

Dar Lyon could not have been nicer to me or have made me feel more comfortable in the lunch intervals when, as the only amateur in the Leicestershire side, I had to sit with the four Somerset amateurs. I was lucky neither to misfield nor to be hit on the arm, which I had protected with voluminous cotton wool, but I did have to force my arm to straighten it, leaving the muscle ever after strained. It had nevertheless been an experience in which I had revelled, euphoria indeed — out in the middle of my beloved Aylestone Road ground — thanks to Ewart and Haydon. So that was how near I was to the county team at the very last minute.

Even with the South Seas now about to become my background I only wished that I was not on the verge of putting 12,000 miles between myself and the milieu of my now receding earliest youth. But I would be back for long leave in four years' time — or so the Colonial Office regulations proclaimed unswervingly.

Meanwhile, the scenery was certainly going to change. I could not begin to imagine what and whom I should come across far beyond the horizon from England.

2

To the Back of Beyond

I waved goodbye to my mother, who was standing in the bay window at 40 Richmond Road. To me, four years did not seem too long to wait for my six months' home leave to come round. She was stoical. I realized only much later how affected at her age she would have been. So insensitive is youth with a whole future to peer towards. We of course dared not ponder on war intervening disastrously. When I parted from Charles he said that he would visit me within a couple of years. Anne came with me on the journey from Fenchurch Street station, London, in dismal workmen's carriages, to the George V docks. There, at Silvertown (an ironically romantic name for a grim blackened area, overwhelmed by the smell of what one guessed to be hooves being converted into glue — and later devastated as a strategic target in the Blitz) we looked over the 10,000 ton ship, *Port Jackson*. It was one of the Port Line's latest oil burning vessels and carried only 12 passengers. With more than that figure a medical officer would have had to be employed. I saw Anne back down the gangway to the train for her return. Before we could meet again I had, besides learning my job, to have passed the examinations in Fijian, law and local and colonial regulations. Then she could come out at my expense. When would that be?

The ship cast off on 12 August 1938. It was the only time I had been on the sea, other than a day trip as a child across the Bristol Channel, and, therefore, was the first time I had left England: this, at the age of 23, is astonishing no doubt to the so much more fortunate (in that respect) present young generation. The English Channel was smooth. Now there was time to survey the other 11 passengers for New Zealand via Fiji. The list showed three prefixed Miss, which raised one's hopes inordinately that the month-long voyage to Suva, the capital of Fiji, might have some highlights. They turned out to be over 50, except for one of about 30 who was going to marry a prison officer in Fiji. Three of the remaining eight were cadets, like me, going to the South Seas: they had been on the course at Cambridge. One of them, Dave Collins, was easy going and comfortably entertaining: after some vicissitudes he met the ultimate one by being drowned when a dinghy in which he was travelling overturned in surf while attempting to land on an island at nightfall, against the advice of the Fijian captain of the ketch, the *Adi Maopa*, in which I had travelled so often.

The Bay of Biscay, as I was to find on every crossing of it, was wretchedly confused. It put me off my food for three days, but thereafter I was at ease, playing deck tennis (at which, having played it a great deal on land, I was too proficient even for the officers, who unjustifiably felt superior about it before being deflated: spin of all varieties and technique, even swerve, baffled their simple, straight, flat-out hurling). The radio reported that Hutton had scored 364 against Australia, but my thoughts were now forward rather than back to home.

The ship tore apart the massed clogging seaweed of the Sargasso Sea in the Caribbean, the air became sultry and scented and when the ship, now in the Dutch West Indies, was alongside a jetty in Curaçao to have oil pumped in it, I absorbed every detail. Seeing my first palm trees, which have never ceased to embody the exotic for me, the pale blue bay, the white house with arched verandahs on the hill, the dusty, clay road to Willemstad, Curaçao's colourful capital, the intriguing sound of *Papiamento* (the mixed Creole, Spanish and Dutch language of this Dutch colony) and the brachycephalic Negroid faces, mostly cheerful, I realized that foreign parts were for me. This was reinforced by the spectacular violet lightning over the quite visible peaks of Venezuela and Colombia. Then there was the sedate, intricate transit through the

Panama Canal, passing a large Hitler Youth ship (the blond youths crowding the decks to jeer arrogantly at our smaller vessel carrying the Red Ensign, while Nazi flags embodied animosity), thick jungle practically touching the sides of the ship, psychodelically coloured wild birds, dozing alligators on the banks, the locks and Culebra Cut ravine excavated with so many deaths from yellow fever (for which I had no inoculation), excitable West Indian Negroes (George Headley, the superlative West Indian batsman, was born in Panama) on board to handle the chains leading to the donkeys or mules (the electric cars) that pulled us through the series of locks. After Panama City and Balboa had finally been passed and we caught our first glimpse of the Pacific and the ocean's islands (Archipelago de las Perlas), I much regretted that we had not stopped at a port at either one end or the other of the Panama Canal. Although I learnt to my surprise that Panama hats were all made in Ecuador, I would have been able to buy one within the Canal Zone: but hats seemed redundant when one wanted to acquire a tan — and when it was too scorchingly hot for that one sat in the shade of a tarpaulin. We passed close to Pitcairn's Island(s) at night — a maddening miss to be made good on a later voyage — and saw nothing but gigantic albatrosses thousands of miles from land, flying fish that leapt on board or through portholes, whales sporting exhibitionistically and dolphins gleefully cavorting. The appearance of a really high island with steep waterfalls, no beaches and no sign of habitation — Taveuni (where I was years later to be in charge) — constituted impressively my first view of Fijian land.

We had crossed the International Date Line, losing a day by the calendar being put ahead (and put back if moving eastward thereby gaining a day). This line passes over the ocean but used to cross Taveuni Island, which is where the 180° meridian crosses. Before the date-line was swung out to sea by a Fiji ordinance of 1879 'to provide for a uniform date throughout the colony' so as not to cross any land, a Taveuni storekeeper had kept his shop open all days of the week in defiance of the Sunday Trading Law. He claimed that he could have customers on one side of his store straddling the line where it was Saturday and have them in the other half the next day when it was still Saturday, Sunday having passed across his premises. Or, one could actually have one leg standing on Monday and the other on Tuesday.

I suppose that I could have been told 'Go west, young man,' but that should in any case have been 'furthest west', because this is what it was. Fiji was precisely on the opposite side of the world to England at 12,000 miles' distance. New Zealand and Australia were at 11,000 and 10,000 miles' distance respectively. Having reached Fiji, if one went further one would in fact be returning in the opposite direction. This was veritably 'the beyond'.

As the vast Suva Bay, with its encircling jagged peaks of the majestic interior as backdrop (this was the main island of the 300 or so in the archipelago), loomed ahead my keenness was now intense. You should not approach land in the Pacific without a fittingly slow anticipation of delight. This means by foot, launch or ship. By air you miss all the essential aura, aromas and aspects. A launch carrying the pilot, the harbourmaster and two administrative officers drew alongside. One of these two was P. H. Nightingale (known mostly and inevitably as Bird: he was Percy Herbert but never addressed as such). Senior by about ten years and a Christ's man, he was to become a friend (I called him P).

The other was one of the six destined for Fiji with whom I had spent the last year at Cambridge — a New Zealander, H. G. R. McAlpine (known to all only and unoriginally as Mac: like Nightingale his Christian names, Hector Gordon Robert, were never used), who had left the administration of Western Samoa. He was later to share with me a 'batch' (bachelor quarters). Soon after I had left the Pacific finally, he was nearly assassinated on a government station (Lautoka), where I had once been posted, by someone who was never caught. The motive is therefore not known but the incident, which caused McAlpine to be invalided out of the Service with serious groin injuries, was unique in Fiji's 96-year history as a colony from 1874 to 1970.

As we were conducted through the coral reef entrance past the hulks of a couple of wrecks, buildings of disparate sizes came into view, pristine in their whiteness and intriguing as to their function. A self-important administration official came briskly up the gangway when it was lowered at the wharf and then, just as briskly, led us four cadets immediately down it. At the bottom he turned and said, 'I'm Mr X, Establishment Officer, you're now touching Fijian soil' (it was actually tarmac). 'One word of advice: keep your mouths shut.' Fiji proved to be pretty full of ironies. Here was a first. As one got to know him he had a reputation for being just about the most voluble and undiplomatic person in elevated positions in the colony. His staccato manner took me years to get accustomed to and to know how to treat. He and I were to have many working contacts, seldom comfortable, and it was not until we had both retired from the Service's competitiveness that he mellowed and I enjoyed his company in the last years of his life.

It was a Sunday, exactly a month after leaving London, when we arrived in Suva. The capital was enticingly languid, but not languid enough to prevent Dave Collins being promptly put on a small slow cutter for stationing in distant Taveuni, which we had passed. The boat would return with copra — flesh of the coconut used for oil, margarine and soap, holding, for me, a delightful cloying smell, for ever after nostalgic. The other two cadets went to government stations some distance from Suva almost as swiftly. McAlpine had already, a week after arrival, been posted to be with a district commissioner 30 miles away and had come in specially to help welcome us. In the opposite direction from him I was to be attached to the senior district commissioner in the colony's principal government station, Naduruloulou, about 15 miles inland from Suva across a magnificent iron bridge, constructed only the year before to eliminate a pontoon. It spanned the Rewa River, as wide as the Thames, which was surprisingly large for a South Sea island. As the house I was to occupy was not quite free, I was accommodated in the Hotel Metropole near the Suva wharf, reeking alternately of copra and Australian beer from the noisy bar under the first-floor verandah. No one else seemed to be staying there overnight except Moira, the buxom attractive daughter of the rather Teutonic Lance Dietrich, the manager, who had no difficulty keeping order in his bar or anywhere else. When His Excellency the Governor one day could not fail to conceal a beautiful black eye, it was rumoured that

Lance had exercised order in high circles. It would have been diverting (and in the circumstances perhaps not without peril) for me that this outstanding allurement (one learned later that she was the reigning belle of Suva) was in the room next door with a connecting balcony, had she not already patently been earmarked by a sleek brilliantine-haired, jutting-jawed, dashingly handsome Jew working in one of Suva's banks. Moira later became Lady Hedstrom, marrying the knighted son of Sir Maynard Hedstrom, whose Swedish father had been successful in commerce in Levuka, owning a chain of stores throughout the colony.

After dinner I was sitting alone on the road-level verandah sipping coffee when a moustachioed European came up with his coffee cup in hand, saying, 'I'm Gilbert Cowan of the Audit Department. You must be a new cadet.' He had a distracted look in his eye and a disjointed form of conversation. Suddenly he rose from the cane chair, still carrying the coffee cup, stepped out on to the pavement and, without a word, proceeded along it as far as a traffic policeman on point duty a hundred yards away. I could see him turn round and return still holding his cup. Out of it he took a sip as he resumed his seat next to me as though there had been no break in our talk. I was beginning to hope that not all Europeans in Fiji were quite as odd, comforting myself with the contrast offered by Moira Dietrich's fundamental normality. Later I accumulated hosts of stories about the unpredictable Cowan, whose auditing (in the green ink reserved absolutely for the Audit Department, like the red ink regally for the Governor) was, however, the epitome of the orthodox. He was known to have rung up the Lands Department, asked if Mr Cowan was there, only to be told: 'No, he is at the Customs Department this week,' and to reply 'Oh! That is where I am supposed to be, is it?'

At my first Fiji breakfast an orange-fleshed fruit with a mound of black, round seeds in the centre was new to me and I did not like my tentative taste. Pawpaw, papaya and mummy apple were its various names. Quite a long time later I acquired a distinct liking for it, which was also my experience with avocado pears. Pawpaw is renowned for a specially digestible pepsin constituent.

Before my first official engagements on the Monday, a woman

with a quite beautiful, almost ethereally so, dreamy-eyed face had come in and ordered some refreshment. I gathered that she was Aileen Leembruggen, the wife of a man of Dutch-Cingalese descent in the districts. She was an artist of outstanding skill and rather reclusive tendencies. The array of female beauty, judged from the only two seen in the first 24 hours, was as startling as the clamminess of the heat, day and night.

That morning I reported to the Secretariat in the old wooden Government Buildings (about to be demolished as a huge new stone palace of a replacement took shape along the road). The Colonial Secretary (head of the Service after the Governor, who had not yet arrived on new appointment) was away and I did not take at all (I never did: he lived to be 90) to 45-year-old Assistant Colonial Secretary C. W. T. Johnson. I knew him later to be unctuous, even oleaginous, to superiors — a repellent sight. When I saw that attitude also exhibited by others I could never stomach it. Some of those not mentioned in these reminiscences are omitted for that very reason — their two-faced sycophancy and disloyalty to superiors in office. Trevor Johnson was on this occasion transparent smoothness. From his origins, which he kept obscure, and from having risen from a local fifth-class clerkship, he had a complex about officers appointed from England. I never found anything in common with him. All his life he had been in Suva: he never knew the districts or the languages and one could not communicate the feel of Fiji to him, which was one's duty when stationed in the districts. Next below him was a former Christ's man, Charles Nott, of a different calibre. Very understanding, at first primarily a Secretariat type, he later proved himself to be an outstanding district commissioner radiating calm wisdom.

I was invited to pass along the open corridor of power to what was then termed the Native Department. There I had my first bowl of *yaqona* — *kava* made of a powdered root of the pepper family, like no other drink in the world outside the South Pacific. It had to be swallowed in one go and was all the better for not being sipped. I grew to like it and to drink vast quantities of it, socially and ceremonially. It is a first-rate diuretic. I did not realize it at the time, but I had been specially honoured in that the first bowl given to me was handed to me by Ratu George Kadavulevu Cakobau, the great grandson of Ratu Ebenezer Seru Cakobau, the first and only King of Fiji. Ratu (meaning chief, but in this case and a few other exceptional instances, high chief) George was to be a friend ever after, asking a few years later that I should drop the Ratu and call him Kadavulevu. Fijians always called him Ratu George and later Vunivalu, not even Ratu Sir George which he became.

His father, the handsome Ratu Pope, a gentleman philanderer (pronounced Po-pay, Fijian for Bobby), had recently died: I was sorry not to have known him. He had been a cricketer of the very highest quality but, with his athletic days over, died of cirrhosis of the liver in 1936. It is said that before he died he accused Ratu Sukuna (Schooner), of whom we shall hear a good deal soon, of *draunikau*ing him. *Draunikau* is Fijian witchcraft, still powerful today but never known to have an effect on Europeans. It involves letting your enemy or intended victim know that you have an intimate object of theirs, such as a lock of hair or a nail paring. Such an object has a spell worked on it by semi-professional sorcerers. Once victims are made aware of this they turn their backs on the world and their faces to the wall to die rapidly from wasting away as they give up eating or drinking. I knew quite a few such cases, alarmingly some of them whom I thought to be too sophisticated to allow themselves to be affected. They listen to no reasoning from a European or anyone else: they just give up. I did manage to save one person from it. She was our housegirl (that is, cook and general help). Wati Witherow, as her name implies, was part European, part Fijian: very fair-skinned, she alternated between being more European than Fijian and vice versa. One day she did not appear from her house in our grounds to prepare meals. As this had happened before when she had a cold (on Fijians this lies heavily: their resistance is still not as tough as that of Europeans), no notice was taken. But when it extended into two days I went to her house and found it locked. I forced the lock and found her turned to the wall, practically unconscious to this world. I did not think that I could get through to her but I reasoned and implored — and ridiculed *draunikau*

31

(which I knew it to be). She thought that the *draunikau* was because, as she was attractive, she had been more successful over a Fijian man's affections than a rival girl now arranging a spell on her. Within a short time she rather shamefacedly came from her house and was strengthened with food and drink. It had been a near thing.

Back to Ratu George. Square and not tall, with the protruding eyes of King George V and a dark brown skin, he was a clerk in the Native Department learning administration, but would ultimately succeed Ratu Pope as Vunivalu of Bau, the title held by the highest chief in Fiji although Bau Island is no bigger than a large sports ground. He was to have distinguished war service in a Fiji battalion fighting in the Solomons (it was said that he would have received a decoration if he had not been disliked by his commanding officer, Colonel F. W. Voelcker, later a New Zealand Administrator of Western Samoa and a one-eyed man of forbidding appearance, gross stomach and total lack of charisma).

Before the war, about the time of our first meeting over the bowl of *yaqona*, Ratu George had captained the Fiji rugby team touring New Zealand, but was reported to have had insufficient control of his drinking to be entrusted with another visit overseas. A decade later, when I was elected captain of the Fiji cricket team to tour New Zealand, Ratu Sir Lala Sukuna, then president of the Fiji Cricket Association, asked me if I would take Ratu George who was, like his father, a fine all-rounder. I assured Ratu Sukuna that I would not only take him but that I also wished him to be vice-captain; I said I would look after him and guarantee to get the best out of him on and off the field. (Later, Sir Pelham Warner told me that, on touring Australia as captain of England, he had been given the same challenge with Len Braund and had accepted it with gratifying results. Coming to know F. R. Brown later, I was surprised that this admirable England captain declined to take W. J. Edrich, a similar risk, on his tour of Australia when he might have made all the difference between defeat and victory.)

On the field there was no problem. Off the field, after the end of play, it involved taking Ratu George as much as possible to cinemas. For the mass of autograph collectors he signed his name in the list below mine as 'G. K. Thakombau', which is how Cakobau is pronounced. There was never the slightest trouble, even when we were joined midway through the tour by his cousin, Ratu Edward Tuivanuavou Tugi Cakobau, illegitimate son of King George II of Tonga and the leading Fijian chieftainess Ranadi Litia (Lydia) Cakobau, who was the granddaughter of King Cakobau and herself half-Tongan, truly regal as well as beautiful. He, however, signed autographs 'E. T. T. Cakobau', to the understandable bewilderment of collectors comparing his signature with George's. They may have spelled their names differently but they were both indisputable first-class all-rounders. George had an inferiority complex about Edward, which was strange in that George held the higher and more pure Fijian rank. But being less sophisticated by nature, he could not emulate Edward's magnificent, eupeptic, tall, light-bronzed, splendidly proportioned presence. Who could? It prevailed in every circumstance: Edward was perhaps my closest friend in Fiji. We were Ted and Phil. George called me 'Skip' (for skipper) and Philip.

To my disappointment, Ratu George's drinking resumed after the tour. I was now stationed far from him. His first marriage had been unsuccessful, but he had become Vunivalu. In 1956, however, he married Seruwaia Lealea, who had no rank and came from a humble sector (fishermen's clan) of Bau; her striking appearance (pretty with a very light skin), calm intelligence and ambitions for their new family helped work a transformation. Liquor was replaced by orange juice for ever after. His appearance changed from a rather dark, sometimes sullen countenance to one of permanent benevolence. He had learned to suppress his violent temper. I never witnessed any of his well-known liquor-inflamed outbursts, but they had now evaporated utterly. His skin seemed to lighten as his hair turned white and his features improved markedly.

When Fiji gained independence and became a Dominion (an apparent contradiction in terms but in fact replicating Australia's and New Zealand's status: it was the first country to become a Dominion since New Zealand had changed its status from that of a colony to a Dominion in 1907) he was appointed Minister without Portfolio, but showed no predilection for executive work. When the last British governor left, Ratu Sir George Cakobau, GCMG, GCVO, OBE, JP was the natural choice as the first Fijian Governor-General, if one accepts that Ratu Sir Edward Cakobau, KBE, MC, probably could not have been appointed because he had separated from his wife and, unlike George, had no consort. As the elder, Edward should perhaps have held the appointment for three years. Indeed, I feel that he was mortally hurt to have missed it. Ratu George's benevolence, once he was Governor-General and the Queen of Fiji's representative, positively radiated itself. He was kingliness, calm discipline, dignity, presence, worldliness, all combined. He looked the part absolutely and carried out his governor-generalship with consummate ease, to which Lealea contributed remarkably. In culmination, the Queen of England (as a descendant of Queen Victoria, who had reluctantly accepted the cession by the Fijian chiefs of the islands in 1874, she was also Queen of Fiji) on a visit to Bau gave him the highest honour that she can confer. The Royal Victorian Chain is limited to foreign, well-disposed royalty — virtually monarchs alone.

By coincidence, on my second visit to the Native Department shortly after my first, the person who offered me a bowl of *yaqona* was eventually to become Ratu George's successor as Governor-General. Ratu Penaia Ganilau was then a clerk. This tall, genial, pale-skinned figure of width enough to be a rugby forward (which he was) became Colonel Ratu Sir Penaia Ganilau, GCMG, KCVO, KBE, DSO after commanding Fiji's forces in Malaysia during the emergency in the 1950s where he had succeeded Colonel Ratu Sir Edward Cakobau. Peni, as Penaia asked me to call him, was to become the first President of Fiji — but that is another story to be alluded to in the volume following this.

While awaiting my move to Rewa I was encouraged to visit departments and observe the Supreme Court sitting under the Chief Justice. It was there that I first saw Reginald Caten acting as registrar of the court. He was to become a lifelong friend. The ceiling fans scarcely moved the air. In the heat Reg's attention would meander at less important moments. Like Groucho Marx, he had a physically wandering eye that softened the occasion and endeared one to a man of exceptional humour, dry wit and deep humanity. He and George Cakobau, two of my longest and firmest friends, died at the ends of 1988 and 1989.

My first district, known as Rewa, but incorporating the native provinces of Tailevu, Naitasiri and Rewa, included the Cakobau royal dynastic home, Bau. We shall visit it soon. Interpolated here is an extract from my first letter to Charles from my Naduruloulou office dated 3 November 1938:

> I have been in Naduruloulou for a month and so far the sun has appeared on three days only while the prevailing characteristics have been unrelieved grey clouds and heavy rain or perpetual drizzle. Nor has it been warm. Apart from the rather astonishing weather (accounted for mainly by the fact that Rewa and Suva are the wettest and greenest parts of Fiji while the other side of Viti Levu has continuous sun and arid brown Spanish-looking land) life is good if escapist. The signs of eminence and respectability among the Fijians are (a) sunglasses (which are worn principally when it is raining); (b) wristwatches, which they consult knowingly but unprofitably as the timepieces do not work; (c) striped ties which resemble the Hawks' tie.

Like all rapid first impressions, it was not altogether accurate. I was to welcome the greyness, rain and coolness often enough later on in Fiji in place of the everyday certainty of grilling sun and dazzling light (in which I never once wore sunglasses).

Now a word about the District Commissioner whose assistant I was to be. It was crucial that, as a first working experience in closest proximity, I should find him *simpatico*. I had been sent to Rewa partly because it was close to Suva and I could travel in on Saturday afternoons and occasionally on Sundays to play cricket on the magnificent Albert Park alongside Victoria Parade opposite the imposing Grand Pacific Hotel. I was helped to do this by direction, as Acting Governor, of the Colonial Secretary, Juxon Barton, himself at nearly 40 a ferociously fast bowler in Suva's intense, humid, dank heat and one of the few Europeans in the colony to play regularly.

But I could not have received more encouragement than by having Ernest Laidlaw Baker in charge of me (no better man was left without an official honour — at that time sparsely and, frankly, ungenerously conferred). He was an Australian and a complete gentleman. He was quietly spoken (there is no more lasting way to earn respect of Fijians than never to raise one's voice: their own chiefs never do), a top-class Fiji cricketer and a splendid tennis player — smooth-complexioned, blue-eyed, white-haired, he could not have been nicer to a raw cadet from England. He let me study the languages as hard as I could.

I had decided to try and put the Hindi examination behind me first, although I had six years in which to do this, compared with a maximum of four for Fijian and law. While it was still fresh in my mind from tuition at Cambridge I concentrated on it, helped by the court clerk, Gajadhar Singh, an Indian with en brosse hair flecked with grey whom some found abrasive but who entertained me with much of the essential gossip of a new country and was to be a friend for life (even visiting me in Rugby 30 years later after he had had three serious heart attacks). With him behind a machine in the courthouse emblazoned with the arms and inscription 'IMPERIAL TYPEWRITERS, LEICESTER' and his idiomatic, cultured use of English, I felt straightaway at home.

Having learnt it at Cambridge from an academic, I found myself speaking a grade of Hindi higher than that of the peasants and storekeepers to whom I lived close. I also used the Devanagri (Sanskrit) script exclusively, its characters attracting me with their quintessential Orientalism and also helping in conciseness of diction. In my view, there is no substitute for learning by use of the native script the language strictly divorced from Roman characters. When I took the examination after a few months in Fiji I was the first ever to do so in the Devanagri characters and the first to pass with distinction (I understand that no one ever did subsequently). I remember that for the oral, conducted by two highly placed Indian civil servants and a veteran European inspector of schools (from India, he was, incredibly enough, apart from the Director of Medical Services and the Secretary for Indian Affairs, Dr Victor McGusty, the only European to know the language in its pure form as opposed to that of the Colonial Sugar Refining Company's overseers, who spoke it fluently but ungrammatically, inexorably so as to be understood, at cane-cutter level), I had to describe my voyage from England through Panama and my first impressions of my arrival in Fiji.

Mr Baker, as he was to me (I was Mr Snow to him), was inspiring. I was only sorry that he was to retire to Australia in six months (he did not look 58 with his boyish face and clear, frank eyes) but I am glad that it was my idea that he should be given a walking cane surmounted in gold with an inscribed ivory whale's tooth (of which more later) handle, which was subscribed for among the government station staff. Ernie Baker was not the type of district commissioner Willie Maugham (as he was always known to fellow writers who avoided the use of 'Somerset') could have envisaged. (Charles abhorred his habits and saw little of him, but I wish I had met him in his younger days.) Maugham might, however, have found a place for his successor, Aimé John Armstrong (who was also 58 but looked his age — trimly moustached, unathletic, slow moving with brown eyes rather weary of the world). Of local origin, A. J. (as he was known: we were Mr Armstrong and Mr Snow to each other) had been divorced twice: periodically there would be female 'cousins' staying with him. Speaking so softly that one could hardly hear him, he would never raise his voice in his occasional rages. These would take the form of tearing the telephone (which he loathed) off the wall or snapping in half a dozen pencils handed to him for taking to an Indian advisory committee meeting (he was not fond of Indians and specialized in Fijian affairs), all with muttered curses. I saw another incidence of rage, contained though it was.

Driving his underpowered tiny Morris Minor up and down quite steep hills from Naduruloulou to Vunidawa, the capital of the inland district of Colo (meaning interior) East now added to the jurisdiction of the Rewa district, he would swear at the vehicle softly but persistently. Eventually, its radiator would start to steam. It was the duty of Ismail, his rascally cook and houseman, to keep in the car two green George IV whisky (Australian brand) bottles, one full of whisky and the other of water. A. J. reached to the back of the car, got out and poured abstractedly into the radiator from a green bottle, which proved to be just what the car needed. The trouble was that it was also at this stage that A. J. needed whisky. He always carried it with him for a long nip but now his supply was in the radiator. Whisky and *kava* were what he drank: water never. A. J. swore *sotto voce* in English and Fijian for the rest of the long day. For a man of 15 stone A. J.'s car was absurdly small, but it nevertheless took the leading part in what, for me, was an unforgettable occasion.

Like so many men of dubious morality in important office, he liked to be seen as a regular Sunday churchgoer. It was because he had been invited on a Sunday to open a road constructed at their own expense by Indian peasant farmers that broodingly he took the fortunately short distance to Verata for the purpose. Bearing away from the river round a bluff full of foliage, he was on the newly gravelled road before he knew quite where he was. The car dutifully did a dramatic skid on the loose surface and straightened out before it could be braked to shoot ahead through a red, white and blue ribbon, thereby severing it rather prematurely. All the numerous Indians on each side of the road loyally started to sing God Save the King, no doubt considering that it must be a new imperial style of road-opening. An Indian boy scout, hearing the approach of the car but not seeing it, was obviously already at the salute — only to scatter out of the way of the skid and fall into one of the new ditches full of water at the side from which he emerged sopping wet — and loyally saluting. We then led the way down the new road and almost at its end, at a spot too narrow for other cars to pass it, A. J.'s car, which had a mutinous individuality of its own, developed a puncture. This was immediately mended by Indians with impressive solemnity while A. J. and I were garlanded and regaled in a palm-leaved pavilion at the side of the road by every conceivable Indian of any status making repeated deep gestures of obeisance with hands pressed together in front of them and enunciating interminable complimentary speeches about A. J.'s interest in the history and accomplishment of the road which, if the truth were known, was pretty minimal. We were given cherryade to drink but A. J.'s mind was on another beverage. With Indians embarrassedly rising, squatting, covering and uncovering their heads alternately in their confused desire to pay their most courteous respects, A. J. made his excuses and, before it could be involved in further aberrations and mis-adventures, the little car sped back along the gravel, dust rising behind us and the Indians still no doubt discussing the great providence of their God in giving them Englishmen to guide their ways grandly if sometimes mysteriously.

A. J. was not to enjoy Ernie Baker's sedate retirement. He retired two years later in 1942 to the Fijian island of Kadavu as a sort of part-time district officer and soon died in some loneliness with the solace of his favourite tipple but little else to interest him. His long government service went, like Baker's, officially unhonoured. I remember them as unfailingly courteous and kind gentlemen. I could not have started under more sympathetic expert tutelage.

Both Baker and Armstrong were only too glad for me to take over entirely the court work. The law part of the Administrative Service course at Cambridge had been quite intense — criminal, civil, tort and contract: it was considered to represent half an LL B. At first I sat with Baker on the bench while I was learning the Fiji court law code known as ordinances. He would patiently consult my view about the defendant's guilt or innocence and, to my reassurance, he nearly always said that it was his view too. On passing an ordinances examination set by Baker, I was confirmed by the Governor in my appointment, ceased to be a cadet, and was granted by the Governor a commission under seal to be a district commissioner. I was now a magistrate with restricted powers until I passed the Law examination. Baker let me take the court — it was virtually a daily duty — in which I was most helpfully guided by my new friend, Gajadhar Singh, the much-experienced court clerk, a little short with his Indian social inferiors and not ingrati-ating to his superiors, who included the principal lawyers, Samuel Ellis, Robert Munro, Maurice Scott (all three ultimately knighted), Said Hassan and W. L. Davidson, who had come out from Suva. They were the cream of their profession (with one or two excep-tions in Lautoka on the other side of the main island of Viti Levu), but I did not feel daunted by their presence, which was always helpful and courteous. Their 20 or 30 years in the colony were never hinted at by them as against my single year.

One day the court clerk had to absent himself. Something almost without precedent had occurred. Abdul, the Romeoesque son of Ismail, the Muslim houseman of A. J. (why such an Indophobe chose an Indian as his houseman was never clear to me), had attempted to abduct Kamla, the elegant Julietesque daughter of the Hindu court clerk, Gajadhar Singh. Such cross-religious happenings were virtually impossible. Ismail engaged the leading Muslim lawyer, Said Hassan, to defend his son, while Gajadhar engaged the doyen of the legal profession, Samuel Ellis (who was Jewish and when knighted after having donated the funds to provide a bomber during the war chose to style himself Sir Howard) to protect the virtuous name of his daughter, who was kept in relative purdah. I could not find the case proved beyond reasonable doubt. This disappointed Gajadhar greatly. But it was not long before he resumed his invitations to me to his house for playing ludo with Kamla, her rounded, vivacious and equally bright-eyed sister, Devi, and young brother, Hari, after curried goat, which I thought wonderful in my spartan existence as a bachelor. Gajadhar's wife was in strict purdah, tantalizingly passing behind a beaded curtain of the verandah where we played. I was teaching Hari Latin, which he took to rapidly through the syntactical similarities with Hindi, while Gajadhar coached me in Hindi. There were frequent invitations like this. It was rare for Europeans in those days to enter Indian houses and mix with the families. I gained much.

It was during the Muslim–Hindu case that Maurice Scott, who was awaiting the next case in which he was to participate, got up to one of his tricks. Said Hassan, waving off the heat with a handkerchief, had a habit of jumping up on to his feet, 'With respect, Your Worship', to interpose an objection with the handkerchief flicked perilously close to constituting assault on fellow lawyers sharing the table. In a dull moment of legal wrangling Hassan duly jumped up only to upset the whole table and bring the four lawyers seated there down on their knees. Unobserved, Maurice Scott, next to him, had leant down and, with a handkerchief, managed to tie Hassan's leg under the table to one of its legs. Hassan, a solemn Arabian-looking Muslim of impeccably dignified demeanour, was not amused.

When war started in 1939, Scott, handsome son of Sir Henry Scott, by then largely retired as the colony's leading solicitor and politician who had married a missionary's beautiful daughter, left Fiji to train as a pilot. He returned from the RAF with a DFC, resumed his profession with a slight accretion of dignity, followed Ratu Sir Lala Sukuna as the second Speaker of the Legislative Council and was himself knighted. Always euphoric, he was married after two divorces to Fenna Gatty, the Dutch widow of Harold Gatty who had been the first to fly round the world as navigator with the one-eyed American Indian, Wiley Post, as pilot and had then settled in Fiji. Scott's predilection for sociability sadly led to a fatal excess of drinking.

A colonial government station, so important to its residents and of interest to visitors and historians alike, needs to be described. It had little in common with Indian Civil Service administrative district headquarters. So, before its singular nature passes out of the Empire's history this is the time to describe such a place and its personnel. Thick in nostalgia, there is no better example than Naduruloulou, the seat of Fiji's senior district commissioner. Approached on a gravelled road on the side of the Rewa River, there was, first of all, a bungalow on the top of the highest hill, 72 steps up in that humidity of 90 per cent and a temperature of 85 to 90 degrees. The sub-accountant's compact house was reclassified as the district officer's residence when I occupied it five years later. Along the road, but on the level next to a grass tennis court and thatched summer house, a short path led to the district commissioner's sprawling bungalow. With a hill immediately at the back, it was dark, an effect increased by the verandah round two sides of it being encased in thick mosquito wire gauze. It was the oldest extant administrative officer's house in the colony. On a flagstaff the Union Flag hung limply in the airlessness and a superb spreading weeping fig shaded the entrance to a private door into the DC's office. The Administration office was so close to the road that it was possible to step off a horse right on to the verandah entrance. CSR Company officials sometimes did that. Inside was one large room, with the DC's office on its own through a door.

Miss Bertie Lovell Hilton (as she was officially styled) was the first person to greet one on arrival. With her grey hair and rimless spectacles she looked like a matron in a South Carolina homestead. Under a wide-brimmed floppy straw hat her face was the whitest one could imagine in the tropics, almost luminously so. As the postmistress, she was the only official not to have government quarters: she lived with her widowed sister up a steep hill down the road from the Government Station, with one of the finest views in Fiji. Over a right-angled bend and a ferocious whirlpool of the river, they looked straight up a wide stretch of calm water reflecting magnificent orange sunsets and orange moonrises (the moon used to rise as a huge golden globe, with the land shapes on it clearly delineated before it became a dazzling silver orb) to the mountains of Colo ahead. The most prominent shapes on the horizon were a couple of curved peaks formed like a woman's breasts — known in the Fijian language as Medrausucu, meaning just that for they couldn't have been anything else.

After Miss Hilton's welcome, one of polite, deeply concealed curiosity (she did not see many Europeans), at the office entrance was Kitione (Gideon: many Fijians' first names are adapted from the Bible) Lalakomacoi, a tall, imposing, extremely handsome and stately Fijian from the commoners' segment of regal Fiji on Bau Island. He was married to a Bau chieftainess, sister of Ratu Sukuna (soon to be referred to as the outstanding Fijian of all time). Kitione, who was the leases clerk, dealt mostly with Indians in Hindustani (the unaristocratic, ungrammatical structure of Hindi which no Fijian ever spoke in pure form) over their leasing land which, by skilful direction in the late 1870s from the first Governor, Honourable Sir Arthur Gordon, remained for the most part in Fijian hands. Kitione rose to the rank of Roko Tui Bua and his son to Assistant Commissioner of Police.

Then there was Choy Raman, the dark Tamil (southern Indian) revenue clerk. This was a rather ironical term because, behind unfailingly gleaming teeth, he was (this was not discovered until

42

two years after I had left the station) methodically embezzling — for which he served a prison sentence.

Yet, within touching distance of him and next to a massive safe was his superior Terry Fenton, a slender Irishman with a moustache, wire-rimmed glasses and infectious laugh. He was the sub-accountant (there was no accountant as such except the Accountant General in Suva) and I was to sit with him, as part of the training set for me by Baker, picking up what that post involved — mostly clerical drudgery and really quite heavy financial responsibility, as I was later to experience. Fenton relished me as a diversion, a rapt new audience for his fund of stories about people in Fiji. He had been in the government since 1924 and what he did not know about Europeans in Fiji, as I judged better after 14 further years' knowledge, simply was not worth knowing. He had an insatiable interest in the human scene, but it was mostly European, for he did not have anything like a DC's immersion among non-European people. Though his stories were not very historical — only dating from about a decade before his own arrival — they were strong on current personalities. In later years, on researching issues covered by the *Fiji Times*, I found that most of his accounts of the 1920s and 1930s were corroborated by the written word — at least those of his stories that could be printed without risk of libel. It could not have been a more congenial introduction for me.

At times I would go and sit on the little jetty alongside which the DC's launch, the *Ruve* (Woodpigeon), was tied. This was an old but impressive craft with graceful lines and sash windows but little used now that there were a few roads. Unless engaged in other duties for the DC, the busybody Muslim, Ismail, was inevitably its engineer. He considered himself the captain and did not take kindly to being the navigator for anyone other than the DC, being most put out at the wheel when I took Gajadhar Singh's entire Hindu family (apart from his wife) on a jaunt up the river.

Just as Muslims and Hindus hardly ever intermarry, Fijians and Indians were also physically and psychologically antipathetic. Indians often had such fine features that Europeans would feel inclined to cohabit with them, but could not overcome the family's protectiveness or ostracism, which also tended to occur in Fijian–European marriages or liaisons. Chinese–Fijian relationships were more common in country districts. Fijians were more tolerant of ethnic mixing among their own kin than either Europeans or Indians. The skin colours of Indians varied as remarkably as one would expect from a huge continent, ranging from a European colour to the almost black hue of Madrasis and Tamils. But none had quite the blue-black tone of the elderly little men who had settled in Fiji from the Solomons and who kept their tobacco in holes in their earlobes. They were gentle and came in periodically from primitive settlements to pay a token tax. I picked up their expressions for steam train (big fella firesnake); aeroplane (big fella all same b'long Jesus Christ); piano (little fella you smack 'im in teeth 'im sing out ting ting); and violin (little fella you scratch 'im in belly 'im scream). The pidgin English of the Solomon Islands varied from that of the New Hebrides (Vanuatu) and Papua New Guinea, where it was also spoken with robust profanities.

Apart from sightseers in taxis from tourist liners varying their day's call in Suva with a visit to what they considered the real Fiji, virtually the only European visitors to the Administration Office would be officials from the Colonial Sugar Refining Company, the cane planting, crushing and refining divisions of which dominated the sugar-growing areas of Fiji. These officials were all Australians, apart from the general manager, Henry King-Irving. He, being driven around by a chauffeur in the only other Humber limousine besides the Governor's, was a very English, deaf, moustachioed, dignified, courtly and noble-looking curiosity. Industry and commerce in Fiji were led almost exclusively by Australians, but they (and New Zealanders) occupied only a minority of the most senior of the Colonial Service posts. Other than a few veteran antipodean DCs and heads of departments, these were the prerogative of English appointees.

Visitors to the adjacent Provincial Office were exclusively Fijians, either to pay native taxes or to deal with general Fijian affairs, which were attended to by the provincial scribe, Uraia (Uriah) Koroi. A commoner from down-river Rewa, he was a great wit as much in English as in Fijian. Since a certain amount of democratization and further delegation of responsibility were evolving in Fijian society and measures of independence were growing — which I always understood to be our colonial purpose — I thought that he would go far, for he was a natural public relations man. He eventually turned to that, but only after having served a short prison sentence for embezzling government money. For some Fijian officials, this was sadly and inevitably an insuperable hurdle to overcome (after all, theirs was but a recent cash society, which some regarded as fair game).

That had happened some time after my second posting to Naduruloulou ended in 1944 and I had left for the Secretariat. He had a first-rate intellect; he just should not have been given financial responsibility. I doubt whether even better pay would have suppressed the temptation. I never understood how so agile a brain could have thought that he would not be found out.

This puzzled me with many of the brightest Fijians, among whom I placed highly Ratu Alipate (Albert) Naucabalavu (long nose: his wasn't markedly so) Naulivou. He was a minor Bau chief and had helped me to uncover an embezzlement by one of the highest chiefs, but then later indulged himself. Too large a proportion of high, some of them the highest, chiefs seemed not to regard government money as different from private money and therefore did not see themselves as stealing it, but saw it as theirs to borrow, at first temporarily, then of course irreplaceably. This seemed to me the most vivid example of bronze idols having clay feet (I once thought of writing a general book on Fiji with the title *Bronze and Clay*, but the clay part diminished with the passage of time). Koroi's assistant was a high chief from Bau, Ratu Joni Kikau — dignified, if rather stiff physically and mentally. Throughout my period in Fiji, when Ratu Sir Lala Sukuna was the only Fijian to be so recognized, I could never have guessed that after independence in 1970 Ratu Joni would be knighted among others (so some, looking for disparagement or believing themselves overlooked, inevitably thought in their vanity) rather capriciously picked out. But the honour did seem to fit his dignity and he had become Roko of three provinces. Meanwhile, the more imaginative and vivacious Uraia Koroi languished underemployed (quite rightly not in a financial capacity) after independence and died in his sixties with his gifts never properly brought out to Fiji's advantage — like those of some other commoners with the right balance.

Between the Administration Office and Provincial Office was the courthouse. It was precluded from any slight zephyr of air by the two buildings and a hill immediately at the back. Often intolerably hot, with its corrugated iron roof (all the buildings except those at Batiki, further along the road, had these roofs, traps as much to attract the full beating down of the sun as for channelling the torrential rain siphoned off into tanks), it had a large *punkah* (a wide stretch of canvas suspended from the roof). This was swung back and forth languorously by a prisoner — the *punkah-walla* — squatting on the grass behind the magistrates' door to the courthouse with a cord stretching from it to his toe, which he wiggled periodically.

The Police Office housed an inspector or superintendent (at that time always a European), a beturbanned (invariably Sikh) Indian or Fijian sergeant in scalloped-edged *sulu* (skirt) with a Fijian or Indian corporal and about four constables. The inspector lived on a ridge in a house set back along a well-mown path, on one side of which was the station cow (free milk for all) and a compound containing houses for the junior policemen and gaol warder, as well as the gaol holding about a dozen perpetrators of relatively minor offences. Major offenders — serving more than six months' imprisonment — were always sent to the gaol in Suva. The lawns around and in front of all the houses on the station were well-mown. On passing the prisoners in their thick shirts and shorts made of sacking, it took me a while to lose my apprehension about the wicked-looking machetes they wielded to cut down thicker grass. The group of up to a dozen were supervised by a single warder — often a Sikh, like the Indian police sergeant or corporal. He carried a token baton sometimes (no one had ever known of a warder being attacked) and they could easily have committed mayhem before fleeing into the bush. But they preferred to remain with their rations of tinned corned beef and salmon, superior to the daily food in their villages and settlements.

The police inspector would supply the court with criminal cases; I, as magistrate, sometimes supplied prisoners from them if a short sentence was appropriate: it carried little or no stigma among their own people. Can I be sufficiently convincing that the station's need for prison labour — the prisoners also carried big blocks of ice in sacking to the houses and dug pit latrines — and my judgement in the cases were unconnected? I can only say with hand on heart that they were. I was too fond of feeling that, just as I had no racial prejudice whatever, my judgements in all aspects of my work, while they might sometimes have been wrong, certainly contained no whiff of favouritism. This sounds pompous but they were the principles without which one might as well have thrown in the job. It was as near pure justice as one was ever likely to find.

No house had electricity or indoor flush lavatories. Inside sentry boxes a few yards from the houses were deep holes surmounted by wooden seats under which the vicious centipedes and large, inquisitive but harmless spiders lurked while giant, dark brown, shiny cockroaches flew from there to scavenge in kitchens unless vigorously controlled by a 'flit' (DDT) hand pressure gun. Torches or hurricane lamps fuelled by kerosene or petrol (benzine) lanterns (their delicate mantles partly covered) were an essential accompaniment to the latrine at night. At the courthouse there would be a separate *vale-ni-vo* (house of the po, as the Fijian words described it, 'v' being interchangeable with 'p' not quite accurately since there was no po as such), with a key available only from the court clerk for the lawyers; similar discrimination (key in the care of Miss Hilton) existed for European officials and visitors and high chiefs at the Administration Office, with an unlocked *vale-ni-vo* for others. This was about the only instance of European discrimination on the station. Maugham would never have understood that: he was writing about stations in Malaya and perhaps circumstances were different there. A fine writer, supremely so in short-story form, he was never to be trusted.

The river was close to one side of Naduruloulou with the gravel road running parallel to it and then in from the river and road there were a number of low hills. The revenue clerk and the court clerk lived next to each other on one of these mounds, but

Gadjadhar Singh had nothing to do with Choy Raman. Separated from their Indian homeland by thousands of miles, a gulf of breeding and background, underlined by colour, lay between a near Brahmin Hindu and a Tamil, the former yellowish brown and the latter like the blackest of Indians, so nearly Solomon Islander in hue. The spectrum of colour sensibility and prejudice was as wide among them as between Fijians from the coast and interior and between half-castes, quarter-castes and three-quarter-castes (generally termed Euronesians or part-Europeans). I had friends in all classes.

Then, on a little plateau, was the house of the Fijian provincial constable, Ratu Simeone (Simeon) P. Vugetia. As his neighbour, I came to know him well. He had jurisdiction over Fijians to the extent that he delivered summonses and warrants; he would also act as my *matanivanua*, literally, eyes of the land. By tradition, each chief — European administrators enjoyed such status — had a *matanivanua*, a herald through whom communications with other chiefs would be made.

He would squat cross-legged at one's feet at ceremonies to be handed, after a presentation to the chief or administrator, the ceremonial ivory whale's tooth, which in earlier days held the power of life or death and now was a symbol of unbreakable trust. Receipt of the presentation, which would be made with the wish for a good relationship or for a favour (never related to pleas for leniency in court or to court matters at all), meant that the spirit in which it was given had to be honoured strictly. When it was handed on to him after the chief or administrator had said in Fijian 'I accept these riches in order that the land may prosper,' or words to that effect, the *matanivanua* would expand on the gratitude and honour. Ratu (wherever Fijians had the title Ratu it was the nadir of manners not to use it in addressing them. For reasons of space in this narrative it sometimes has to be omitted) Simeone had the poker face, thin and creased, of Victor Borge and beneath its solemnity lay Borge's kind of deadpan humour. He knew no English except two nonsensical phrases spoken with deliberate and near-perfect diction: 'I want to play tennis with the girl guides,' and 'I love the sweet smelling para grass' (these are plumes like pampas that grow in the sugar cane). Koroi had mischievously taught them to him in order to amuse me — I don't think Simeone used them to any other European. Simeone knew he would be guaranteed a laugh. The phrases would come out of the blue as we sat round a bowl of *yaqona* in his house.

When we became great friends (Simeone would give me yams and pawpaw from the vegetable garden behind his house: in front of it was a lawn on which I taught Fijian and Indian members of the station to play deck tennis) he invited me to the village of which he was chief — Vuniniudrovu, just off the Rewa downstream in the Waimanu tributary. The day came. He had gone on ahead. I followed in a punt across the Rewa along the Waimanu. It was dark but I was greeted at the landing on the bank with a row of bearers of flaming torches stretching back in two lines to the ceremonial house. It was a Cecil B. de Mille scenario.

Alternately, between the bare-chested torch bearers, their faces blackened with soot, were men carrying clubs over their shoulders. Their torsos glistened with coconut oil: they wore skirts of leaves. I walked between the two lines (it was the most impressive physical reception I ever received at the hundreds of villages I visited) and took my place on the one chair in the house where a squatting array of similarly blackened faces and oiled chests, arms and legs was already congregated. Like most races of brown or yellow pigment, they had no hair on their backs and very little, if any, on their chests, which were extremely well muscled. In deep unison they called out a monosyllable of respectful welcome.

Immediately I was seated I noticed that Ratu Simeone had discarded his khaki shirt and khaki, scalloped-edged *sulu* and was squatting in a skirt of glistening leaves with black circles on his forehead and oiled shoulders. Hanging from his neck was a superb, large, ivory-lined, mother-of-pearl shell breastplate. It was the best I was to see in Fiji, even superior to the one or two at the great ceremonies on Bau. It shone in the orange light of the hurricane lamp suspended in the centre of the house by wire from a rafter. Ratu Simeone's skirt was of variegated green, scarlet and yellow croton leaves. An identical skirt was also worn by the man approaching in a crouching position with a whale's tooth, for which I had learnt the acceptance speech and which I handed to the *matanivanua* (on this occasion this could not be Ratu Simeone as he was my host) squatting closely at my feet. He took it and made a short speech. It was the finest whale's tooth (only cachalot whales have teeth) — rich brown, polished caringly over the years — I ever had. It was unfortunately to be lost in an earthquake-cum-tidal wave. I have always missed it.

Then followed the ceremonial presentation of *yaqona*. A huge root, hauled into the assembly, was touched by a man who offered it to me: it was in turn touched by the *matanivanua* who broke off a small root while thanking them for it. Then one of the three round the large bowl who faced me, flanked by two others with blackened faces and glistening torsos, started to knead the *kava*, previously pounded into powder, with the water that was poured in from behind him out of a hollowed-out bamboo tube. A handful of hibiscus fibre sifted out any nodules of *kava* and, after being thrown dextrously backwards by the mixer, caught and shaken outside, it was again brought crouchingly to the bowl where the mixture was turning khaki-coloured.

The archaic, unmelodious chanting, which had started with the mixing, continued. After a number of throwings, wringings out and kneadings, the officiant declared, 'The chiefly *yaqona* is prepared.' The *matanivanua* replied, 'Pour it.' The chanting had stopped. A young man in the same apparel as all the others but with a necklace of split whale's teeth bent down to the large bowl, inserted in it a small polished half coconut and approached in upright style. Taking a half coconut cup, which the *matanivanua* offered me, I held mine out to the cup-bearer. He filled it up with the mud-coloured liquid and squatted on the floor while I drank it as custom dictated in one gulp, after which they all clapped and called out, 'It is dry.' The young man rose to take another cup to my *matanivanua*. Then to Ratu Simeone, his *matanivanua*, and to lesser chiefs with *matanivanua*s following. Ratu Simeone had done his new friend proud.

It was then back to Naduruloulou Government Station. Up a hill of 39 steps off the government road was my bungalow, with Ratu Simeone's house below. It had wooden sides with glass windows in front of mosquito gauze. The front door and doors between the rooms — verandah, dining room, two bedrooms, kitchen — were all mosquito protected. Inayt, a Hindu of about 65 but looking older, had been found by the police inspector to look after me. He had a large, grey, walrus moustache, tousled white hair and wore a *dhoti* — a white cloth pulled up between his spindly, unsteady legs: he was benign and supremely respectful. It might have contributed to his liking me that I never ate anything but poached egg on toast and tea for breakfast, the same for lunch and the same for dinner plus tinned strawberries and tinned cream. I lived on this because I preferred it to anything else and it was my initial chance, living on my own for the first time and therefore able to indulge in my preference, to do as I wished. But it was a surprise to me when, after a couple of months, I felt weak getting out from under the mosquito net round my bed and found that I could not stand. Fenton, Dennis and Molly Hill (the Fiji-born police inspector and his Tasmanian wife with whom I had stayed for the first week while the faithful Inayt was being found for me as cook — Ernie Baker was away and his wife was in Australia) all decided that I must have — promptly — changes in my diet. Inayt was told and he started making curries with vegetables and frying sausages, and I soon felt better. Fenton had given me the salutary warning that a cadet two years previously, William Pakenham-Walsh — alone on the isolated island of Kadavu — had died (they were pre-penicillin days) from the combination of a hornet's sting in an open carbuncle but also more fundamentally of malnutrition. This was not to be the first case of a rather similar death that I was to know of relating to a bachelor in the solitude of the Pacific. Gerald Gallagher, a district officer in the Gilbert Archipelago, was another tragedy — from coral sores, malnutrition and galloping consumption on the exceedingly remote Gardner Island in the Phoenix group.

One day I had occasion to retrieve a ball from the corrugated iron roof whence it rolled down to lodge in a gutter. I climbed up alongside the large tanks into which rainwater would pour (there was no piped water on the station: these tanks were our only source from the corrugated iron roof of the house along gutters) to collect it. I was revolted to find with the ball two decomposed rats — of a size which only the Fijian species can attain. All the water that I had been drinking (even though by strict injunction from my European co-residents it was boiled and then stored in the chest containing sometimes a block of ice) had palpably soaked in and flown over, round and through these murky corpses. It cannot have done my health, psychological if not physical, a great deal of good. But apart from that day off through weakness at Naduruloulou, I worked every day including Saturday mornings and sometimes Sundays without illness throughout my time in Fiji. That is, except for about a week off in Vunidawa with dengue fever in 1944 and a plague of carbuncles on Taveuni in 1948. My regular games playing, I am sure, was responsible for this good fortune.

The legs of the government-provided ice chest, like the gauze-fronted meat safe, were mounted inside empty meat tins containing water and a little kerosene to deter mosquitoes from laying larvae in them and to frustrate climbing ants. Ice came sporadically from Nausori, the township four miles away, by a decrepit open station wagon and was deposited by the driver in the empty garage at the bottom of the steps, later to be humped up on sacking by a prisoner. Meat came by the same vehicle. Despite the huge river being at the bottom of my house there was never fish — remarkable, considering that one was living in an archipelago of 300 islands.

The zinc-lined ice-chest would usually be filled with Australian beer in bottles and with bottles of boiled water. I was not to have a paraffin-fired refrigerator before living in Lomaloma when I was only able to obtain the height of such expensive luxury (paid for, paraffin too, by government) for the purpose of storing anti-tetanus serum for the hospital.

Translucent gecko lizards occupied the house with me. With suction pads on the feet of their four fragile legs, they would periodically fall from their upside-down habitation on the ceiling. If any creature is to lose its grip and plop down into your soup, cream or curry, then let this inoffensive, companionable one do so. Should its tail be caught in a closing door or window, another

52

would be grown. With their delicate, dainty, timidly inquisitive ubiquity one could not feel alone in the utter stillness of Fiji's rural tropical nights.

On the other hand, one would have preferred the most deafening silence not only to the hostile whining hum of the mosquitoes but to the crazy swishing about of the giant cockroaches with long waving antennae — permanent inhabitants of kitchens. The cockroaches (their name is suitably repellent) glistened brown; they crawled all day, which was preferable to their flying at night when they collide with your face and emit a stale odour. Squashed, they oozed a white liquid which also smelled stale. No kitchen, even Government House's, would be without them: boiling water was the only way to be rid of them. The only slight deterrents to them were giant spiders, not poisonous like some of Australia's but larger. When they were not in the lounges, verandahs or bedrooms, they would go on safari in the kitchen and catch a token cockroach. If they themselves were threatened, they released the sacs carried underneath in a cocoon containing hundreds of small ones which fled to all quarters dementedly.

Centipedes would insinuate themselves in the house from the latrines. The first time I had a close look at one was after I had woken up in the early hours of the morning saltily thirsty after a beer session in Suva. In the kitchen sink, where I was pouring water from a tap — there was no bottle of boiled water available — I could not believe my eyes, which were not until then focusing. A long shape, with short, spiny legs which could well have totalled 100, counting both sides, and sharp, hooked mandibles at its head and tail, was lurking, not disposed to conceal its menace. It had to be got rid of. I had heard that boiling water was most effective. But there was none immediately available. So I cut it in half with a knife. Each half walked off. Thereupon I cut it into quarters, which did not extinguish the repugnant, sinuous interloper. I finally had to cut it up completely. Centipedes have a habit, I had been told, of selecting specially comfortable places, such as under one's pillow or in slippers, where scorpions in other countries are reported to make for. I always went barefooted, so they were deprived of them in my house. But I always checked under my pillow, without ever discovering one there. If bitten, the only known prophylactic or alleviator was the application of washing blue. Centipedes did seem to prefer one's external earth latrines, the most menacing of locations. In that habitat I saw them but could not catch them. Dissected stomachs of giant toads, introduced from Hawaii just before I arrived in Fiji to eliminate an insect damaging sugar-cane leaves, showed that centipedes were not out of reach of a toad's enormously elongated quick tongue.

The Hawaiian toads soon proliferated to the stage where roads were greasy with squashed, spread-eagled silhouettes. Queensland, which shares the species, goes to the extent of having road signs warning of skids where toad colonies exist alongside roads running through sugar plantations. It was impossible to walk on lawns in Fiji at night without treading on their spongy resilient backs. They would rise again like cats' eyes on roads to bound about unresentfully in giant undiscouraged leaps, sometimes flapping against your knees. One would nonchalantly walk barefoot in the hot nights on the grass: the sensation of contact in that form was not, however, wholly anodyne to the human sole. They put dogs in jeopardy. Toads' defence mechanisms are poison glands which inquisitive dogs lick with lethal results. And toads would jump into Fijians' cooking pots on kitchen floors. Fatalities among Fijians occurred when the intruders had not been noticed in the food. In Queensland, as in Fiji, toads eat everything but what they were introduced for. In that State it is regrettable that youths deliberately run them down in their vehicles: on the other hand, a worthy Queensland mayor is trying to gain public support for a statue to Toad in the main square of his township. As Ernie Baker said of toads to me, trying to avoid them in his car: 'They sit and think; sometimes they just sit.' Their best trick is to form a pyramid, about 20 standing on each other's backs, taking their turn, with their long sticky tongues, to catch hornets under nests beneath the houses built on squat concrete stilts. They have certainly taken, in their exile from Hawaii, to a new country with an enthusiasm which they conceal behind impassive, thin-lipped, quarter-to-three countenances. There is, nevertheless, with all their pros and cons, the fact that the giant toads make a meal of centipedes, if they are so lucky as to encounter them on their nocturnal rounds. Centipedes and giant toads are specially unexpected features of the generally imagined paradisiacal life in the South Seas.

Not in Rewa, but in islands near the sea, other cohabitants of the house besides toads, lizards, spiders, cockroaches, centipedes and mosquitoes (and never excepting the bloated flies) were land crabs, which were extremely difficult to eject from the house, into the corners of which they would retreat, brandishing their claws like punch-drunk boxers. Fijians could manage to find a way of evading their pincers and extract them. Land crabs were delicious to eat.

An occasional addition to my diet, albeit a not very substantial one, was pigeon. A Sikh, Thakurdin Singh, who lived up river as a sugar-cane planter and who, with his imperious-looking turban, bristly, grey, walrus moustache, weather-beaten and martial features looked as though he had come straight from the North-West Frontier Province of India, became a friend through Gajadhar Singh's good offices.

On passing the Naduruloulou office during his periodic shopping visits to Nausori, he would bring Gajadhar a brace of pigeons and, on returning home, would stop the station wagon he had commandeered at the bottom of my steps and call out (a Fijian would never call out) *'Hakim sahib.'* This literally meant 'Doctor, sir,' but to Indians district commissioners were regarded as such — a comforting salutation from a race I habitually got on with as much as with Fijians from whom they were so different in temperament, tradition and style. Thakurdin Singh, a cheery, robust character, was always highly amused when I referred to him as *Khubutar sahib* (the pigeon gentleman): he would never come up to the house and I would descend to accept the brace proffered for me. I visited his house once. He was the epitome of Indian hospitality, though I think he tended to lord it a little over his less well-endowed Indian neighbours.

We have not quite completed the survey of human life on the station.

Opposite my house over the river at Navuso was an agricultural station, consisting simply of a few little huts for research and experimenting on varieties of crops. It was eventually to be moved across the river and to take over the whole of the government station. The agricultural officer's house was the next one after mine along the government road (he had to cross by precarious punt to his station each day), but it was some way past it, after two or three hills as high as the one on which my own house was perched, and I never got to know him well during my first posting to Naduruloulou. He was a little withdrawn, as was his wife, and was almost not part of the government station. Bayard Parham, who came from New Zealand, was a botanist of the highest quality and a man of deep integrity.

It was only a few years later, during my second posting to Naduruloulou and then in Suva, that I got to know him and we became good friends. We were both members of the small Fiji Society, which had been set up to gather all forms of information about Fiji. He had mellowed as success inevitably rewarded his diligence, becoming deputy director of agriculture and eventually transferring to Western Samoa as director. His mother wrote a standard work on Fijian plants, as did also his son. His two spinster sisters in Suva, living behind a screen of exotic shrubbery, were eccentric but not recluses; wearing dresses down to their ankles and behatted at all times, they were long-lived, truly Victorian women who never made the transition into this century.

The last part of the government station was at Batiki, just beyond the agricultural officer's house. This was the provincial compound housing the provincial scribe (Koroi), assistant scribe (Ratu Joni) and the native stipendiary magistrate, whose eternally and broadly smiling daughter, Nanise (Nancy), was everyone's (but particularly Koroi's) friend. There was a stretch of hand-mown grass here where I could coach the Fijians in a little cricket. Sometimes we played on the government road itself. It carried almost no traffic as there was a cul-de-sac about ten miles up, which ended in the river near Thakurdin Singh's property.

The native stipendiary magistrate's jurisdiction was confined to Fijians and for that purpose he would sit jointly with the administrative officer in a Fijian house in various villages in the provincial as opposed to the magistrate's court where the administrative officer sat alone. It was a dichotomy that worked harmoniously. Proceedings were in Fijian, with the provincial constable acting as orderly. Our joint powers were limited to imposing up to six months' imprisonment or a £50 fine. The cases were mostly of assault and battery, non-payment of native taxes and divorce — seldom theft. No one in Fiji ever locked a house — there were no locks — and one could not possibly shut out the air from windows and doors, even if it was partly obstructed by mosquito wire-gauze. When one considers how much of a fortification a house has to be made in 'civilized' society, it is astonishing that at least up to very recent times houses were left permanently wide open in both sophisticated and secluded places. Secluded and lonely these places could certainly be, though the Rewa Government Station (which we have now encompassed) was less so as it was the largest.

On looking down the slope from my house there was always a come-hither quality to the lights of Ratu Simeone's compound. Having dined, he and his family would chat round a bowl of *kava* or play cards. Fijians scarcely ever read: there was little literature in the language. Even with the conviviality of and perpetual welcoming by Fijians one was aware, at least as a bachelor, of isolation during the long hot nights. There were repeated tales and incidents of Europeans living alone, perhaps with temperaments different from my own, suffering physical and mental anguish that would culminate in alcoholism and/or suicide. Though aware that Miss Hilton down river would have her binoculars focused on the irresistible spice of colonial country life — a bachelor establishment — I encouraged people of all races to visit my house. The Indians, in that they were not a cohesive group within Fiji's society and had strong internal yet divisive customs and complexities, tended to be more individualistic than the Fijians. Their intelligence could be sharper, if less intuitive. The contrast could be stimulating in the company of either. Indians could be proud and inhibited with both Fijians and Europeans. For example, Gajadhar Singh would never bring his family to my house to return the numerous invitations I had received to his. Instead, he would come up on his own for an hour before dusk for an iced beer, which he would drink with me overlooking the superb curve in the river against a background of rain trees, weeping figs, giant tree ferns and gracefully spraying-out clumps of bamboo.

3

Pandanus Mats and Parquet Floors

With dusk coming down like a shutter between 6.00 and 6.30 p.m. all the year round, lights would pierce the hot blackness. Most Europeans' houses and those of wealthier Indians would have benzine lamps. From my bungalow two incandescent mantles surrounded by a glass globe open at top and bottom gave out a steady brightness created by pumping the petrol (known as benzine in Fiji) in the base. Hurricane lanterns, thick glass protecting lighted wicks above kerosene (paraffin)-filled stands, were mostly for use in Fijians' houses and in those of poorer Indians: their light was insufficient for the handful of people who wanted to read. They were the only ones that one could safely carry about outdoors.

After having served my dinner, Inayt, lantern in hand, would meander down the 39 steps and turn in the Batiki direction where he had his corrugated iron hut. I was left on my own in the deep undisturbed quiet, the river below too black to be picked out from its banks. Until I passed the examination I would spend this time poring over my Hindi books and occasionally updating the list of books on the Pacific that I had read or was devouring. Charles — it was typical of one of his sagest pieces of advice — maintained before I left England that I should do this as I would need to refer to the list from time to time when, as he considered inevitable, I would want to write about the people and places. Little did I think

59

that eventually, after I had completed over 10,000 entries, the list would be unique by the widest possible margins and would be published in its own right as the *Bibliography of Fiji, Tonga and Rotuma*. (While I was doing it I should have extended it to Samoa as that group was linked to each of those three countries.) The first list of a few hundred entries was devoured in flames when my flaming lamp mantle was shattered on to it by a giant moth with incandescent orange eyes. The second draft was swept out of my garage by the river flooding over the road. Inauspicious starts for a work that has found its way into a number of the world's major libraries and, if found now in catalogues, a copy is priced at £120.

After an hour or two of studying Hindi, the occasional, ephemeral light below my window would beckon irresistibly and the urge to broaden my knowledge beyond Hindi would triumph. I would feel impelled to leave the house — all windows and doors open — and to stroll in shorts with a small torch along the government road past the unidentified fragrances disseminating from the river bank on one side and the scattered houses and station offices on the other. Through the gauze of his house I would observe A. J. alongside his petrol lamp, with rolled-up sleeves, pen in hand and a whisky at his elbow, bent over his letters or files. He would come to the office every morning with a tin box of papers, but I did ponder over his need to work on them at night — possibly it was his way of occupying those long black hours, or perhaps the papers contained a fair proportion of letters to female 'cousins'.

I would then pass the DC's house and, beyond the seemingly limitless steps up to the Fentons' house, would walk as far as the junction of the Naduruloulou Road and the King's Road, which then led northwards on Viti Levu for the 150-mile journey between Suva and Lautoka. Even this gravelled circuminsular artery was totally quiet at night. The junction was Kasavu village, a rather scruffy collection of thatched houses where some of the housegirls who worked for European wives on the station lived. I was made manifestly welcome in any house, but was always escorted to that of the headman, who was a rascal in appearance and tended to be — harmlessly — so in manner.

A single, hard-backed wooden-seated chair would be placed in the middle of the hut and I would present my packet of *yaqona* roots. The house would soon fill up as the pounding of *yaqona* was heard. Everyone would sit cross-legged on pandanus mats, which smelled cosily of sun-dried raffia beside the thatched walls and, as such visits were always informal, women were present. My Fijian would improve nightly. I found that women, especially young ones, would enunciate the most clearly. Perhaps it was the result of agile tongues on perfect teeth and full lips. I had left the guttural Hindi sounds of Asia at home and was now luxuriating in the labial and dentilingual areas of Oceanian languages. I would stay until 1.00 or 2.00 a.m. before wandering back after having swallowed many half-coconut cups of *yaqona* and smoked a few cigarettes. There was no doubt that *kava* not only loosened the tongue and induced a pleasant numbness but that it did also create a need for a cigarette. In addition to the roots of *kava*, on most visits I would also take a round tin of 50 Players cigarettes to distribute: they soon vanished within the house. Not a soul disdained to smoke. It was, I suppose, after about six months that it clicked all of a sudden. By this I mean that the Fijian I was attempting to use throughout these long sessions was now spontaneously flowing. Effort and the need for concentration had diminished. I began to think automatically in the mellifluence of Fijian and, while I find that speaking is always marginally easier than understanding a foreign language, they were both now either comprehended or comprehensible. I could relax — the Hindi, in which I was further advanced, had been firmly left in my house: the Fijian had now come along, the unacademic way.

Invariably, the most comely female poured out the drink and one of the regular attenders — and servers of the *kava* with her long delicate fingers — was Litimai, who was half-Chinese, half-Fijian. Adjacent to the village of Kasavu was a small Chinese store from which I bought my *yaqona* roots for 3*d.* a time. It was a branch of Wing Zoing Wah's main shop in Nausori four miles down river, but I do not think that Litimai was the manager's daughter, although he had been in that lonely location keeping cheerfully to himself for some years. It was astonishing where one would fiund Chinese storekeepers — often in infinitely more isolated places than this. Sometimes they persuaded Fijian women, not impressed by short men but probably impelled by the steady contact with cash, to live with them. It would be their only contact with the outside world other than the Fijian customers, with whom the Chinese would make it a point to be on good, even if not profitable, terms. The mixture of Chinese and Pacific Islander was always attractive genetically.

The talk in the village hut consisted of news or gossip. As Fijians had no newspapers or radios, information about current and historical events was passed round by word of mouth. Humorous incidents would be told and retold with relish. Edward VIII's abdication two years earlier provided a never-failing source of interest — as did the effect on Britain of the First World War. The eccentricities of Europeans were always a popular subject for discussion — rarely of Fijians whose communal society did not lend itself to aberrations. They would never mention the polygamy or enthusiastic philandering of chiefs, which the missionaries had fortunately failed to eliminate.

The population of Indians, in the main introduced to cut sugar cane while Fijians concentrated on the demands of their communal system, had many years previously surpassed that of Fijians who needed every possible stimulus. (Only recently have Fijians come again to outnumber the Indian immigrants.)

It was taken as a matter of course that if a chief's fancy were taken it would carry on to its logical conclusion. There was no stigma whatever attached to illegitimacy and this liberalism extended to commoners. Discretion prevailed and it was not easy to be aware of the progeny of chiefs outside marriage, even though it was useful to have private knowledge of this so as not to put one's foot in it during one's relations, official or otherwise, with one's new neighbours. Three quarters of the population of the regal island of Bau was believed to be lacking legitimacy. Monogamy was quite an illusion: its rarity could be just the fillip needed for the wobbly birth rate. Fijians loved chatting unmaliciously before occasionally dozing off round the walls of the house on the soft mats of plaited pandanus leaves. Sometimes card-playing would replace conversing, which would never be done standing up. A pillow would be supplied for me to lean my back against as I moved from the hard chair to sit on the soft floor: I could never, to my permanent regret, master the squatting, cross-legged position adopted by all the others. Euchre was their favourite card game, but it was very difficult, if not impossible, for Europeans to comprehend. Simultaneously, a ukulele was often being strummed with some light singing accompaniment by a small circle of young men. Occasionally, young women would take their place. Talk, card-playing and music would alternate or overlap. There were never gaps in these activities. In the completely relaxed atmosphere following the consumption of *kava*, natural tiredness would take over and, to the quiet humming sound of the murmurings of the half dozen or fewer who were still participating, one eventually succumbed to all-embracing sleep.

After these late but beneficial nights I would experience diffi-culty making it to the office shortly after 9.00 a.m. I never men-tioned that I had spent the evenings in the village. Miss Hilton, Fenton and Baker or Armstrong would have disapproved in prin-ciple, although Armstrong might have recognized its appeal and usefulness and may possibly have acquired his fluency in Fijian from sleeping dictionaries.

Towards the end of his period in office (when Armstrong was about to take over as DC) Baker did not want to accept an invita-tion to open a Fijian school on the Waidina (a tributary of the Rewa) at the village of Wainawaqa. He suggested that it would be an experience for me to substitute for him and that Koroi could accompany me. I prepared a speech in English. Koroi translated it into Fijian for me and I learnt it off by heart, for under no circumstances could one ever give a speech at a Fijian ceremony from notes.

When we reached Wainawaqa, which was up a steep bank on the edge of the Waidina, the village was keenly awaiting us. We were taken straight to the chief's house, Koroi acting as my *matanivanua*, for the ceremonies — the presentation of a thick yellow whale's tooth, the offering by the hosts of a huge *yaqona* root and the mixing of the chiefly *kava*. These were followed by my speech delivered sitting on the single chair — one never stood up to make a speech: it would have been the height of bad manners — while everyone else squatted out of respect. The speech was understood and I was thanked for it by the chief's *matanivanua*. Then the head teacher invited me to put a key into the lock of the school building (only schools and churches were ever locked up or had locks. I was never sure why — it seemed to be a token Europeanism for a wooden structure). I led the way in and was respectfully followed by the elders who sat in the classroom to observe a lesson for the assembled children. After this there was the mildly bizarre touch of Fijian children dancing with coloured streamers round a gaudy maypole on the village green. A more conventional form of dancing (*meke*s) followed — some as animated as squatting postures allow. Comic relief came from inquisitive dogs with no ear for the plangent cadence. Then, after dinner in my house alone, as was the custom, there was a scarcely catalytic but nonetheless companionable *taralala*.

This too, like the maypole, was a European derivation, thought to have evolved from the missionary-taught maypole dances. A girl or woman would come and lightly touch one's foot or knee, making a zz-zz-zz noise between her teeth — a sweet susurration like a robin trying to attract attention without disclosing its whereabouts. You then stood and, with an arm round her waist and hers round yours, you shuffled in step over the springy, thickly laid mats (so cool for the feet) to an infectious clapping rhythm reinforced by a tapping with verve on a hollowed-out piece of wood known as a *lali*. Movement was in a circle round the kerosene lantern on the floor of soft mats. Nothing was said. It was mesmeric and not very exciting, but sufficiently unusual — the Fijian sexes otherwise never openly touched each other — for men and women to revolve semi-hypnotized for hours until 3.00 or 4.00 a.m. or even cockcrow, which typifies so many bucolic Fiji dawns and leaves one with little energy for the rest of the day. The elders would sit outside the circle, watching, dozing off, and quaffing *yaqona*, which was brought regularly to add to the soporific aura. One could of course never refuse an invitation to shuffle round in the *taralala* (I would have taken off my shoes to avoid catching them on one's partner who lived a totally barefoot life), but naturally one hoped that if someone attractive were present she would come along more regularly than others. It was never done to pick a partner oneself or for couples to monopolize one another. So the long nights on tour from one's headquarters were seldom lonely, if hardly lubricious, even in missionary eyes, which could not, however, penetrate the environs of the bush. Fijians simply did not believe in solitude. As we returned to Naduruloulou, Koroi blithely (considering his lack of sleep) told me that I was the first European ever to spend a night in Wainawaqa, as I had been at Vuniniudrovu. Though neither small village was far off the main Rewa River, the exceedingly rare European travellers on the tributaries passed them by.

On tour, white shorts, a white shirt and white socks were worn; at the office one wore white trousers, a white coat, shirt, tie, socks and shoes. The material — a thick, starched drill — was inelegant and uncomfortable (I felt that I looked like a milkman), but the tropical outfitters in London had said that it was *de rigueur*. When I went into Suva I noticed this not to be so. Palm Beach cloth, much thinner and neater, or shantung — shiny and ultra suave if one could afford it — was used and I supplemented my drill wear with a couple of suits of this material, cream-coloured for smarter occasions. But for one of my many early visits to Suva I wore shorts because I had been telephoned by Juxon Barton, the Colonial Secretary, to play squash with him.

He was Acting Governor and sent the number two Government House car (with a gold crown on the front and no number plates) — a Chevrolet — all the way out to Naduruloulou to pick me up and return me. I had played very little at Cambridge, but was reasonably quick on the court, although Barton — six foot six and thickset with it — stood firmly in the middle and I had to keep running round him. He explained that he had sent for me as he took daily exercise and all his opponents, weaklings he crisply called them, had succumbed to influenza. He exuded strength in every sense.

All his 22 years' experience had been before Fiji in Kenya. He had been sent from Whitehall as Colonial Secretary in 1936 to carry through a reorganization of the civil service into senior and junior divisions, splitting up in the main those who had been recruited from England and those who had come in by other means. As can be imagined, it was a misshaped, hefty boulder, intensely unpopular, thrown into what had been a placid mill-pond. Barton seemed impervious to other people's opinions. He was not a character suited to Fiji. A story I could not believe, however, was to the effect that soon after his arrival in Fiji he was having a drink in the Defence Club in Suva when Ratu J. L. V. (later Sir Lala) Sukuna, CBE, *Médaille militaire*, District Commissioner of Lau and the first native of any colony to become a district commissioner, walked in. It was alleged that Barton exclaimed: 'My God! They allow niggers in here.' After that his time would have been doomed. In all my years in Fiji I never heard the word 'nigger' and I am sure that it never entered the head of any European, including the handful with no time whatever for Fijians, who in any case bear no resemblance to Negroes. My belief is that Barton's reference was to 'natives' (unforgivable enough) and that the term had been pejoratively distorted by his European enemies. Nevertheless, the allegation persisted, notably as testimony to his unpopularity for the invidious reorganization.

When, a year or two later, I was appointed as DC Lau to succeed Ratu Sukuna, Barton instructed me to find out whether he had been in the habit of flying the Union Flag at the Government Station: he had heard that the custom was not carried out (it wasn't). I was also generally to report to him personally all that I heard of Ratu Sukuna's show of independence, as he believed it to be (I didn't). But then, while I was in Lau, he was transferred back to East Africa — to Nyasaland — as Colonial Secretary, which was not a promotion and from where he retired in 1945, missing out on a governorship.

This hard man had a soft spot for me and thought that I was tougher than most of my colleagues. Many years later, during his retirement in Sussex, he sent me some papers to keep (with a note saying that, approaching 90, he had been advised to sort out his documents, though he asserted this to be premature), but added a typical Bartonism: 'Ironical that all Fiji's native leaders are illegitimate.' He went on to name three, including Penaia whom he claimed to have hand-picked for the Secretariat. So what? Even if true, which the sweeping generalization wasn't, it made not an iota of difference in the estimation of the Fijians or of the world. Barton even wrote a letter on the subject to a national paper. He omitted to say, however, most probably out of ignorance of Fijian society, which was surprising in a man of his elevated status in the Service, that it was of no significance at all. In any case, this was self-evident because the leaders were of the unsurpassed quality that Fijian society produces.

Barton did not get on well with the Governor, Sir Harry Luke, a quite different personality. Aged 54, Luke had arrived in 1938 from being Lieutenant Governor of Malta for eight years and, before that, Chief Secretary of Palestine, after having been a district commissioner there. His experience was of the Middle East, on which he was an historical expert and about which he had written a number of books.

Though his first publication (in 1910) was a *Bibliography of Sierra Leone*, I own one of his earliest Oriental works, *The Fringe of the East: A Journey Through Past and Present Provinces of Turkey*. This, like his *Bibliography*, is by Harry Charles Lukach, the name he used in the early part of his career and recorded as such in the first *Who's Who* in which he appeared (later editions of *Who's Who* included the entry that his father's name was 'J. H. Luke'). Although he refers in his three-volume autobiography, *Cities and Men*, to his mother, Eugénie, being Viennese, he makes no reference to the name Lukach and there is only a passing note about his father being connected with British insurance interests in the Austrian Empire. In a three-page eulogy of his prepossessing father who died in Austria, he nowhere states what the initials 'J. H.' stand for. Was it Johann Heinrich? Nor in the three volumes is there any reference to his grandparents. It is a little mysterious.

After Sir Harry Luke had died I corresponded with his eldest son, Peter, whose valour (his father, whom he physically resembled, was not short of it himself in gaining an Italian medal for it as lieutenant-commander in the Royal Navy in the First

World War) in the North African campaign resulted in wounds and an MC and who, after many false starts after it, was the writer of the highly successful London West End play, *Hadrian VII*, when my sister-in-law, Pamela Hansford Johnson, came to know him well, and of a rumbustious autobiography.

I hoped to discuss with Peter family ancestry, but he lived in Spain and we never got round to it before he died in 1995. He was a Catholic and his eldest son was a student of Buddhism in Kathmandu — a polychromatic family indeed. Sir Harry had stated in his autobiography that he himself had been baptized in the Church of England in London soon after birth: in his Fiji domain he was leader of it after the Bishop in (*sic*) Polynesia.

Here the reader may rightly ask me to pause for a paragraph or two to offer the *mise-en-scène* to a theme of reflections and observations running right through my writings over the years. From earliest days I have been fascinated by individuals' racial (and especially mixed-racial) and social-class backgrounds the better to understand them, the more to admire them and the easier, if called for without, I trust, being patronizing, to sympathize with them. Where applicable, I am also fascinated by their tribal origins and, to a lesser extent, by their inherited or acquired faiths, especially when these faiths have been discarded. To this end I became a Fellow of the Royal Anthropological Institute and contributed to its journal, *Man*.

Practically all his life, my brother Charles was similarly engrossed and the subject would invariably run through our conversations *entre nous*. Witness the best of his non-fiction works, *Variety of Men*. There would have been further concentration in the succeeding volume, which he asked me to help him research, to outline the origins of, and express his admiration for, individuals such as Isador Isaac Rabi, Werner Heisenberg and J. D. Bernal. To this essential knowledge, as he regarded it, of genes, he would add luck, in which he was ever a believer, to account for a person's achievements (or a lack of luck in the absence of them). He and I were not original in accepting the old axiom of being in the right place at the right time or, putting it perhaps more forcibly, in not being in the wrong place at the wrong time. This knowledge was centred on basic, inescapable facts with which one, after all, had to live. While I couldn't swallow exhibitions of an excess of pride, I could sympathize with any reticence shown where ostracism, or that dreaded and only too frequent historical occurrence, persecution, were in the air.

Was J. H. Luke (Lukach, as he must have been) an *émigré* from the Austro-Hungarian Empire, even possibly a Jewish one? The antecedents of his son, who was to rise in the British Colonial Service from first appointment as ADC to the Governor of Sierra Leone in 1908 and in the Colonial Office from 1911 to the top position as a governor through the pre-First World War and later prejudices of the English Establishment, an unusual progression given those times and no doubt a tribute to his exceptional talents, are intriguing to perhaps a unique degree. (A predecessor, Sir Everard im Thurn, Governor of Fiji just before the First World War and Swiss-German by birth, alone approaches him.)

Sir Harry Luke had been to Eton and was much disposed to wearing its striped bow tie, which I think I was alone in recognizing in Fiji where he always styled himself on the complete English gentleman. He was unique as a governor in writing books on the Pacific nearly half a century ago. His slight but entertaining *From a South Seas Diary* uses some of my pictures and refers to coming across me in remote parts of Lau. Harry Luke had an extremely strong aesthetic taste, not least in women. A small, dapper, vain man with extremely bright, brown, beady eyes and a smoothly turned down nose, which tended to infer disdain, he was a cultured person, entertainingly exhibitionistic while host at Government House functions.

We played Murder there once in the large reception room. I did not know the rules — they were either not explained or I was not listening. He had rigged the cards to the extent that he was the detective and Mrs Y, his beautiful, vivacious companion with a retroussé nose, was his assistant. Lights had been extinguished. There was much fumbling and groping. Someone surreptitiously pushed a card into my hand. I could just make out that it said 'Victim'. It meant nothing to me until a good while later a shape approached, that of His Excellency who hissed, '*You* are the victim. Lie down.' It was he who had originally handed me the card and I was supposed to be recumbent on the parquet floor.

Like the giant moth in its distraught state after demolishing my petrol lamp mantle in my bungalow, I wobbled and assumed a glazed look before sinking down. I could have done with a pandanus mat. Anyway, the delay enabled him and his assistant, hand in hand, to lose themselves in Government House for ages, so it seemed, before the lights came on again — now with me, I judged it advisable so to remain, prone on the parquet surrounded by the captivated assembly. As he had handed round the card in the dark he knew the murderer. This tended to be forgotten as he impressively eliminated all but the perpetrator.

In his dual capacity as Governor of Fiji and High Commissioner for the Western Pacific, he had a preference for South Seas' pandanus mats rather than shining Government House parquet floors. He especially liked the Micronesian Gilbert Islands and Polynesian Ellice Islands and took every opportunity to visit them, not least to view the topless women. He also liked Lau — the more Polynesian part of Fiji; the Melanesian side appealed to him less than I would have expected of a man of his wide interests. By the same token, the Solomons and New Hebrides did not appeal to him — admittedly the women there tended to be too indigo. Fijians were not impressed by him.

To them he did not look gubernatorial. More like a pianist of Jewish continental origin, indeed, he resembled as he aged the Russian maestro, Vladimir Horowitz, in nose, small sharp eyes and protuberant lower lip. He made no attempt to invite powerful European commercial figures to functions in Government House. It was his undoing. When there were different circumstances and opportunities for criticism they were later to petition London for his retirement. His favourites were much younger. Perhaps because I was one, working in his office and feeling free to venture a few unorthodoxies, I liked him for his own really distinctive, kind and considerate individuality. His 'bachelorhood' certainly enlivened the occupancy of Government House.

4

Plumes of Feathers and Ruffled Ones

Right from the first in 1874, when the Honourable Sir Arthur Gordon, son of the British Prime Minister, the Earl of Aberdeen, became Governor, Sir Harry Luke's predecessors were a markedly assorted variety of men with splendid names — a panoply which, as an historian, I constantly reflect on and about whom I have collected material that has never been published. But I must for reasons of space resist making this the history towards which I am otherwise tempted. Let me just mention their names in date order. Following Gordon, who after his Fiji days applied unsuccessfully for the viceroyship of India and became 1st Lord Stanmore, were Sir William Des Voeux, Sir Charles Mitchell, Sir John Thurston, Sir Henry Jackson, Sir George O'Brien, Sir Everard Ferdinand im Thurn, Sir Henry May (whose daughter became a friend of mine), Sir Bickham Sweet-Escott, Sir Cecil Hunter-Rodwell, Sir Eyre Hutson, Sir Murchison Fletcher and Sir Arthur Richards, later 1st Lord Milverton.

Now for a brief story about Richards, whose sallow, saturnine features earned him the sobriquet 'Old Sinister' when he went on to be Governor-General of Nigeria. He was more than a match for his number two, Juxon Barton. An ADC to Richards in Fiji reported overhearing Richards saying contemplatively: 'Barton, there are two things a cadet must have — a refrigerator and a native woman.' Barton's upright, forbidding frame reeled back.

71

'My God, Sir. I understand about the refrigerator but really, Sir, a native woman?' Richards retorted exultantly: 'To look after the refrigerator, of course, you damned fool.'

Sir Harry Luke took no trouble to conceal his dislikes, one of which I saw first hand. This was Sir Julien Cahn, the philanthropist owner of the celebrated cricket team. The animosity between the two English country gentlemen, which was how they presented themselves, was intense (but more on Luke's part than on Cahn's) — with me as the unlikely intermediary. I had played against Sir Julien's team of international players on a few occasions in England and witnessed occurrences so unusual that they were probably without parallel.

Going in first for the Gentlemen of Leicestershire against Cahn's team, with the first ball of the match I was hit high on the thigh by R. J. Crisp, the South African and Worcestershire very fast bowler (later to gain the DSO and MC with dashing exploits in the North African campaign and to become an eccentric recluse in Greece). I was about to rub the spot when the close-in short-leg called out: 'Hold on! Hold on!' He came up and pointed out that the gilt crown on the new ball had applied itself as a transfer to my flannels. Apparently, the ball had landed on the pitch on the opposite half bearing the maker's name, leaving the crown side to imprint itself pristinely on me. Denijs Morkel, another fast South African Test bowler, was to bowl from the other end, with Ian Peebles and Walter Robins, both England and Middlesex bowlers, to follow with their spin. They were among the fielders who gathered round to look and marvel at the gilt crown. No one had seen anything like it (my bruise seemed to be of no concern).

Nor had anyone experienced what was to follow in the second incident now recounted.

Sir Julien of unsmiling countenance and gravel voice was no performer at the game, but he was the world's greatest enthusiast; no doubt, part of this was to gild further his image as the complete English gentleman in the way that he had managed to become a master of foxhounds and live in a baronial hall. He had greatly increased the worth of the business of his father, Albert, formerly Nottingham Furniture Company, latterly Jays & Campbells, the earliest hire-purchase firms with branches in every town. He himself, after being knighted in 1929, had become a .baronet in 1934 as a result of considerable pressure by Stanley Baldwin on Prime Minister Ramsay MacDonald. This was Cahn's reward for having paid off Maundy Gregory (who, with Baldwin, arranged titles for those offering funds to Conservative causes) to keep quiet about some recipients — the whole matter was distasteful to MacDonald and exceedingly so to King George V, as the latter's biographer, Kenneth Rose, revealed.

Cahn had fragile bones. While fielding, he would place a brilliant man behind him at mid-off so that his letting drives go past him would not look disgraceful. In fact, the unwary batsman, taking a run on the ball going through Cahn's legs, would often be run out by the hidden figure behind throwing it in with alacrity to the stumps at the bowler's end. For batting, Cahn would have his chauffeur inflate in the balcony pavilion (at West Bridgford) or a striped marquee (at Stanford Hall) special huge pads with a bicycle pump and strap them round his legs. Slowly he would make his way to the wicket at number nine or number ten. As his sole movement was to put his leg in front of the wicket, he was highly likely to be l.b.w. This leg would invariably be struck with a stifled thud as the pneumatic pad absorbed the shock. If John Gunn were the umpire having to answer the inevitable appeal for l.b.w., Cahn was safe. Gunn, the former England and Nottinghamshire player, was his employee. Should it be the visitors' umpire he would have been previously advised by Gunn to let Cahn have the benefit of the doubt if they wished to renew the fixture and to enjoy Cahn's magnificent hospitality — at a separate table from that of his own team, whose accessibility to the wine with which the visitors were plied was strictly limited.

In one match at Stanford Park, Cahn had just reached the wicket and was about to take guard from the umpire when there was a loud hissing noise. I was at silly mid-off with instructions that if he gave a catch I was not to take it unless it was absolutely unavoidable. Cahn's left-leg pad shrank visibly. Exceedingly annoyed, he stalked off the pitch to the marquee where, it was reported, but could not be seen, he sacked the chauffeur on the spot. There was a long delay (the two-minute rule was regarded as being in abeyance for diplomacy's sake) and then from the marquee he called in his other batsman, declaring the innings closed, with Sir Julien Cahn 0 not out. 'Deflated' should have been added. As a bowler, he lobbed the ball higher than anyone I ever saw. Its trajectory did not make it all that easy to hit. But if the biggest hitters did strike it, he was backed up by probably the best fielding side in the country and would frequently have analyses resembling 3 for 70 — all his victims would be caught or stumped.

In a talk with him at Stanford Hall he had asked me what I was going to do on leaving Cambridge and if I would like a match or two for his team. I told him that I was going to Fiji. He then said that he hoped to take his team to New Zealand and he would try to stop off in the capital, Suva. He remembered this the following year because when I was in Naduruloulou I was telephoned by the Governor's ADC who told me that Cahn, his wife, Phyllis Cahn's brother, George Wolfe, his secretary, Cyril Goodway (the wicket-keeper and later chairman of Warwickshire) and his wife, would be passing through and that the Secretary of State for the Colonies had asked the Governor (whom I hardly knew at that stage) if I could look after them. My instructions were that, after meeting them off the Matson liner, the *Monterey* (18,685 tons), I was to take them to see a little of the countryside not too far from Suva. The Governor's number two car would be at my disposal for the length of their stay in which they and I were to have lunch at Government House.

In the programme I arranged, there was time for me, after the *Monterey* had tied up at the wharf, to take them to Naduruloulou where I had not long been stationed. I showed them my humble house and Kasavu village where the party were given a taste of *yaqona*, which almost no one likes the first time but nevertheless considers a talking point for years after. Cahn took lots of film on a movie camera (not often seen in private hands in those days) and then we returned to Albert Park where I had put on a match displaying Fijians. He was speedily impressed. It did not take him long to tell me that he would pay for the Fijian team to make a first visit to England in about two years' time (the war was to

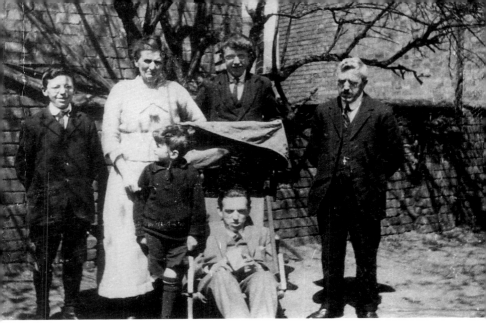

ABOVE. The only picture taken of the whole Snow family, Leicester, 1922. C.P. Snow at back on right of father. Author standing in front of mother. *(Photo: Lucy Parker)* BELOW. May Ball at dawn, Christ's College, Cambridge, 1937. Author and fiancée (later wife), are seated ninth and tenth from left (Martin Clemens fifth). *(Photo: Stearn's, Cambridge)*

ABOVE. Government House, Fiji, 1938. *(Photo: Rob R. Wright)*
BELOW RIGHT. Sir Julien Cahn, 1938. *(Photo: C.C. Goodway)*
BELOW RIGHT. *Seated:* Sir Harry Luke. *Standing, left to right:*
Col. Ratu Sir Lala Sukuna, Hon. A.D.C.; Capt. F.R.J. Nicholls,
A.D.C.; Lt. Col. C. Brewster Joske, Hon. A.D.C. *Squatting:*
Governor's *matanivanua*, 1939. *(Photo: Rob R. Wright)*

prevent that, and Cahn had died before the end of it). While the match continued — we were able to see more of it after lunch — we went briefly into the centre of Suva where Cahn filmed urban life to contrast with rural Naduruloulou. A Fijian policeman with a huge head of hair, in blue tunic, white *sulu*, scarlet cummerbund and bare feet was on point duty in a stand under a concrete parasol. Cahn naturally filmed him and, to my astonishment if not to that of the rest of the party, the constable then held out his hand for money. I told Cahn not to respond. I thought that it was the end of the matter. But at lunch with the Governor, which was already short of easy conversation, Cahn mentioned the policeman. He had not warned me that he was going to do so. Luke was irate and instructed me to find out which constable it was. The Commissioner of Police quickly discovered the culprit and sacked him. Not a happy lunch, with Luke increasingly frigid towards Cahn, whose invitation to tea at 4.00 p.m. on the *Monterey* before the liner sailed he nevertheless accepted.

Cahn, his party and I were in Cahn's deluxe suite with tea all ready. Then Goodway and I set off at 3.50 to meet Luke and his ADC at the top of the gangway. It was slow going as there was a considerable contraflow from returning passengers swelled by people seeing them off in an hour's time. Goodway and I could not see Luke who was in mufti and had had to push his way, after having enquired of an officer where the suite was, among the jostling crowd: when we ourselves returned to the suite a quarter of an hour later dead silence was reigning. Luke had frozen up, Cahn's gravel voice was not to be heard, Phyllis Cahn was struggling to break the ice, while Luke fixed me with a disapproving stare. The shortest permissible protocol time for the stay, half an hour, expired; Luke and the ADC parted stiffly from Cahn and retinue while Goodway led the way to the gangway. As we reached it Luke went down and the ADC turned round to me to say 'You're in deep trouble. Fancy not meeting HE!' There was time for no more to be said as they were whisked off. I followed ashore and, having given the ADC time to return to Government House, I telephoned him with my explanation. To my horror, His Excellency — unprecedentedly — answered the phone himself. Off balance, I tried to clarify that we had left the suite in good time to meet him and take him to Cahn but had been obstructed by sheer human weight in the passageways. I ventured to say that, as a guest, I was myself in Cahn's or Goodway's hands and had not expected to be asked to meet him. Luke fulminated that it was one of the worst examples of bad manners and certainly of discourtesy that he had experienced as the King's representative. 'No more than would be expected, I suppose,' he added with thunder in his voice, 'from your poisonous friend.' Well, I knew that Cahn was *persona non grata* with many — including the hierarchy of MCC, which unforgivably never elected him to membership — in the all too unpleasant attitude of that era towards those who might not have the requisite ancestry (it has given me pleasure to propose his grandson for election to the MCC), but I was not wise enough at that stage to foresee that Luke, with a cosmopolitan Lukach background, could conceivably have a similar hostility of reaction. He concluded with no diminution of asperity: 'I'm off out of Suva for a few days and you are to draft for me a letter to Cahn expressing my acutest displeasure.'

For two weeks while he was away I sweated over the effort. It was the more arduous because I wanted to incur the least opprobrium possible from the affair. I hoped to keep open my chances of a future relationship with Cahn because I liked him and was sure that he would honour his promise to have the Fiji cricket team visit England. Eventually, I submitted to Government House two drafts, one stronger than the other. Enormous was my relief to have a prompt reply personally from Luke to me, a humble cadet, as I then was, saying that he had thought the two drafts aptly articulate and absolutely admirable but had decided not to use them or write at all. 'Matter forgotten.' The fortnight away had done the Governor a lot of good. Not that the glacial episode was entirely forgotten. More than once afterwards Luke mentioned whimsically to me something about 'Your friend Cahn', but the 'poisonous' was never repeated to me and I enjoyed favours from Luke as I knew him better.

From Naduruloulou I would make sorties by broken-down station wagon to Nausori, the township four miles down the

Rewa River. The genial Vivian Dunstan was manager of the European store, Morris Hedstrom, at the near end of Nausori's single gravel road. He would personally dispense bowls of *yaqona* and Viv (he insisted, like all Australians, on being known by an abbreviated first name) would call me Phil. Indeed, I was called that throughout my time in Fiji by those Europeans and part-Europeans who knew me, as I was by Anne. Phil Snow was about as short a name as could be devised. Like places, such as the Grand Pacific Hotel (GPH), Colonial Sugar Refining Company (CSR), Colonial Secretary's Office (CSO), the Public Works Department (PWD), Queen Victoria School (QVS), Central Medical School (CMS), Colonial War Memorial Hospital (CWMH — the only four-letter one in Fiji), the two main European chains of stores, Burns Philp (BP) and Morris Hedstrom (MH), Government House (GH) — and persons, His Excellency (HE), District Commissioner (DC), Chief Justice (CJ), all directors of departments, such as the Director of Public Works being DPW, as many as could be were cut to the briefest identifiable form possible. No doubt it was to save energy in Fiji's heavy, humid heat. Dunstan used to talk to me with enormous pride of his son, Don, at school in Adelaide. I think that he at least believed that Don, when a qualified lawyer, would take up politics and reach the apogee of Premier of South Australia, but Viv would have raised his eyebrows at his son being the first premier in Australia to abolish the honours system and appoint an Aboriginal as State Governor. Don, returning from University to be a lawyer in Fiji, had a health breakdown in 1951, thence to go back and make his often criticized political mark in South Australia.

Such shopping as I did in Nausori (to the incredulity of Viv Dunstan who believed that Europeans should support fellow Europeans) was at the opposite end of the road in the Chinese store of Wing Zoing Wah, where prices were perceptibly cheaper. It was in the dark recesses of this store that I first met the medical officer, Dr Humphrey Silvester Evans, who was to become one of my closest lifelong friends. He did not live on the Government Station at Naduruloulou, but near a hospital adjacent to the much more populous Nausori. Dressed all in white — shirt, shorts,

77

socks up to his knees and shoes — with a gold-rimmed monocle dangling from a thin black cord, he had blond wavy hair (which I later believed to be dyed golden), startlingly light blue eyes, a hawk-like nose and a brisk walk. Front face, he was strikingly good-looking. In later years, when the features of Thor Heyerdahl, arguably the world's greatest living explorer, became familiar, I thought that Evans looked like him, but with a beaked nose. He recognized my Cambridge Hawks' Club tie and mentioned that he had been at Trinity. Humphrey Evans was probably the most cultured man in the Fiji archipelago and was certainly a fine eccentric. He had been conjoint Medical Officer/District Commissioner in isolated districts like Lau and Taveuni, and was later to have a period in Rotuma. As I got to know him, it became evident that he would never have gone into medicine had his father not been a doctor. Administration *per se* was his consuming interest. For a while he was acting Director of Medical Services, but was disappointingly prolix and could not be steered towards priorities. He was a skilled photographer and expert entomologist: these were but two of his interests. Only stuffed shirts bored him. When he was District Commissioner in Lau and on Taveuni, he would walk about with a long, ivory-topped Roko's staff of office, which was strictly the perquisite of the office of Roko, the highest government-appointed Fijian chief in a province. That was an indefensible usurpation, justified, however, he claimed by the fact that as DC he was also PC (Provincial Commissioner) in charge of a province above a Roko. His first marriage had failed because he spent too much time away from home in the districts. His work, visiting villages for weeks at a time, was all-absorbing. Hypersensitive to female beauty, he had a Lauan woman live with him. Indoors, he would wear a cream *sulu* (far less a form of European dress than now), the calf-length skirt, which he maintained was the essence of comfort, particularly for sleeping in during the nights that were often hotter than the days.

On leave in England in the late 1940s he advertised for a young woman to accompany him back to Fiji as his second wife. Several responded: all were interviewed. He chose a Swiss, Hélène, who was charming. But when he took her to the isolation of Rotuma and again absorbed himself in the affairs and the exceptionally intelligent people of those islands, she committed suicide. This tragedy created every sort of difficulty, for Humphrey was the only doctor-cum-magistrate within five or six days' distance by sea at the quickest. There were no other Europeans in this minute island group, so he had to act as the certifying doctor, coroner and officiant at the funeral. When he himself died in Suva in 1965, the Rotumans undertook the burial according to their rites. I found him an enormously stimulating person — there was no one like him — although some thought him fundamentally a cold man. I can only say that I could not have had a more unusual friend. When he died the discontinuance of his stream of culture from Fiji in his letters — Sir Julian Huxley and Dorothy Tutin (whom he adored from afar after seeing her in London in *I am a Camera*) were among his correspondents — left me with an unfillable gap. I was touched when he left me £100 in his will as a contribution towards producing my *Bibliography of Fiji, Tonga and Rotuma*. It was by his example that I had discarded carrying about a topee and for the most part changed from white drill as a material to cream Palm Beach shantung, which was so much cooler and, I hoped, perhaps even a little prepossessing.

I would spend some evenings with him and on others, when in Nausori, would, armed with my rubber sponge-faced table tennis racquet from Cambridge days, play at the CSR Company's Part-Europeans' Sports Club. When Europeans heard of this and my friendship with Humphrey Evans, some of the CSR Company Europeans, who lived as a self-contained community on the hill at Nausori at heights strictly corresponding to their rank — with the general manager, Henry King-Irving, at the top in about the second largest house in the entire Fiji archipelago — tended to look down their noses. Since he was the doctor, Humphrey Evans, similarly regarded as non-conformist, to put it mildly, could not be denied membership of the company's exclusively European tennis club: he was very fond of the game and immaculately clad for it. I was too busy with cricket to play much tennis, but I had been generously invited at the outset of my appointment to Naduruloulou to join that club.

At the company's Part-Europeans' Sports Club, a corrugated iron building near the sugar mill, I found a table tennis table and Lily Edwards, whose father was part-European (with a European father and half-caste mother) and mother pure Samoan. There were beautiful Samoan women in Suva living in the sleazy shanties of Naiqaqi, which were demolished shortly after my reaching Suva to make way for the sharpest possible contrast — the colossal, quite magnificent, neoteric, glistening white stone Government Buildings. These were alongside Albert Park where, every late afternoon, the sinuous South Sea embodiments and their older female relations used to play a kind of cricket that resembled rounders. It was a picturesque sight. The Naiqaqi shanties themselves did not make the most impressive approach along Victoria Parade to the nearby police sentry box at the entrance to Government House. I developed a soft spot for Samoa. I always wished that I could have been posted there, but this could not happen as it was a New Zealand dependency, a connection with Polynesia that I considered New Zealanders did not appreciate sufficiently. Lily Edwards proved to be an adept pupil at table tennis. She was very fair and her features perhaps an improvement on the pure Samoan. Voluptuous and the colour of coffee with cream, she was a most lithe performer of solo Samoan dances (with large flashing knives) to which I was entertained in the Edwards' home at the very foot of the CSR Company hill where the part-Europeans (known as *kai loma*s, Fijian for 'middle people') had precedence — just — over senior Indian mill employees such as engineers, launch drivers and crushing operators. The sweet smell of burning emanating from the lofty chimney of the mill where centrifugal spinning machines separated the syrup from the crystals and waste, megass, out of which rum was made, pervaded the atmosphere: it lent an enchantment to the still, intimate nights.

I had to catch, somehow, an old station wagon making an unlikely journey to Naduruloulou late at night. Sometimes I had to wake up Bechu, the faithful Indian whose wagon humped ice and meat — and half a dozen passengers — once daily from Nausori to Naduruloulou. Nocturnally, I would have the wagon to myself and he would only accept a shilling. Travelling in the daytime with a full wagon, which might include a goat and chickens, it would be sixpence a passenger and I would unfailingly be given the front seat alongside Bechu. The unwritten custom of being invited to sit in the front of a wagon or bus was a favour accorded to Europeans and Fijian chiefs.

While there were not many examples of manifest discrimination, liquor, however, could be drunk by non-Europeans only if they held permits (the highest chiefs, high Indian officials and wealthy Sikh store owners were permitted up to 12 bottles of beer and three bottles of whisky a month). The amounts, which varied, were decided by district liquor permit committees — in my district presided over by myself with the police inspector, two worthy Indian and two worthy Fijian citizens. Such embarrassing discrimination was abolished about 20 years later when it was thought that heads could now hold liquor (of course some could and some couldn't). The permits had to be shown at hotel bars or stores selling liquor. Apart from the selectivity of membership of drink-selling clubs (which I eschewed anyway as they were totally European except for the occasional highest Fijian chiefs — not even part-Europeans were admitted) there was little racial differentiation in daily life. This will disappoint those ready to criticize colonial administration. But I can only speak of Fiji.

On one occasion soon after first meeting Humphrey Evans in Nausori, I went further along the road down river and then turned to Bau. My companion was Victor Bunge, sanitary overseer, and the vehicle was his open-backed van. Our mission was to investigate a report that the single Indian living on Bau Island in its only store, which he occupied under licence, was in the habit of sleeping at nights, no doubt luxuriously, on top of the unbagged flour in a huge bin. This meant an overnight stay. In the event, Bunge, after taking me to Bau landing, had to return to Nausori for some serious report. I was punted across the mile to the island, relishing the slowness of approach to all its dominant history. My punter was Filikesa (Felix) Balekiwai (this translates unpropitiously as fall-in-the-water), a fine-visaged commoner of dignified geniality, who was to become the father of Lady Lealea, second wife of the Vunivalu, Ratu Sir George Cakobau. The sentry boxes, which

were strung around the coast of Bau on platforms over the edge of
the sea reached by narrow planks, were the lavatories — not at all
obviously so, as Filikesa, the ferryman, laughingly told me, since
lady tourists would always presuppose that they were watch-
towers.

The Roko Tui Tailevu, Ratu Isireli (Israel) Tawake, was a tall,
avuncular man of quite immense dignity, which he managed
to retain absolutely unperturbed when he purchased a second-
hand car — the only Fijian at that time to own an automobile —
and tried to drive it along Nausori's road bumping into this
stationary vehicle and veering off that approaching one. He was
never prosecuted for his shunting, dodgem style of staccato
progression and never did get the hang of driving. Ratu Tawake, a
favourite of mine and the ultimate in military figures (he had been
in the labour battalion in France in the First World War) who
looked, with his aquiline nose and head held high, like a very
superior North American Indian chief, vacated for me his superb
thatched house with thick layers of fresh smelling plaited mats
exuding welcome.

At about midnight I received a message that the Indian could be
seen dormant in the bin. The door was pushed open by a Fijian
with sufficient speed for me to catch the offender red- (or rather
white-) handed. In any case his shape was clearly delineated in the
flour. I immediately withdrew his licence, had the store shut up
and him evicted. Bau was storeless for a while, but at least
hygienic.

Meanwhile, the weather changed and the sole radio on the
island — in the regal Cakobau compound — reported a hurricane.
In any case, the channel was too rough for a punt to take me back
to the mainland. This plainly and delightfully meant staying on.
There was a women's *meke* practice the next evening which, after
I had been given an escorted tour of Bau, I was invited to attend.
It was quite a beauty chorus. The best looking among them was
Adi (Lady) Vasemaca, betrothed to Ratu Edward Cakobau (who
was not at that moment on the island) and later to become the
mother of the first Fijian brigadier, Ratu Epeli (Abel) Nailatikau
— in 1987 to be ousted from command and to become Fiji's first

ambassador to Britain. As soon as I sat with my back to the thatched wall, *yaqona* was distributed and I was garlanded with a necklace of frangipani, hibiscus, gardenia and something else which was splendidly pungent. I never experienced the equal to this ambrosial aroma in subsequent garlands. The fourth component was identified for me as the split orange nuts of the screw-pine tree (pandanus). The fragrance is most closely recaptured by Guy Laroche's perfume *Fidji*. Although *Fidji* was said to be manufactured from Fiji perfumes, and gardenia (which grew wild on Bau) is specifically mentioned, I suspect that pandanus is the main ingredient used by Laroche, who died in 1989 and was as famous for his scents as for his *haute couture*. This was another enchanted evening.

After two more days the hurricane had not materialized and there was no excuse for me not to return to Naduruloulou. I was to go to Bau a number of times before one had to obtain permission (as one now does) to do so, but this first trip was utterly memorable and no other was quite so heady. On it I had met the leading chieftainesses of Bau, as well as Ranadi (Queen) Litia Cakobau, who, as mentioned earlier, on a tour of Tonga had had an affair with King George II from which my great friend Ratu Sir Edward Cakobau had resulted. Although, in the mid 1940s, Ranadi Cakobau had once given a sermon in Bau church in which she accused me specifically of influencing Fijians to play cricket on Sundays, this did not affect our personal relationship.

Saving all I could for Anne's passage from England, I could not buy my own car. So Ernie Baker used to drive me in his Vauxhall from Naduruloulou to and from Suva to play cricket. Since there was a lot of beer drinking after the heat of the play, it was perhaps as well that I did not have to drive back, especially past a totally unprotected whirlpool (in which drowned cattle from up the flooded Rewa River would circle bloated and stinking for days). This was deep below Miss Hilton's house on the bluff at the right-angled turn of the Rewa. Negotiating this spectacular bend was always a hair-raising experience. Then Baker retired and A. J. Armstrong did not go into Suva on Saturday afternoons, so I became totally dependent on a rather unreliable station wagon (its unsteady steering and wheels caused it to lurch off the gravel road into the cane fields) from Naduruloulou to Nausori, where I had to catch another wagon across the Rewa bridge for Suva, and similarly for the return journey. There were no timetables for these 'buses' anywhere in Fiji: when they were full at their termini they moved — and not before. By the time I got back to Nausori, the terminus, it was so late that I had to wake the uncomplaining, dutiful Bechu from his sleep.

In Suva, at the age of 23 — this is still 1938 — I immediately became a cricket administrator. In 1996 I completed 58 years of uninterrupted service in cricket administration (not counting two years in charge of Christ's cricket) and am currently vice-patron of the Fiji Cricket Association of which the President of Fiji is patron. Because of the very early age at which I started as an administrator, it has been pointed out to me that this is probably a record in any country where the game is played. I decided to merge the exclusively European and part-European Suva Cricket Club, of which I was secretary, with the entirely Fijian and Indian United Cricket Association, whose sixes would land with impressive monotony on our neighbouring pitches on Albert Park to remind us of their existence. My decision caused a lot of European opposition; some European players dropped out in protest and one or two of my friendships with Australians and New Zealanders cooled off. However, I knew exactly what I was doing. It was going to make it harder for Europeans (myself included) and part-Europeans to retain places in the Suva representative team. I would gain popularity among Fijians and Indians, but, more importantly, it would improve the standard of play.

Thus the Suva Cricket Association was formed, with much moral help from Clive Brewster (formerly Joske), a nephew of Adolph Brewster Brewster (formerly Joske) who was the son of a pioneering German Jewish merchant, Paul Joske. A. B. Brewster, who served as a district commissioner in the interior for many years, was the author of one of the best books ever written on Fiji, *The Hill Tribes of Fiji*. At this time, after a divorce, Clive Brewster was sharing accommodation with Johnson — the unesteemed bachelor Assistant Colonial Secretary and a friend neither of mine, nor, I discovered, of many others. Clive had had a distinguished career as an aviator during the First World War. He became a colonel during the Second World War, but on his return to Fiji in the late 1940s inexplicably fell to his death over a balcony at the Taj Mahal Hotel in Bombay. He was a tall man and it was a low balcony: suicide seemed out of character and vertigo improbable. A charming natural diplomat, he had been a genially and quietly dominant figure, the Don Juan in the Suva of the 1920s and 1930s.

Administering cricket in the heat-induced lethargy had its problems, personalities and ethnic groups apart: even more so, playing. Mats of coconut fibre had to be stretched over lush grass difficult to mow or reluctantly out of apathy so tended by the Suva Town Council. This was so in all my time in Suva until, through my friendship with his part-European daughter (Police Inspector Probert's wife), I found a most willing ally as groundsman in the goatee-bearded Captain Norman Macdonald.

I used my spiked cricket boots from England but found that the spikes adhered to the matting and I could not move my feet quickly enough. After a few slow, uncomfortable innings I followed the example of everyone else (except Fijians who played barefooted, as I did if a tropical deluge had half flooded the mat) and wore rubber-soled shoes. The grass on the outfield was of a thicker, broader-leafed variety than any I had encountered before and, to score quickly, one had to lift the ball higher than was my style. This was contrary to my training and, throughout my time in Fiji, I never succumbed to what I regarded as a technical weakness, especially after having seen that Bradman never played his impeccable range of shots in the air. It took me a little while to make my place in the representative Suva team secure. While the matting took time to get used to for batting, it helped my slow bowling. I discovered Fijians strangely vulnerable to it, despite their propensity for huge hitting — in a Naduruloulou versus Bau match I actually took ten wickets for ten runs in the innings. I had to be sure to pitch it on the narrow mat and at the same time hope that the googly did not spin too wide to miss the wicket.

Other than Juxon Barton, I was the only Englishman playing and, because I was English, there was some Australian and

Euronesian (part-European) edge to make me have to fight all the more for my place. This was only five years after Douglas Jardine's legside theory tour of Australia, emotively given by Australians the label 'body-line'. Fiji cricket circles and even dinner parties were still full of that shock to Australia and my views were constantly sought. While they might have found a Jardine-like character in the ultra-English Barton, I think they felt I was unabrasive.

As a bachelor newcomer to the colony I was invited to rounds of European dinner parties, particularly if there was an unattached daughter. It was surprising how many there were in Suva and they were attractive too: the tropics seemed to have the same effect on women as on buds and flowers. That an English administrative officer might be a nuptial catch, perhaps eventually to acquire a plume of feathers in his helmet, was not disguised by parents, who were mostly Australians but unashamedly imperial, often more English than the English. They had my career in view more clearly than I had. As for my own feelings, I was only too conscious of being physically in competition in Suva with husky sailing, swimming, beach-type Australian and New Zealander bachelors in the Bank of New South Wales and the Bank of New Zealand. These macho types might have been expected to, but didn't, play rugby, which was dominated by burlier Fijians, or soccer, which was monopolized by Indians.

The dinner parties had two features in common. One was that, being not long after the abdication, I was repeatedly asked what it was like to be in England then and what I thought of Edward VIII. From what I knew about him at that time, I was pro him. But from his virtual toadying to Hitler, from allowing Negroes only the back-door entrance to Government House in the Bahamas, from his Philistinism and naïveté (excepting his judgement of the Maginot line which the Supreme Command foolishly ignored), I have since found little in favour to add to his remarkably good looks, despite his five-foot-five-inch stature.

The second feature was that my arrival in Fiji had somehow been preceded by a report in the *Fiji Times and Herald* that I was an international table tennis player for England. Although I had participated in the preliminary round of the world tournament at Wembley and had played for both Cambridgeshire and Cambridge University, this was a distortion of the truth. I was well short of England standard. I disabused my hosts as much as possible of the legend, but they always expected me to perform on their verandahs where, surprisingly, there was always a table. I therefore used to take my racquet with me and only wished that, in the unaccustomed heat, I could have been in shorts and a short-sleeved shirt instead of dressed for dinner. The narrow verandahs were cramping to my style, both for long-distance defence and for smashing, so I did not always have it my own way against either masculine or feminine knowledge of local conditions. While I did not lose, I had the feeling that I was expected to be a perpetual whirlwind: a few marks, if not points, were lost, I'm sure. Enticing and charming as many of the young European women were (pre-eminently the five Kearsley sisters whom I was privileged to know), I ineluctably found that the part-Europeans, particularly of a Samoan and Tongan mixture, more closely approximated to the beguiling types I had expected on leaving England for the South Seas. French administrators in the South Pacific had no complex under the skin on this score. Does this help to account for their managing to contrive a colonial presence in Polynesia to this day?

With so much happening, my letters to Charles, with whom I had promised to keep regularly and fully in touch, were lengthy. We had agreed that we would keep each other's letters. His I did manage to preserve, but after his many moves in London throughout the Blitz most of mine to him went astray (purloined or destroyed or both by no friend), possibly in a Cambridge cellar with more valuable letters. I did keep copies of some of mine to him. Sadly for many, I like to feel, Charles never kept a diary. But how many major writers did? They were too occupied producing other and truly creative works. It was also a pity that he was not given to reminiscing as such at any time in his life. The nearest he came to it was in his *Variety of Men*.

In one of my letters to Charles that did survive (from Naduru-loulou dated 1 September 1939) I wrote as very much a first impression full of hope:

I'm very anxious to introduce you to the one race that is to a man courteous, pleasant and happy, even if happy only because of a complete lack of neurosis. No advocate for them (the Fijians) could plead that their happiness sprang from deep intellectual sources. It's simply due to complexes not yet having worked their way through the generations to the surface. ... At present they are unspoiled (except for some of those whom missionaries have ruined) and free in outlook and honest in concept and I want you to see them before one of the last races representative of these characteristics disappears.

A note is perhaps necessary here to explain my missionary policy about cricket among Fijians over and above my own predilection for the game. As soon as I saw them playing it in a rather limited manner I was impelled to foster it (or, where it did not exist, to introduce it) as an activity that seemed so naturally to match their innate dignity, their alertness of eye, their muscled agility and sinewy grace of movement. Rugby football, requiring almost no equipment and little technical polish and coaching, was easy to organize: it had a majority following but also, to me, sometimes a rather worrying element of aggressiveness about it. Fijians, like Samoans and Tongans, were successful at it with their physique and it was easy to comprehend — for spectators and players alike. But as it did not cultivate anywhere near as much the rare combination of attractive native qualities just mentioned, I felt that cricket was a thoroughly worthwhile outlet for both *bravura* and finesse, as well as interracial *mélange*.

5

Colossus and Some Odyssey

The Ribbentrop–Molotov non-aggression pact was the inevitable precursor to Germany feeling free to overwhelm countries to its west. I had just been posted to Vunidawa, the administrative centre of Colo East Province, to run it by a series of week-long visits from Naduruloulou, answerable in theory to A. J. Armstrong there, but for most practical purposes on my own. Colo (the interior of Viti Levu) was divided into three parts: Colo West, under the jurisdiction of a DC on the coast at Nasigatoka; Colo North, under a DC stationed in the hill station of Nadarivatu; and Colo East. The DC in charge of Colo North used to combine it with Colo East, but their interconnection by river or through rugged mountains was formidable and unfair to the third inland component.

I was very excited by the prospects of my new district. In *The Hill Tribes of Fiji*, Adolph Brewster largely described the wild times of his position as Governor's Commissioner for Colo North and Colo East 50 years earlier and there had been little reason in intervening times between his and mine for the introduction of much change. There were almost no roads and the beautiful Wainimala and Wainibuka rivers, the main tributaries of the Rewa, provided the principal means of making personal contact. Fijians were almost the sole human beings there and they used bamboo rafts and, in some areas, floated on currents down the rivers with a bamboo for buoyancy under one arm. There were few horses or other animals and scarcely any European-style buildings — merely the odd school and church. The pagan temples had disappointingly vanished. Otherwise, there was nothing to differentiate the view from that of earlier centuries.

I had gone to Vunidawa on 1 September 1939 and was taking court on 5 September when the telephone (the only one in Vunidawa) on the court clerk's desk rang. The call was for me. I adjourned court and retired to the extension wire in my office. It was A. J. saying in muted tones that war with Germany had started (Fiji was 12 hours ahead of London's time) and that the Governor's ADC had telephoned him to say that I was to be transferred to the Governor's office that day. Though A. J. had explained that I was up river, he was requested to have me moved to Suva immediately. I returned briskly to Naduruloulou, packed all my effects in a couple of suitcases and a tin trunk, paid off a tearful Inayt, clutched my kitten Lulu and, for the last time, descended the 39 steps. A waiting taxi took me through the back entrance of the Government House drive to the adjacent cadets' quarters known as 'the Batch' (short for Bachelors' Quarters), the only quarters, apart from the gubernatorial buildings, lying within the Government House grounds. There I joined two contemporaries, one (McAlpine) working for periods at Navua, and the other, who was inclined to be sycophantic, sanctimonious and tendentious, in the Secretariat.

From the Batch there was a superb view down an avenue of royal palms over to Joske's Thumb on the opposite side of Suva Bay. This volcanic plug — an irresistible, twisted challenge to mountaineers such as Sir Edmund Hillary (who eventually tackled it in the 1970s) — was covered with bush extending as far as to Colo, to which I had expected to devote myself. The view from my office, which was attached to the Governor's, was no less grandiose.

My duties were to decipher secret telegrams and to act as an extra ADC to the Governor and Commander-in-Chief. Second Lieutenant Jocelyn Nicholls, the ADC who had spoken out of the corner of his mouth at the top of the *Monterey*'s gangway after Cahn's tea party, was a regular army officer and automatically had to return to England without delay: he was later killed in

Burma. By being called to work with Sir Harry Luke, my relations with the King's representative had been totally restored. In the changed circumstances, to have stayed in Colo East would have quickly made me feel a recluse: now I was as close to the vortex of Fiji's war as could be. But it was, of course, without assessing it as such at the time, a strangely phoney war. I was with the Governor for its duration up to the early summer of 1940. Fiji did not become important in the war until the bombing of Pearl Harbor 18 months after that, but it was, all the same, deluged with telegrams from the Secretary of State for the Colonies and from New Zealand forces' commands, and with occasional alarms over a rogue German raider being likely to bombard a defenceless Suva if it had passed a New Zealand army battery overlooking the entrance through the reef.

I had to be on call 24 hours a day and to work five and a half days with readiness for some emergencies on Saturday evenings and Sundays. The cable office had instructions to telephone me outside working hours should anything marked *en clair* 'IMMEDIATE' arrive for the Governor. Were it to prove to be something that could not wait until the morning (always remembering that we were 12 hours ahead of Greenwich), in that event I was to wake the Governor. I would have to walk down to the office adjacent to the Governor's to meet the Fijian carrying the cablegram and extract the cipher books (to be destroyed before invasion and, in the case of ships, before surrender) from the Governor's giant safe. I remember an all-change of books when the Germans captured a submarine intact. To reach the office meant passing a police sentry with a bayonet.

One occasion combined drama and melodrama sublimely and ridiculously. Dreamily, at 4.00 a.m., after having been woken up in the Batch by a telephone call from the cable office, I was making my way down the hill towards the Governor's office when I was brought sharply to reality by a sentry with a guilty conscience because he had evidently nodded off and had not heard or seen my approach, but, more to the point, he had the edge of his bayonet just short of my throat. He had given no challenge. I rocked back on my heels to avoid the bayonet: then he recognized me. The cablegram bearer on his cycle with a lamp made a safer approach. I opened the long cablegram and started the laborious decipherment. Marked 'IMMEDIATE. GOVERNOR SUVA [Those three words were *en clair*. Then began the most secret cypher, all in numbers.] FROM LORD HUNTINGFIELD' (this is no invention but his actual name — he was 5th Lord, William Charles Arcedeckne Vanneck, Governor of Victoria), it read: 'I regret the delay in sending you this notification through misunderstanding at this end. As president of the British Red Cross Society in Australasia, I now inform you that Red Cross Day this year will be ... [in two months' time] and trust that you will make every endeavour to maintain Fiji's excellent record of help.' There was plenty more. I went no further and, never before or subsequently given to throwing books (or anything else) about, I hurled the cipher book straight through the open safe door, locked it and stormed off back up the hill, leaving unheeded Huntingfield's urgent plea that had been sent with a fine disregard for Melbourne's time scale in relation to Fiji's and with an equally fine disregard of the sacred prefix 'IMMEDIATE' as well as so imperious a use of the most secret cipher. The decoding chore was generally tiresome and bad for my mathematics, as one of the tricks of deciphering (it is no breach of confidentiality to reveal this, meaningless as it is here) was to crack all the messages, which were totally in figures, by sub-traction without carrying a figure forward to the next column and then look up the resulting numbers for words in the secret books.

Nicholls's substitute had been a lieutenant commander who was a slightly more senior administrative officer than I was, but why he, as a naval man, was not called up I never knew. He and I had to work together in the same room. He had an odd habit of swivelling on his heels: his countenance matched this versatility as he was just as two-faced. Obsequious in the presence of the Governor, he would, when away from him, bite the hand that literally fed him. I have never grown accustomed to hypocrisy of this kind. He had curt manners with Fijians, not least with our bright, cheerful Fijian police orderly, Joni (John) Gu, who was permanently smiling and the husband of the highly photogenic Roma Tripp (a name we shall see later). Ratu Sukuna told me, with the glee Fijians reserve for pricking pomposity, that when he had been DC Nasavusavu the lieutenant commander had over-turned his district boat in the course of a smart manœuvre to impress a visiting Governor, and had had to present himself to His Excellency in dripping condition. He was imperious but there were aspects of kindness behind his vanity. For example, there were excellent opportunities to play cricket on Saturday afternoons and Sundays on the adjacent Albert Park, and in any emergency he would stand in for my decoding during the season from October to April: in return I would deputize for him to suit his inclinations.

When Queen Salote of Tonga passed through Suva *en route* to New Zealand for a health checkup (she was then unknown outside the Pacific but in 1953 became one of the Empire's best-known figures on the coronation procession in London — she lingers in the English public memory), in the absence of the Governor and ADC I, as acting ADC, had to visit the 40-passenger ship, the *Matua* (4000 tons), conveying an invitation to Government House for lunch. On my way to her cabin I passed a large deck window and saw her, as few outside her household might have, with her greyish hair down to her shoulders. For all public appearances it was braided and fastened up. With genial charm, she asked me to explain that unfortunately she did not feel up to coming ashore.

Again while acting as ADC, on looking through the safe to see if it contained anything I had not been shown but might need in a hurry, in a cobwebbed recess I came across the following circular to the Governor, Sir Everard im Thurn, from the Marquess of Crewe, Secretary of State for the Colonies. Wise man that he was, im Thurn never circulated it — at least not in any of the districts in which I served (virtually the lot), for I never saw a copy of it or ever heard anyone mention it. Marked confidential and sent from Downing Street in January 1909, it was a classic of its kind.

1. It has been brought to my notice that officers in the service of some of the Crown Colonies and Protectorates have in some instances entered into arrangements of concubinage with girls and women belonging to the

    native populations of the territories in which they were performing their duties.

2. These illicit connections have at times been a cause of trouble with native populations; and another objection equally serious from the standpoint of the Government lies in the fact that it is not possible for any member of the administration to countenance such practices without lowering himself in the eyes of the natives and diminishing his authority over them.

3. I will not for a moment believe that such practices receive anything but the gravest condemnation from the members of the Service. Their admirable work and excellent conduct are fully appreciated by His Majesty's Government, and I feel sure that this Circular will be accepted by the Service as an appeal for loyal co-operation in vigorously reprobating and officially condemning all such cases of concubinage between Civil Servants and native women whenever and wherever they are detected.

CREWE

It is nicely apposite that the Marquess's father had embarrassed his family when, on moving house, a suitcase he was carrying burst open to reveal on the ground in very public view part of his vivid collection of erotic literature, lavish in its range of *risqué* illustrations.

Now there was reorientation to European girls. I was no good at dancing: I had some sense of harmony and melody but little of rhythm. This was a real disadvantage in Fiji. I have always had an acute inferiority complex about it. Nevertheless, I took Joyce Kearsley, fourth in the arresting line of Constance and Bill Kearsley's five daughters and later to marry an American major-general, to Grand Pacific Hotel dances. On one occasion I wore, out of a desire somehow to cut a dash, a bow tie of cerise, mauve, orange, magenta, ultramarine and green stripes, admittedly a rather sickly mixture. They were the colours of a Christ's College drinking club — all right in Cambridge but perhaps not for the then *de rigueur* evening dress wear for GPH dances. Sir Harry Luke's cavorting with Mrs Y (his accomplice in Murder at Government House) did not prevent his bright parrot-like eyes spotting it. Next morning, as soon as he had taken the few steps from Government House to his office, he walked into mine next door. 'I do not want you to wear that abomination ever again,' he said, and turned on his heels.

He did not welcome competition in his own often spectacular wardrobe. He adored dressing up and being photographed in his Knight of the Order of St John of Jerusalem robe and cap, in his MA and D.Litt. gowns and hoods and both the blue and white gubernatorial uniforms, as well as, when informal, Etonian bow tie and flashily banded Panama hat. Australians thought him ornate (not the word they used): they were correct but this assessment did not diminish my opinion of his qualities.

Things suddenly began to whir. Events in Europe deteriorated fast. It became alarmingly and translucently clear to me that if Anne did not come out now she might not be able to before the end of a long, probably disastrous war. And would she survive it? Actual invasion of England did not then seem likely, but bombing certainly did. The deterioration reached a crisis when Luke was in New Zealand. The chilling Johnson was still Acting Colonial Secretary; the formidable Barton, Colonial Secretary, was on leave in England. John Craig, the Officer Administering the Government (so appointed by Luke in preference to Johnson), to whom I was acting ADC, was only marking time before his retirement as Financial Secretary and Colonial Treasurer at the age of 56. It was no good expecting him to make a decision.

By letter, Charles warned of the European danger — he had no confidence in Chamberlain and Halifax in the forefront of affairs, or in the anti-Semitic Londonderry set who ran the country from the rear — and offered to pay for Anne's passage as his wedding present, for I myself had not saved up enough funds. So, without local permission, I asked Charles to arrange for her to come out. I determined to wait for Luke's return. Then, seizing the first moment, I told him and was relieved beyond any words that I could express by his crisp 'Of course, she must come out.' I reminded him that I still had a year or more in which to have to pass the Law and Fijian examinations, but had passed an extra one, Hindi, long before the due dates and with distinction. He said that he would have difficulty replacing me in his office, particularly as the war was hotting up. Since there was no married housing available in Suva, it would be necessary for me to be transferred. A day later, he delighted me further by saying that he was appointing me DC Lau, and that while Anne was making her inevitably painful, slow 12,000-mile way out (there was no air transport) I was to go out straightaway to Lau to take over from Ratu Josefa Lalabalavu Vanaaliali Sukuna, CBE, *Médaille militaire*, who had been DC for the almost unprecedented length (for anyone in any district) of eight years. He was 52: I was 25. The experience was to be unique — succeeding a Fijian. (He was the only Fijian district commissioner and, as said earlier, had the distinction of being the first native in the Empire to hold that position.)

Before hardly anyone in Suva knew, I was on my way to the administrative headquarters of Lau (bearing the euphonic name of Lomaloma) in the 50-foot district cutter *Adi Maopa*. This was a new vessel, named by Ratu Sukuna after his mother, Adi Litiana Maopa, who was of the highest Lauan rank; his father, Ratu Joni Madraiwiwi (Sour Bread), had been a chieftain of Bau. After a couple of nights' sailing, the *Adi Maopa* anchored off the imposing white office building made of burnt coral. Three cannons pointed out to sea through a gap in the white coral wall surrounding the spacious Lomaloma Government Station compound just behind the beach's casuarina and palm trees.

Ratu Sukuna was standing on the beach in his cream *sulu*, silk handkerchief tucked in at the wrist of the sleeve of his Savile Row silk shirt, waiting for me to be rowed ashore in the dinghy. He was very like both his father and mother in appearance, not conventionally handsome but absorbingly interesting with a long face rising to a pointed dome in the shape that Fijian mothers and relatives trained children to have by constantly pressing round the crown at an early stage. What little hair he had was grey-white. Not more than five feet nine inches tall, he was sturdy: the calves of his legs bulged enormously. He smiled with his eyes. 'Hello, Snow. Welcome to Lau,' said the extraordinary mellifluent voice, totally Oxford, from lips pleasantly pursed for perfect enunciation, emphasized with lines on the sides of his mouth. In all the 20 years I knew him (from 1938 when he was 50 to his death in 1958) I never once heard an English word mispronounced or given a Fijian intonation. His Fijian was, like his English, uttered unfalteringly — and softly, so much so that one had to be on the *qui vive* to avoid the discourtesy of having to ask him to repeat himself.

When all my worldly goods in the tin trunk and two humble suitcases followed with Lulu being carried by one of the crew, Ratu Sukuna took me over the finely mown grass of the Government Station compound and along the wide, velvet-like grass path through the profuse coconut groves to one of the two sets of steps curving up to the little plateau. There stood the DC's house, unusual in being in concrete, with the conventional wooden shutters, glass doors and corrugated iron roof. His wife, Adi Maraia, a Bauan of high rank (but not of the highest in that remarkable island's hierarchy), appeared soon after with a beaming smile, but not to stay. No explanation was given but I deduced — and saw it later confirmed — that she did not eat or drink at the same table if they had visitors.

Ratu Sukuna and I sat, whisky and soda to hand, on the verandah to take in the immortal panorama of a huge ex-crater, now Lomaloma Lagoon, all blues and greens, with its backdrop crescent on the horizon of the islands of Namalata, Susui (a traditional picnic resort, uninhabited except by stingrays in its lagoon), and Munia (owned by the striking part-European daughter of the recently deceased H. H. Steinmetz of Germanic birth, Harrow education and nearly 50 years on this model copra plantation), Cikobia-i-lau and Avea. All of the islands were different in their craggy, green outlines against the sunset of gold. But foremost in the lagoon, with a spit of sand stretching almost to touch the Fijian village of Lomaloma and the Tongan village of Sawana, which were obscured from view by the wealth of coconut palms, was a pyramidal island, Nayanuyanu (meaning The Island).

Uninhabited, it had been the refuge, with a cannon he had brought with him for protection, of William Hennings, a German trader who had eloped with one of King Cakobau's relatives, Adi Mere (Mary) Tuisalolo. Cakobau's sourness over the impertinence of the elopement was in no way diminished by the fact that he had had her father, Ratu Kamisese Mara Tuimacilai Kapaiwai, who was also his cousin and who had led a coup against him, hanged on Bau in 1859. More of that and of the island's present owner, Ratu Sir Kamisese Kapaiwai Tuimacilai Mara, will follow soon. Suffice it to say here that this was the only hanging ever known to have been performed by any person in Fiji outside Suva gaol, or by Ma'afu (soon to be referred to) of his enemies, and that it was Cakobau's manner of demonstrating his new Christian ways. His victim was Ratu Sukuna's grandfather and the fact that Cakobau was the great-grandfather of Ratu Sir George Cakobau may always have been not far from the minds of the victim's and the King's descendants, Sukuna and Pope. (You will remember the *draunikau* hypothesized in an earlier reference.) Fijian memory, as in the cases of some people who do not write things down, is very long.

On that verandah I dared scarcely hope that, in a month or so, this and its view would be Anne's and my honeymoon home and official residence.

Ratu Sukuna did not like Suva in those days. He used to return to Lau, the only district to which he was ever appointed, with astonishing celerity for a laid-back Fijian, after the numerous pressures for attendance in Suva requiring his unique knowledge and his position as senior Fijian member. Enduring and demurring to the banalities and postulations of the Legislative Council had its limits for him.

Brought up with an Indian family of standing in Ra, where his father Ratu Joni Madraiwiwi was Roko Tui, Ratu Sukuna had been to Wanganui Collegiate School in New Zealand and had represented the school at cricket.

In view of Sukuna's most eminent career, it is interesting and reassuring for any wrong-footed at the start of careers to record two very early inauspicious episodes, previously unpublicized and unpublished. Government had acceded to the request of his father for a post as fifth-class clerk in the Secretariat for his son, who replied to the Colonial Secretary:

Sir,
I have the honour to acknowledge the receipt of your letter dated January 30 informing me of my appointment. While thanking the government for their magnanimity I at the same time beg to submit my resignation to the same since under the present circumstances I am unable to remain in the service after February.
I have the honour to be, Sir,

Your humble servant,
J. L. V. Sukuna

On 4 February 1907, the Colonial Secretary, A. W. Mahaffy, minuted the following to 'His Excellency, The Governor':

Respectfully submitted is a letter from Ratu J. Sukuna regarding his appointment to this office. The Governnent have spent a considerable sum in educating this youth and — at the special request of his father — an appointment was found for him in this office. At some inconvenience the appointment was kept vacant for him for six months. Without any explanation he now resigns. His father should be asked to use his influence to advise the boy to remain in the service for a year or two — we deserve some return for our trouble.

On the same date, Sir Everard im Thurn then minuted the 'Hon. Colonial Secretary', saying that 'The lad's action ... tends to discredit the advice of those who advised our keeping him longer in New Zealand or even sending him to Cambridge.' And later, on 14 February 1907, that 'I have spoken to you and Mr Sutherland on this very disturbing subject. Mr Sutherland seems to think that he may possibly be able to do something further by personal influence to break down the very obstinate and bad mind of this lad.'

Native Commissioner W. Sutherland reported on 26 February that: 'Sukuna spent an evening at my house and I went over the matter of his future with him again. The following day he decided to express regret to you for the hasty step he had taken and to ask you to allow him to withdraw his resignation.' The next day, Sir Everard im Thurn again wrote to the Colonial Secretary saying that: 'I'm glad, for the sake of the lad and his race, that he has asked to withdraw his resignation and I comply with that request. I should like Mr Sutherland to bring Ratu Sukuna to me — say at 3.30 p.m. on Friday afternoon.'

Sukuna's headstrong nature was to mature, but a liberal, almost imperial, attitude towards money was with him all his life. Crown Agent for the Colonies Sir William Mercer wrote on 24 July 1914 to the Colonial Secretary, Fiji:

> I have the honour to acknowledge the receipt of your letter of 1st of June respecting the funds available to enable Ratu J. V. Sukuna to complete his education in this country. It is certainly the fact that Ratu Sukuna has been spending money at too great a rate. As soon as he landed in April last year and before I met him he went to a very expensive tailor who had been recommended to him on the steamer and incurred a heavy bill and throughout he has had an exaggerated view of the style in which he should live. I have several times warned him as to this but without any particular effect. . . . In other respects he has been entirely satisfactory. The Warden of Wadham wrote to me recently that he was 'A great success' there and very popular.

He then wrote to Sukuna on 27 July 1914: 'It seems to me that you cannot carry out both the Oxford and the Bar courses and I think that it would be best for you to take two years to take the Oxford LLB degree and to give up the idea of the Bar.' Mercer was himself a Wadham product.

When the Crown Agent's dispatch reached Fiji, it contained the following letter from Sukuna to Mercer dated 2 August 1914, two days before the war began:

50 Rue des Ecoles,
Paris.

Dear Sir William,

I am glad you have written about final schools and the Bar. The position seems to me to be the same as in June 1913. There was then likely to be insufficient funds to do Oxford and the Bar except by much pinching in every direction which I was not prepared to do. . . . I wrote on 28th July asking for money. I am now on very short commons with five francs in my pocket and my landlady pressing for payment in advance.

Yours sincerely,
Lala Sukuna

(Note the signature, commented on later.) In the margin against 'which I was not prepared to do', the Governor wrote 'Why not? Others have to pinch. E. im T. 1.10.14' and minuted it to the Colonial Secretary, adding: 'Sukuna's letter shows that he retains the worst features of Fijian character and is careless in many matters and self-indulgent.' When he had retired as Governor, im Thurn became one of Sukuna's unreserved admirers, not least of his war exploits. One must be thankful that officialdom was to restrain itself in the unprecedented reactions of the first Fijian to life abroad.

At Wadham, Oxford, Sukuna continued to play cricket and read law. When the First World War started he asked to enlist in the British forces but these would not accept native colonial troops. So he slipped away from England, joined the French Foreign Legion and, having been in battle with a whole regiment that had been awarded the *Croix de Guerre* (not conferred on individuals in it), gained the *Médaille militaire* in 1915 near Arras in France, sending back vivid letters of trench life and death before he was seriously wounded. On discharge from a Lyon hospital four months later, his return to Fiji was in heroic style, except for his stern father ordering him to take off permanently a turban that

101

Sukuna had found comfortable for his great bushy head of hair in the trenches. Fijians of pre-Cession times wore them made of thin mulberry bark, but only if they were of the highest rank. Ratu Sukuna was of that status but the headwear had long been eschewed.

While all chiefs must be addressed as Ratu unless a friend gains dispensation and can use a more familiar name, I shall drop the title for convenience periodically. Sukuna was to give me the privilege of asking me to call him Jo, short for Josefa (Joseph), which his family used, after I had known him closely for about four years and he was then officially Ratu Sir Lala Sukuna, KBE. Barely a dozen Europeans were ever invited to address him as Jo. I never used the privilege in company. In 1917 Sukuna returned to Europe as quartermaster sergeant with a Fijian labour battalion in Marseilles and Calais: the army authorities allowed native troops for dock unloading but still not for combatant duties, despite the astronomical Allied losses in the war. The war over, he assumed perfunctory humble work in the Native Department, interpreting and the like, before returning to England in 1919 to read for the Bar at the Middle Temple. Incidentally, his *Médaille militaire* was the highest French decoration, given only in cases of bravery amounting to VC standards to non-officers and somewhat anomalously to those of general and marshal rank. He used to tell Maraia that he gained it for cleaning latrines.

Just after my arrival at Lomaloma, Sukuna made his final tour of the Lau Archipelago and I had the unparalleled advantage of being asked to accompany him. Maraia stayed behind at Delana (the name of the house: it meant Hill Top). He used to take with him a silver-topped, elegant little crystal bottle of very hot chilli vinegar to pep up the food on board. He would never sleep in the two-bunked cabin. It was airless and, even after a servicing in Suva when it would be sunk in shallow water to drown them, the *Adi Maopa* was overrun by large brown scuttling and flying cockroaches. This was a deterrent shared by all inter-island schooners, ketches and cutters, however often they were treated with salt water and fumigation.

Sukuna would sleep on a bunk suspended under a canopy next

to the helm and would wear a bright red, flowered *sulu*, always with a long-sleeved shirt. The only severe scar from the war I noticed were two indentations in his wrist as he raised it out of his sleeve. We shared at the stern a shower-cum-lavatory. There was no lock on the door and once I opened it, thinking Sukuna was up in the bow of the boat, to see him showering clad in a bright red slip. I apologized, was greeted politely and invited to follow him in as he was about to leave. I could not observe the considerable groin wound he was reported to have received in the 1915 battle in Champagne, for he always wore a red slip under his *sulus*. These would be washed by his cook and suspended for drying on a line as though they were scarlet pennants decorating a vessel.

All Fijian men wore thin cotton shorts beneath their calf-length *sulus* and, incongruously, also under their skirts of leaves when taking part in *mekes*. Women wore only ankle-length *sulus*, which they would tuck in at the waist very securely. When sailing with Sukuna I was relieved that the weather was not too bad and that I could keep up with his input of stiff whiskies and *yaqona*, glass for glass and bowl for bowl. I did not equip myself so well when I was touring with Anne later, but the weather was not quite as favourable for most of our tours together.

At each island he and I visited, Sukuna was given the special Lauan ceremonies. It was of vital importance for me to see them in case they were to be repeated to me in somewhat similar style when I had taken over. Practically the only difference between what was accorded to him and what was to be extended to me was that in the speeches he was always formally addressed as Tui Lau (King of Lau). There had been only one before — Enele Ma'afu'otu'itoga, the Tongan who had conquered the Lau Archipelago in the 1850s and who gained the title for his lifetime in 1869. (It was Ma'afu who had brought the cannons now in front of Lomaloma Government Station.) Previously, Tui Nayau had been the highest traditional Lau title. Sukuna's mother, who died during Sukuna's district commissionership, had been the Tui Nayau's sister. The then current Tui Nayau was Ratu Tevita (David) Uluilakeba, father of the future President Ratu Sir Kamisese Mara, who himself succeeded as Tui Nayau and in 1969 was also installed as Tui Lau. Ratu Mara, six foot eight inches in height and lean from earliest days as a Central Medical School student when I coached him at cricket, to this day is recognized as only the second Tui Lau since Ma'afu, for Sukuna was never formally installed as such, but was so cited in the ceremonial by hosts and *matanivanua*s during my time in that archipelago.

There is nothing in Fiji like Lau chiefly ceremonial. Varying in divisions of Lau, it has not been recorded in its full panoply. It starts with *cavuikelekele* — an invitation to bring an anchor near to the shore, represented by the presentation on board the vessel of a whale's tooth. This occurs in other maritime provinces. For very rare inaugurating occasions, the women on shore wave long ribands of *tapa* (decorative cloth handmade from tree bark) as a tantalizing prize for the first among the visitors to catch a woman holding any; this custom, known as *cere*, is restricted to Lau and Bau. Then, on shore, is *roqo tabakau*, when strips of matting presented by two men crawling forward are received by the *matanivanua* almost contemptuously. Next is *i vono*, when a man bearing over his shoulder a stalk with two green coconuts waddles awkwardly on his knees to put them before the chief guest, for whom they are accepted, as in the case of the teeth, by the *matanivanua*. It represents the offering of the fruits of the land and is confined to Lau. A whale's tooth is then offered as a welcome for landing. Presented on board or on land, this is known as *qaloqalovi*, and is not peculiar to Lau. *I luva ni tawake*, when a further whale's tooth is offered as a request for the war flag on the visitor's craft to be lowered, is peculiar to Lau. This is followed by *sevusevu* — the presentation of a huge root of *yaqona*. It is general in Fiji but what follows is a Lauan and Bauan (and in tribes related to Bau) custom only. This is *vakamamaca* — the presentation of folds of fine mats symbolizing a change into dry clothes after nautical discomforts. It is often accompanied by a whale's tooth with *tapa* or sinnet (teased out fibre from coconut husks). The *yaqona vakaturaga*, in form common to other parts of Fiji but differing in detail from province to province, follows with *kava* mixing accompanied by archaic chanting and the approach of a couple of bearers of cups, one for the chief guest and the other, following, for the *matanivanua*. During the course of the differentiated stages of the ceremony, about half a dozen whale's teeth would have been presented, compared with one in nearly all Fiji's provinces, truly an *embarras de richesse* for the Lau administration. To round off the welcome, *magiti* (presentation of food) and *mekes* are ubiquitous throughout Fiji.

Sukuna always gave a short, grave reply in melodious tone to the welcome before we walked off at quite a pace to see any particular part of the environs involved in some or other land question. It is a mild shortcoming, but I learned when I succeeded him that, in ordering repairs, he used not to inspect the interiors of village houses. According to Fijian custom, he held too high a rank to be able to do that. On his walks, he would lead the way, for he knew Lau inside out, along paths so narrow that we had mostly to go in single file. Following immediately behind him, I would be hypnotized by his calves, which bulged larger than any I have ever seen.

His statue outside the Government Buildings in Suva, by a sculptor who never knew him, gives for posterity the absurd impression that he had elephantiasis in both legs. His legs were finely formed, but his calf muscles were pre-eminent. Although the statue may — and rightly so — aim to be Olympian, it is frankly unbecoming. Sukuna has been as unfortunately treated by his sculptor as by his first biographer, who suffered from the crippling disadvantage of knowing neither Sukuna nor the language — on top of its inaccuracies, the account was so opaque, obscure, convoluted and unstraightforward as to be virtually impossible to interpret.

Sukuna was always immaculately dressed, even for bush travel, though more so before than after the Second World War. His silk shirts buttoned to the wrist and his *sulu* in light grey or Palm Beach brown would be tailored. He wore no headgear. Some chiefs, including his younger brother Ratu Tiale (Charlie) Wimbledon Thomas Vuiyasawa (who looked like him and had managed to pass himself off as a Maori in New Zealand and fight on the Somme in the First World War) and Ratu George Brown Toganivalu, rather demeaned their features, I thought, by wearing khaki or even green topees.

All the way up hill and down dale, in measured deliberate tones interspersed with soft chuckles, Sukuna would chat evocatively about persons and places. His favourite reading was biography and history; his most comfortable position for it in all weathers was in that bunk above the small cabin next to the helmsman. At one stage he told me that he contemplated writing a book on philosophy, but he never got round to it and the world is the poorer for that. Also, extracts from two consecutive entries in his 1933 diary as DC Lau, describing a 'customary welcome from chiefs and people of Totoya' on 14 February, in which in the '*meke*s by women' there were 'three or four really pretty girls in the last one' and then, on 15 February, how he had 'had *yaqona*' and that 'as the pretty girls were making it [he had] lingered over extra bowls', show an uninhibited eye for pulchritude.

In my 20 years of knowing him, I never saw him express displeasure by a look or word. He had a deep knowledge of, and respect for, cricket: it was almost a euphemism for entertaining manœuvres with decorum, specially applicable to Fijian leisure activity. For him, Raymond C. Robertson-Glasgow's *Cricket Prints* achieved the perfect balance between deferential humour and exquisite English. Sukuna was himself a master of both these gifts, although I think that his famous take-off, tongue in cheek, of some Europeans in a talk entitled 'A Fijian's View of the European', given to the Defence Club with the Governor present in 1939, is not as subtle as his style could achieve. An extract, after all his quips, nevertheless represents a weighty judgement:

I have given you something of the Fijian's view of the European. You will have observed that it contains nothing uncharitable; there is no envy and no malice. The view is, of course, critical but not hostile. Indeed it is to the credit of the European community that they have and hold the good will of the Native Race. It is an achievement of which you may justly be proud in these changing times of strikes and riots, of normality and reorganization, of novelty and dis-organization. ... There are few places in the Empire where relations between governors and governed are better and

ABOVE LEFT. Author and wife at Lomaloma, 1940. *(Photo: C.G.O.T. Parr)* ABOVE RIGHT. Author as officer in charge of Police. Lau, 1940. *(Photo: Anne Snow)* BELOW. Author's wife with young friend on the beach at Lomaloma, 1940. *(Photo: Author)*

ABOVE. Author's wife with women's *meke* on Lakeba, Lau, 1940. Adi Veniana Puamau is on her right. *(Photo: Author)*
BELOW. Author explaining, in Fijian, about the Pacific War and the Japanese threat to Fiji. Nadi, 1942, Brigadier E.T. Seltzer, U.S. Air Force Commander on his right, Colonel A.H.T. Sugden, N.Z. Army on his left with author's wife. *(Photo: U.S. Air Force)*

more harmonious than in this colony. Your predecessors — governors and overseers, merchants and civil servants, planters and traders — have laid a sound foundation and on it they have started an edifice whose pillars are the humanities and common sense.

Being so much in demand, he should have retired earlier or been given leave by government (he had only just retired as Speaker of the Legislative Council, after onerous years as first holder of that office and suffering a stroke in that time, when he died in 1958 from cerebral arteriosclerosis at sea on the *Arcadia* off Ceylon *en route* to England aged 70) to write his reminiscences: they would have been supremely well written and uniquely constituted. He was too acquiescent to have tried to direct his later life along the most appropriate course. Had he been appointed Governor in 1948 — at the age of 60 — he could have retired in 1951/2 and had ample time, not overtired, for writing. Almost Olympian in his hero's return from the First World War, he inexorably made an increased mark on Fiji. From the 1930s Europeans, Fijians and Indians recognized the growth in Sukuna's stature. No one could be compared with him. By the time of his death, Ratu Sir Lala was the colossus of Fiji. He straddled the cultures of both hemispheres. Now, nearly 40 years on, he is historically established as Fiji's greatest figure — a seemingly unsurpassable one with Ratu Sir Kamisese Mara approaching closely in his shadow and perhaps, given the different circumstances, already in the vanguard.

One night, having completed most of the tour with Sukuna of the main islands and in Tui Nayau's Lakeba house drinking whisky — not a favourite of mine but on this occasion meriting the production from Ah Jack Browne's Chinese store of more bottles — I heard a message over Suva radio: 'To Phil [*sic*] Snow in Lau. Anne arriving May 2 *Mariposa*.' The last name was that of the American companion liner to the *Monterey*. As it was the end of April and I had heard nothing of Anne having left because of blackouts of messages in the now severely dangerous stage of the war, I had now to hurry into Suva on the *Adi Maopa*, which Sukuna allowed me to use while he patiently waited for its return on Lakeba, the island of his late mother and where he was himself to be buried.

I was lucky that the message got through to the only place on our tour with a wireless and that it was one of those rare days when the battery was charged. I reached Suva with a day or two to spare. This was sufficient for Luke to change my mind — there was no question of my refusing — and to arrange for the marriage to be in the pro-cathedral rather than in the registrar's office, which Anne and I had always intended, not least in consideration of Anne not knowing anyone in Fiji and of our not having clothes appropriate for anything grander.

Luke and the ADC arranged for the Government House gardener to provide a bouquet and Kingsley and Jane Roth, referred to later, insisted on being the hosts at the reception, for which Luke gave the champagne. He also presented us with a turtle-shell cigarette box monogrammed 'S' in gold. It was too delicate to survive numerous rough moves, though the ADC's large cut glass jug miraculously has — the only wedding present to do so except for silver tankards from my Indian friend, John Amputch, who had helped me found the Suva Cricket Association.

Now for a word about Anne's journey, as I learnt about it from her when we had a moment after her arrival. In such circumstances, it was a minor epic for a woman of 20 who in England had hardly travelled more than a few miles from Leicester. Charles had very generously bought her London–Fiji tickets. The odyssey began on 20 March from 32 Jellicoe Road and the railway station in Leicester. She then took the boat train across the English Channel from Folkestone to Calais in a blacked-out ferry with all passengers wearing life jackets. From there the train was blacked out to Marseilles. Charles had thought of asking Richard Aldington, living in the south of France, to help her on this part of the journey, but Aldington had already escaped to America.

She was able to share a sleeping compartment with a young girl going to Malta. It had been thought safer to travel over land than from the P & O *Strathnaver*'s embarkation point in London via the Bay of Biscay. Feeling certain that she had boarded the correct ship at Marseilles, in a letter to my mother of 2 April, which I saw years afterwards, Charles reported that Anne had sent him 'a postcard when she got on the boat at Marseilles — so I think you can take it that she is safe'.

From Marseilles there was once more a total blackout throughout the whole 10,000 miles to Melbourne. But there was plenty of fun, at least as far as Port Said where a posse of Palestine police who had made a fuss of Anne disembarked. The *Strathnaver* was the last civilian ship to have been allowed through the Suez Canal, only a matter of days before the German breakthrough at Sedan, over the Meuse and in Belgium. It was a close-run thing.

On arrival at Melbourne on 18 April, after the long black nights through the Red Sea, Indian Ocean and Great Australian Bight, Anne was wonderfully looked after by Philip and Margo Bowden, Charles's Tasmanian friends in Cambridge, now trapped by the war in Australia. Other than Cahn, Philip had been the first and only friend from England to have visited me so far in Fiji (I had taken him from Suva to Naduruloulou). There was a scintillating dazzle in Melbourne's harbour — an American liner (the USA had not yet entered the war) was proclaiming its neutrality with every conceivable light. Anne never forgot that spectacle. She was furthermore to embark on it for ten floodlit nights from there via Sydney and Auckland to Fiji.

At last, at 7.00 a.m. on 2 May 1940, Anne was duly brought in by the 18,563-ton *Mariposa*, a brilliant white sight swinging through the coral reef entrance to the turquoise Suva Bay with apparently only 20 passengers on board. She had gone from one Jellicoe Road to another. The names of the two roads alongside the wharf were Jellicoe (like her home address) and Harris (like her own for this last day) — one coincidence followed by another. (Incidentally, Harris was Anne's adopted name. Her mother, Mary Anne Gee, had died three days after her birth as the tenth child and her aunt and uncle had brought her up.)

We were whisked off in the Governor's number two car to the vicar, H. Mayo Harris, for proclamation of the banns for the marriage under special licence at 5.00 p.m. Kingsley Roth gave her away, for she knew no one. Although late afternoon and evening weddings with dinner jackets were usual in that antipodean setting, I wore a grey pin-striped suit. The Governor wore a Palm Beach suit and Panama hat. Alone among the guests, the seemingly elderly (he was 58) Chief Justice Sir Owen Corrie wore morning dress. It was rumoured that it was thought that he was the bridegroom.

From the cathedral, which was full, we went by the number one GH car, the Humber limousine resplendent with gold crown (this time and perhaps for the only time in his Fiji career the Governor was in the number two car) to the Roths' house, where Luke, who had insisted on countersigning the register, made the speech with toasts. I was more nervous over my response than I had been in the cathedral. Ironically, the Colonial Secretary, Juxon Barton — who would, had he been in the colony, certainly have opposed our marriage because of his inflexible attitude towards administrative officers not marrying until all their examinations had been passed — had travelled on the same liner as Anne without realizing it (he in first class, Anne in tourist).

At dinner afterwards at GH with a large number of guests, there were considerately no more speeches other than Luke's announcement that, to his knowledge, this was the first time that anyone would have 'signed in' to GH under a single name, only to stay the same night under another name. Anne, sitting between Luke and Barton, was not spoken to once by the latter. After such a day, she was glad to have time to breathe.

A breakfast next morning of pawpaw, scrambled eggs and coffee on the verandah overlooking Suva Lagoon and Joske's Thumb was memorable. We stayed a week there and then moved to the GPH for two days until the *Adi Maopa* returned with Sukuna from Lau. It was late doing so and when it did come in Luke circumspectly would not let us leave for Lomaloma until a radio telephone had been fitted (Sukuna never wanted one). This was to be a godsend in Lau but it took quite a while for it to function properly, in fact not until three days after we had moved from the GPH on to the cutter tied up at the wharf. After constant farewell parties and the bathos of go–stop false alarms as to the machine's readiness to operate, we were finally passed fit for sailing to Lomaloma, reaching it two nights later. Anne, not yet of independent age, had found home — after six weeks and 12,000 miles alone, in the back of beyond or precisely the opposite side of the globe. I had at least a little idea of what we had been slowly plunged into. She had none.

6

Frailties in Paradise

From here on I kept a diary through most of my time in the Pacific, primarily because it was an official requirement for administrative officers in districts (until one had to economize on paper) but also because it was useful to record less than official happenings. For only the periods in Suva were there no diary entries of any sort. With hindsight, I regret those intervals but doubt if I would have had the residual energy at the end of the day, after hours of writing Secretariat minutes and dispatches, to keep it up. I did keep a diary on sea voyages to and from England: there was plenty of leisure for that.

The only key waiting for me at Lomaloma was to the small safe, which Ratu Sukuna had left in the care of the senior of the two clerks. The office on the beach consisted of a small room, which the clerks shared, and my large, virtually empty room, which led through a door up three steps on to the courthouse Bench. None of these was locked day or night. On looking back, it never ceases to astound me that no home in Lau, or anywhere else in Fiji, was ever locked or even had windows and doors that could be locked; and in Lau, for instance, given that we could be seen sailing off on the cutter for a week or a fortnight away, our frequent absences were never concealed from the public. It would simply never have occurred to anyone to steal. Anything purloined would be too easily identified in Fiji's communal society. Government cash was, however, regarded as public property for embezzlement by occasional impetuous employees of His Majesty's Service: after all, it was likely to have emanated from the public. But that was the exception: there was a safe none too large in each office and it would not have been beyond the strength of a couple of men to abscond with them. But it never happened.

The front of the office looked past the three mounted cannons over the beach to the lagoon — at high tide a few yards away. The thatched open-topped sentry box on the sand was a primitive urinal: it had no door, only a curve in the side for privacy. There were in fact two — one for the DC and visitors, the other for clerks and station officials. There were no notices of course: it was all a matter of custom. Villagers passing by would have used the all-enveloping bush.

My new life as DC (and PC) Lau was paradisiacal. In Africa, one had to be in administration for about 30 years before being designated a provincial commissioner. In India, the culmination of a life as an administrator often carried no more romantic a title than collector of taxes, deputy commissioner or deputy magistrate. Until 1913, in Fiji, apart from Colo where there was a governor's commissioner, the highest position in a district carried the title of stipendiary magistrate. That year, however, they all (about a dozen of them) became district commissioners. A district commissioner in Fiji had jurisdiction over all and everything in a district, whereas a provincial commissioner (and a district could contain more than one province) held the supreme position in a province in all matters purely Fijian. I was to be the last PC Lau resident in the province.

This is the time to explain why I was not at the war. As soon as it started with Germany, government laid down that no employee could leave for the war without resigning first from the Service and with a clear indication that afterwards the post could not be resumed. This applied even to the odd person who had been previously in the armed services. I suppose that this had deterred the Lieutenant-Commander who was ADC.

It did not deter Commander William Burrows, a DC of 18 years' standing, but he was 57. When he did return after the war to retire in Fiji he was virtually blind, having been blown up on the docks at Bari in Italy, to where he had moved as a port officer. One who did resign was the distinguished Cambridge oarsman Neville John Bradley (he had been stroke of the 1934 Cambridge crew winning in record time), but he was related to the Cadburys of Bourneville and so was rich enough to be independent. Although a Quaker, he nevertheless took part in combatant duties as a patrol boat leader in the English Channel.

Oddly, there was a connection between Burrows and Bradley, or at least there should have been but wasn't. Three years before the war, Bradley had been posted on first appointment as a cadet to Navua where there was only one house, the DC's. Jack Bradley had to reside in it with Burrows, whose wife was not living with him. After a week Burrows could no longer tolerate the intrusion. Willie Maugham would have liked both the situation and the solution. Burrows marked out in chalk a line on the floor of the beachside bungalow, not dividing it into equal halves but giving himself three parts, with a quarter for Bradley, who was not to cross the frontier. The border lasted until Bradley was moved to a district on his own, several months later.

As for myself, with neither private means nor a job to return to, I could not afford to resign and had to accept that Fiji must be my home until the war finished. The official ruling was that the country had to be administered and there was no spare personnel qualified to deputize in what was, after all, a shoestring staff. After Pearl Harbor, the wisdom of this decision could be more plainly seen; with Fiji likely to be invaded by the Japanese it was vital for administrators to be responsible for defence, civil order and avoidance of anarchy.

As the bombing of England started in earnest in 1940, my conscience in beautiful remote Lau was deeply stirred, not least when I heard that the area around our Richmond Road house in Leicester was almost the first to be bombed. A single German plane had dropped its bombs near the gasometers and all along the unbroken line of terraced houses in Cavendish Road, which was at the bottom of our garden: flying fragments had smashed our third-storey windows and some people living parallel to us had been killed. The pilot, brought down in Northamptonshire on his return route to Germany, claimed that he thought that he had been releasing his load on Birmingham: either implausible or bad navigation — a 30-mile distance error in daytime and a location scarcely similar in size.

In his letters, Charles did not think that Lau was too escapist. He probably thought that the war would catch up with it anyway. There was always a chance, as there had been in the First World War, of a German raiding vessel, which I would have been powerless to deal with and on which I could be expected to be transported. One of my first acts in Lomaloma was to call in all the village heads of Vanuabalavu island, asking them to be ready at a moment's notice to try and hide any livestock — the handful of cattle, horses and poultry — if a German ship turned up. I was not to know until after the war that for months a German raider, the *Orion*, had been crisscrossing very close and attacking vessels with success and impunity.

As I now had a radio telephone on the *Adi Maopa* anchored in the lagoon, I might receive advance notice. This was assuming that the *Adi Maopa* was with me, for it often happened to be away from Lomaloma on survey, repair or requirement by officials waiting to come to Lau. It was a comfort, as Luke had rightly insisted, to have it at least some of the time. There was a radio operator in the crew of ten needed to handle the huge sail of the cutter rig. It was later to be ketch rigged when, after carrying not Anne and me but the Adviser on Native Affairs, Charles Edward de Fonblanque Pennefather (who had been visiting Lomaloma), the single mast broke, nearly drowning some of the crew and almost capsizing the vessel. Livai (Levi) Tareguci, with dimpled cheeks, who looked like a deeply tanned Clark Gable, attended to the radio telephone. His English had yet to improve.

One day a periodic trouble of mine since having scarlet fever at the age of 13 — wax in the ear — flared up. NMP (Native Medical Practitioner) Luke Savu was portly but athletic, very genial, most conscientious and highly competent. NMPs were much later to be designated medical officers, like fully qualified European medical officers, although they had no qualifications other than three years at the Central Medical School in Suva. He asked Livai to request the Medical Department in Suva to send out on the next boat an instrument he did not have. Fijians apparently did not produce ear wax. I have done so prodigiously all my life. If it had the same value as ambergris, which whales produce, I would have been worth a lot over the years. Back came the reply from the Medical Department: 'Sorry we cannot predict the future but have sent what we believe you need.' Luke's use to Livai of the word 'auroscope' may well have sounded like 'horoscope'. 'H' is an unknown letter in Fijian, but in neighbouring Tonga and parts of Lau it appears frequently. I later saw a record of Livai's transmitted message: he had confidently asked for a horoscope, which was a word he *had* heard of.

Anne set about putting the house in shape. There should have been at least a bare minimum of government furniture, but almost the only items were Sukuna's. He had generously left them behind temporarily — rattan cane chairs and settees on the long verandah together with his shelves of books — unique items for a Fijian to possess. He had also left Maraia behind in a *bure* (thatched hut) at the rear of the house for a few months until he had settled somewhere on the main island of Viti Levu in his job as Commissioner for Native Land Reserves. Her staying on could have been an embarrassment: a wife left behind was without precedent in the history of transfers of DCs. She was, however, amiable and self-effacing. Although of a different generation we got on without difficulty: large though she was in size, she even took a hand in deck tennis.

Of the fisherman tribe on Bau, she possessed a European strain: this helped her in Sukuna's multiple cultural associations. The essence of diplomacy and hospitality, Adi Lady Maraia was a member of the fine Toganivalu family. She was much liked by Anne and me. When she predeceased him, Ratu Sir Lala was greatly distressed. She was 20 years younger than he was. In reply to my letter of condolence he mentioned that she was particularly fond of us. We certainly felt honoured to be held in her regard. Custom prevailed on him to marry the Lauan, Adi Liku, who was 46 years younger than him. She was with him when he died at sea on the voyage after which they had been due to stay with us.

Sukuna had obtained a cook-houseboy for us, Mataiasi Uluiviti, who was of an unusually high rank for a person in his position. He was about 20 and knew no English. Anne had to learn Fijian fast. It helped that I was working hard for my examination in that language; getting her to check what I was learning each day accelerated the process. Meanwhile, directions from Anne to Matai (as he was known) and what we might receive were likely to be at variance. Similarly, communication with the very pale-skinned, elegant, ever-smiling housegirl, Losalini (Rosalind), had to be totally in Fijian.

Vanuabalavu's principal villages were Sawana and Lomaloma. Their inhabitants always seemed to remember us when there was any special occasion for conviviality, which they strongly believed should be shared. At Christmas, apart from the fish drive off Nayanuyanu conducted with peals of laughter and ripostes between the sexes, badinage that was too quick for me to understand, we were visited at night in turn by the choirs of each village on the lawn in front of our house. Fijian and Tongan songs would be interspersed with carols such as Silent Night in either language.

We would present the squatting figures with foot-long bars of red carbolic soap, containers of cream cracker biscuits and tins of kerosene. Once emptied, the kerosene tins would unfortunately be used to add to the cacophony of noise lasting from a few days before Christmas until the New Year; in a custom peculiar to Lau and Tonga, they would be beaten with sticks throughout the day and night — a sound (known as *qiri kapa*, beating the tins) from which we were moderately insulated when up at Delana and one that we could have done without at beach level, where most of the tin parading occurred. It was impossible to sense the purpose of this relatively modern mania when they had such natural sweetness of melody in their singing.

The tempo of life, special occasions apart, was as marvellously languid as one wanted it to be, except for my necessarily being tied in the evenings to the study of the Fijian language and customs. With Anne testing me from the textbooks, I soon put the examination in these behind me, as well as the Law examination, hence completing the lot which, together with the previous Hindi distinction, placed me ahead of all my contemporaries — one of them never did pass the Hindi. There was no end to a DC's versatile duties. Sometimes there would be aids to doing less than the minimum. Returning after lunch down the hill from the house to the office, I noticed a jet black mynah bird flying out through the open window with a piece of foolscap paper in its gold beak. I found that it had taken from the top of my pending box an audit query relating to Sukuna's period of office and had disappeared with it into the bush. When I had a reminder about it months later from the Audit Department, I reported that the query had been dealt with by a mynah. My reply must have been sufficiently unorthodox for me not to hear anything further about that query.

There was little enough office work. Touring the 30 inhabited and 20 uninhabited islands forming the Lau Archipelago (the whole colony is reckoned to have 300, of which 100 are inhabited — not counting 500 islets and reefs) was the most important and most demanding part of one's duties. After all, the 10,000 Lauans were dispersed over 44,000 square miles of non-pacific Pacific and I had to face the fact that they were entrusted to my charge.

Anne and I would often be away on the *Adi Maopa* for nearly a fortnight at a time, especially if we were visiting southern Lau. If possible, I would take the Roko, who slept on one of the two suspended bunks near the helmsman until Anne and I found existence intolerable in the two parallel bunks within the cabin. Anne woke up once to find cockroaches crawling in her hair. That was enough. We left the cabin to them while each of us took a suspended bunk up in the air above on deck where Ratu Sukuna had judged it best to recline. While Ratu Jekesoni Yavala was delighted to take our place inside the cabin, his snores, as effectively as the cockroaches, prevented our being able to sleep. If possible, I would take the travelling NMP to islands that did not have one and he would share the cabin with Ratu Jekesoni. However, such is the Fijian capacity for heavy sleep in whatever location that he had no difficulty in being lost to this world.

Our food on board would be brought to us by Matai. It was invariably tinned pilchards in tomato sauce, with bottles of the sauce to add to their palatability. Chicken, pork, occasionally beef and sometimes turtle would be tried, but were invariably too tough to masticate. Very large fish caught by the crew would ring the changes, but there were no puddings — nothing sweet at all except condensed milk with tea. We always took chocolate, for the food was predominantly salty, not least when the sea was rough and the spray filling the air dampened our exposed bunks. It was an unbalanced and unenticing diet, but we endured it without ill effect.

Aged 25 and in the first district to be my own, I would have been insensitive not to have been conscious of my heritage, if that is not too purple a term. My historical training had not been for nothing. At its most awesome I was third in line of responsibility — answerable to the Governor who was in turn the representative of the King. The Colonial Secretary was technically to one side of that chain. In Fijian ceremonies, I was honoured to be addressed as the '*I Sosomi ni Kovana*' (Governor's Deputy). This is what the Fijians understood one to be in the district and I would hear the Governor referred to as '*I Sosomi ni Tui*', that is, the representative of King George VI.

We had only been at Lomaloma for a day when the Fijian village of that name, just outside the Government Station, performed the conventional Lauan ceremony of welcome, the preview of which I had experienced so comfortingly on Sukuna's farewell tour.

Not to be outdone, next day the Tongan community of Sawana, which is adjacent to Lomaloma (with a teacher and missionary imported from Tonga: that language was spoken daily) gave me its welcome. I expected only slight differences, but there was a main one of which my *matanivanua* had given me no prior knowledge. When the *yaqona* was mixed the cup bearer stood up, poised himself before me and then twisted round to give the first cup to someone squatting on the right in the *bure*. The second cup went to someone I assumed to be the *matanivanua* of the first recipient. By this time I was worried that I had offended in some way. The third cup came to me and the fourth to my *matanivanua*. When the mixing bowl was empty and the ceremony had finished they looked expectantly towards me and I made a brief, reserved speech of thanks because I suspected that there had been some intended slight.

119

As we were walking back past Lomaloma village to the Government Station I asked the clerk who had been present what I had done wrong. He said: 'What you did was absolutely correct.' I asked why the first cup had gone to someone else. He explained (and I should of course have been told of this in advance) that I had been given the royal Tongan ceremony. The first cup always went to one of the hosts, as did the second, to show that the drink was not poisoned. Even in Tonga, it would be the third cup that Queen Salote would receive. I was always exceedingly careful in all ceremonies never to be critical. One was of course always in the position of an honoured guest.

In some villages — never the unsophisticated ones, more likely where Europeanisms had crept in — water would be poured into the mixing bowl from a tin bucket instead of from a bamboo tube. But I did not act as a hot-headed colleague was reported to have done in another district by getting up, kicking the bucket over and refusing to have the ceremony performed in his honour. On another occasion he considered the offered whale's tooth unworthy in size and threw it across the *bure* before stamping off. It was inevitable that, sooner or later, it would be recommended that he be retired from the Service, which he was — prematurely. Such unforgivable conduct had, it was understood, never been known anywhere before or after in the 96 years' history of district administration from 1874 to 1970.

Both in and out of my office I would be consulted and interviewed by every kind of person, a tall order for one of my limited experience both in life and in Fijian customs. With no one to consult on a non-existent telephone (in 1989 Margaret Thatcher was reported as saying at a dinner that 'the British Empire would never have grown up if we'd had the telephone; it grew up because people had to make their own decisions on the spot and not refer them to headquarters') or by letter (which would have taken months given that the sailing vessels carrying mail were three months apart), many were the times when I would have welcomed a second judgement. I couldn't help wishing that Charles was looking over my shoulder, not least to advise me about persons whom I sensed were not far from being rogues. It took me time to pick them out. The few who existed among the kind, genial, uncomplicated Fijians were little more than minor dynastic intriguers, petty land squabblers and small-scale cash manipulators in a virtually cashless society. But I cannot recall having been taken in by any of them. Luck was on my side and, of course, without Charles or anyone whose assessment I valued being at hand, it meant that I had to mature and sharpen up the more swiftly.

There are of course dubious characters in all races. It did not seem to me unusual that in those days I had a completely colour-free approach to all individuals. After all, one of my best friends at Cambridge, Arnold Kelshall, was a native Trinidadian. And I had made lasting friends in my first station on the Rewa River among the Fijians, Indians, part-Europeans and Europeans alike. To me, if they were friends they *were* alike. My test for friendship was natural good behaviour. If that existed they were welcome always in our house — if not, not. Anne shared my absolute lack of racial prejudice. She would drink (unusual for a woman) *bilo* for *bilo* (coconut cups) of *yaqona* with me on a nightly visit each week to either Lomaloma or Sawana villages. She would not stay as long as I and would return without a light through the palm trees to the house 500 yards away — such was the predominance of trust on all sides.

She and I would hold open house every Saturday night we were at Delana. The Government Station handyman, Josua (Joshua) Raitilawa, with some European strain in his dominant Bauan character, had a small billiards table which he lent us. He also made a full-size table tennis table and soon we had Fijians — the two clerks, the police sergeant (I was officer-in-charge of police) and the three constables from the coral-walled station compound down below, NMP Luke (whose name was pronounced Loo-kay, as opposed to the Luke in Sir Harry's name), villagers from Lomaloma and Sawana and the *Adi Maopa* captain, engineer and crew — filling the house for these games and cards. They revelled in Pit, the old auctioning card game recently revived. I would circulate 50 Players cigarettes in round tins and in addition to *yaqona* there would be cakes and biscuits. We enjoyed ourselves and we liked to think that they found the new DC and his very young wife an interesting change, not simply in generation because those of Sukuna's age would be foremost among those joining in the fun. Politeness was never transgressed: jollity abounded, often reaching hilarious proportions. There would be wiping of eyes with mirth.

On 1 July 1940, Anne had an unconventional twenty-first birthday. Maraia, who was more sophisticated in European ways than any Fijian woman of her era anywhere, knew the European significance of a twenty-first (it was not a Fijian or Tongan observance at all) and presented a large home-made cake. The Lomaloma villagers brought Anne a roll of ornamental *magimagi* (laboriously thinned-out coconut fibres stained black and red and used for tying and decorating house rafters and canoe decks). A huge polished turtle shell was brought up from Sawana village. Other gifts included an elongated Fijian comb for use on high heads of hair and a wooden pillow rest moulded to fit the nape of the neck and avoid crushing bushy hair on the back of the head — visitors to our house often ask us about these highly unusual objects. A *sevusevu* (presentation of *yaqona*) and *magiti* (presentation of pigs, fish and vegetables) followed. Maraia joined Anne and me at our dinner table, and the Fijians put on *meke*s (dances), outdone in melody but not in vigour by the Tongans who took their place. There was no alcohol and no Europeans were present.

Our nearest European neighbour was the storekeeper who lived between Sawana and Lomaloma villages. His Tongan wife, a forceful character at loggerheads with Maraia, was a descendant of Wainiqolo, who had been Ma'afu's lieutenant. I persuaded her brother Wiliame (William) to give up being assistant to the storekeeper and to become Buli (district head) Lomaloma and, eventually, Roko Tui (native government head) Lau. He had acted as guide to an American zoologist visiting Lau in the 1930s and impressed me with his knowledge of that subject and with the English he had picked up. On a casual saunter over the coral shore reef at low tide I noticed a sea-hedgehog, the spines of which invariably cause serious poisoning, probably because of the effect of coral on flesh cuts. Wiliame Wainiqolo said in English: 'Yes, that is indeed a fine specimen of echinoid.' I had to look up that word in the dictionary.

His brother-in-law, the storekeeper who also traded in copra, was Thomas Osborne Umphrey (*sic*) Stockwell, JP. Of Lincolnshire origin, he had resided in Lau for about 30 years and lived up to his name, but would be annoyed if we obtained some articles at lower prices from the sole Indian storekeeper in a shanty outside the lime-painted coral walls of the Government Station. It would not do to let him have the monopoly. Stockwell always wore a ragged singlet, through which a big beer stomach protruded, and small shorts. That was all. He had been barefooted so long that when I persuaded Sir Harry Luke on his only visit to Lomaloma to include him in the invitation to us to dine on the viceregal yacht, T. O. U. Stockwell could not find any shoes to fit: he wore a tie and shirt and light trousers used for going into Suva about once every third year, but no coat. It was his shoelessness that disturbed Luke, who was not easily shaken by human peccadilloes.

Trader Tom Stockwell, who had strong racial prejudices despite having a Tongan wife, would not have fitted into Anne's party. He made home-brew beer with a quite pleasant taste — I preferred it to the bottled variety — and every evening that we were not away on the *Adi Maopa*, by standing invitation Anne and I were expected at Stockwell's. In a gloomy inside room beyond the store — he did not believe in sitting on his little outside verandah being looked at by villagers passing or calling in at his one-roomed store — he and I would drink large quantities, though Anne disliked the taste or effect of all forms of alcohol. Mrs Stockwell would remain at the back of the room and he would have his receiver tuned in to the news. This was at the height of the Blitz, with extraordinary scores being claimed for German planes destroyed. They could not have been correct, or Hitler would have given up the raids, but at least the propaganda department's efforts to convince us over the radio had a soothing effect (though the bombing of Coventry, which was too close to our Leicester homes, did shake us). As did the home brew. We would return tranquillized for dinner in the moonlight or on darker evenings by torch — it never rained for our visits to him.

For guidance and also for aesthetic enhancement I had the prisoners put boulders of coral, painted white with lime, at regular intervals on each side of the track from the store along the beach across the creek bridge and up the path to Delana from the Government Station compound. I understand they still exist 50 years later and that my name is associated by older Fijians and Tongans with the path: '*Na Gaunisala nei Misi Sino*' — 'Mr Snow's Road'. The Stockwells would dine with us on occasions. At one meal with them Anne and I were offered octopus. It was beyond Anne's capacity. Tasting like sweet crab, its purplish red colour and the slight roughness of its suckers on the palate tended to diminish the pleasure of taste. For no obvious reason, a rat is presumed to be the object most antipathetic to an octopus. Acting on this presumption, Tongans dangle over their canoes stones disguised as rats, which the octopus will seize with all its ability for embrace and is then itself captured by Tongans who turn it inside out.

Our friendship with trader Tom lasted for most of our stay in Lau, but it was irrevocably strained when he put pressure on me to have Fijian government employees buy only from his store. This I declined to do and, sadly, it was the way our relationship ended. I could be under no obligation, official or personal, to him. There was no doubt that he could be irascible. Although he was in commerce among natives not disposed to thinking along economic lines and I was in government, I could never understand why he and his wife did not have better relations with his immediate neighbours or, alternatively, why he did not seek a different life. To have elected to live it as he had chosen must initially at least have meant that he had — or thought he had — an element of adaptability so fundamental to the atmosphere.

There was a near neighbour of his, but he was part-European and T. O. U. Stockwell did not have the same respect for him. I liked Howard Swanston Tripp greatly. His father had been the last Collector of Customs (and Consul for Belgium, Norway and Sweden) in the days when Lomaloma, Suva and Levuka were the three ports of entry into the colony. His mother was Samoan. He and his part-Lauan wife were the parents of Roma, the wife of my orderly when I was part-time ADC at Government House. Post-

124

cards with her glamorous and alluring face were bought by tourists in Suva. Many years before, H. S. Tripp had briefly been Clerk of Works on the Government Station, a post long since abolished.

Now he was literally a beachcomber. He used to roam the beaches near his hut in the hope of finding something to pep up his bartering existence. From a few coconuts sold to a trader he earned the odd pence: the land was his wife's — it was less than a quarter of an acre. He bore his penury with a gentleman's dignity. One day a message came to me from his wife. Would I please see him as he was very ill? Anne and I immediately called on him in his broken-down thatched hut. I found him gaunt and emaciated, ashen and in deep pain, sometimes delirious. As there were no stretchers on the island, I arranged for four Fijians to put him on a gate and carry him to the hospital. There, Luke extracted from his thigh a huge elephantiasis ulcer.

About two months later an etiolated figure shuffled on crutches into my office. Howard Tripp solemnly put on my desk 6*d*. He said that it was for the war effort towards helping to buy an aircraft. He had heard the appeal on the hospital wireless. It was probably the only cash that he was to see in a year. Receiving gravely the official receipt from me and saying that if it had not been for my insistence on his going to hospital he would not be alive, he gave a weak, atrophied smile, swivelled round almost animatedly on his crutches and shuffled out of the office. But before doing so he put a hand inside his shirt and gave me a brown envelope, saying that it was for me personally. It contained a sun-browned, very faded and rare sepia photograph of Grant's Hotel, Lomaloma, one of many hotels of thatch in Lomaloma's great days of the 1870s and 1880s, when it had a botanical gardens as well as its port. This picture is still the only one extant of a Lomaloma hotel, its European patrons reclining in pyjamas on its verandah.

In those days there were about 50 resident Europeans. Now there were only Stockwell, Anne and myself and Tripp, whom I never ceased to regard as anything but every bit a European. Tripp reminded me of the past more graphically than anything except a drunken-angled signpost on the beach, skywards inclined and declaring 'TO THE BOTANICAL GARDENS'. I straightened it out and had the prisoners cut away the undergrowth. Revealed were a cannon, which I caused to have removed to the front of the Government Station, and exotic shrubs struggling to survive, including one identified by Sir Harry Luke as a persimmon bush. He bravely tasted its fruit and confirmed his identification. I took him to see the restored botanical gardens when they were fit to sit in again, but no one sat in them afterwards when the jungle had resumed its takeover. Before the liana creeper and sensitive grass reclaimed them, I had tulip trees, flamboyants (flame trees) and Persian lilacs planted to provide some modern history alongside the mahogany, cocoa, cotton, Norfolk island pines, crotons, traveller's and royal palms, which I also introduced.

Lomaloma and its botanical gardens were the favourite retreats of the first Governor, Sir Arthur Gordon, when Ma'afu, who had been Viceroy of Lau during Cakobau's reign, was drowning himself in gin in the village. The historian in me cannot forbear to recall that in taking over from that most distinguished of all its DCs, Ratu Sir Lala Sukuna, I had some of our predecessors in mind. The very first, from 1874 in Lomaloma's heyday, was stalwart enough to become Sir George Ruthven Le Hunte, Lieutenant-Governor of British New Guinea and Governor of South Australia and Trinidad. Sir William Lamond Allardyce had a fine trawl of governorships round the world — Falkland Islands, Bahamas, Tasmania and Newfoundland. Sir Basil Home Thomson became governor of Dartmoor prison and, as assistant commissioner at Scotland Yard, secured the pro-German Sir Roger Casement's execution. Not quite so prolific and versatile a writer as Thomson was Dr Sir Thomas Reginald St Johnston who, after Lau, became Governor of the Falklands and Leeward Islands. Walter John Foster Hopkins was, through a less robust mind, driven by the rustling of the casuarina trees round the house to end his life up at Delana: I came across his grave while clearing the botanical gardens of its jungle. My great idiosyncratic friend, Dr Humphrey Silvester Evans, was Sukuna's immediate predecessor.

Some of the Europeans living almost solitary existences in the Lau Archipelago also had rather heterodox family histories.

Naitauba island is outside, but not far from, the vast lagoon containing the various islands that once formed the rim of a volcano, including Vanuabalavu, of which Lomaloma is the capital. Naitauba was owned by Ratu Gustavus Mara Hennings. Fijians called him Ratu out of respect for his grandmother, Adi Mere Tuisalolo, who was a cousin of King Cakobau. As has been noted briefly, his father, William Hennings, had eloped with Adi Mere to Nayanuyanu, the cone-shaped island just opposite Lomaloma, and had mounted a cannon to warn off those who wished to take Adi Mere away from him.

Left uninterfered with, he then occupied Nabavatu, a rocky high refuge along the Vanuabalavu coast, before buying back into the family Naitauba island from Walter and Herbert Chamberlain, fifth and sixth brothers of Joseph Chamberlain, Secretary of State for the Colonies from 1895 to 1903. Joseph, who was the eldest brother, married three times. Sir Austen, later Chancellor of the Exchequer and Foreign Secretary, was the eldest son of Joseph's first marriage. Prime Minister Neville Chamberlain, as a son of the second marriage, was Austen's half-brother. The wife of the ultra-solemn Neville was improbably the sister of Horace de Vere Cole, whose hoaxes achieved worldwide notoriety. Walter and Herbert were therefore uncles of Austen and Neville.

They had made a fortune from the sale of a Birmingham screw business and had bought Naitauba from William Hennings for £7250 in 1877 during the course of a hunting, shooting and fishing trip round the world from 1875 to 1879: I have their unpublished diaries full of rough and ready comments and undiluted Victorianisms. They visited Naitauba again in 1881 and recorded having 'Cleared much jungle, planted many thousands of cocoa (*sic*) nut trees and 300 ac. of South Sea cotton, the proceeds about paying the costs. Then, as the government regulations enormously increased the expenses of labour and we deemed it hopeless as a paying proposition under vicarious management, we sold it in July 1899 for £4000.'

Ratu Gus was Hennings's only son. Amid a few dalliances, this good-looking half-German half-Fijian married Elizabeth Vogel from Germany and ran a model copra plantation with excellent labour relations helped by his Fijian rank. There was a setback in the First World War when he was obliged to surrender his launch engine to Sir Reginald St Johnston at Lomaloma, while his wife and two eldest daughters of celebrated looks, Adi Elizabeth and Adi Sofia, were exiled to New Zealand.

It was in the course of looking for Hennings that, in September 1917, the freelance German raider, Count Felix von Lückner, after his 1571-ton clipper, *Seeadler*, had been shipwrecked in a tidal wave on the coral reef of Mopelia in the Society Islands of Polynesia, turned up some 2000 miles away at Katafaga island in Lau, then owned by Hennings and managed by Stockwell. Appearing in a *Seeadler* lifeboat named *Kronprinzessin Cecilie* and finding the island empty except for a Fijian caretaker, von Lückner and his half-dozen crew refreshed themselves and left this note addressed to Hennings:

Dear Sir,

We are sorry that we have not met you here. Although we had a good time in your island I and my mate sleept [*sic*] in your house, we had a good wash and are now quite fit to proceed on our sporting trip. The wonderful stroll around your little island we shall never forget. Perhaps we shall call at your island again and hope to meet you the next time. All the things we took is paid for — a turkey 11*sh*. Bananas 2*sh*. Me and my man are thankfull [*sic*] to you and your Maciu.

With best regards,
Yours truly,
M. Pemberton

Sir Max Pemberton, popular romantic/historical novelist of the era — with *The Sea Wolves* (1894), *A Gentleman's Gentleman* (1896), *The Gold Wolf* (1903) and *The Diamond Ship* (1907), which no doubt appealed to Count von Lückner — would have been entertained by the global reach of his fame. Von Lückner had known that the owner was part-German. He went next to Wakaya island near Levuka to which a message was sent without von

Lückner knowing. A small cattle steamer, *Amra*, set out from Suva with coconut palm logs alongside the rails as decoys for guns, which they did not possess on board. To von Lückner's chagrin, he found that he and his more heavily armed lifeboat had surrendered to this craft and to Police Inspectors A. E. S. Howard (later a district commissioner and the only one besides myself to devote leisure substantially to coaching Fijians in cricket) and J. C. Hill (later the *Auckland Star* caricaturist who covered my 1948 Fiji cricket team's tour of New Zealand), after which he was interned in New Zealand. He had been ultimately outwitted (but not by Hitler in the Second World War: he was resolutely non-Nazi).

Sukuna told me that in the First World War an uncle of Gus's in the British army had been killed in the same sector of the Western Front in the same battle opposite another uncle in the German army, also killed there. Gus, like his wife and children, had no English blood. By the time I knew Gus and Elizabeth Hennings in the Second World War, their German links had worn thin. On my first visit to Naitauba in 1940, his two elder attractive daughters were away in England, one of them (she lived ten miles from me until her death in 1991) ferrying planes in the Second World War like Amy Johnson. The third, Adi Joyce Irene Taivei Mara, with exotic olive-skinned, oriental, Dorothy Lamour-like features, lived with her parents. Her loneliness as a 16-year-old on an island having almost no visitors of any kind was as extreme as could be. Lau, at this time with copra a mere £3 a ton compared with its 1930s price of £30, attracted no vessels. Their cousin, Jo Sukuna, as they called him, used to visit them as often as he could.

James Sawyers Kidston Bradock Borron and his wife Zena were other Europeans (this time pure ones) whom Sukuna used to call on as much as possible. Jimmy Borron was more in appearance than in character an island eccentric, understandable after a visit to his island, Mago, an extinct volcano with a lake in the centre. One could not see the ocean from their homestead. Borron had a reputation for discouraging visits of government officials, except Sukuna, by leaving dead cattle across the narrow switchback of a track down which his brakeless, open-backed lorry would hurtle at alarming speed, with ravines on either side of the wheels, to draw up purely by running out by its own volition at the edge of the sea. That fairground adventure was not to be relished, but I did enjoy seeing Jimmy Borron: we became lasting friends.

Tall, with a goatee beard and silk muffler, he had an ulcer practically eating through his shin. He hankered deeply for the 1930s when he had been wealthy enough to tour the world's nightspots. On our return to Lomaloma, we would be accompanied by sackfuls of avocado pears (which grew almost wild on his estate: it was years before Anne and I acquired a taste for them, though they now never fail to entice us) and of oysters from the inland lake (the only ones in Fiji). A most generous personality, Borron owned Rairaiwaqa, a fine Government House-like concrete villa on a commanding site above Suva, in which, after he left Lau and was posted finally to Suva, Sukuna lived at a peppercorn rent until his death. Now it is the number two residence in Fiji (number one being Government House) and is used for visiting VIPs.

The one European on Kanacea island was Reginald Philip Little, who was the manager for the owners, Morris Hedstrom. He had been distinguished in the First World War by being awarded both the Military Medal and the Military Cross, a rare happening.

This, then, constituted the European population of Lau except for Captain James R. Grey and his wife on Nabavatu, separated from the Lomaloma end of Vanuabalavu by impenetrable bush and approached only easily via its dramatic fjord-like lagoon. Grey had been an irritable copra planter in Tahiti: he was no less so in Fiji where the natives (I use that word with precision, not pejoratively, just as I would expect to be called a native of England) would not work for him. He was deaf and knew no Fijian: his wife, who was much younger than he was, seemed lonely. On one of our returns to Lomaloma on the *Adi Maopa* we were greeted with the staggering news that she had died while giving birth to a daughter. Had the *Adi Maopa* been in Lomaloma I would of course have lent it to take her to hospital in Suva, but apparently it would not have been her wish after an extremely rough voyage to Suva a short while before. It would have been too late as well as useless, since medical opinion confirmed later that she could not have survived anywhere. Captain Grey went off to Australia to become port superintendent in Townsville, Queensland, and the daughter was brought up in Suva by our great friends Reg and Clem Caten, who were devastated when Captain Grey later took her away. I had not liked him; nor did Sukuna have any time for him. Grey was a misfit in Lau, as contrasted with the interracial Hennings, the individualistic but philanthropic Borron and the adaptable Little.

I have omitted so far from the Lau group one other European, a plantation manager, not an owner of an island. On unlovely Cicia island, I. D. Cammell was a thin, totally unprepossessing person (although he had been awarded a Military Medal in the First World War, not lightly bestowed) with a continuous whine about everything. I don't know whether it was the stifling heat or his depressing presence trying to take up all my time, which I wanted to give to the Fijians of Cicia, but it was on this island that Anne, inspecting a village with me and with Cammell unshakeably in tow, fainted — the only time she succumbed to anything during her stay in Fiji. Certainly the heat sizzled. I was reminded of a dry entry (of 16 February 1933) in one of Sukuna's diaries as DC (I had read them all from 1932, his first year in Lau): 'Heat intense. Appreciated the feelings of the natives of Baluchistan who were officially reported as having been loud in their praise of a new telegraph service because of the shade cast by the telegraph posts.'

So much for the Europeans of Lau. Of course, against the background of isolated remote islands, they made a more positive impression as persons than might have been the case in a less remarkable environment. Indubitably, islands encourage eccentricity, though of those mentioned Hennings, Borron and Little were the essence of calm normality and of notably firm friendship.

In the communal society of villages inhabited by commoners with an occasional high chief, eccentricity among Fijians was rare, almost non-existent, as was homosexuality in my time, when the fundamental nature of their society did not encourage marked individualism. It was also not in the nature of Fijians to be eccentric, although his friends used to say approvingly that Ratu Tevita Uluilakeba, son of a Roko Tui Lau, Ratu Alifereti (Alfred)

Finau, of Sukuna's time, had markedly individual facets. Sukuna, who was a cousin of his, had made him Buli Lakeba (head of the island), but had passed him over as Roko Tui Lau (government head of Fijians of the whole province) in favour of a stocky, most cheerful Lakeban of perceptibly lower rank, Ratu Jekesoni (Jackson) Yavala, who has been mentioned before and who was a loyal and enthusiastic supporter of mine. When I was Provincial Commissioner Lau, he was my assistant in charge of native affairs. Small, rounded, with a smile full of teeth and an appealing modesty in his dignity, he was as extroverted as Ratu Tevita (six foot six inches tall, lean, almost cadaverous for a Fijian) was introverted.

Ratu Tevita's lugubrious countenance contrasted, like the Arctic and the Equator, with Ratu Jekesoni's broad beaming face. Why his countenance was so mournful is not obvious. It was common belief that he had many female attachments, paramount among whom was Lusiana Qolikoro, a lady from Sawana with Tongan antecedents. Their son, the six foot eight inch tall Ratu Sir Kamisese Mara, became President of Fiji with a host of honorary degrees and foreign honours after his GCMG, KBE and MA. Ratu Mara was the second Fijian to go to Oxford, following Sukuna at Wadham and later made an honorary Fellow by that college.

When I gave him a little coaching at cricket he was a lean Central Medical School student (he is still lean at 76) known as Ratu K. T. Uluilakeba. In trying to work at the succession to himself, Sukuna steered Mara away from his Uluilakeba name to the simpler one for Europeans and Indians to pronounce and from the medical career he had started at Otago University. Knighted at Holyroodhouse as Chief Minister in 1969, Ratu Mara stayed his first night as a knight with us in Rugby.

It might be an understatement to say that his father, Ratu Tevita, was undoubtedly and understandably not disinterested in women. This was noticeable from the animation in his features when he joined Anne and me in playing cards at the house of the strikingly beautiful Veniana Puamau, the half-Gilbertese daughter of a former Lau Roko who had been stationed as a doctor in the Gilberts.

Staying on Ratu Sukuna's farewell tour of Lau, on which I had accompanied him, in Ratu Tevita's charming thatched, framed-windowed guesthouse in his compound on the boundary of the great *rara* (the village green where I was on a next visit to do some invigorating coaching of impressively keen cricketers of all ages, with Ratu Tevita electing to participate — irrefutably Lau is and has been for more than 50 years Fiji's champion province at cricket) while Ratu Sukuna resided in his own house on the Lakeba beach not far from where he is buried next to Ma'afu and Ratu Alifereti Finau on the very edge of the sand, I saw through a side door a vision I shall never forget.

With hair in copper-tinged, erect spikes, the figure of Veniana — yellow bronzed, as with the most expensively acquired Riviera tan — in only a long scarlet *sulu* from her feet to her waist, her pyramidal unrestricted breasts gently swaying, sauntered with a bucket and all the time in the world, from her house to a stand-pipe tap outside Ratu Tevita's compound. The sinuous elegance, the colouring, the insouciance, to a European the exquisite naturalness of poise were the personification of South Seas allure. I saw a good many instances of most of these qualities in a number of Pacific women and girls: but none quite encapsulated all to this extent as Adi Veniana Puamau.

When Sukuna handed Lau over to me he said that he had set in train the machinery to have Ratu Tevita relieved of his relatively unexalted position of Buli: as it was, implementation of what might have been an uncomfortable task fell to me. But Tevita held no grudge against me. He always showed as much affability as he allowed his features to express and we would share polite drinks on Lakeba and in Suva. His undoubted intelligence never found an official outlet. Of course, traditional life around Lakeba centred on him. Administration bored him when there was apparently such ease and delight elsewhere, even if undemonstrated in his countenance. The villagers regarded him, not unnaturally, as a man-and-a-half, indeed semi-divine. Roué was how Sukuna described him to me, but Tevita never lacked mana.

I was not unaware of it in a Vanuabalavu versus Lakeba (of which he was naturally captain) match at Lomaloma when, during a brief whirlwind appearance at the crease, he hit a googly of mine for the tallest six I have ever seen. It was temporarily lost in the sky, of which his followers would regard him as overlord, and fell in the sea (also, one felt, part of his domain). Following the habit of high chiefs, he opted not to bowl or field — traditional tasks of commoners to which he did not stoop from his great height. Mana did not save Lakeba: we managed to win. Incidentally, mana makes the third Polynesian/Melanesian word after taboo and ukulele to be absorbed into English. Ratu Tevita is credited with having written the words for that most melodic farewell song *Isa Lei*. Composition of the tune itself has not been traced but was first put to musical notes by Reg Caten's father, Lieutenant Abner Caten, bandmaster of the Fiji Defence Force. It was of course in Ratu Tevita's Lakeba house and on his radio that I had heard of Anne's impending arrival in Fiji.

After Anne and I had been five months in Lomaloma, Sir Harry Luke announced that he would be visiting us on his large new viceregal yacht, the Royal Colonial Steamship *Viti*. This vessel, with a single gun, had just turned up, but the Governor was not to have it for long before it was commandeered for use in the New Zealand navy and it was never to return to Fiji. Governors ever after were bereft of fitting vessels. When Luke came in the *Viti* all the viceregal party had to wait about an hour longer than planned for lunch at our house after the welcoming ceremonies and *meke*s as, unbeknown to Anne and me, Matai, our cook, had been watching too in the assembly. It was not the only thing to go awry.

Luke had asked me to arrange for him to see a unique ceremony, of which I had told him, at Tota near Mavana, in the rugged limestone cliffs between Lomaloma and Nabavatu, and I had accordingly passed this on with the date to the Buli. When we arrived to witness it, it was all over. Only sulphurous fumes hung about around the dark lake. We should have seen a traditional pagan priest summon the fish, in a lake filled with men stirring the bottom, which would leap up stupefied on to the banks. But all the fish (a particularly delectable species) had been taken by the special tribe and eaten. Luke looked at me for an explanation.

I was nonplussed. Sukuna, who was in the Governor's party, then rather shamefacedly admitted that he had been approached in Suva with news of the impending visit to the lake by a Lauan of that area and sent his approval with directions. But he now realized that he had got the date wrong and had told the tribe that it was for the previous day. It was a near thing for me. If Sukuna had not been present and had not owned up, my name would have been as muddy as the lake water. Anyway, I was able to write up a detailed description for Luke — small compensation for a man who liked to see everything for himself, not least anything in any way unusual — and for the official Lau history kept in the Lomaloma office. Sir David Attenborough, on a prolonged visit years later to Lomaloma, saw it and brought the unusual custom to wide notice in his *Quest in Paradise*.

This episode marked the beginning of a sad estrangement between Sukuna and me which was to last for a couple of years until we were both working in Lautoka, he as Native Lands Commissioner and I as District Officer. It was through the benevolent offices of Shiwabhai Bhailalbhai Patel, the diminutive Indian lawyer (atheistic rather than Hindu) whose intellect, wit and shrewdness were quite out of proportion to his five-foot height, that we were brought together again in Patel's garden at tea on its comfortable garden swing. A memorable visit of both to my house at Natabua, Lautoka, for tea followed shortly afterwards: their conversation that afternoon gave me cause for the greatest regret that it could not have been recorded for posterity. They argued ethics and altruism on a philosophical level above my head. S. B.'s was the more agile and broad mind, Sukuna's the more balanced and diplomatic, but mine, even with the discussion being all in my — and not their — native language, pedestrian and lame.

Sukuna and I resumed where we had left off to become the closest of friends until his death 14 years later. His permitting me this honour — he put it on a more equal plane than that — for me always remained a treasured and illuminating privilege until it was closed by his far too early death.

He used to wear his BA Oxford gown to take court in Lomaloma. Impressive no doubt but hot, although Lomaloma's was by far the coolest courthouse in the colony because it was the nearest to the sea at a yard or two off the beach. No need for a *punkah* there when they were absolutely essential and mostly non-existent in every other of the diffuse courthouses in which I presided. It was in the course of a case at Lomaloma with a police sergeant prosecuting that I confiscated something I still have.

A man had been having an argument with a woman and the *turaga ni koro* (the unpaid — only services in kind — and unfortunately habitually unthanked head of the village; I always felt a small stipend would have encouraged quality and standing for these posts at grass-roots level) stepped in to stop the quarrel. The man in his rage took out a heavy throwing club from the rafters and hit the *turaga ni koro* on the head, fracturing his skull. Blood was still flowing through four or five thicknesses of bandage two days later. The club was exhibit A and I decided to put it out of harm's way. With its blood stains now faded, it lies in my library. The *turaga ni koro* was treated by the admirable NMP Luke and recovered, while the offender helped his prison colleagues for six months to keep the grass cut round the Government Station.

In my position as magistrate, I was answerable not to His Excellency the Governor but to His Honour the Chief Justice. The most serious judicial matters — beyond my summary powers to impose up to a £50 fine and six months' imprisonment — were heard first by me, but then transferred to the Chief Justice for judgement if I had found a *prima facie* case to exist. Appeals against a magistrate's decision could also be made to the Chief Justice.

There was cricket coaching by me on the fine ground outside the office every afternoon from 4.00 to 6.00 for whoever wished to turn up. They did so at all ages. In fact, one villager did not think himself too old at nearly 60. There would be matches on Saturday afternoons — we worked in the mornings.

I have described what mostly sounds like play: so it is time to restore perspective with the briefest of summaries of work, bearing in mind that it is not exactly riveting entertainment. My duties as registrar of births, deaths and marriages and in compiling jury lists and lists of voters could be left to my two clerks, one of whom was revenue clerk and whose receipt and cash books I had, as sub-accountant, to check regularly. One could never escape the chore of cash checking. Sukuna relished it no more than I, as two droll entries in his diary as DC show. On 19 June 1933 he wrote that he 'sat at the feet of Great Diana of the civilized — Money — counting and recounting cash but, like the fickle goddess she is, refused to agree with the recorded Oracles — the Cash Book'. On 8 August 1934 he was 'still endeavouring to answer letters and the sheaf of queries. Of the Tribe of sub-accountants I must be the *bête-noire* of the Treasury both in metaphor and fact.' As provincial commissioner, like him, I too had the financial records of the provincial scribe (at Lakeba) and various native stipendiary magistrates to check. There were also warrants to scrutinize.

As officer-in-charge of the police I had a corporal and four constables, varying individuals but likeable. For them Lau was a backwater stationing, but they did not exactly exude ambition. The rungs in the police ladder of advancement were (1) Constable, (2) Corporal, (3) Sergeant, (4) Sergeant-Major, (5) Sub-Inspector (a gigantic leap), (6) Inspector, (7) Assistant Superintendent, (8) Superintendent, (9) Assistant Commissioner and (10) Commissioner. By 1940 no Fijian had been promoted beyond rung four.

I was, in addition, superintendent of the gaol. Lomaloma Government Station was a large one to keep trim. Its surrounding wall of coral had to be kept white with burnt lime. Prison labour did this. I built up from scratch a station garden with pawpaw and lemon trees, pineapples and bananas. Prisoners, with one of the constables who took turns to act as warder, kept large areas of grass mown. I managed to obtain green paint from the Public Works Department with which they could obliterate the clashing red corrugated iron roofs of the buildings. Green tops on white buildings — that was my aim for all stations over which I had control and accomplished as long as paint was available. The colour scheme transformed station appearances as effectively as pure white does for English doors and window frames in the place of off-white, which looks dirty as soon as applied.

No inmate of the gaol was there for longer than six months: most offences had been non-payment of taxes, minor peculation and relatively mild assault. Their food included assorted tins of fish and meat, which were luxuries they couldn't afford to buy in their villages. In this lotus land one evening the warder reported that one of the six prisoners was missing at the end-of-the-day count. He couldn't escape from the island: there was no panic. The certainty was that he would be outside the gaol door waiting to be admitted for his breakfast of tinned salmon. He was. He had fallen asleep on the edge of the bush and, to his annoyance on his night of slumberous liberty, had missed his evening meal of tinned pilchards.

I was also appointed Deputy Sheriff of the colony but not told why or what my duties might be. This was just as well, as will emerge later. In addition, I was chairman of the Board of Visitors for Hospitals: there were two in Lau. All this was on top of being both provincial and district commissioner for the length and breadth of Lau, from Munia to Ono-i-Lau and from Totoya to Cicia, listening to pleas for assistance, adjudicating in disputes, seeing all corners for myself and aiming to be as completely *au fait* as was humanly possible. As if there were not enough *de jure* if not *de facto*. Another duty I had was the comic-sounding one of Receiver of Wrecks. Even given Lau's maritime nature the post did not seem likely to call on one's attention to the point of exhaustion and I was beginning to wonder if it was not a euphemism for receiving wrecks of the human variety when one day a Fijian showed me on a beach a grey, war-camouflaged-painted, large life raft marked MARIPOSA. I had not heard that the liner had been wrecked, but then there was censorship, although America was not in the war. I reported it on the *Adi Maopa*'s radio telephone in my capacity as Receiver of Wrecks. I never knew of another DC who had a thing to do in that most singular of one's multiple jobs. Nothing further transpired, but years later, after America had been through the war, I learned that the *Mariposa* had been a troopship and had never been sunk. After the war was over, this graceful liner was never to resume its San Francisco–Melbourne run.

Early on in my time as DC, the Lomaloma village elders asked me to give an address on the war in the church, which everyone, including neighbouring villagers, attended. It was packed. Some dogs walked up and down inside like self-important ushers: others sidled in shamefacedly as if not wishing to attract attention for being late. Hymn after hymn, with superb singing from the congregation, swelled the atmosphere. After what must have been half a dozen lay preachers successively holding forth as interminably as Fijian (and Tongan, for they were also present) lay preachers do — there were no prayers — it was my turn to go to the pulpit. I gave a realistic, if melancholy, account of the Germans' success on land in sweeping back the British army to Britain in utter defeat (Calais and Dunkirk had both just been captured and Paris was about to succumb). I thought that they should know the worst. And I gave it to them. I said that I could promise no reversal. I was then criticized by another half-dozen lay preachers for being so pessimistic. Britain could never lose a war. Germany was second rate. Faith would ensure victory. And so it went on. The dogs curled up and went to sleep despite the tone of the preachers becoming more vehement. After it was all over I considered that I had done my duty and could at least never be accused of covering up the inevitable. They were proved right — in another four years' time — and I wrong. But I never regretted my straight-from-the-shoulder contribution. And I never went to church in Fiji again (or anywhere else, except inescapably for funerals, memorial services, weddings and baptisms).

In a letter to Charles of 5 September 1940, I wrote:

For such as us I suppose the world has never looked blacker. ... I am filled with little but the most abysmal gloominess and inner coldness at the thought of what the future holds in the case of every alternative — whether we win the war straightaway, whether we win it in ten or more years' time, whether we lose it immediately or in the course of another decade, or whether it will be stalemate. ... Anne and I have great concern for your safety. ... The mail from Suva here is less frequent now as the copra trade (the carrying of which is about the sole *raison d'être* for the communication by cutters between the Lau Group and Viti Levu) has become virtually non-existent. I suppose the average is once every three months. As a cutter is about to leave I shall have to stop prematurely, leaving very much unwritten.

Charles had written to my mother on 13 April, 'I shall be surprised if the Germans attack Leicester except by accident at this stage of the war [which is precisely what happened, as early as in August]. You'll find that we shall bring down more and more bombers at night as the war goes on [a hint about his inner knowledge of scientific defence].' He was Director of Scientific Personnel under Lord Hankey, Minister without Portfolio in the Cabinet, and later Ernest Bevin, Minister of Labour and National Service. On 18 December, he told my mother, 'Philip is well and happy apart from worrying over us here.'

I was later to have to meet Sir Harry Luke on another visit from him, not to Vanuabalavu but this time almost in Tonga. The rendezvous was to be at Vatoa island, named Turtle Island by Captain James Cook, FRS (why was he never knighted? — surely the most distinguished omission ever from government honours), which was the only part of Fiji he visited, having been warned of the archipelago's cannibalistic predilections when in Tonga. Luke's visits are described in the most diverting of his books, *From a South Seas Diary*. Between his first visit (to northern Lau) and his second (to southern Lau, in which his pleasure on visiting such surpassingly beautiful islands as Fulaga and Oneata — although he thought Vanuabalavu hard to beat — was a delight to share), he and I had been in direct touch, quite unconstitutionally short-circuiting the Colonial Secretary.

Luke was as concerned as I was that part of the presentations of food on his visits included turtles live on their backs. I had seen them lying on land in the hot sun for days or weeks, upside down, gasping for breath and uttering soft sighs. Tears could be seen oozing from their protuberant eyes but, in addition to looking lachrymose they seemed to attempt to appear philosophical, which added to the pathos. They were given nothing to eat or drink. I had also learned that, once presented, they were killed as slowly as possible with incisions. In this way their blood flowed less quickly and, it was claimed, more taste remained, particularly in the head, which was always ceremonially reserved for the highest-ranking guests and was the last part to be severed from the body. Among the most antediluvian-looking and out-of-this-world creatures, they are possibly among the most sensitive. Their treatment frankly sickened me.

I had also told him that the Lauan girls who performed the *meke*s (sitting down, with delicate gestures of arms and fingers and with tapping toes) did so in singlets surrounded by garlands and that if caught in the rain they kept their singlets on, which I felt predisposed them to the consumption that had reached almost epidemic proportions. (The eradication of tuberculosis was sensibly made the prime memorial aim instead of a monument at the end of the war; it was successfully accomplished after huge sums of money had been raised by bazaars.)

Luke directed me as provincial commissioner to send to all Bulis throughout the Lau islands an edict prohibiting (1) the slow deaths of turtles and (2) the wearing of singlets for *meke*s. I do not think that (1) was ever taken notice of to this day, except perhaps in 1995, the International Year of the Turtle, when some token restriction was proclaimed — for all too short a time no doubt when capture of the creature is so assiduously sought in and away from the Pacific. I had little hope of (2). There was too much missionary influence. My surprise was considerable therefore on arriving at Lakeba, shortly before an isolated rendezvous with the Governor, to be greeted on the beach at night by girls returning from *meke* practice wearing garlands of exquisite fragrance over bare breasts gleaming with scented coconut oil.

When Harry Luke himself turned up at Lakeba next morning on the *Viti*, he was astonished to see that (2) had been complied with. It was the only time I ever came across it in the performance of a *meke* anywhere in Fiji. The response had been most enthusiastic. It patently appealed to the all-powerful Ratu Tevita Uluilakeba's regal roving eye: he would have had to indicate approval in his domain for compliance with this gubernatorial edict. But I presume that the missionaries learned of it and had the trend stopped, for wet singlets have been redonned and if it had not been for the special focus on it, which brought rapid and improved diagnosis, tuberculosis would undoubtedly have swept through the Fijian people.

Elephantiasis (the swelling to monumental size of limbs, especially arms, legs, scrota or breasts, but generally more common among men than women) was spectacularly prominent in Lau. Filariasis, as it is sometimes called, usually starts with a red streak down the leg. One or two Europeans had experienced it: the only known cure was a very long leave in a cold climate. To my horror, I noticed a streak on my leg. NMP Luke advised bandaging round it. This I did for a month or two, after which it vanished as suddenly as it had come.

The mosquitoes causing it were virulent in Lau. Their incidence was partly due, at least in the gardens below our house at Delana, Lomaloma, to Fijians planting their stock root vegetable, *taro*, in water made stagnant by the embankment of plots. I could not change that traditional Lauan style of planting; nor could Sukuna. Those *taro* beds close to the house worried him. As an entry in his Lau DC's diary of 13 October 1932 stated: 'The matter is a serious one for a DC who does not wish to leave Lomaloma with an awkward and protruding encumbrance between the legs.' I never saw, but he might have done, a case of a Lauan's mobility relying on suspending his scrotum in a wheelbarrow. Often enough legs the size and shape of an elephant's were seen. There was no relief from mosquitoes day and night at the house. When I caught the pests alive I would pull out their stinging proboscises and let them go, hoping that in the fullness of time a species would be bred without the wherewithal to puncture the skin. Looking down at my DDT-covered ankles (sprayed with Flit guns, the main constituent being kerosene) in the dark under the table, I would find on each about a dozen mosquitoes standing on their heads, their proboscises inserted through the oil. I could squash half of them at a time, but it was futile: replacements took up position. It is remarkable that one did not develop a permanent twitch, so perpetual was the need to counterattack.

The only solace, such as it was, was that the mosquitoes were of the culex type, which in other countries carry yellow fever — this has never reached Fiji where the conditions are rife for it but had been rampant in its death-dealing effect on the construction of the Panama Canal — while in Fiji they convey dengue fever (in the last 50 years developing lethal effects) and elephantiasis, which was a special danger in the South Seas. Providentially, they were not the malaria-carrying anopheles species. There was some relief from the irritation of the monstrous regiments near the sea, as in Lau where one was seldom far from it, or Taveuni where the land rose nearly sheer to avoid the usual configuration of beach, mound, low plateau (where the pests abounded) and hills.

River banks, especially in the wetter zones of Viti Levu such as Rewa, were notorious harbingers. Mosquitoes' backs and legs would be flecked with silver: they looked like test tubes when their bodies were full of blood. To add insult to injury, they not only deprived one of blood but left in the unwilling donor a yellow fluid that was maddeningly itchy. The invitation to my skin was greater even than to Anne's, although women's skin is generally more susceptible. One could not avoid scratching and spreading an infection. Iodine was said to be inadvisable for use in the tropics, so one went about with wrists and ankles covered as with red ink, which mercurochrome so closely resembled, even to its iridescent green sheen.

As to why mosquitoes make life almost unbearable for some and not for others, no one seems to know. I subsequently theorized that it depended either on the relative thickness of the skin into which proboscidiferous mosquitoes thought twice about injecting themselves, or the blood group of the victim, or even a combination of both. It is extraordinary that by the end of the twentieth century this mystery has not been solved. None of the various anti-mosquito gauzes, thin to allow in maximum outside air, often thick for internal doors, have ever been made mosquito-tight. That was nearly always only achievable under a mosquito net. In Suva, alone of all parts of the colony, where ditches were sprayed with larvae-killing oil, there were some houses, like the last one of concrete occupied by us, that were practically immune.

So far as Lau was concerned, the mosquito was a veritable serpent in paradise. It could put one off the South Seas for life.

The only relief if not at sea was in the office alongside the beach. Anne (whose blood group, A negative, is rare but not quite as rare as my AB positive) would come down, write assiduously in the separate diary she kept, and type for hours there to escape from them.

She typed the letters to our parents and to Charles. We always felt guilty describing what were obviously out-of-this-world experiences to those enduring bombing, threats of invasion and rationing, all in increasing quantities and with no end in sight. We could only complain of lack of meat (which was made up for by an abundance of fish and crabs), of the primitiveness of the transport, lighting and latrines (Lau, lacking toads, had its quota of centipedes lurking in their favourite abodes and harmless but repulsive giant cockroaches) and of the mosquitoes.

And there were also hurricanes. We had two in Lau. Our first was really an experience and a half. The night before, the sky at sunset was purple (later I came to recognize this as a prognostication). The wind rose suddenly after dark at about 8.00 p.m. and increased with palm trees and casuarinas swaying so violently that it was unsafe to go outside. At about midnight there was a storm with intense horizontal rain. We were worried about a lofty palm near our bedroom and moved out of its possible range with a decision to spend the night on the verandah. We had pulled down the shutters. Soon there came knocks at our outside door. It was Josua Raitilawa and his family from the *bure* on the slope behind us, asking for the greater safety our concrete base gave us. They said that our latrine had cartwheeled down the hill.

Maraia, Sukuna's wife, had left Lau by this time: otherwise we would naturally have invited her up from her *bure*. There were more knocks. This time it was the police corporal and the constables with their families and the three prisoners who feared a tidal wave: their wooden houses and the wooden gaol were on flat ground within the walled compound alongside the beach. They were drenched. Then there were more knocks, this time of villagers whose thatched and wooden houses had collapsed. There were about 50 in all. At around 3.00 a.m. there was an utter lull. The rain had stopped. There was no noise from the trees.

Then, a quarter of an hour later, the wind came up with even greater power and the rain slanted from exactly the reverse direction, completely uprooting the palms that had leant over the full distance the opposite way. It was intensely hot. All thought that it was the worst hurricane they had known. We were thankful that we were in a house flat on a concrete base. This was unusual, for most European-style quarters were on concrete stilts, in theory to allow for the circulation of cool air. It was a space used for storing battens for shuttering up the buildings in hurricanes (and as cool, daytime hideouts for toads, as we have seen, but not in Lau). By dawn, at about 5.00 a.m., the wind velocity was showing signs of abating. One could just gingerly open a door to test the wide open world outside. The villagers decided to go down to the flat land with the Government Station officials and their families. Corrugated iron roofs — which I learned later were the most menacing feature flying through the air and known to slice people into halves and pieces — seemed to have stopped circulating and trees were no longer coming down.

I went to the government office. A tidal wave about four feet high had swept through it, swamping books and papers, but had not penetrated the police quarters or gaol, which were on concrete stilts, unlike the office. Then, after passing the hospital, to find that, battened up but on stilts, it had escaped with the loss of only a few outbuildings, I went to the villages of Lomaloma and Sawana. The thatched houses there were a sorry sight. About half of them had fallen in; some had palms lying over them. There had miraculously been no injuries or deaths. A little cutter had been blown ashore. It had been the one empty boat at anchor and the captain could not reach it from the shore before it was beached. Fijians had told me that the safest, if not exactly most comfortable, place to be in a hurricane was the open sea on a craft with an engine ploughing bow first. We were to experience on average a blow a year throughout our time in Fiji, but none seemed as threatening as on a small Lauan island.

Other curiosities for Anne to describe in her letters to England were leprosy and the fauna. Carrying out my provincial commissioner's duty on village inspections to look at each house, I would unfailingly ask the owner first if I might do so and I would always be welcomed since, if it needed rethatching or other repairs, my instructions could achieve a priority for him. But, hearing of my presence in the village, the inhabitants would tend to hide any leper. They knew that any discovered would be sent to the leper island of Makogai, probably never to return. I would often hear that I had just missed one who had been taken to a cave or deep into the bush, but I did not have the heart to follow it up, merely reporting to NMP Luke, who himself was more than busy at his hospital but had a periodic travelling assistant.

Apart from my occasional blockage of an ear (treatment now facilitated by the auroscope), I only had occasion to consult NMP Luke professionally once. This was, when wearing trousers rather than shorts and stepping over a grass ditch, something started stinging me repeatedly behind the knee. I could not manage to squash the hornet, which it obviously was, through my trousers. There was only one possible course of action. Dropping my trousers, I managed to kill it but not before — inevitably, of course — a bevy of young girls came into view and could scarce restrain their amusement in front of me, their chief. Luke's application of surgical spirit quickly removed injury from the insult. Anne, picking roses round the Lomaloma house, was once attacked by eight hornets, four of which stung her distinctly painfully.

As chairman of the Board of Visitors, I had to inspect Luke's hospital periodically, but it was a formality. Luke was too conscientious for there to be any shortcomings. This was generally true of all hospitals in other districts where I was chairman of the boards, but it was not a task to which I looked forward. The tropics and hospitals are not comfortable bedfellows and I am full of admiration for doctors and nurses who have to work in that heat, with inferior equipment, smells and insects among the disadvantages. When hospitals were first established by government, Fijians would only go to them when *in extremis*: so they named them *vale ni mate* — houses of death — since no one seemed to return from them. It was a real triumph when they came to call them *vale ni veivakabulai* — houses of health.

I have frequently mentioned the duty of provincial commissioners to inspect villages. It was a prime function to see if the thatched houses were watertight, that ditches were not stagnant breeding places for mosquito larvae and that the village greens were not overgrown. I would be accompanied by the village head (*turaga ni koro*) (he received wrongly, I emphasize what I said earlier, no cash payment for his onerous job) and sometimes additionally by the Buli and the Roko. As villages were invariably three or four miles apart, and allowing for the welcoming ceremony and a different speech from me in each, one would perhaps visit as many as six a day. The average village contained about a dozen houses, entirely of thatch — roof and sides.

During overnight stays I would hear the work required called out by the village head strolling through the village after dark like a town crier and announcing the day's work for the morrow in order of priority. In addition, there was a calendar of work for men and women, sometimes interrupted by emergencies like hurricanes or preparations for chiefly visits.

There was little leisure after fishing, collecting firewood and food, maintaining gardens, weeding, thatching, plaiting mats and making *tapa* — tasks split between the sexes. Yet some Europeans thought Fijians lazy. Life was such that they had to pace themselves.

Ratu Sukuna could scarcely be faulted. His gravitas was statuesque, even if he always had a quiet chuckle about himself, one felt, never too far away. That was one of his cluster of endearing facets of which he would allow a friend the occasional glimpse. But, as I have alluded to earlier, there was one duty he declined to carry out. Because he was a chief of the very highest status he could not go against custom and enter the houses of the humble. I had to report that some houses in Lau — nearly all were thatched — showed a lot of neglect, particularly on the principal island of Lakeba. It only required a personal visit on inspection by the Roko or Buli to put to rights a quite serious exposure to physical ill-being. Of course, the thatch exteriors (roofs and walls) could be seen by Ratu Sukuna and he would direct their repair, but some defects could only be seen from the inside — including mats that needed to be renewed.

The villagers seemed pleased with this aspect of my work: they were certainly not offended and welcomed the chance of a chat. This might have been the only aspect, apart from physical encouragement of and involvement in sports, in which I was naturally ahead of Ratu Sukuna in points through youth — perhaps relatively minor points too — though I was merely doing my job. In other aspects, compared with an indigenous leading chief, a young Englishman must have signified a step down for the Lauans who could, however, be philosophical and were always impeccably mannered, never for a moment revealing that they were long-suffering, if that is indeed how they felt. With hindsight, I am sure that they must have been, not least because these random reflections and off-the-cuff observations show me to be the person I was. They certainly seemed, however, to enjoy being invited to our house, which was not possible in Ratu Sukuna's time except in the most formal style.

There were other informal visitors to the house: they included land crabs. These were delicious to eat, more so than sea crabs if one could be sure that their scavenging localities were not near latrines, but they inflicted no damage. Anne's diary records that she found one waving its claws threateningly behind the bedroom dressing table. It took a Fijian to know how to expel it. In Lau alone might be seen a giant coconut robber crab, about three feet long with enormous mandibles. One was caught, just before Sir Harry Luke's call on us, in Vanuabalavu. It was kept in a large empty kerosene tin with a rock on top of the lid, which it almost succeeded in pushing off. Primeval-looking, they are the world's largest terrestrial crabs. They are caught by means of a platform of ferns fixed halfway up a palm tree. Having knocked down some coconuts — its favourite diet — the crab descends backwards, reaches the platform, thinks that it has reached ground level, lets go, falls 30 or 40 feet and is discovered stunned by delighted Fijians. This pleasing trick was later disappointingly exploded as a myth when I met the father of Corporal Sefanaia Sukanaivalu, awarded a VC posthumously for action against the Japanese in the Solomons. He came from Yacata island, one of the last refuges in Fiji of the crab, and I got to know him in nearby Taveuni in 1949 — and the elder brother of Sefanaia in England later on.

An expert on coconut crabs, Lote Sukanaivalu claimed that they could not climb trees, but did confirm, when I asked him whether it was true, that the hapless creatures took up stones or sticks with which to fight when cornered. In that dilemma, moisture is seen to drip from their eyes. They are trapped by embers being pushed into their holes: although they often crush these with their nippers, the continuous protrusion of embers makes them sweat and they emerge to be captured by only the most skilled, deft hands obtaining the sole grip that is possible — behind the claws. Lote also told me that they stand with their great claws upwards in rain, catching it in sockets for drinking purposes.

Sir Harry Luke asked to be given the particular crab in the kerosene tin after he had offered it a stick as wide as one's finger to snap off. This the crab bad-temperedly (not unnaturally) did. A finger would have been mutilated beyond repair. Sent to the *Viti*, with some humanitarian reluctance on my part, it was served for dinner. Stockwell in his bare feet relished it, but Harry Luke and I thought it a little over-rich. It had been fed on more coconuts while in its kerosene tin. This crab is now extremely rare. Virtually extinct in Fiji, it is also now endangered in the Seychelles, its sole remaining habitat half the world away. Had I been as aware in 1940, at the time of Luke's visit, as I was in 1949 of its habits (not unendearing) and of its being nearly an endangered species (as it certainly is now) I would of course have had it released.

I used to let it be known that I would welcome seeing anything unusual found on Vanuabalavu. A Fijian duly came on to the back porch of Delana with a five-foot-long land snake coiled round his neck. I do not remember its fate. Snakes are a chiefly food on Taveuni where they are kept in deep pits. At Wairiki on that island I once saw a collection of them, perhaps about 30, writhing in the near dark, waiting to be served before the Tui Cakau (King of the Reefs) who has a hereditary right to them, a privilege I in no way begrudged. Like everything else one has never tasted in the carnivorous world, land snake is supposed to have the same flavour as chicken.

On a coastal walk from Lomaloma I once saw a nest of sea snakes sunning themselves on a boulder. I counted about 15.

Handsome creatures with gold heads and black and white stripes like Newcastle United's in equal bands, they are not eaten. Their bite is poisonous, unlike that of the land snake.

Where sharks were known to come right up to the reef shore we kept out of the sea (in any case I could not swim), but barracuda, with their pugnacious, protruding, teeth-lined jaws and unfrightened by any noise, were the greater menace. They could bite without changing position, whereas sharks, with jaws that receded so much as to be chinless, had to turn over to be able to grasp and, in any case, would be frightened off, Fijians asserted, by any noise made in the water.

As Anne and I discovered to our surprise, the most peaceful little piece of land could be awesome. Not knowing that we would be going there later for a Christmas fish drive, we could not postpone any longer going across the sand spit to Nayanuyanu conically dominating the view from the front of Delana. We had practically completed a half-hour stroll round its coralline beaches when, from out of the bush forming the pyramid, there was a dramatic crashing of undergrowth and the emergence of a wild sow. I later learned that Fijians regard them as the most dangerous of land animals. It was probably protecting young pigs. Its teeth snarled as it came for us. There was no alternative but to rush into the sea, sharks and barracuda notwithstanding. There we stood helplessly while, on the sea edge, the sow stood belligerently. Half a dozen young women from Lomaloma village saw our predicament. (They may have been following us at a discreet distance out of curiosity, for Anne was the first European young woman to have lived in Lomaloma for a score of years — in fact since Humphrey Evans's first wife, Phyllis, which was before they would have been born.) Grabbing sticks from the bush, they drove the enemy back, ending what could have been a most ambivalent future complicated by an incoming tide.

Absorbing as our new life among the handsome and amiable Lauans was in every respect, it was a pleasure to have the occasional European visit us. Charles Pennefather, Adviser on Native Affairs, came for a week to preside over the Provincial Council meeting at Lomaloma, to which delegates came from all over Lau.

I always liked him immensely and respected his vast experience as a DC, although he clearly had a mental block about spoken Fijian. He did not have much vocabulary: what he did have he produced in an affected English (it used to be called Oxford) accent, mocked in private by Fijian friends of mine like George and Edward Cakobau, whereas his own English, although first-generation Australian, was impeccably classless.

To my surprise, with my knowledge of only two years, a situation required me to have to translate some sentences for him. He could understand Fijian, but could not be understood easily by Fijians. He had been an inspector of police before becoming a DC. As ANA, he was soundness itself. One felt comfortable with him: he was a delightfully easy guest, with humour tucked not far away. George Cakobau, captain of the 1938 Fiji football team touring New Zealand, used to tell me gleefully about how nocturnally active Pennefather, their manager, was and that his movements in hotel corridors would be mischievously monitored by the team from doors slightly ajar.

A different sort of visitor was Dr W. G. MacNaughton from Levuka who used to take a bottle of whisky to bed with him after having imbibed all evening. Next morning it would be empty. He was in other ways an unexceptional character, but on an ill-judged transfer to West Africa he was to die of cirrhosis of the liver. Virtually all the medical officers in Fiji were friends of mine. The sad coda is that a surprising number of them drank very heavily and died early of cirrhosis. I think it must have been their way of combating the smells and sights of tropical diseases and the sweltering heat in the absence of fans or air conditioning in their hospitals. They always seemed thoroughly to enjoy their trips away from them. No wonder. They had all my sympathy.

It was in Lau that my cat, Lulu, which had been with me in Naduruloulou and Suva, had to be put down after a severe injury caused, it is believed, by a wild cat's attack. Matai acquired a mongrel dog with a black head and white body who became so attached to us that we had to take him on all our *Adi Maopa* voyages, which he literally revelled in, nose pointed eagerly forwards to inhale the breezes.

151

Lau could indeed be isolated. The longest we were without mail was three months. Ketches simply did not find it worth their time to come for copra. On one of our returns from the entrancing Fulaga, Kabara, Totoya, Moala and Matuku islands, taking about ten days, we were greeted with the request from the NMP that Tom Stockwell be transported on my *Adi Maopa* immediately to the Suva hospital: otherwise he would die from blood poisoning. He returned about six weeks later in robust shape. No thanks were forthcoming. It had cost him not a penny. He had little sentiment in him.

Life in Lau — wild sows apart — was not without proximity to danger. One of the most obvious instances of this was when a sub-standard launch returning Anne and me from visits to Susui and Namalata islands went aground on a sandbank. Villagers saw us and took us ashore in a flimsy outrigger canoe. We then set off to walk nine miles back to the Government Station along the beach, but misjudged the rate at which the tide was coming in and, without timepieces (we seemed to live happily without them), under-estimated the amount of light left before nightfall. We were forced to leave the beach and, as dark descended, clambered holding hands through and over jagged limestone crags in single file and complete darkness. Corporal Tevita (David), Constable Marika (Mark) and the short-sighted veteran clerk, Solomone (Solomon) Tuwai, all barefooted, were with us.

We were confronted in cavernous gloom by a chasm. Two narrow, rounded coconut trunks stretched across it with the sea jostling, we estimated, about 20 feet underneath. Tevita went first, sideways, over what he reported to be a length of about 25 feet. Then he returned separately to carry Anne and, on another return, to lead me with my feet sidling sideways by his hand; somehow the toes of his bare feet gave him the necessary balance. Marika and Solomone helped each other across. Once over the worst, though we could not be sure that we were until we had moved much further on, we plucked glow worms from the bush and put them on our clothes and blew on them to increase their radiance, which was just enough for picking out the thin twisting path through the bush. Anne and I were never more glad to see the light or two from houses in Sawana and Lomaloma glimmering ahead. Next day I wrote to the Commissioner of Police recommending Tevita's promotion to sergeant.

Anne and I had only two jaunts away from Lau in 1941. The first was when we went to Suva for our routine checkups with the Indian dentist and for me to put the Fijian and Law examinations behind me. On the other occasion, I ventured, as captain, to take the unsophisticated, raw Lau cricket team I had been coaching to Levuka, the old capital of Fiji, with its half-dozen run-down, dingy stores in which, one is reminded by Anne's diary, she was immeasurably thrilled by the thought of shopping. There, we had been bold enough to challenge Suva. To our intense surprise, but their greater astonishment, we beat them easily before a large crowd. The ground was the only one outside Suva to have a stand (I had had built a thatched pavilion on tiers, a novelty in Fiji, in the station grounds at Lomaloma). It was full of excited spectators who all seemed to be on Lau's side, sensing a real cricket coup. NMP Luke, stout though he was, was one of the team to perform nobly. Four of the team had never played the game until I taught them three months previously. They took to it as to the manner born. It was my first major cricket success in Fiji.

We were charmed by Levuka where P. H. Nightingale was the DC and he and his wife looked after us cordially. Anne's diary records that we saw 'Ratu Edward who was "well away"'. It was uncharacteristic of Ted Cakobau to have been even slightly out of control. My belief is that for 'Edward' one should read 'Penaia'. My recollection is that the young high chief, eventually to gain the DSO and to become Governor-General of Fiji and its first President, was learning how to drink — or how not to: they are part of the same process — and that Edward was holding him up in the Levuka town hall foyer awaiting a taxi to take them home. Ted Cakobau by 1941 was too much of an old hand (at 33) and I am sure that he was avuncularly seeing Peni through the unavoidable initiation of youth (at 18 or so) in drinking.

Touching the edge of civilization whetted our appetite for a taste of a little more of it. We had been nearly 18 months in Lau, absorbing its charms and affection. Sadly, I had to reconcile myself to the fact that I was no natural mariner. With some trepidation, but all my examinations behind me, I asked His Excellency for a transfer (it was irregular to approach a Governor directly, but my relations with him were as different as could be from those with the Colonial Secretary). He readily granted it in August 1941. When he heard that I had asked for a transfer, Jimmy Borron, on his freehold island of Mago, implored us to stay. He was later to give me for Albert Park, Suva, a fine scoreboard with revolving numbers, the only one to be seen in Fiji.

Anne and I left the Lomaloma village beach in a dinghy for the last time. Handshakes, tears falling down cheeks, not least of NMP Luke who knew all about transfers (he had himself come to Lomaloma from Nadi) and a wonderfully harmonious rendering of the most touching of farewell melodies, *Isa Lei*, by the crowd on the beach affected us deeply. Such faithful friends we were leaving. We sensed that it was forever. We, of course, did not know that the war was soon to take a violent, serious turn. With hindsight, I am glad that we elected, or asked unconsciously, to be more part of it than would have been possible if we had stayed in Lau.

7

Blacked-Out

No two areas in Fiji could have been more different than the Lau and Nadi districts. We had moved from serried ranks, like so many asterisks, of bottle-green coconut palm crowns (one took a risk every time one walked in the groves: the valiant Little told me on Kanacea that he was doing so when the next he knew was that he was trying to get to his feet and was brandishing his fists — he had been knocked unconscious by a falling nut during a period of slight labour unrest) to orderly masses of pale-green, sharp-edged sugar cane leaves; from lush green land cover among light blue lagoons to sun-baked brown clay almost bare of vegetation with no sea visible; from practically unrelieved Fijians and their customs to areas overwhelmingly inhabited by Indians and their way of life; from communalism to individualism; broadly speaking, from Polynesian to Melanesian Fijians.

A 360-mile-long road went round the island of Viti Levu. Half of it was Queen's Road, a 180-mile section from Suva to Lautoka via Nasigatoka and Nadi. The other, going round the opposite side of Viti Levu from Suva to the same destination via little Kasavu village and Ra, we have already seen to be King's Road. It was Queen's Road that passed through the centre of Nadi township. This was a one-horse, one-taxi settlement with Indian shopkeepers sleeping at night on the open ground-floor verandahs in front of their shop doorways. Dust rising from the pavement-less, gravel road gave it an American Wild West appearance.

Kwong Tiy's Chinese store was the best in the township. Before Christmas, its owner used to leave ivory mah-jong sets on Nadi administrators' doorsteps, until this was interpreted as close to bribery: no matter, we always shopped with them — Indian competition was no obstacle. Nadi was famous for its violent lightning. Taking shelter during one storm in Kwong Tiy's, I remember purple-red, lethal-looking streaks dancing like demented illuminated crackerjack dragons down the middle of the empty road glistening with torrential rain. There were more fatalities from electric storms in Nadi District than anywhere else in Fiji. Trees overhung both the road and the avenue leading from it through the Government Station (consisting of police quarters, gaol, clerks' quarters, courthouse and provincial compound) to the district officer's house.

As I wrote to Charles on 13 November 1941:

The Nadi house — pleasantly set in lawns and near the only trees in miles of sugar cane — not only overlooks the cricket ground here but just fails to overlook the sea. It is a pity that, as a rule of paper economy, diaries are discontinued for that was an easy way to outline my activities to you. ... Just before my transfer to Nadi an obviously psychological complaint attacked me which was diagnosed as pyelitis (an excess of crystals in the stomach). ... Getting away from the sea and disposing finally of examinations (Law and Fijian) have probably cured what was at worst only incipient. ... Your letters are being religiously kept here: meanwhile, we in Fiji are now prepared well enough to resist any likely form of attack (that is, raiding parties). ... Incidentally, if you should wish a letter to reach me with celerity, Suva has this week become part of the route of the Pan American Airways Clipper Service from San Francisco to Sydney.

Unfortunately, this new airline facility was only to last a fortnight. The Pacific world was about to change — for ever.

Fortunately, copies of my letters to Charles were retained. His letters, such as reached me (there is no means of knowing what might have been sunk), have been reproduced in my *Stranger and Brother*. He had reported separate observations to Mother through 1941. On 4 January, he told her 'My lumbago has been very troublesome', on 14 May (apocalyptically) that 'the Hess affair is very extraordinary, one of the most extraordinary things that has ever happened in a war. It is really good news of course for us: but I hope people won't bank on it too much. This war is going to last a long time yet.'

On 11 September he mentioned that he had 'been in bed for ten days with lumbago' — was this the demon ulcer referred to much later? I can't help thinking that it was — and that 'the Russians are fighting more bravely than any people ever have'. On 26 September he said of lumbago that no one really knows the cause. 'It is one of the rheumatic diseases and they are very mysterious. All the rheumatic diseases are hereditary, apparently. There is no cure at present.' Then, on 9 October, he wrote that 'If the Russians are beaten the war will last a very long time.'

We had no car for a while, but Bhaskaranand Basavanand, the gentle Indian sub-accountant — quiet, partly deaf, reliable, the acme of honesty and a perfect gentleman — used to lend me his. It was with Basavanand's father that Ratu Sukuna had been brought up in Ra. Of Brahmin stock, Basu (to his friends) was an Indian Christian. Opposite him on the Government Station road (but so wide was the disparity between them that the road could have been the Grand Canyon) lived Abdul Ghafoor Sahu Khan, the administrative assistant (a post in only three districts and filled by three Indians), a Muslim, puffed up into a choleric sphere with self-importance and not one to inspire confidence in his impartiality of judgement.

The police inspector was Australian, as was the dominant element of European society in this district. The overseers of the Colonial Sugar Refining Company — all strong, cooperative Australians hardened to comparative isolation and with an unfailing disposition towards sport — lived amid cane fields in managerial-type houses surrounded by brown stalks to be cut and crushed for sugar. Their wives were keen to pay their calls on Anne because my predecessor had been a bachelor. They came in their hats, wearing gloves and carrying visiting cards, the dust from their cars on the drive swirling up to the end of the cul-de-sac terminated by our house behind hibiscus bushes set in a large circle under the Government Station flagstaff.

Below our garden opposite the imposing *bure* in the Native Stipendiary Magistrate's compound was a large ground owned by the CSR Company and benevolently lent to me for cricket. The pitch was a concrete one so fiery that when a large Fijian bowler pitched the ball on the mat covering it there almost seemed to be a burst of smoke from its bounce as from a great aircraft's tyres touching down. It was so formidable, every ball being chest or more high, that I put a thick lump of cotton wadding in the left breast pocket of my shirt over my heart. Apart from spiked rubber batting gloves, leg pads and my abdominal one (Fijians never wore an abdominal pad and were intrigued by my doing so. The folds of their *sulu*s cushioned the blow for them, or their testicles were made of iron), I had no other protection.

Although it was devised for concrete wickets, I always henceforward went to bat with the wadded pocket. I was never hit on it, though both sides of my chest were at times hammered black and blue, but I never had a rib cracked or indeed any bone broken in my quite long playing career; I relished playing against the fastest bowling, which seemed to move off my bat the quicker, especially if hooked in front of my eyebrows. This sounds like bravado, but it was no more than my modest method. Fijians' limbs always seemed infrangible, with the exception of a royal toe in New Zealand, referred to later.

Fielding at slip closer than I should really have put myself, I was dazzled one afternoon at Nadi by the back of a raised newly oiled bat reflecting the glare of the sun. A ball off it hit my cheek near the side of my nose with considerable velocity, astonishingly not fracturing a bone. It was just before a meeting that had been arranged in my house for representatives from all over the archipelago to form the Fiji Cricket Association. Such a national body had never been set up and therefore teams properly representative of Fiji could not be selected. The Suva Cricket Association, created by me three years earlier, boycotted the meeting, which nevertheless saw the tentative beginnings of the foundation that marked time until formally established by me in 1946, with the warm support of Ratu Sukuna.

The experimental foundation in 1941 made me a controversial cricket figure (only in a few Suva eyes) for two or three years, a letter to the *Fiji Times* of 1 April 1942 from the Suva secretary J. D. Hallum, a New Zealand teacher, referring to that 'august body brought into being by that master-genius, Mr P. A. Snow' — rather unsubtle with a whiff of sour grapes. Cricket authorities in the capital had also been peeved by the defeat at the hands of the team from the jungle — Lau — at Levuka. Hallum himself was soon to disappear into an obscurity from which he never really emerged — ironically into a country district himself — and to have to eat his complex-ridden words.

Local affairs had anyway receded into oblivion when, without declaration of war, the Japanese destroyed much of the American fleet and air force at Pearl Harbor, Oahu, adjacent to Honolulu in Hawaii, on 7 December 1941. We did not know then that by a fluke — a great stroke of luck, absolutely life-saving considering that the Pacific campaign was so dependent on such craft — the vital American aircraft carriers, *Lexington* and *Yorktown*, were at sea and not in harbour when the cataclysm supervened. And it did not occur to us for a long time also that the stunning (but as it turned out only partially successful) Japanese action at Pearl Harbor impelling America to enter the war and at last to become an open ally of Britain was the best thing to happen for Britain since Hitler's mad failure to follow up the débâcle at Dunkirk with invasion of a virtually defenceless Britain and his equally insane decision to invade Russia.

Instead, we thought it to be an utter disaster. Reports coming in could scarcely be sifted from rumours, but there seemed to be no doubt that the Japanese had swept like a whirlwind right down to the very doorstep of Fiji. After all, the Gilbert and Ellice Islands were, after Tonga, just about our nearest neighbours.

Only a month before Pearl Harbor, Sir Harry Luke had personally (highly unusual for a governor to do so) telephoned me at

Nadi: 'You're an adventurous person, Philip,' he said. 'I would like you to go to Ocean Island as assistant to Resident Commissioner Ronald Garvey. When can you leave?' I spluttered out that I had been in Nadi only three months and that we were both beginning to enjoy the touches of 'civilization'. Could I be permitted to forgo his considerateness for my tastes? I was not that adventurous. Disappointedly, Luke said that he would offer the chance to someone else.

This proved to be Dave Collins, who had no sooner reached Garvey (ultimately to become Governor of British Honduras and, surprisingly for an administrator, to return to his jumping-off place of Fiji as governor before seeking in retirement, rather surprisingly again, to be Lieutenant-Governor of the Isle of Man) than the Japanese, immediately after Pearl Harbor, bombed Ocean Island (Banaba) in the Gilbert Islands group. This was a strategic target because of its production of phosphate — guano, the droppings of ocean birds, a priceless fertilizer, from which the Banabans who lived there profited through royalties before being deported under brutal treatment by the Japanese to Nauru, the Caroline Islands and Tarawa and then, in reduced numbers, buying Rabe island in Fiji after the war. The Japanese lost no moments in bombing it.

Garvey and Collins just had time to throw themselves into slit trenches outside the Residency, which had its roof blown off. Collins lost his couple of suitcases of belongings: he was a casual, laid-back bachelor but the experience shook him for a long while. He had been a companion on the way out to Fiji from England in 1938 and it was he who was to be drowned in the 1950s when the *Adi Maopa*'s dinghy overturned. He had married a nurse who was later awarded the GM for having saved her housegirl from a Fijian man armed with a cane knife, attacking her so severely as nearly to amputate the girl's arms before running off to electrocute himself on a cable. But Collins was relatively lucky in that instance in the Gilbert and Ellice Islands' headquarters on Ocean Island, from where virtually all Europeans were evacuated.

The administrator left behind in charge, Cyril George Fox Cartwright, was transported to Japan and died of malnutrition.

On Tarawa atoll — after the war displacing Ocean Island as the headquarters of the Gilbert and Ellice Islands — 22 Europeans, including two traders, a missionary, a teacher awarded the GM for his courage in operating the radio and 17 New Zealand servicemen were beheaded on the beach before an audience of Gilbertese forcibly summoned to be witnesses by the invading Japanese.

My first action after Pearl Harbor was to have slit trenches dug as rapidly as possible — in zigzag shape as learnt from experience in the Spanish Civil War and Malaya so as not to be raked by cannon or machine-gun fire from aircraft — in the township, on the station and at schools. To signify approaching air raids, a number of discarded plough discs were installed to be clanged: for the all-clear I managed to obtain a number of whistles. Bombing was expected at any time. Chinese storekeepers, with the genocidal record of Japanese in their homeland in the 1930s on their minds, comprehended the position better than Indians who have, however, a strong survival instinct.

The Japanese were not slow in spreading propaganda that the British (and Dutch) imperial presence was going to be displaced by the Greater East Asia Co-Prosperity Sphere. This was aimed to attract Indians (it did to some extent in India, but was pellucidly spurious). Some pondered over whether a Japanese landing in Fiji would turn the Indians on the Europeans who, like the Fijians and Chinese, were of course to a man anti-Japanese. It is an idle thought. The Japanese would have eliminated all but the Indians, so there would have been no Europeans for the Indians to exterminate, even if any had had the wish. I personally found Indians the most unbellicose of people — still under the Gandhi precept of non-violence. To them, war and force were repellent.

Their support for me in what I tried to do on the community's general behalf was, I believe then and still do, totally sincere. There might have been, of course, as in India, the odd disaffected political type like Subha Chandra Bose (whose force went from Burma to India to be defeated), but Fiji was too small for that kind of concept. Some local opportunism, with possibly A. D. Patel as a leader, might have been shown, perhaps in the form of strikes and/or civil disobedience, but I am sure that the Japanese would have taken matters wholly into their grasp without too much racial differentiation.

Invasion could now be only round the corner. The pace of the Japanese approach was unbelievable. Hong Kong surrendered on Christmas Day. But there was always Singapore as a base from which British warships could make forays. At least there was until 10 January 1942. Police Inspector Jack Probert, the hard-faced, normally impassive Australian, came running up the drive from his house at the bottom to ours at the top, panting out that the *Prince of Wales* and *Repulse* had been sunk and then burst into tears. This was certainly one of the more traumatic moments of the war for me — it was so incredible then, though not at all so after the war when one knew the facts. For instance, I had never known that after France's surrender to Germany, Japan had immediately secured air, naval and military bases as close to Singapore as French Indochina, which had been used for the sinking of the two battleships: that vital fact had been kept from us. We also did not know that, aware that American aircraft carriers had escaped the Pearl Harbor holocaust, the Japanese pilots after the raid had tried unsuccessfully to persuade Admiral Chuichi Nagumo, their carrier fleet commander, to let them return to finish off the oil storage and harbour installations and to catch the American carriers. Nagumo thus allowed America to recover.

The advance of the Japanese (numerically inferior, we learned later, to the defenders), with comparative ease on bicycles and in rubber shoes, down through the thick entanglements of Malayan jungle, culminating in the surrender of Singapore on 15 February, made the beginning of 1942 — and the rest of the year — the blackest period of our lives. Not only did we never pause to think when the war with Japan, so cataclysmically begun, could possibly end, but we were now single-mindedly overwhelmed with the question of surviving at all. We appeared to be wallowing in limbo. The real and the apocryphal were inextricable: the future seemed to extend no further than the next day. Today was no more than the day before tomorrow.

Fiji had no navy and merely a modicum of New Zealand and local volunteer European troops. The Royal New Zealand Air

Force in Fiji at the time of Pearl Harbor consisted of half a dozen ponderously slow Vickers Vincent fighter biplanes, rather more than, but similar to, Malta's three Gloster Gladiators. They were based four miles out of Nadi, at Namaka — the airstrip there being the humble beginnings of what was after the war to become the international airport, now known as Nadi. The commanding officer was Squadron Leader G. R. White, a diminutive figure with what we came to recognize as the inevitable bristly air-force moustache, the first we had seen. His number three was Flying Officer Ian Salmond, a cultivated New Zealander (and nephew of Sir John Salmond, the noted law expert, and Louis Salmond, the architect of the Grand Pacific Hotel) with whom, and with the number two, Flight Lieutenant Eric ('Grif') Griffiths, we became firm friends.

A fine sight was the arrival — at a speed I had to that date never visualized — of about a dozen American P39 Bell Airacobras. These fighters, disembarked in pieces at Suva wharf and floated in barges up to a primitive grass strip at Nausori where they were assembled for dispersal to Nadi, were passing over Nadi to land at Namaka, there to form with about half a dozen New Zealand Air Force Lockheed Hudson bombers and the humming-bird-like Vincents the total aerial resistance to the Japanese. I had not seen monoplanes (now an out-of-date term) before: they seemed faster than sound compared with the Vincent biplanes, which resembled dozing dragonflies.

At lunch time the day after their arrival (about which Grif had, at dinner with us the previous night, been most enthusiastic), the frenzied, speed-inspiring sound of an Airacobra was heard right above the Government Station. It was having a dogfight with a dignified Vincent, like a streamlined hornet buzzing a ponderous bumblebee. Suddenly the character of noise altered. An engine seemed to have cut out. Looking straight up, I saw smoke like an inverted water spout coming out of the rear of the Airacobra as it plummeted towards earth while the Vincent hovered. With a dull thud, it hit land just beyond the cricket ground, which I raced across, at the nearby Fijian village of Namotomoto.

Practically the first there out of the handful attracted by the spiralling noise of the Airacobra's engine, I saw that the Airacobra had nearly straightened out on to the road but had hit the end of a Fijian *bure* and ploughed into the small village green. It seemed that a desperate attempt had been made to miss the Government Station, township and Namotomoto village. Although it was an American plane, I somehow feared that the pilot was Grif. And so it was. He could be seen bent forward with the engine, sited behind the cockpit (a unique feature of the Airacobra), embedded in his back. The plane had not caught fire, but there was nothing to be done before, within about five minutes, a RNZAF vehicle came along with a guard to cordon off the crash, warning us away from the machine guns, which might fire from it automatically.

I had turned to the Fijian house that lay exposed to view. A lunch for three had been disturbed. A child was crying within a few yards of the propeller, which had injured a man. A woman was distraught. I arranged for the man with a crushed leg — it was later amputated — to be put into a car on the nearby road and taken to the hospital overlooking the cricket ground. Their *bure* had fortunately not ignited. Ian Salmond quickly turned up in a car. He had rushed back from Namaka airstrip after marking the spot where the plane had fallen. He told me that Grif's borrowed Airacobra had stalled in correcting too tight a spin, a manœuvre his Vincent with its slower speed and apparently greater buoyancy could manage comfortably. He had had time to reconcile himself temporarily to the loss of Grif and was most concerned for the injured Fijian.

He had not realized in the air that it was his close friend, Grif, who had elected to engage him in a mock dogfight, but had a shrewd suspicion that it might be. It was his sad task to convey the news to the woman in Grif's life, Dorothy Kearsley, who was heartbroken. Later, when I held the coroner's death inquiry, it was confirmed that Grif's extreme familiarity with the slow-turning Vincents he had been flying had misled him into thinking that he could manœuvre the infinitely faster Airacobra into a tight spin round an adversary. In doing just that, his engine stalled. Since the Pearl Harbor shock, this was the third most traumatic experience of the new war, after the destruction of the British warships and the fall of Singapore: it was also the first poignant impact on a personal level. Through me, the RNZAF was quick to compensate the Fijian family as best it could.

I was now up an hour before every dawn until an hour after dawn (when I returned to bed for a couple of hours) watching the skies — not in the mood to admire the spectacular sunrises — and looking down the avenue towards the trees on the horizon. The sea was about two miles away: probably the first I would have known about any invasion would have been seeing Japanese infantry clumsily shambling unimpeded up the drive.

Despite regarding Fiji as its front line, New Zealand had few army battalions. One or two coastal batteries had been put up to overlook approaches through the reefs, but for the first four or five months of 1942, until American reinforcements arrived, there could have been little armed resistance. Meanwhile, we came to know the New Zealand army officers well: they would welcome the chance to escape from their camps for dinners with us and I found their reports of the utmost value. To while away the boredom of waiting, the troops would patiently train mongoose (introduced in the previous decade to eat rats in sugar-cane fields and now just as prolific but not damaging) to sip milk sophisticatedly from saucers. Their battalion teams would enjoy matches against my Nadi team on our cricket ground, even though they were invariably defeated despite including some Test players.

My pre- and post-dawn watches from the verandah of the house, with the telephone nearby, were for the purpose of being ready to take specified action in the case of an invasion. It had become a byword that Japanese landings invariably occurred at dawn to achieve the maximum surprise. By being awake, I could get Anne and her Fijian assistant female cook (Matai had accompanied us from Lau) on to the path, with their suitcases, through the sugar-cane fields at the back of the house, up towards the Fijian villages five or six miles inland, or as far as they could reach towards the interior. Long after that, we heard that among the first actions of the Japanese in Malaya, the Dutch East Indies and the Philippines were to set fire to the crisp, brown sugar stalks and dry leaves, creating an inferno and incinerating all refugees.

When the Pacific war started, wives of Europeans were officially urged to evacuate themselves to Australia or New Zealand. A few government officials' wives did so: many of the commercial ones went because they had relatives there. In Anne's case, we cogitated over the problem — to take the chance of being torpedoed or mined *en route* (a large liner, the 13,415-ton *Niagara* of the Canada–Australasian Line, which called regularly at Suva, had gone down full of gold bullion when hit by a mine just off New Zealand, but all the passengers were rescued) or to await events in Fiji, although the latter seemed hopeless. It was found later that at least two Japanese submarines were rampant around Fiji.

Enough women remained for a little mixed tennis to be a Sunday diversion. There was little or no night-time entertainment: the blackout and lack of petrol made it too difficult. The hot evenings behind black material over every door and window, cutting out all the air and light, seemed endless. We held open house for Americans and New Zealanders with vehicles and enough petrol for calling to play cards, or to share meals or drinks. As I wrote to Charles on 18 April 1942:

> The position of Fiji is rather acute. More than that I cannot say as a very rigid censorship now exists. ... In the midst of it all, there is amusing local news which shows that we keep the traditional sense of proportion expected of us to offset the feverish rash of air-raid precautions and defence works — of which more, when it is all over, that should provide us both with plenty of material for writing. ... Anne and I send our love.

It was the sole letter I had time to write to Charles in this bleakest of years. Charles had written to Mother on 18 December 1941:

> The Russian victory is the greatest in the war and I think it must mean the beginning of the end, however far away the end. I am worried about the Pacific, partly for Philip (though he is personally in no danger yet — not until the Japs are certainly in possession of Singapore) and partly because I dislike seeing the British Empire temporarily over-

run by Japanese. But it will only be temporary — our fleets will get there in time. ... [This must have been deliberate optimism to buoy up Mother.] Meanwhile, we shall be as anxious about Philip and Ann [*sic*] as they were about us last year.

On 1 February 1942, Charles wrote reassuring her that 'I ... think the Japs will go West (towards India) rather than East and, altogether, I am not desperately worried about Fiji for the moment.' His guess was wide of the mark. This was followed, however, by letters home dated 15 March, in which he said, 'I am naturally worried about Fiji. It is possible that the Japanese will attack it to cut the Americans' route to Australia' (this adjustment was closer to reality) and, on 25 May, that 'I'm glad Father still trots down to church and his organ. That is the way to keep young.'

My war-liaison duties were crowded on to my ordinary administrative work, but I still had no nostalgia for the nineteenth-century pace of Lau. The war was on one's doorstep in Nadi, salving properly, I felt, my conscience. I had to link myself with the New Zealand army headquarters next to the air force at Namaka and was expected in any way possible to obstruct Japanese movement towards capture of the air-force base and army headquarters.

This meant blocking roads with lorries and station-wagon buses that, with my authority, I was able to commandeer. Bridges too could be obstructed. At least that was the theory. When Suva realized, not altogether quickly (it was slow in orientating itself towards believing that, for invasion purposes, localities with airstrips had priority over those with wharves) that Nadi would be the prime Japanese target because it contained the vital single airstrip of size in the colony, I had been authorized to set up what was unique in Fiji — bridge guards.

I was officer-in-charge: the guards, unpaid of course, were Fijian villagers living near the bridges shared (even to this day) between road traffic and the single-track, narrow-gauge, sugar-cane railway. I explained the strategy to them and they were thrilled at the possibility of participating. I had been issued with yellow armlets bearing the letters BG (standing for Bridge Guard) in black. The letters were incomprehensible to their wearers who knew no English: if anything, they should have been VK (*Vakatawa ni Kawakawa*), the Fijian for Guardians of the Bridges. They had no arms of course. Their armament was, in fact, fishing spears and *meke* clubs. However, the black candlenut dye from the bush with which they ornamented their faces for *mekes* would now serve to take the gloss off their faces and so avoid detection at night.

Eventually the signal came through. The New Zealand brigadier in command at Namaka, Leslie Potter, CBE, DSO, telephoned to say that the enemy were on their way. He would not go further on the telephone than to state that there were believed to be half a dozen aircraft carriers in the huge force. He did not know any estimated time of arrival. I got out my car. There was a magnificent silvery moon. The narrow country roads were lit up as if by the best city lamp standards. We had all been compelled to find black, thick curtaining with which to black out every window and door. To check on the efficacy of that in the township and elsewhere was another part of my duties. Anyway, that night headlights or sidelights were superfluous. There were no other vehicles: a curfew was in force. Loaded with Players cigarettes in their rounded tins of fifties, I called at the villages near the bridges. Delightedly, a score or so of Fijians, blackened on their foreheads, cheeks and round their eyes, sallied forth with their fishing spears and clubs to the narrow, short bridges. I said it would be an overnight stay, possibly to be repeated the next evening and so on until further notice.

Nothing happened. Certain Indian cane cutters would not agree. To relieve the tedium near Nadi River bridge the Fijians leapt out at dawn with war cries as Indians half-asleep trudged towards the fields where they were to cut the cane. Startled out of their minds by the figures previously concealed under the bridge, the Indians leapt into the river. It made the Fijians' day at that particular strategic spot.

I waited all day for news. Nothing happened the next night and then Brigadier Potter rang me to say that he thought that the invasion was now unlikely, at least for a while. Further than that, he could not go. Much later, I realized that it had been the Midway sea battle that had interrupted — and perhaps done more than that — the Japanese armada's progress south to the New Hebrides, Fiji, Tonga, Samoa and New Caledonia. When we did learn something about the Midway sea battle, it became clear that, like Dunkirk, Kursk on the Russian front and Guadalcanal in the Solomon Islands, it had been one of the major turning points of the global war.

The Americans had shortly before the battle cracked the Japanese code. The Commander-in-Chief Pacific, based in Hawaii, Fleet Admiral Chester Nimitz, cool, incisive, quiet and modest, had interpreted the Japanese attempts at side-tracking correctly. Admiral Raymond Spruance, the self-effacingly competent and underestimated right hand of Nimitz, carried out the remedial action effectively.

Chaos inevitably marked phases of the battle, the last great one to be fought in any war by naval forces without the ships on either side catching sight of each other. It was the first and most decisive air–sea Japanese–American engagement, at times so confusing that Japanese aircraft would land through smoke on to American aircraft carriers to refuel and, recognizing their mistake, fly off again pretty smartly. This happened in reverse with American planes on Japanese aircraft carriers. The satisfactory outcome was that more aircraft carriers, the key to Pacific success, were lost by the Japanese than by the Americans. Pearl Harbor had been avenged.

Whatever had happened to defer the threat, my dawn watches nevertheless had to continue. I have never liked dawns since. New Zealand, to strengthen further its front-line position behind Fiji, sent over what was to prove to be a real headache. The Civil Construction Unit came to put up more army and air-force buildings, but principally to broaden, strengthen and extend the airstrip and provide a second one. This was to enable American Boeing B17 (Flying Fortress) bombers to land and refuel.

For me the finest sight in the war was the flight over Nadi Government Station of a Flying Fortress. It was of a colossal size compared with anything I had seen before in the sky. At this stage

I think I believed that, however long it would take, the war would be won. Japan simply could not have anything on that scale. The bombers were to fly from Hawaii through Fiji, where they had to refuel, to New Zealand and Australia, a vital life line which the Japanese had to sever in order to make them go the other way — from America to England, Egypt, India and Australia, a vastly longer route which would have added years to the war. That was the nub of Fiji's strategic importance in the war — and it was centred in my district.

To augment skilled labourers (plasterers, carpenters, electricians and builders) and to supplement non-skilled Fijian labour assembled by the New Zealand Public Works Department (Fijians were now also being recruited for possible fighting either in Fiji or overseas: I had been the first, so I was led to believe by the Native Department, to recommend them as born commandos), the New Zealand government had opened its prisons. Nadi was suddenly filled with 1000 working-class Europeans (all 'white' men were called Europeans whether from Europe or the Antipodes: Americans were always 'Americans') strolling about perspiring in dark blue serge long trousers, collarless shirts, braces and big black boots. I was fearful for the European image, not too chauvinistically I think in view of what I now recount.

Neither Fijians nor Indians and Chinese (they were a few shop-keepers from Canton) had ever seen this type of European before, some of whom were as degraded in behaviour as in dress (for which they could hardly be held responsible; there had been no time in New Zealand to issue them with any tropical dress and this could not now be procured in Fiji, given the shortage of such material). Every sort of crime short of murder was committed by the rougher elements. Being outside courts-martial, they were subject to my court (perhaps it was someone tried and convicted by me who had been my potential assassin — perhaps that is putting too fine a point on it — in Wellington in 1948, about which there is a note later). Consequently, I was in the courthouse on the Bench five days of the week: my normal work piled up. The Secretariat in Suva thought of no assistance for me in any form.

On top of this, Fijians were drafted in from other provinces to carry out strategic construction work in Nadi, where they both overcrowded the villages and had to be fed. When not taking court, I was now having to escort lorries carrying bags of rice and tins of meat to the villages where I would dish out portions. For this work I did have the assistance of a cadet in Lautoka, Thomas Lascelles Isa Shandon Valiant Iremonger. He had been in the Ellice Islands and proved a cheerful companion in our humble joint effort, but it seemed a long way from helping to win the war.

It was with the incitement of the Civil Construction Unit (which paid its own craftsmen handsomely) that the Fijians from other provinces staged a go-slow and then all-stop of work on their vital construction of the runways for the Flying Fortresses. Delay could not be tolerated: those bombers could not be more urgently needed. Commissioner of Labour Charles Stuart de Cairos Reay, a DC of local origin with considerable experience of Fijians, accompanied by the Roko Tui Nadroga and Navosa (Colo West), Aisea Vasutoga, were brought in to settle the strike.

They asked me to accompany them. The mood was black. More money, better rations and housing were asked for, with a certain legitimacy. But I had never seen Fijians so recalcitrant, especially in front of a leader of such strength of personality and dignity as Vasutoga, not of high rank but of long standing and widely respected as a Roko with a commanding presence, deep judgement and constant common sense.

Reay decided to adjourn until reason prevailed. As we withdrew to our car, stones were thrown, to Vasutoga's intense disgust but well-controlled fury. He realized there was more to this than Fijian impatience: he had seen the CCU characters in the background. As Deputy Sheriff I had a copy of the Riot Act, but since in the whole of Fiji's history it had never been read out publicly (the Sheriff, Deputy Sheriffs and JPs had the power to do so), it was always left in the office safe.

The Act requires that the Proclamation be read in full, regardless of missiles and aggression in any form, audibly to the assembly. It is not absolutely brief and is in somewhat convoluted language. For those who have never seen it, this is it.

171

Proclamation under the Riot Act, 1716, to be read by the Sheriff,
Deputy Sheriff, or a Justice of the Peace

PROCLAMATION

Our Sovereign Lord the King chargeth and commandeth all
persons, being assembled, immediately to disperse themselves and peaceably to depart to their habitations, or to
their lawful business, upon the pains contained in the Act
made in the first year of King George the First, for preventing tumults and riotous assemblies. God Save the King.

It had been emphasized that the wording of this proclamation had
to be followed *exactly*, or the efficacy of subsequent proceedings
against the rioters could be jeopardized. The Act provided that
if 12 or more persons were unlawfully, riotously and tumultuously
gathered together to the disturbances of the public peace it was
the duty of the Sheriff, Deputy Sheriff or a Justice to go as near
to them as he could with safety and, after commanding silence
from them, to read the proclamation. If persons to the number
of 12 unlawfully, riotously and tumultuously remained together
for an hour after the reading of the proclamation they were guilty
of felony. Even if I had had the Act with me, reading it would
have been an unenviable task to perform.

By the next day, passions had been soothed, the inevitable com-
promise was reached and the airstrip work proceeded. The Flying
Fortresses were so heavy that they required reinforced concrete
platforms of the thickest quantity fastest produced.

Throughout all this Stuart Reay, shrewd and imperturbable, had
been able to indulge his custom, after lighting his chain-smoked,
hand-rolled cigarettes, of flicking the unextinguished match between
two fingers about a chain's distance — a flamboyant reflex action
that bemused the Fijians.

Sometimes there were incidents, assaults, attempted rapes or
thefts by CCU men that called for the use of Fijian and Indian witnesses. As magistrate, for the defendants in these cases to follow
what was being alleged, every word of Fijian and Hindustani had
to be interpreted and recorded by me in longhand. This was a hell

172

of a sweat, not least in the absence of any air conditioning. The speed required to write every word verbatim helped ruin my script. But it was necessary in case there were appeals, when the court clerk would have to type the evidence written by me.

Because the Indian solicitors knew no Fijian, the interpretation was also necessary for them. These included the restless, saturnine A. D. Patel (an uncertain ally of Britain but friendly enough with me) and S. B. Patel, my close friend who kept out of politics or in the shadows behind them — his life was too much fun in other respects, not least gossiping about persons, to dabble with dogmas. They also did not know all the Indian languages, such as Tamil (of south India), Telegu, Pushtu, Urdu and Malayalam. Very few of the European lawyers knew Fijian, Hindi or any other language and there were no Fijian solicitors. In criminal actions, the European police inspectors would prosecute and their Fijian or Hindi was often limited or non-existent. It was important that the magistrate knew the main languages also in order to check the interpreters. I occasionally had to pull them up, at least in Fijian and Hindi, for a misleading rendering.

The lawyers were invariably courteous. Only once was a short fuse displayed. This was by a very young, zealous New Zealand lawyer, Kenneth Stuart, later to become a puisne judge after Fiji's independence. We had something of a set-to before a not very crowded court. Afterwards he came to my house and apologized. Over an iced beer we mutually blamed the heat. From that single day (starting with our being the only Europeans to exercise at cricket on the *rara* when the day's work was done) to this, we have been the best and longest of friends.

After I had founded the Nadi and Lautoka Cricket Associations and had left these districts, he became the mainstay, indeed the motivator, of cricket in the northwest of Fiji — from 1944 for more than 40 years. This was a considerable achievement in such an independent-minded area, requiring great determination and diplomacy over and above his personal standing, for which he was respected by Fijians, Indians and Europeans alike.

Oath-taking was diverse. Sikhs took it on the Grantha, Hindus on the Ramayan, Muslims on the Koran, and Europeans, Fijians and Christian Indians on the Bible. Rarely did a European attest. Chinese were asked to blow out a match or drop a saucer on the floor, failing which they were free to tell a lie. So it was insisted on. The Chinese seemed to understand a significance claimed for it that, if they blew out a match or cracked a saucer and if they then did not tell the truth, their souls would be extinguished as easily as the match had been blown out or the saucer broken.

At last, both the Colonial Secretary (after repeated reporting of the state of affairs to him by me) and the Chief Justice took action to relieve me of the court onus. Cyril Higginson, a former DC of long standing before returning from a transfer to Africa, was belatedly found to be doing next to nothing as resident magistrate at Lautoka, 22 miles away. He now came regularly to relieve me of all but about a day a week. In a white topee he would sit upright at the wheel of what can only be described as a matchingly upright vintage car (it was totally square), beside which my second-hand Ford V8 Coupé looked positively rakish.

Meanwhile, my duties shifted almost entirely into liaising with the United States Air Force, Army and Navy, and with the Royal New Zealand Air Force and Army. To help the Airacobras disperse from the Nadi aerodrome in the event of an attack, a host of airstrips were acquired around it. This meant visiting flat sites (or less flat ones that could rapidly be levelled by the bulldozers that had arrived with heartening force) with American air officers such as Captain W. L. Wilhelm, a gentleman with a quiet assurance about his minimum requirements. Wilhelm was shot down while leading dive bombers off the aircraft carrier *Hornet*, but he hit Admiral Chuichi Nagumo's flagship, the aircraft carrier *Shokaku*, thereby preventing its aircraft from operating and putting it out of action for nine months. This was the Battle of Santa Cruz on 26 October 1942, when the *Hornet* was ablaze, six months after Wilhelm had had dinner with us in Nadi.

Compensation for land taken was arranged instantly with the Fijians and Indians concerned — one of the rare examples of red tape being cut in the Service. It made for a friendly reception for the Americans in my district; the Indians tolerated the lightning-like upheaval in a way I could not have anticipated. Bulldozers would take over within a day and, in less than a week, the strips of metal carpeting (containing holes treated with weedkiller to prevent the undergrowth coming through) were there for the planes. One of my most hair-raising experiences (literally) was being taken by a burly and non-communicative Lieutenant Harry Viccellio — there were few Anglo-Saxon names about now although there were plenty of Anglo-Saxon expletives — in an open-sided, windscreen-less jeep (they now flooded Fiji) from one end of the metal carpet to the other, testing it out at 100 miles an hour for safety and take-off (which we nearly did). Viccellio, who seemed to have no nerves, died as a fighter pilot some months later.

The commander of the American air corps was Brigadier Edgar T. Selzer, whom Anne and I took to warmly. Like a more senior Wilhelm, he was one of the few Americans to have a moustache — a short fair one. Reserved and calm, he had what can only be described as a sort of English dignity, reserve and calm. When Selzer sent his khaki-coloured limousine for us, in returning a dinner we had given him, we were astonished by the inner luxury of the vehicle. It was the one comfortable ride I had during the war. I had put on a ceremony jointly for Selzer and his American forces and the New Zealand battalion commander, Colonel A. H. L. Sugden (whom with his black Groucho Marx moustache we also liked). This was not only to give them an opportunity to experience (but not fully comprehend since my speech was in Fijian) the sincerity of a Fijian welcome, but also to enable me to explain to the Fijians, in their principal village in Nadi at Narewa, what the war was about and how it was going and to request their cooperation with the American and New Zealand services, a cooperation readily given then and, impressively so, for long after the war to both countries.

Soon after the death of Grif (the first dead person I had seen), I had to attend to the consequence of another calamity of a different type. Amenayasi Turaga was probably the best of the many Fijian fast bowlers. At 33, he was quite the fastest, using his six feet four inches bare-footedly to thump the ball down left-handed directly at one's chest (or, on concrete, head). He came from Nakavu — the village next to Namotomoto — and his fame was colony-wide.

A fortnight after an astounding bowling performance for my Fiji team against the New Zealand forces' representative team (which we dismissed for a total of 22, despite their having first-class players and a Test all-rounder in it), he had returned to his clerical job in the gold mines at Vatukoula and, at lunch time, idly swung his arm over while holding a small piece of iron wire. This connected with a low electricity cable and, in an instant, he was electrocuted. The mines manager rang me and asked me to inform his family: an unpleasant task.

Next day, Turaga was brought to his village and I gave the funeral oration in Fijian at the burial ground just beyond the village green. His coffin was open for his grieving family, among whom were a CID sergeant from Suva, Aisea (Isaiah) Turuva (as fine and intelligent a man as his elder brother) who, five years later, became a member of my Fiji team touring New Zealand. This was the second dead person I had seen — and in quick succession — but in his case I found it hard to believe that he was not simply asleep. There were but two small black marks on his chest where the electrocution had somehow shown. It was a tragic waste of a superb physical specimen in his prime — just as tragic as Grif's, though in a different way, for Grif's life courted death daily whereas Turaga's could hardly have been more removed from risk.

Also at this time there was drama of a different kind, but it turned out to be a melodrama. The Governor's ADC telephoned me from Suva requesting that Anne and I vacate our quarters for a night, which we were to spend as government guests at Lautoka Hotel, to accommodate a VIP and his suite. No other details could be given. It was a viceregal command to be complied with unquestioningly. Not that we minded: a night in the hotel would be a refreshing change. Our curiosity mounted as the day approached. Exactly on the minute in late afternoon, RNZAF outriders on motorcycles flanked as large a khaki-coloured automobile as I had seen. While one of the outriders took down the Union Flag from the flagstaff at the entrance to our drive, the RNZAF pale blue flag was hoisted. Out of the limousine stepped an ADC, followed by a trim-moustachioed, slender, slight figure in air-force uniform and gold braid. The ADC advanced and enquired, 'Mr and Mrs

Snow? May I introduce His Excellency Sir Cyril Newall.' We
invited them in to tea.

Marshal of the RAF Sir Cyril Newall had become Governor-
General of New Zealand in 1941 at the end of a wearying period
of office defending Britain in the Blitz. He was Chief of the Air Staff
from 1937 to 1940. After five years in New Zealand he became
Lord Newall of Clifton-upon-Dunsmore, a village just outside
Rugby where my daughter was later to live for a while. Newall
could not have been more self-effacing, pleasant and apologetic.
He explained that there was no accommodation for him at
Namaka, where he had been inspecting New Zealand army and
air-force personnel. He regarded it as an unpardonable intrusion,
or rather extrusion, to put us out of our own house: he added that
Sir Harry Luke, with whom he stayed in Suva at Government
House, knew that we would understand. After giving him a drink
and showing the ADC where there was more liquor and where, if
it were needed, the petrol can was housed in the garage for the
lamps (already fully fuelled) that would soon have to be lit, and
explaining about the blackout curtains, we left for Lautoka.

Late that evening, which Newall had spent as guest of honour at
the army mess at Namaka, his ADC rang me at the hotel to say,
half jokingly: 'You're a fine one. We had to dress for dinner and
return to the house in the dark. The petrol lamps wouldn't work.'
I said that this was extraordinary. I could only think that he had
not mastered the pumping of the lamps. They had had to use
torches. Next day on our return I tried to get the lamps to
function. They refused. I emptied out the petrol, substituted more
from the can in the garage, with the same lack of result. It took me
some time and another can of petrol to find the fault. Someone
had substituted water for the white petrol, which was in use at
that time, but petrol fumes had lingered in the can and the lamps.
One never locked a garage — indeed it had no door — but,
although scarce, petrol had never been interfered with before. The
first time would, of course, have to be when visitors were taking
over the house. The deed must have been perpetrated that same
day, although New Zealand sentries had turned up after lunch to
patrol the house.

Within a week the following letter had arrived:

Government House
Dominion of New Zealand
Wellington

8 June 1942

Dear Snow,

His Excellency the Governor-General has asked me to write and thank you and Mrs Snow for your great kindness in allowing us the use of your house during our visit to Nandi.* We were most comfortable there, and are indeed grateful to you. His Excellency trusts that you were not put to too much inconvenience by our 'invasion', and apologises for turning you out of your own home.

Yours sincerely,
C. J. Holland-Martin
Major, Military Secretary

P. A. Snow, Esquire

Seeing the cavalcade raising the dust on the road, the inhabitants of Nadi township had decided that the figure in the car was either a captured Emperor Hirohito, General MacArthur, or one of the King's brothers.

Petrol was really short now in Fiji and was to remain so from 1942 to 1945. My official duties secured a little more than the ration. Surprisingly short was currency. Not so much gold, which Indians buried in their compounds, but the colony's treasury ran out of the 1*d*. nickel coins with a hole in the middle for stringing round one's neck (I never saw anyone so wearing them). Further supplies could not be shipped, or if they were, they were sunk *en route* from the London Mint. So the Government Printer had to

---

* Note the spelling Nandi. That is how it is pronounced; the Fiji-language sound requiring 'd' to be preceded by 'n', 'b' by 'm', 'g' by 'n' and 'q' by 'ng', while 'c', as we have seen from Cakobau, is pronounced 'th', as in Spanish.

print 1*d*. notes. They were two inches square at most and, remarkably, managed to contain three signatures. As can be imagined, resembling fragments of soiled toilet paper (sometimes one wondered about this use), they quickly became grubby, torn and despised. Unfortunately, I had to pay out substantial amounts of money in small denominations — of less than £1, or as little as 1*d*. (there was no halfpenny or farthing) — to Fijians for leases paid by Indians. Fijian landowners were paid scrupulously detailed proportions of the total value of lease money (paid by Indians) calculated in relation to their status from high chiefs down through minor ones, clan leaders to members of tribes with rights to parcels of land: hence the fragmented distribution. Lease pay-outs were a biannual chore, but the money was naturally awaited with eagerness by Fijian landowners for whom this might be the only cash that they ever received. With conditions now as they were, these lease payments became one of the more niggling tasks of the war. There was no short cut. Those 1*d*. notes had to be meticulously counted and disgustingly handled.

I never dreamed that they would become one of the numismatological rarities of the world and only wish now that I had kept a handful of them, instead of the mere half dozen a more prescient friend gave me years after the war. They were soon replaced by the coins with the holes in them once the war ended. Circumstances created by the war in the Pacific had their share of oddities.

8

The Dark and the Light

T he pace was severely hectic in Nadi, but energy had been
stored up for it by our sojourn in Lau. It was satisfying to
know that, in contrast with being in Lau, one was now as
close to the action as possible in Fiji's conditions. The Japanese
were the vicious enemy to be defeated and eliminated forever.

The cadet in Lautoka, T. L. I. S. V. Iremonger, no longer able to
tolerate the Provincial Commissioner there, resigned from the Service. He had the private means, it was understood, not to need to
have to return to the Service, which one knew was not possible if
one resigned. Junior to me, Tom joined the British navy and later
became an English MP for many years. Apparently the importance
of Lautoka's position as the second major port after Suva was
being increasingly recognized in the capital, not least in view of
Lautoka's 18-mile distance from the mass of airstrips and Nadi
aerodrome. I was transferred to Lautoka in June 1942 at a critical
phase of the war — just about the sharpest knife-edge period in
the Pacific. There I was to be Assistant Provincial Commissioner
Lautoka and the Yasawas (the latter a string of islands near Bligh
Water off Lautoka, now a prime tourist region, then virtually empty).

The provincial commissioner was a contrast to the Ernie Bakers,
A. J. Armstrongs, Charles Pennefathers and Stuart Reays I had
been delighted to work with and for and to know. An Australian,
he had risen from being a police sub-inspector. He was fluent in
Fijian and Hindustani — ungrammatically in both — which he

spoke in a rasping voice that pleased neither Fijians nor any others. What I could not forgive in him was that, apart from never uttering a compliment about anyone and being generally rebarbative, he was abominably and inexcusably otiose for so dangerous a state of the war, which he seemed not to recognize. Had it not been for the war he would have been close to being retired: he was 53, with two years normally to go. Now he was simply marking time. I had to keep a distant relationship with this curmudgeonly (the *mot juste* that regretfully has to be applied) character on our journeys together, enforced by the rationing of petrol: we would share cars between Natabua, the government station four miles out of Lautoka, and our conjoint office in Lautoka.

His relations with the English resident magistrate and the Fiji-born district engineer, both of whom constituted the European settlement on the station with the PC and me, were characterized by mutual animosity. The Australian superintendent of police (the epitome of no-nonsense forthrightness), the New Zealand medical officer and the English medical officer of health, all three living in Lautoka Town, disliked him, as did the Australian manager and officers of the largest CSR Company compound in the colony. Fijians were only frigidly polite to the PC.

In short, he had no friends except, I learned without surprise, C. W. T. Johnson of the Secretariat. He was lucky to keep his job and luckier still, seven years later when he was over 60 and after several transfers to further paralytic inaction in other districts, somehow to be given a CBE on retirement (via the Mason–Johnson line?). Contrasted with the worthy, unrewarded Baker, Armstrong, Pennefather and Claud Monckton, it can only have been through longevity. It was so unusual for me to have dislikes of fellow creatures that the unfortunate episode of this man stands out in my memory. The local correspondent of the *Fiji Times* ran a regular column fulminating against his serious inactivity, yet somehow the PC was retained, escaping removal with cunning.

These observations are recorded to confirm — lest I have so far given any opposite impressions — that persons were of course no more perfect in my part of the Pacific than in any other segment of the world. In a career one inexorably, I suppose, comes across someone of his type with whom one has to have close contact. Alone of all the senior PCs with whom I worked, he was the only one I found it impossible to respect, apart from a later one who was a nonentity. Shockingly, he wasted my availability at such a hazardous time, with which he nevertheless would not dispense: it suited his *amour propre* to have an assistant, although it meant sharing an office. About all he would delegate — because he had nothing to delegate — was to make me officer-in-charge of the gaol. And, as he did not like court work, I would also take an occasional case when the resident magistrate paid once-a-week visits to Nadi. The chore of counting the revenue clerk's cash at the end of the day was mine.

A week after my move (the PC was impervious to being disliked: otherwise, I cannot imagine how he encouraged or indeed engineered my being stationed alongside him), Sir Harry Luke resigned, to be replaced by Major-General Sir Philip Mitchell, formerly Governor of Uganda (it was normally considered a step down to move from there to Fiji) whose military rank was more honorary than real. This was due to his having been political adviser to General Sir Archibald Wavell and chief political officer on the staff of the General Officer commanding East Africa. His whole Colonial Service career had been in East Africa apart from this period in Fiji.

Luke had been the subject of a secret petition to the Secretary of State for the Colonies from a cabal of leading commercial European figures. These included Alport (later Sir) Barker, a New Zealander editor of the *Fiji Times*, Sammy (later Sir Howard) Ellis, a leading lawyer married to a Joske, Sir Henry Scott, a retired lawyer and father of the playful Maurice, and Sir Maynard Hedstrom, head of the mercantile colony-wide firm of Morris Hedstrom. They felt that they should have been encouraged to visit Government House (they probably should) both governmentally and socially and thought that Luke spent more time in the outlying islands than was good for the war effort. In fact, with the Japanese occupying much of the Western Pacific, that region's High Commissioner (Luke) could now travel very little. Of course, the opposition to him knew less of the islands (including Fiji's) because they virtually never moved out of Suva. Perhaps the most hurtful action of Luke's was not to entertain them at Government House. And there were Luke's well-known inclinations towards women and other tendencies, judged to be peccadilloes in a society that nevertheless could not really afford to throw stones. He was thought not to be the man to welcome the American forces now overwhelming Viti Levu's strategic spots.

But I was personally sorry about his manner of departure. Had it not been for the war he would have retired by 1942 in any case. Few would deny that Luke was (perhaps, with the first, Gordon) the most cultured of all governors of Fiji. He had been kind to me.

Both Mitchell, a big-jawed, strong-looking man except for a barrel stomach protruding below the belt of his military uniform (which he invariably wore, putting aside his gubernatorial finery) and his diminutive South African wife were little known during their stay of approximately two years up to 1944. He declared that he had come to wage war and spent all his time (probably correctly) with the forces. He knew nothing of Fiji's districts and did not want to learn. This blind spot was to be his downfall when he left Fiji to become Governor of Kenya, where he ignored reports from DCs that the Mau Mau movement would break out at any time. He got on with Sukuna who never viewed Luke with respect. But then Luke failed to recognize fully what an ally Sukuna could be: perhaps his greatest mistake. It was increasingly important, if one was to be successful in Fiji, to have Sukuna on one's side. I met Mitchell only about four times: he did not deign to take notice. I did not greatly mind. There was now much that I found to do, creating it myself.

With some CSR Company backing, I put pressure on the PC to allow me to organize Lautoka's civil defence. My appointment as Air-Raids Precautions Officer, Lautoka (conjointly with that of DO Lautoka) was demanding. I had to set it up from scratch. Astonishingly, during these months after Pearl Harbor, Singapore, Hong Kong, the Philippines, the Dutch East Indies and all the other multiple calamities, there were no slit trenches, no alarm signals, no corps of emergency first-aid helpers and no wardenship in zones. There was just nothing. It was almost the same in Suva. With very ready support from the Lautoka urban population (almost wholly Indian and European), a sizeable organization with tiers of responsibility and set procedure for action in the event of raids or other emergencies (such as crashes of American or New Zealand planes) was established. I managed to compose a booklet, *Civil Defence Services, Lautoka*, and have it published by the Government Printer. It was circulated to all the leaders in the town, which was later to become Fiji's second city after the capital.

The warmest encouragement was given me by Major C. L. R. Griffiths, the only Englishman — a lean, hungry, slightly aloof one — on the considerable staff of the CSR Company Mill in Lautoka where he held the humble position of storekeeper. By way of compensation he was a keen Territorial Army soldier and very efficiently organized the few, somewhat recalcitrant European residents of the town outside key jobs in the company or government into a military company commanded by him with real intelligence. Griffiths had no faith whatever in the PC. He was one of those whom I met and judged to be living his life far below his gifts. Unpopular but discerning, he would, I estimated, have been more than a match for the Japanese, officer to officer, which is what mattered.

The PC would have liked the power of being in charge of everything, but hadn't the energy, imagination or judgement to stir himself. It was no surprise to find that the PC Lautoka and the PC Ba, Nixon Caldwell (who were next door to each other in major districts), did not get on together at all. Caldwell, of the same seniority, had no respect for him. On starting to organize civil defence, I found that over his only war idea, which was to evacuate Europeans from Lautoka on a single-track sugar-truck railway to Ba, the Lautoka PC had never consulted Caldwell, who had planned for evacuation from Ba to Lautoka on the same, signal-less, curved, single-track railway — simultaneously, with a fair-size collision midway fairly certain. Finding this out (he had never made it public), my confidence in him moved from zero to several degrees below zero and — to apportion the censure fairly

— my confidence in Caldwell was also shaken (but that did recover later).

The war did not seem to be losing its momentum. It had been learned that wherever Japanese landed their first act was to shoot as spies administrative officers who were inevitably, as I was, in closest liaison with armed forces. It was believed that had they been in uniform they might merely have been imprisoned and no doubt tortured. So an edict came from Suva that the PC and DO Lautoka, PC Ba and DO Nadi (the latter somehow wriggled out of it) — in regions now recognized, with Suva, as the prime areas for invasion (plans captured after the war showed demonstrably that Nadi was target number one, with Lautoka as the nearby port number two, well before Suva) — were to wear uniform of a material that was about to be sent.

When it turned up, it had obviously emerged from a museum cabinet of Boer War relics. Attired in it, we looked as though we might be in time for the Relief of Mafeking. The thick treacle-brown khaki material had to be cut at our expense, adding insult to injury, to make a short-sleeved tunic coat, long trousers (which for years after never seemed to wear out when gardening) and knee-length shorts, which were *de rigueur* in that era. There came with it long khaki socks and a huge topee. (I was at one with the PC, which was rare, in experiencing disgust. It touched his vanity more than mine, for with an astonishing burst of energy he unsuccessfully tried to scrounge some thin, glossy, light-fawn, material from the American stores.)

A little to relieve the musty appearance, we fixed the brass Royal Coat of Arms from our white Colonial Service solar topees in the *pugree* of the khaki topee. I found the helmet too heavy to wear. Epaulette markings were, for the PC, two dark-blue stripes surmounted by circles, and for the DO one such stripe, an insignia, which most closely resembled, I noticed subsequently when I saw one, that of an air commodore, but his was in gold. This insignia could never be fathomed, any more than our uniform could, by the American forces, by the New Zealand forces, or by anyone.

Paying a joint courtesy visit to practically the only British ship to visit us at this time — HMS *Engadine*, a seaplane tender — at

Lautoka wharf, at the top of the gangway we were asked for confirmation of our names. We simply said 'Provincial Commissioner' and 'Assistant Provincial Commissioner'. When we were taken down to the captain this had been changed by our escort, looking hard at our insignia, to 'Vice Admiral' and 'Rear Admiral'. We were alone in this garb among our colleagues in the frontline of Fiji (Suva and Nasigatoka, like Nadi, somehow evaded it) and chose at the earliest moment to discard it, still smarting at having had to pay for what we insisted was of course government issue and pre-1900 issue at that. The PC Ba, the holder of a First World War MC, seemed to find merit in it. I was the first and perhaps only Fiji magistrate ever to hold court in uniform.

Reverting to the civil defence of Lautoka, when all was as near ready as possible I arranged with the American air-force command to stage a mock raid of the town. Timed for 4.25 p.m., the planes were meant to return to Nadi at 4.35 p.m. At 4.25 p.m. the new siren was sounded. American army, air force and navy personnel, including some Negroes (as they were officially and by themselves called at that time) shopping in the town or drinking at the hotel, dived into the zigzag trenches, leaving the residents with no room to join them. That was something that had not been predicted — troops were only in town on certain days. The slit trenches were full up to the top with the previous day's torrential rain, which did not deter the alarm-conscious troops. Nor did the fact that the giant Hawaiian toads were in the trenches before them. When the troops climbed out on the all-clear being given from the fire brigade-cum-siren-tower, from which hoses were hung to dry and was later to be known as the Snow Tower, they did so drenched to the skin with toads squatting triumphantly on their backs and heads.

The four Airacobras put on a duly frightening performance — strafing, diving vertically, swooping, side-slipping and skimming off with their slipstream the leaves of the mango trees along Vitogo Parade just above the royal palms. So rapid was the alternate horizontal crisscrossing of the pairs of fighters with only feet to spare, simulating the machine-gunning of the rectangular civic layout, that the heat of the town seemed to be rent asunder and the sun momentarily obliterated as the planes' shadows flitted

along and across the tarmac streets. The continuous aerial scream-
ing was alarming, as was the likelihood of crashes.

I had invited the Director of Civil Defence of Fiji, Dr Victor
McGusty (who lived to the age of 99), from Suva to watch. He
was so energetic, personable and versatile as to hold also the posts
of Director of Medical Services and Secretary for Indian Affairs
conjointly — he had been joint DC/District Medical Officer in a
number of areas — and on occasion Officer Administering the
Government. Ever alert naturally to promote the interests of his
son-in-law in the Service, Ronald Garvey to whom, remarkably,
during his postwar retirement, he was ADC at Government
House, and seldom without correspondent two-tone shoes, he was
normally loquacious. Now he was speechless in his admiration for
the performances. When he had regained his breath, he was his
customary magnanimous self. I felt reassured.

Meanwhile, some Indians in the town had been marked with
cards that pinpointed them as 'casualties'. The first-aid teams were
then to collect them on stretchers and take them to first-aid stations.
One of these posts was, by collaboration with Police Superintendent George Kermode, the police station on Vitogo Parade,
which happened to be where Anne, who had been awarded a first-
aid certificate in Nadi, was second-in-charge to Clarence Angleson
Adams, the New Zealand pharmacist from along the Parade.
Smooth and calm, 'Gerry' Adams was quite the wittiest of all our
friends and was later to become the first mayor of Lautoka. Anne
said that one 'casualty' brought in was not marked as having a
broken leg or arm or other war-like injury, but was an Indian boy
covered with sores who had asked to be taken to them for
treatment. The only fire-engine, driven by the chief (and sole) fire
officer, Desmond Tilley, with four voluntary unpaid Indian
assistants, would rush up to me with brakes screeching to
supplement the self-important clanging of its sublimely polished
brass bell. Puffing and huffing, as was Tilley's wont, this loyal and
energetic officer would salute with an astonishing reservoir of
alacrity, then depart in a flash to dowse here and extinguish there,
relishing his all too rare phase of publicity, and finally return to
sound the all-clear from the fire station.

One of a number of incongruities was the narrow-gauge steam sugar-cane train running alongside the main Lautoka street in the middle of the sheer hell. It was quite oblivious of the air-raid alarm signal having been sounded, but, sensing a rare occasion, added to the cacophony with its own rather hysterical steam whistle, which did not fool the residents — only the visiting forces unfamiliar with it — into believing that it was either the alarm or the all-clear. The town whirred with excitement. The air-force pilots got carried away by the exuberance of their practice stunt, for they exceeded the split-second timing, continuing their hazardous exercises until 4.55 p.m. It seemed never-ending and I naturally could not authorize the all-clear till then. But all judged it a valuable and successful exercise, not least the American pilots who had lingered so long, but confessed, in reply to my thanks, their absorption in the affair when so felicitous an opportunity was offered.

One day, driving along a high section of the road from Lautoka to Nadi, where I was to take court because the DO Nadi was in hospital and the resident magistrate was occupied in Lautoka, I could scarcely believe my eyes. Across the whole of the vast Nadi-Vuda Bay was an entire American fleet. I could pick out about three aircraft carriers from the 50 or so warships. It was an exhilarating sight. On my return in late afternoon, they had all gone.

In 1942 the Pacific Ocean's naval battles certainly swung about. Those of Savo island in August, Santa Cruz in October and Tassaforonga in November were undoubted defeats for America. The battle of the eastern Solomons in August was a marginal loss for Japan, while the battle of Cape Esperance in October and the naval engagement of Guadalcanal in November were slight victories for America. These battles were of course only learned of after the war. That the fleet's stay in Nadi-Vuda Bay was so evanescent was, I suppose, because it was too concentrated a target for Japanese aircraft and submarines. In fact, as the date of its visit was 28 November 1942, it must have been the American fleet from the last of those battles taking a momentary rest out of aircraft range under Vice Admiral Harry W. Hill and including the

188

aircraft carrier *Saratoga* and the battleship *Colorado* before leaving probably for the Guadalcanal sea battle.

The Japanese had landed on Guadalcanal Island in June. Soon after this Martin Clemens, my friend from Christ's, now DO Guadalcanal, had reported to the Americans that the Japanese were surveying an airstrip. Then, on 7 August (my twenty-seventh birthday), Major-General Alexander Archer Vandegrift landed with marines to capture it and to name it Henderson Field after Major Lofton Henderson, a marine flyer killed at Midway.

Clemens had been appointed as a Colonial Service cadet in the Solomon Islands simultaneously with my similar posting to Fiji 1000 miles away from him, but close neighbours by the standard of the Pacific's astronomical distances. His part in the Japanese war was significant. Estimating more accurately than most international experts that war with Japan was inexorably drawing near, he anticipated a siege. Only part of the following legend is slightly wrong.

Crates of mixed tinned foods were ordered from Australia and lay unopened until war followed the Japanese bombing of Pearl Harbor on 7 December 1941. The Japanese swept down into the Pacific with a formidable fleet at astounding speed. Admiral of the Fleet Earl Jellicoe, on a world survey of potential bases immediately after the First World War, had prognosticated the importance of the Solomon Islands. He had picked them out as a most likely source of conflict and for the construction of a major base. Nothing was done there. The Solomon Islands remained a backwater and Singapore was selected as the fortification. The Solomons were there for the taking — and, ironically, so was Singapore. In the centre of where Jellicoe had anticipated an almighty showdown, Clemens was appointed DO in charge of Guadalcanal.

He decided that when the Japanese reached the capital of the Solomon Islands group, across the straits from him, he would take a handful of trusted Solomon Islanders (11 police and a dozen government servants) with a radio transmitter up about 3000 feet into the mountainous terrain of his island. His bearers carried the scores of huge cases of food. Clemens told me: 'It was no good going any higher because of morning mist obscuring the view. . . .

189

The mist caused my radio switches to stick.' After their capture of Tulagi, the capital of the Solomons, the Japanese moved across the straits to Guadalcanal. From under luxuriant tree cover, between 18 May and 15 August Clemens watched the Japanese movements and reported them to the Americans who were following.

Meanwhile, as there was nothing to eat but wild yams he started opening his crates. To his delight, the first contained tins of scallops. 'My favourite,' he exclaimed exultantly, 'this is not going to be too bad after all.' After a few meals of scallops, he opened a second crate to sample a change. This contained scallops. So he opened a third. More scallops. And so on until, after about a dozen had been opened — now with some frenzy, he realized that all 30 crates contained nothing but hundreds of tins of scallops. That is the legend. The truth, which he has given me, is that he had one emergency case labelled '48 x 12 oz Assorted Meats'. He resisted opening it for as long as possible. When opened it contained 48 x 12 oz tins of Tasmanian scallops. He had most of the 48 cold (awful, he told me, shuddering at the remembrance), others fried or curried, until, gloomily yearning for but one tin of meat, he could not face another single scallop — and this despite nothing else but wild yams.

On this diet he survived, losing three to four stone in weight, until he observed American landings and ventured down from the mountain hideout. Unshaven, dirty and ragged, his appearance had to be in broad daylight along the beach carrying a large Union Flag with his followers in military order so that he was not shot by the sentries for whom there was no password. Clemens stayed with the American forces, advising them of Japanese positions, completely loyally served by his Solomon Islanders. One of them, a repeatedly bayoneted and left for dead sergeant major, Jacob (later Sir) Vouza, was awarded the GM for refusing to give information under torture from the Japanese. Clemens was awarded a meritorious MC.

I did not know until long afterwards that Martin Clemens had so valiantly been helping Fiji. I have never ceased to be thankful for his imperturbability and his very individual style of bravery.

He had demonstrated his physical courage at Cambridge as one of the leaders of the night climbers who scaled astonishing heights without lights between and over buildings, hoisting improbable objects such as commodes and an Austin 7 on to conspicuous pinnacles.

In this crucial year, Charles had been keeping Mother as well informed and encouraged as he could. He wrote to her on 18 July 1942: 'Philip is expecting a Japanese attack but that was before the American victories in the Coral Sea and at Midway: for the present at least, they are pretty safe.' He was still exhorting Mother to be optimistic. The Coral Sea battle was a highly dubious victory. Later, on 30 September, he wrote, 'In the Far East I agree with you that the position is better, and Fiji certainly out of danger for the moment.' And then, on 2 October, 'I am looking forward to hearing from Philip. They are probably kept pretty much absorbed by the New Guinea and Solomons battles. The New Guinea one has not gone as badly as I expected.' It preoccupied us less than other parts of the Pacific, although MacArthur's success there certainly released some of the Japanese grip. On 17 December, he wrote to her to say that 'Winston has offered me a CBE. I hesitated about accepting it (it hasn't any bearing on my real ambitions) but decided to.'

As the year changed to 1943, a most impressive chiefly ceremony was performed at Viseisei village, Vuda, halfway between Lautoka and Nadi, for Vice Admiral Hubert Fairfax Leary, US Naval Commander-in-Chief of Task Force, who had been in the Pearl Harbor débâcle. The only naval commander to land officially in Fiji during the war, he was in command of naval forces in the Southwest Pacific (with Halsey in a similar post in the South Pacific). Accompanying him were Vice Admirals Monroe, Mason and Harry Hill. For this array, Adviser on Native Affairs Charles Pennefather was present in white Colonial Service uniform, the PC and I in our antediluvian khaki. I had done most of the arranging and, after the ceremony, Leary, in thanking me, asked what his name now was after 'my induction as a Fijian chief'. I had to disillusion him that, unlike the recipient of an American Indian ceremony, no named chieftainship followed.

With the PC, I also attended close to this time a rare installation of a Roko. Ratu George Cakobau had given up being Roko Tui Lautoka and the Yasawas to join the Fiji Regiment. Ratu Jovesa Tana, whom I nicknamed absolutely privately Chief Sitting Bull from the resemblance of his square jaw and unamused face to that figure, was appointed in his place.

He was a favourite of mine and I was glad to have found in an abandoned provincial office a Roko's staff of office — an ivory-topped, six-foot long stick. We knew of no precedent in our time for an actual installation, but after the *yaqona* ceremony, in which he was, to his reluctance in our presence, presented the first bowl, the PC asked him to receive the staff. Ratu Jovesa had less standing than the high chief of nearby Vuda, but he was a sturdy type of man who knew his limitations, aired no graces and was successfully diplomatic.

The PC's wife and elder daughter had evacuated to Australia but his younger daughter invited us to threesome tennis on the court below her house. The PC sometimes made up the fourth player, his participation a shaft of light in so dark a character.

More and more American troops gratifyingly poured in. The scene changed sometimes from day to day. Suddenly a whole sugar-cane field empty of plants was covered with Negro soldiers. I stopped to welcome them. As I did so, a handsome sea-snake, quite a quarter of a mile from the beach, slithered across the road. Before I could stop him, a terrified, wide-eyed Negro decapitated it with a shovel. I had not seen one since Lau and was never to see another. It was remarkable that it should appear in such an area.

One day, returning from the office to the Government Station at Natabua, I found all the land in front of the gaol and contiguous fields a serried mass of tents with Americans in occupation. Two or three were lounging in our doorless garage. Unaisi, our attractive cook-housegirl from Namoli village, was alone in the open house but unperturbed. They were making a great fuss of Bonzo (the black and white mongrel of singular charm from Lomaloma: I was deeply attached to him) and of a female brown mongrel, who had been brought out of the bush in Nadi by Matai as company for Bonzo. I was concerned for their safety with large lorries and streams of jeeps passing a yard or two in front of our house. But I needn't have been. Next day the troops were gone, embarked, it was assumed, for the Solomon Islands, the principal battle area.

The Japanese were at their closest, but this did not deter the commanding officer in Fiji, Major-General R. S. Beightler, peace-time Governor of Ohio, from being as flamboyant a character as General Patton. Somehow he had acquired the shiniest, silkiest form of white tropical uniform (made of shark skin, I think) with a good deal of gold braid; he looked like a Balkan royal family intriguer, or as though a ticker-tape reception were just around the corner. Always accompanied by the most glamorous of nurses, also in a shiny white uniform as trim as that of an air hostess (he was obviously an Eisenhower in his diversions and like Luke in appearance and style except that he was suave and supercilious), he would be seen in his long open automobile, the colour matching his uniform, riding about in western Fiji as though he were on Governor's prestigious business in Ohio.

Unabashed by his female escort, Ruby Evans, the local apex of audacity with a part-European's lack of inhibition, would call out 'Hello, sweetheart,' to which the general would just as uninhibitedly call out 'Hi, Ruby.' How he knew her I can't begin to guess. Moving to the Solomons, he had to sacrifice his grandeur of appearance for the aspects of dirty warfare.

Our house at Natabua was open to all forces: many friends were made, some of them to be killed as they left for battle zones. They, in turn, would invite us to an open-air film arena in a natural amphitheatre near our home where the screen ignored the black-out. Indeed, the military camps were always lit up at night. I felt this to be unfair, for it would induce the Japanese to think that they must be civilian towns and therefore make them more prone to bomb the blacked-out areas presumed to be the military zones, but which were in fact civilian.

The gaol compound was just opposite our house. The prisoners, as usual, kept the lawns of the Government Station houses of the PC, DO, Resident Magistrate and District Engineer spotlessly clean. I inspected the gaol every Saturday and would hear any complaints while the Sikh warder listened disbelievingly as if there really could ever be any complaints. There in fact seldom were: merely perhaps that a prisoner did not feel too well or that the food was monotonous, which it never was.

In the Lautoka court I had to take the preliminary inquiry into a murder of a Sikh by six Sikhs. They had avenged a family feud by the simple process of cutting the person to pieces with cane knives. They were all over six foot and prepossessing figures, with bright multi-coloured turbans and luxurious beards. While they awaited trial for a fortnight in my gaol before transfer to the Chief Justice's court in Suva, I grew quite attached to them as they jokingly and politely worked in my compound, swishing their cane knives at the long grass where the mower would not penetrate — much as they must have done at their victim. They knew that their execution — capital punishment was not abolished for many years — was inevitable. They had happily righted the wrong to their family. I was sad to see them leave for Suva where, within a week, they were hanged without saying a word at the trial.

From 1936 to 1945, the Chief Justice was Sir Owen Corrie, as tall as those Sikhs, but slimmer. Indeed, men do not come any slimmer. He enjoyed his Supreme Court circuit away from Suva, which periodically took in Lautoka. As he was a friend of the bland, anodyne C. A. Adams, they and I, with another, played many tennis doubles. He was so elongated, standing at the net as my partner, that an errant serve of mine once hit him on top of the head. He gave his usual cluck-cluck sound, as he did when entertained (he often clucked at the Lautoka cinema when we were sitting with him and Gerry Adams). He spoke in a dignified semi-drawl and was the best of company. His wife had stayed in England. After becoming a Supreme Court judge in the British zone of Germany and a puisne judge in Kenya, he retired to be mown down and killed by a car while taking a walk along a country lane in England.

Chief justices were not often all that prominent. They kept a respectable, independent distance from governors. One of the earliest was Sir Henry Berkeley, who acted for a while as Governor at the turn of the century. He was an uncle of Fiji-born Reginald Berkeley, author of the successful West End play of 1920, *French*

Leave. I was later given the family album of photographs by Sir Henry's daughter and I had Sir Henry's name commemorated on the Suva street map in a manner related later.

War pressure began slowly, almost imperceptibly, to diminish in about mid-1943. I felt that Fiji was safe unless there were a disastrous reversal of American progress. Among my letters to Charles in that year were two. In the first, dated 13 March, I stated that:

> At last it would appear here that a Japanese invasion would be highly risky. ... As ARP Officer, Lautoka, controlling four thousand mixed peoples (mostly Indians) with a couple of Head Wardens and 30 Wardens (largely the more stable Indians) it is quite my most difficult task to dissuade everyone, even highly placed officials, from relaxing ... into deep smug contentment that nothing can ever happen here. I could call it a Singapore atmosphere that has pervaded Fiji but for the anomaly that my most intelligent associate in Civil Defence (H. R. W. Richardson), my counterpart in Suva, is a young colonial service refugee from Malaya. ... If anyone has any nervous elements in one's makeup at all, there has been a good deal of suspense for the more imaginative and realistic minded of us. No enemy aircraft has been known definitely to appear but they very easily might have. ... Martin Clemens is now a major in command of the Solomon Islands Defence Force and has been given the MC. ... Anne, in good health, sends her love with mine.

In the second, dated 13 July 1943, I wrote: 'Both Anne and I absorb your letters and regret only that they are too few: we shall hope after the five years of war in front of us we shall have you as our guest for half a year (as a minimum) in a Fiji that will not have lost its charm entirely.'

I indeed now managed quite a lot of weekend tennis intermingled with cricket on the CSR ground. It was shameful that in as large a town as Lautoka, the government had no ground of its own except at Natabua School, a picturesque but small and tree-darkened ground near our house. My standard at tennis, with Gerry Adams's coaching, was now not so negligible.

A unique cricketer was a member of an opposing team who would take the field without a leg. Supported by a crutch, he would chase after, and stop, shots with agility. Tribhowan was a Gujrat whose leg had been cut off by the sugar-cane train on the narrow-gauge railway when he was a small boy. Batting, he would stand with his crutch support under his arm and very nimbly and two-handedly make respectable shots. To anything loose on the leg side, he would gyrate and, in swivelling round, propel the ball with some force. He disdained to use a runner. A ball never hit his crutch in front of the wickets, but if it had and that ball were straight, he could not have been given out l.b.w. — manifestly not. But could he have been out c. (crutch) b.w.? Would it have counted as part of his person? It was not connected like, say, a head or torso, for which one *could* be given out — syntactically incorrectly — l.b.w. if they were in front of the wicket when hit by a ball which, if not so obstructed, would have hit the wicket. The crutch might have been interpreted as equipment under MCC Law 36 and hence l.b.w. but, saving much argument, the question did not arise in my matches against Tribhowan who, despite his lowly origins, overcame adversity still further by becoming a puisne judge.

There were entertainers of another sort. With so many American troops still stationed in the Lautoka–Nadi area or in transit from Lautoka wharf as reserves to relieve those in the battle zones, it was not surprising that some celebrities came to them. Anne and I met Joe E. Brown, whose last major part was with Marilyn Monroe in *Some Like It Hot* (1959). His rubbery face was naturally amusing, but his dry wit offstage was just as forthcoming. He was as far as could possibly be from the raucous American comedian type. We were the first English people he had met for ages — he was Anglophile enough — and we intrigued him as much as he entertained us, particularly with a five-minute private imitation of an English fan engaging him in conversation. At lunch a corpulent Australian local dignitary came up to him and said that he was one of Joe's greatest fans, at which Joe looked him up and down and round and round and retorted: 'Well, watch your diet,

Bill. I'd hate to lose one of my greatest fans.' An excerpt from my letter of 13 March to Charles encapsulates the impression of the moment:

> Among the oddest of recent acquaintances is Joe E. Brown, the bouncy comedian who, as you might expect, is a quite serious person offstage. For a day I went round with him, showing him parts of this district and marvelling at his quick-change character when he performed (in front of thousands of American troops). He would not be convinced that I was ... not the Police Commissioner, which was the term fixed in his mind.

It was at this time that the *rapprochement* I have previously mentioned occurred between Sukuna and me. S. B. Patel, always known as S. B., with considerable aplomb and his five feet full of sparkle and bonhomie, had arranged for me to have tea with Ratu Sukuna in his (Patel's) garden at Lautoka. Reg Caten, the droll deputy registrar of the Supreme Court on circuit with the Chief Justice, was present to increase the amiability. Sukuna and I fell into our relationship of up to two years before totally naturally. From then on we saw a lot of each other in Lautoka, Vunidawa, Suva, Taveuni and on his leaves in England when he would stay with us. On one of his visits to our Natabua house, he told Anne and me that he had just returned from a recruiting visit to Lau. There he had learned that an American cargo ship had been wrecked on a reef in unsophisticated Ogea-i-lau where its salvaged cargo of cocoa, a quite unfamiliar substance to the islanders, was mistaken for varnish and used with water for painting the interior of the church — to their disappointment, a fleeting, or rather flaking, accomplishment. Sukuna's soft chuckles over man's absurdities were a delight, no less so the hooting eruptions of laughter from S. B. and the sight of Reg Caten's ready predisposition to slightly wry grins.

When Ratu J. L. V. Sukuna was promoted from CBE to KBE in 1946, all, including his friends perhaps more than anyone, expected him to call himself Ratu Sir Josefa. He caused general surprise by deciding to bring into use the second of his three forenames, Josefa Lalabalavu Vanaaliali. This was shortened to Lala (as in that independent letter to the Crown Agent on 2 August 1914: if he initialled notes he used L. S.), but it was no surprise, although he was the first Fijian knight, that he should put the all-important Ratu before the Sir, a fashion followed by the half dozen Fijians to be knighted up to the folding up of English-style honours in 1987. He later received a second knighthood as KCMG, habitually given in Fiji only to governors.

The end of our short-lasting estrangement, emanating from his upsetting the timetable for the sacred fishing at the lake on Vanua-balavu in Lau in 1941 and from my immaturely presuming to take umbrage with so high a chief, was for me a great satisfaction and a help in many ways. I like to think, from the warmth he showed me subsequently, that he wanted an end to it too.

A welcome visitor to Anne and me at this time was Dr Humphrey Evans, now in smart uniform as Chief Medical Officer in the Fiji forces. For two so intimately connected with Lau as Ratu Sukuna and Humphrey Evans and in their relationship as predecessor and successor there, it was odd that they never made a reference about each other's existence to me and that I never saw them together. The two intellectuals seemed to keep their distance although often geographically close.

Other visitors from Suva included Alexander (later Sir) Newboult, who came in 1942 from being Under Secretary, Federated Malay States, to succeed Juxon Barton as Colonial Secretary. Newboult had been adviser to Duff Cooper in his curious term of office as Cabinet Resident Minister, Singapore, just before its surrender and had left that colony with him. Newboult was a quietly perceptive, most able man, the brevity of whose stay — up to 1945 — before going back to Malaya, retiring as Chief Secretary there in 1950, was a loss to Fiji.

This was also true of John (later Sir) Rankine, a protégé of Sir Philip Mitchell, just as Mitchell had been a protégé of his father, Sir Richard Rankine, a former shop assistant in Suva and then a clerk in the Fiji government who became Resident of Zanzibar. With burning brown eyes, John Rankine was ambitious but discerning and capable. His appointment to Fiji in 1942 as Assistant Colonial Secretary had been one of Mitchell's better moves for the Fiji administration, which were otherwise uninspired and uninspiring. Rankine left Fiji in 1945 to become Colonial Secretary Barbados, Chief Secretary Kenya, British Resident Zanzibar (like his father) and Governor of Western Nigeria.

Newboult judged that I ought to be on my own and arranged for my transfer to be DO Ra, a posting that had been unavailingly declared for me as early as 1939. I would have greatly liked the appointment. It was an attractive station. But the PC blocked it with the scandalous argument that Christopher Legge, the DO Ra, ten years senior to me and a bachelor, would not fit into the establishment. Newboult reluctantly could not make any progress. I have seen the correspondence and it is astonishing that the PC could have had his own way although he was a natural intriguer.

A chance came for me to visit the gold mine at Vatukoula, half-way between Lautoka and Ra. As it is the only mine that I have been down, I do not in retrospect regret the experience. Loaded into a cage with three or four other Europeans, we were lowered at quite a pace down into an increasingly hot hole. Water was pouring in on our unprotected heads all the way down the seemingly bottomless shaft. I believe that this was to keep the lowering wires loose and cool. At the bottom my shirt was soaked with a mixture of the water and the hellish heat. We walked along seemingly endless tunnels to the drilling face where helmeted Fijians (Indians and Chinese do not work in mines in Fiji) were sweating away. What they produced was singularly uninteresting. I was relieved to be hauled up under the streams of descending warm water back to the surface. The only gold I saw were a few blocks in an above-ground guard room. Brick-shaped, they were dull, not at all the gleaming specimens I had expected to see. They apparently saw only a day or two of daylight in their existence before being transported to the gold depository of Fort Knox in Kentucky, there to be promptly put down into the vaults forever. Lunch with E. G. (Red Ted) Theodore followed in his governor-style, decorated *bure*. Part Romanian, he was general manager, having been Premier of Queensland and Commonwealth Treasurer, with in his time some rather dubious happenings (alleged fraud). His period in Fiji was without blemish: he became a member of the Legislative Council. By the time the lunch was over, my shirt and hair had dried out while, internally, I had been well liquidized.

Another diversion was my being offered a lift in his car by Captain H. Ronaldson, commandant of the army training school at Natabua, with three American medical force nurses to the precipitous hill station of Nadarivatu, where A. B. Brewster (Joske) had for so long been in charge just after its cannibalistic days. The stone chimney piece in the house, now no longer occupied by a DC, was an unusual sight, but evidently needed in the cold mountainous mist where this station perched. I would have welcomed being stationed there, but no administrator ever was during and after the war. It was a lucky posting for a clerk-in-charge, who could grow strawberries and, if he or she were the type, could enjoy the ice-cold pool that had been constructed when governors used to transfer residence to avoid the hotter weather, as though from Delhi to Simla. The American nurses exulted in the pool, but Captain Ronaldson and I were astute enough to keep out of it.

A contemporary of mine on the Colonial Service course at Cambridge, David (later Sir) Trench, who died in 1988, stayed with us in Lautoka at this time *en route* from the Solomons on a secondment to Tonga. He was later to become High Commissioner for the Western Pacific and Governor of Hong Kong. He, like Martin Clemens, was an expert in the main theatre of war, the Solomon Islands (where, like Clemens, he was given the MC) and the fact that he was being seconded to Tonga did more than anything to convince me that the war must be turning there away from us. The battle for Guadalcanal, on 7 August 1943, had fluctuated alarmingly, as did the general situation there with its following naval engagements, as we have seen, for some time. Many of the Americans were now leaving Fiji for, we thought, there and islands close to it.

I could not help wondering what permanent effect, if any, so many of them might leave on Fiji. By comparison with the New Zealand forces, which too had diminished, they were handsomely paid and victualled. They had been able to show generosity to

The Dark and the Light

Fijian villagers and had fraternized with them. Only a few American–Fijian children, however, were born and fewer still of New Zealand–Fijian descent: by about five years after the war, one could hardly see any signs of there having been such a preponderance of Americans and New Zealanders in the country. Many districts — the surpassingly lovely Lau for one — had of course never seen them at all.

The Americans had, nevertheless, used the island of Koro in Lomaiviti Province to practise a landing on a Pacific island. It lies in the middle of the Koro Sea and useful lessons were apparently learned, although some were not applicable to the special circumstances of the atoll landings and mountain-scaling invasions of, for example, the terribly costly reconquests of Tarawa, Okinawa and Iwojima.

At last, with my ARP and other work accomplished, relief from Lautoka was secure. Newboult ordered the PC to take as a cadet James Coode, an escapee from the Gilberts and in undernourished condition. The PC protested that Jim Coode, a bachelor (who later with his wife became lifelong friends of ours), was too junior to me, but this time the PC was firmly overruled. All the same, Anne and I were sorry to leave so many friends in Lautoka, especially when their overseas visitors were also departing to receding fields of battle. But the wives and families evacuated to Australia and New Zealand were beginning to return to Fiji.

It had been a close-run thing. To America and New Zealand my thankfulness was profound and eternal for the salvation that they had brought. It was, of course, America that had primarily saved Fiji, partly through Fleet Admiral Ernest Joseph King, Commander-in-Chief, US Fleet, and Chief of Naval Operations 1942–5, absolutely insisting on naval priority for the Pacific against Churchill's reluctance to be involved in it.

America's rescue of the Pacific islands was monumental. Brilliantly achieved so soon after the seemingly irretrievable Pearl Harbor setback, the perilous dislodging at often fearful cost (the marines' setback at low tide on Tarawa atoll was perhaps the bloodiest of isolated actions) of fanatical Japanese occupation could never have been expected on such a scale. Of course the

201

gratitude of those on the Pacific islands is immeasurable. We also had every reason to thank New Zealand for its necessarily smaller-scale but no less speedy and courageous action when that country had been left nearly and dangerously devoid by its manpower being posted to front lines overseas.

At about this time, after a tremendously worrying interval (in which he was as anxious for me as I had been for him in the worst stages of the German war), came at last a very long letter from Charles. He made no mention of his CBE, awarded in the 1943 New Year's Honours for his work relating to telecommunications (I had of course heard about it from Mother).

He blamed his silence on the frustration of his worry for us so close to the Japanese. I had thought that mail between us was being sunk *en route* as we were so nearly surrounded. He had also been having his intense affair with S—, described in the graphic letter to me printed in full in my *Stranger and Brother* and later reproduced by the *Sunday Times* on the whole of its supplement's front page. At about the same time, 30 September 1943, he wrote to Mother: 'The German war should be over by this time next year,' and, on 17 October, 'I've heard nothing from Philip but he's safe enough now. You'll see him before too long.'

Charles was deliberately bringing forward the time scale to dispel Mother's impatience. He perhaps sensed that she was wondering if she would live to see Anne and me again because, on 2 January 1944, he wrote to her at the Aylestone Road, Leicester, nursing home into which she had gone that 'the war news is excellent and the German war will be over by the summer'. But it was too late for Mother's spirit to be sustained for seeing Anne and me again.

Having received Charles's single letter of 1943, my mind was now much freer and I looked forward to a not too long-drawn-out end of the war. I left Lautoka with the congratulations — for my ARP work — of Dr Victor McGusty, as head of civil defence in Fiji. That particular job had been done. Not long after that, the PC was moved appropriately to the backwater of Levuka, the least important of the posts for senior officials.

9

The Interior, Headquarters
and Release

Reluctantly, we had to leave our elegant, slim and shapely housegirl, Unaisi, behind in her native Lautoka. But eagerly we drove in the Ford V8 Coupé with the two dogs the 160 miles on the King's Road towards Naduruloulou. After a call on Christopher Legge, with whom I developed on each meeting an affinity, we had to pass through Vaileka in Ra, which after Lawaqa in Nasigatoka (to which I was, and still am, chagrined never to have been posted) would have been the most pleasant government station for us. Our destination was one I knew so well from my very first posting of all, the Rewa River. For Anne, it would be her first time there, apart from a day visit in 1940 from Suva to show her the Government Station and pay respects to Charlie (brother of Nixon) Caldwell, who had succeeded A. J. Armstrong. I was pleased to return with her to an environment I had enjoyed so much as a bachelor in my first year in Fiji.

We were housed now on the top of the highest of the station's hills, the first as one approached Naduruloulou when the right-angled bend of the river had come into view — 72 steps up and with a superb view of the two courses of the river. The sea was 20 miles to the south (out of sight) and the interior, whose mountains provided a stage-like, jagged backdrop, was to the north. The red soil of the arid sugar-cane fields had been left behind: all was verdant. There were a few cane fields (the first since Ra) and, pulling sugar-cane trucks, were picturesque, ponderous, patient humped-back zebu oxen plodding in almost black soil along the bank of the river, which the road followed towards the delta and Suva.

The dogs bounded exultantly up and down the steep slope from the house, which in my previous time had been occupied by the Fentons. We engaged a housegirl, Bui (as tall and slim as Unaisi: she was broad-faced, pleasant but not so fine-featured) from my old haunt at Kasavu village lying below us. On arrival at the station the news reached us that our very friendly next-door neighbour at Natabua, Lautoka, the wife of the district engineer, had collapsed — immediately after we had left — in a coma and died the same day. Diabetes was the cause and had never been suspected, such is its insidious nature.

Next to the DC's large old bungalow below our slope was the station tennis court, now no longer used by Charles Nott and his wife, who played instead in Nausori, four miles down river, on the CSR Company courts, where we were also honorary members. Charles Nott had been at Christ's a decade before me. As a Secretariat man for years, he seemed likely always to be there, but had not long been made DC. Self-deprecatory, short, with a brisk, dapper, twinkling-stepped walk, he was a congenial and highly competent person with whom to work. There had been a structural change in the office. Instead of my spending time in the large general office, which I knew so well and to which his was attached, I had a small one of my own next to his. He was proficient in delegating.

As I wrote to my brother Charles on 21 March 1944:

> To my pleasure the two interior hill Provinces are mine to supervise — Colo East and Naitasiri. Colo East will mean delightful returns to Vunidawa where I had, after a few hours there in 1939, heard of my transfer to the Governor's office on the outbreak of war, and Naitasiri is little known but mostly mountainous. Of all the types of country which I have had to live in, these Provinces represent the most attractive. For overlong my contact with the sea was too close.

I planned, to Nott's pleasure, to visit every village in each of those underestimated provinces mentioned in my letter. And, in my relatively short time at Naduruloulou, managed to do so. There was a different police inspector, Charles Tucker, local born and pleasant with, however, a reclusive wife: the sub-accountant in Fenton's place (and such a contrast) was A. P. Michel. Melancholy, he and his wife lived in my old house: both tended to be recluses. The sole European from my previous time, Bay Parham, was still in occupation as agricultural officer on the way along the riverside road towards the native provincial compound of Batiki. The provincial staff, I was pleased to find, was still centred round the irrepressibly mischievous provincial scribe, Koroi, the commoner from Rewa Province so quick in polite repartee. His genial, aristocratic Bauan assistant, Ratu Joni (later Sir) Kikau, related to the gifted Toganivalu family, had left for higher office. Koroi had two replacements for Joni, part of a more conscious policy of training chiefs in detail of administrative responsibility. One was a perpetually cheerful and bright young high chief from Nasigatoka, Ratu Aisea Wakanimolikula (Root of the Orange Tree) Vosailagi (Voice from Heaven), who was to die young when in paramount office in his province of Nadroga. The other was Ratu Inoke (Enoch) Takiveikata, looking, so it was commonly said, pointedly in nobility of visage and markedly athletic figure like a young version of the strikingly good-looking and commanding Vunivalu of Bau, Ratu Pope Cakobau. Inoke was in 1988 to act in the country's highest position, President, after having been Roko Tui Cakaudrove. Two court cards and a joker.

It promised to be a happy location. One significant loss was the medical officer in Nausori. Dr Humphrey Evans had, as we have seen, joined the army: he delighted in dressing up as a major in the Fiji Regiment. His successor was another eccentric of a different kind.

Dr Lindsay Verrier (he had changed his last name on coming from the Gilbert and Ellice Islands to Fiji in 1940 from Isaac) was rotund but hyperactive, just as fundamentally disinterested in medicine as Evans (I had less faith in him as a doctor than in Evans, which was not very much) and as overwhelmingly inclined towards absorption in administration. He was full of statistical approaches to his work and in a high-pitched voice cared little for what he said. Unlike Evans, he played no tennis but, like Evans, had little rapport with the Australians of the CSR Company, preferring genetic research into part-Europeans, into which as a doctor he could gain knowledge but which to my regret was never published. He lived to his seventies and at one time was a Suva town councillor.

After independence in 1970 he acted as secretary to the Prime Minister. Ratu Sir Kamisese Mara was to tell me that appointing him was one of his (Mara's) mistakes. 'Clever but crazy' was how I flippantly described Verrier to Mara who agreed, amid much laughter, that it was a just appellation. Verrier had been, unknown to himself, a sort of court jester. Fijian chiefs like to have one attached to them: it is a picturesque tradition in islands where entertainment is in short supply. From Nausori, Verrier was to be posted to Taveuni where he nearly brought that idiosyncratic island to a state of war between planters and government by high-handed actions, often theoretically well-intentioned, like trying to improve the labour lines. The rows of corrugated iron shacks in which copra labourers lived did invite attention. A feature of the tension was Verrier threatening to sue a planter, Duncan Hedstrom (one of the leading commercial firm's family), for assault by being pushed on the Government Road. Life near Verrier was never stable. But in Nausori normalcy reigned.

Miss Bertie Lovell Hilton had retired from postmistressing and from being the accumulator of gossip in the office to being full time with her sister on the bluff overlooking the whirlpool and spectacular view up river, now with no bachelors on which to focus her binoculars.

Next to her on the bluff was now a battalion of Fijians being prepared for war overseas — it was to be Bougainville, part of the Solomons, where the only colonial VC in the war was to be gained, posthumously, by the Lauan, Sefanaia Sukanaivalu, son of the coconut crab specialist. The Notts invited us to tea with the battalion commanding officer, Colonel F. W. Voelcker, the one-eyed New Zealander mentioned previously.

With him were Captain Ratu Edward Cakobau, who was to

obtain an MC, and his less sophisticated cousin, Captain Ratu George Cakobau, both of whom we have met before. Halfway through tea, George tipped over his cup. Edward did not have George's prime claim to the highest native position in Fiji as great-grandson of King Cakobau. But his (and also Queen Salote of Tonga's) father was no less than King George II of Tonga and his mother the leading Bauan chieftainess, Ranadi Cakobau. So he had few inclinations to hold back before his audience. He laughingly leapt in with: 'There's nothing so pleasantly callous as to laugh when anyone tips tea over. Look at George blushing under his brown skin, the clumsy fellow.' Edward's pale cinnamon face was radiant with amusement. It was a classic case of what the Germans describe with a single word — *Schadenfreude*.

That personal dig over, he was as usual in his dignified, softly spoken, witty, urbane style the life and soul of the party while George, not unnaturally, had gone into his shell. But, personal digs or not, this was always so when they were together. I noticed this most when George, my vice captain on the 1948 Fijian cricket tour of New Zealand, who had been easy and outgoing in his manner up to that point, was joined by Edward from England. He then promptly let Edward take the lead unofficially under me while he leant towards the morose, though it has to be said that this was naturally accentuated by his having broken his toe while batting barefooted at Napier.

I had heard much about a fine English eccentric in Tailevu Province at Lodoni (London) — not the sort of name that one would associate with a hamlet of four houses overlooking Ovalau island. There was some pretext for visiting him. He was Lodoni's postmaster, which occupied him for five minutes a day, and a justice of the peace, which occupied him with signing summonses for five minutes a week. Nott encouraged me to know him. Milton Craig's father had been the first Liberal MP for North Staffordshire. His three sons, born not far from my father's birthplace near Crewe, came for some unknown reason to Fiji in the last decade of the century. They lived on remittances from the Staffordshire family: one died soon and Milton's twin brother Willie died in 1930.

Milton, whose eldest brother was believed to have been a

baronet, had a Fijian wife, Matilda, and, through her, a thatched house in Lodoni with a few cows and two horned goats whose horizontal slits of eyes seemed always to convey a hint of mild egotism and to be calculating the best angle and moment at which to butt. Milton eked out an existence as a remittance man slightly above that of a beachcomber. The last time he had been in England was, he reckoned, in 1889. The thatched walls of his house needed renewing and the thatched roof had sufficient holes to allow his tame owl ample egress and ingress. When there were visitors the owl appeared and would sit motionless on a rafter except for a flicker of an eye. Milton had a silver moustache to match his silver hair and a benevolent face. His voice was soft and cultured, his eyes sparkled and he had a ready wit and sense of the ridiculous; it never occurred to him that Europeans and Fijians alike recognized eccentricity in him.

His furniture consisted of two swingback chairs with torn canvas seats, a desk littered with his post office and JP impedimenta, a table and, at it, two wooden chairs. His hospitality was always such that one could never leave without being given a meal. This would tend to be chunks of tinned corned beef and *taro*. Flies abounded. One's effort to get through the meal was helped by two large dogs, one on either side, whose necks would lunge forward to grab, unrebuked, the food being half-heartedly conveyed from plate to mouth. Milton exuded happiness and placidity. As I came to know him, I never heard an ill word from or about him: he had adapted totally to his individual world and found for himself perfect peace. He and his wife were loved and respected by all. Milton died in 1947 three years after my last visit to him. The memory of him is imperishable.

With Nott's wish to encourage local staff in games and my own to refamiliarize myself with matting on grass wickets after three years of matting on concrete, I formed the Rewa Cricket Association using, by courtesy of the CSR Company (that indispensable benefactor of sports facilities), the ground opposite the Nausori mill. The part-European table tennis club — and Lily Edwards — had since disappeared. But Nausori still had an outstandingly voluptuous beauty in the part-European, Jessie Rounds. On the

Nausori ground I managed to set up four teams, one from Naduruloulou and three from the RNZAF at Luvuluvu, just outside Nausori, where an airstrip had been built above flood level for small planes, helping, but not solving for future years, communication over the 140-mile distance between the capital, Suva, and the international airport at Nadi.

In the only season in which it existed, the Rewa competition was won by Naduruloulou — or Rewa CC, as we called ourselves. The team included Ratu Waka Vosailagi, Ratu Inoke Takiveikata and Josua (later Sir) Rabukawaqa, a teacher who was to become Fiji's first high commissioner in the United Kingdom.

I was soon able to resume my cricket in Suva, broken since 1940. My name had been subjected in 1942, it will be remembered, to criticism in Suva for having started the Fiji Cricket Association in the one-horse, one-taxi township of Nadi. Ratu Sukuna adopted that favourite description of mine for Nadi in his gracious Foreword to my *Cricket in the Fiji Islands*. I kept for a while a low profile. With the warm encouragement of its charming captain, Ernie Turner — the manager of Cable & Wireless and a sagacious, dignified, tall Australian with an exceptionally broad mind on the racial level, who was no mean player at 50 — I was welcomed as a member of the 90 per cent part-European team.

The part-Europeans were old friends from before. This team played against the formidable Fijian police side and an Indian team, but mostly against forces' sides of Fijians and New Zealanders, including Test match players. One of these was P. E. Whitelaw, whose third-wicket partnership of 445 in New Zealand in 1936 lasted as a world record for 40 years and who had been nearly selected for the 1937 tour to England. I soon came into form on the Suva wickets. Just as soon, despite the low profile, I was propelled yet again into the post of secretary of the Suva Cricket Association, supported on all sides and quickly able to introduce representative matches with other districts that had otherwise lapsed in Suva's unimaginative organization of the past couple of years.

I was out of Rewa proper quite a lot. With Charles Nott encouraging my frequent absences on tour in Colo East and Naitasiri, I would spend whole weeks at intervals in them, especially in Colo East's headquarters at Vunidawa, from where I could radiate in every direction. In the new liberty of action, war work was almost submerged. Unlike Nadi and Lautoka, the district was not militarily dominated. Danger had now passed from Fiji and the freshness of the air was emphasized by contrast with the now quickly forgotten claustrophobia caused by the proximity of the PC, which I had somehow endured in Lautoka. Nott was all that PC wasn't. The independence felt like Lau's wide open spaces.

The essentially Melanesian Fijians of Colo, in the interior, were quite different from the semi-Polynesian Lauans. Of a darker bronze colour and rugged in features, their looks were not as impressive: and since their chiefs were less powerful, as in all Melanesian society, their ceremonial customs were much less elaborate. Their thatched houses were rectangular or square with right-angled corners, like those in the rest of Fiji, but unlike those in Lau, which were oval-shaped in the Tongan style. The Colo people may have been less sophisticated, but they were sincere and trustworthy once their confidence had been gained. They were not dissimilar from the Nadi and Lautoka Fijians but, being more remote from Europeans and Indians, had not developed a degree of deviousness seen in some Fijians in the west of the country.

The Colo East people were delighted when Ratu Sukuna, as Adviser on Native Affairs, agreed to open the Provincial Council there. Since this would be the eminent Lauan chief's first visit to their area and they had no precedents on how to receive him, they turned to me: we had many consultations and agreed on a programme. As I knew Ratu Sukuna so well they took my word that they were making preparations along acceptable lines.

In the event, a posse of Colo East tribesmen — in black war paint, skirts of coloured leaves, and oil-polished chests over which splendid clubs and a few breastplates were hung — met him and Charles Nott at the river where the road ended and where normally the one station wagon would have been waiting for the three-mile drive to Vunidawa. I had walked from Vunidawa with the ceremonial party along the road to the river where Sukuna was presented with a whale's tooth. Then he, Nott and I walked ahead

210

of the guard of honour from the Waidawara punt-ferry to Vunidawa. I had persuaded the Colo men that this was the most dignified form of approach for Sukuna and, what was more, he enjoyed a walk more than anything.

At the lofty ceremonial house in Vunidawa, elders and *yaqona* mixers waited to perform the ceremony — in fewer stages than was customary in Lau, yet deeply impressive in its rather more primitive aura. Sukuna knew that, while they had received on rare occasions governors, European advisers on native affairs and other administrators, it was a new experience for them to pay their respects to the highest chief by merit in the country. He discerned that I must have had a large say in the deliberations and afterwards congratulated me on the amount of thought that had been put into it. He, Nott and I stayed in the resthouse alone for three days, further increasing my knowledge of Sukuna: Nott was a close friend of his and, like a half dozen or so Europeans (no non-Europeans), was entitled to address him as Jo. It was a happy time. Sukuna listened courteously throughout the council proceedings and replied to requests with the utmost patience and gravity, impressing deeply the men who had come from all the recesses, near and far, of Colo East. Many young men were to join the Fiji army as a result of his visit: one or two of them did not return from the Solomons and it was my heart-rending duty to have to visit the villages and break the news of their deaths to wives, fathers and mothers. That was something from which I would have wished to escape.

After years of only desultory visits by officials and, before that, brief residential occupation by bachelor district commissioners, the DC's house at Vunidawa, now the government resthouse, was in dire need of a woman's touch. Nott wished to encourage its use for local leave (while overseas leave still seemed far away) and, although money was hard to come by in the government's wartime economy, managed to find a sum to give to Anne for curtains and mats. She transformed it enthusiastically.

On one visit to Vunidawa I did not take her but P. V. Williams. He had played cricket for Winchester, Sussex and the Army, in which he had been a major, but for no explained reason was now

211

a leading aircraftsman in the New Zealand Air Force at Nausori. He was still a good cricketer, if fat, sweaty and uncultured: drink may have been his problem. On the put-put (outboard-engined dinghy), which I was using this time in order to get a better view of the river villages instead of taking the car route via Korovou on the King's Road, I began to shiver. By the time of our arrival at the end of a long day sitting upright on the boat, I felt weak and crept into bed at the resthouse. The NMP at Vunidawa hospital, a third-rate establishment, was called: he diagnosed dengue (break-bone fever). I certainly knew I had it because my bones felt stretched and cracked: they also seemed to be red hot. Neither before nor since my time in Fiji have I ever felt so ill. It was never a lethal disease in my time but has become one.

I had gone to Vunidawa to take court, which therefore had to be adjourned *sine die*, but also to see something very rarely witnessed. This was an ivory ornament made from a whale's tooth in the shape of a female. Its male counterpart was said to be in Colo North many miles and mountains away. I had enquired if I could see it, having heard of it after many *yaqona*-drinking nights on a previous visit to Vunidawa. All that was required of me was to present a *bulamakau* (bull or cow, from which the word was derived) as *magiti* (for a feast) to Taulevu village. Before leaving Naduruloulou I had paid for the animal and by arrival it had been presented on my behalf.

All was set except me. I was clearly out of the action. My hot, seemingly shattered bones not only prevented my travelling the short distance to Taulevu (its hill was within sight of Vunidawa), but delayed for a week my attempting to return to Naduruloulou (when I did so I had not eaten for a week and had to be nourished fast by Anne). Meanwhile, I asked if I could send Peter Williams as my stand-in. The Taulevu guardians showed it to him, but as he was not immersed in things Fijian its impact on him was slight. I never did see it. There was so much to do on other visits that I forgot about it, though Sir Harry Luke would have given it priority had he known about it in his time.

On another *raikoro* (village inspection, that prime part of one's administrative duty) in Colo, I took in as many villages as could be managed in a week's walking. This involved climbs I'd never previously attempted — not steep but long, up and down seemingly *ad infinitum*: the nearest had been to Abaca (meaning ABC) village below Mount Evans at the back of Lautoka on to which, as well as on to Nadi, there was a superb panoramic view. In making that visit, I had not realized that I had been following in the footsteps of Cadet A. W. Tedder in Lautoka in 1913, later to become Marshal of the RAF Lord Tedder.

I decided to penetrate as far into the interior as I could and one day I set out from Vunidawa and had the lunch I most enjoyed — river prawns, a mass of them — at Korosuli. On the long, sometimes precipitous walk from there deeper inland to Laselevu, I developed an acute stomach ache. Laselevu was very primitive — only a kind of bush lamplight and no milk in my tea (a piquant lemon-tree leaf served as a substitute). But I felt anyway that I would never eat again. I thought it might be acute appendicitis, perhaps peritonitis (the imagination ran high at that distance from a surgeon). So I drew up for the first time a will, though I had little money to bequeath and there was only Anne, but that was my state of mind: I have never been so pessimistic about myself, even on my medieval bone-breaking rack in the grips of dengue (I at least knew what that was).

To my intense relief, I felt better in the morning. There was no breakfast except lemon-leaf tea and a biscuit cracker. Unlike travel in Lau, where the boat would carry one's meals, I had not brought any food so as to avoid the load and not upset hosts' offerings of it by custom. I was punted up the white foam rapids of the Wainimala River — it smelled of freshwater fish — between gorges to Lutu (where there was a fine river fish for lunch) and to my destination near the Namosi Province border at Narokorokoyawa. On a mountainous path I was met by Ratu Rusiate Doidoi, the Tui Noimalu and a most imposing leader. He had been in prison at one stage for manslaughter: in the course of a fight as a youth, he had struck the chin of a man whose head went back on to a sugar-train line near Nausori, fracturing his skull and causing death. Now he was in his sixties, with a splendidly sculptured face and utterly commanding frame.

213

He gave me his magnificent house, so high on a *yavu* (mound of stones) that I could scarcely negotiate the primitive form of ladder (a semi-rounded tree trunk with intermittent rungs) leading to the side door for visitors of rank. It was narrow: there was no handrail and the little ravine over which the carved gangway was positioned was almost like a dry moat. As I entered on the thick mats between two dozen men squatting and facing each other, a deep shout of '*duo-o-o*' preceded my taking the only chair in the *bure*. The *kava* ceremony was markedly impressive, with the cup bearer rushing in the end door from outside with a wild flourish and a ferocious gleam in his eye. His bare chest and arms, shiny with scented oil, rippled with muscle. Apart from Ratu Rusiate, everyone in the *bure* was attired, like the cup bearer, in scarlet and yellow croton leaves.

The atmosphere made me very conscious of the pre-Christian, pagan times that I would like to have known: it was accentuated by an awareness that this was the dead centre of Viti Levu. Ratu Rusiate went, as hosts' custom dictated always to my shame, to live and eat in his kitchen while I was served at a table by his crouching female family or retainers. For dinner, like lunch, there was again magnificent fish from the sparklingly crystal-clear Wainimala River I could hear jabbling (my own onomatopoeic word for the sound) over boulders just beyond the house. At night, the *yaqona* served was green — fresh, strong and incessant. My stomach was now fully restored. I had brought cigarettes to be presented in this village miles away from any store. To respond to frequent calls of nature after the considerable consumption of *yaqona*, I had to venture sideways gingerly down the gradations of the steeply inclined rustic ladder, quite a manœuvre, probably better accomplished barefooted. There was no moon and anyway it was a sight to which villagers were accustomed, a man standing against a tree. It was cold at night at Narokorokoyawa, the sharpest drop in temperature that I ever knew in Fiji, despite a crackling fire in the hearth at the end of the *bure*.

So few were the signs of European infiltration that I kept feeling that I was in the pre-1870s in the heart of cannibal country. I was the first European to have stayed in the village for over 30 years.

214

An old man remembered seeing Lady Hutson, the Governor's wife, being propelled in a bamboo punt past the village at the end of the 1920s. No other Europeans since then could indeed be recalled as having been seen at Narokorokoyawa. Adolph Brewster Joske used to visit it regularly when stationed in the district in the 1880s and 1890s; and the perceptive, virile young Austrian, Baron Anatole von Hügel, had been fascinated by his visit there in 1875. But this was beyond current memory. Everything, under the strict control of Ratu Rusiate, was of the highest calibre. I was most impressed by him and, in addition, liked him.

The lavatory was a thatched sentry box, not near the river but just inside the boundary between the cut grass of the village square and the bush. As usual, one took one's chance with a centipede lurking under the rim of the seat or in the large concrete section of pipe. I always took toilet paper in my suitcase, together with mercurochrome, bandages, toothbrush and paste, a change of shirt and shorts. The Fijians themselves, paperless, used the rough husk of old coconuts. The lavatory became the urinal in daytime, replacing a tree in the village square of the night before.

Not so much here in Narokorokoyawa, but in other parts of the interior in particular flies were an abominable nuisance. I could write a whole volume on them and mosquitoes. Flies were not so overwhelming, as in inland Australia, as to require the ingenious if uncomfortable and inelegant invention of cotton reels on hats with which to agitate them, or as in the manifestly dirty parts of Africa like Ethiopia, or in India (where even clean faces are seen with flies wandering over them). Nevertheless, food had to be wafted with fans to keep them from travelling on it to one's mouth. I had to learn a method of counteraction. From studying their approach to their repulsive habits, I noticed that flies take off vertically like helicopters. The most effective way of dispatching them was for one's hand to descend sharply and vertically down to squash their take-off. No sideways swipe ever worked. Chiefs in Africa carry fly whisks. They are not unknown in Fiji: I had two or three presented to me. But they could profitably be in wider use.

The village was in pristine condition: it would have been presumptuous to have suggested the slightest improvement, even if I had noticed a need for it. After three days of talk and looking round the food plantations and river scenery, I started the long overland return walk past Lutu, up two or three long mountain sides and down them again and then up and down until I lost count. The severe undulations were daunting — to me but not to the two or three women carrying my suitcase and tin box and maps. They considered the expedition, ordered by Ratu Rusiate, to be great fun. They obviously thought my load negligible. It probably was, compared with the huge shoulder-backs of firewood they would carry in through the bush daily to their kitchens. They sang and joked all the way, never wanting to wait with me for a rest.

The path through the jungle was faint. A male guide helped me to follow it. A disappointment, with the sun scarcely penetrating the massively tall trees struggling to reach it and leaving a pointillism on the path, was the absence of wild life. Not even birds: a few differing calls were heard and identified by my companions, but their sources were never seen. There should at least have been a few parrots, doves or parakeets. No mongoose came into the bush this far to threaten their existence. The mongoose had been introduced to Fiji to catch rats, but had proliferated and was a marked feature of the sugar-cane areas.

Another disappointment was the absence of flowers apart from a few scattered spikes of brilliantly scarlet ginger. All was vivid green — fernery, trees and weeds — and dapples of sun. When we arrived at Naivucini in Nadaravakawalu district, I was dead tired: my unaccustomed muscles were stiff. But the women carriers had not made their trek for nothing — they were to return by the same 3500-feet switchbacks next morning when I would leave by punt for Vunidawa. Their infrequent sorties from Narokorokoyawa in any direction were in their view certainly going to take the opportunity of embracing some lighthearted enjoyment (perhaps away from Ratu Rusiate's eagle eye). So, after putting on a *meke* of their own after their hosts had performed one, they *taralalad* with a positive spring in their steps until close to dawn.

On one of my visits to Vunidawa, I took half a dozen cricket balls and a bat but no stumps or pads. Standing on a well-cut piece of grass, I invited about a dozen Bulis, who had come in to

216

collect their salaries, to bowl at me. The word for 'to bowl' in Fijian is the same as for 'to throw'. One of the younger Bulis, about 40 years of age, almost black-skinned and from the deepest interior, which had been decannibalized fewer than 70 years before, took a ball and hurled it at me with demoniac energy. His action was exactly as if he were throwing a spear — his arm bent a little above shoulder level.

Against a background of jagged, indigo mountains I scarcely saw the ball but nevertheless managed my favourite shot, hooking it off my eyebrows. The ball had not bounced. Nor did all the others that he rapidly picked up to repeat his throws as though at a coconut-shy. The Buli could be persuaded neither to bounce the ball nor to straighten his arm. It would only slow him down, he rightly claimed. When reluctantly relieved of the balls that I fended off with the bat (if I had mistimed by a split second in front of my head I might not be in a position to reflect on this episode), he was replaced by other Bulis who, on their first acquaintance with something supposed to resemble cricket practice, adopted the same approach. For my part I was relieved to call it a day with people who believe almost to a man that a ball is meant to be propelled with all the velocity of which an arm is capable.

Four years earlier I had had a nearly comparable experience. At Tubou on Lakeba in the marine setting of Lau, this time with pads, I had set up stumps at the end of the concrete pitch (no such refinement as a mat on it) and offered a dozen balls to a dozen bowlers who did bowl them straight-armed with one bounce, a ferocious one, nonstop for an hour until I grew weary managing to keep them out of the stumps, lamenting the absence of just one slow bowler. It was no good. Their simple concept was: the faster the action the better. Even when I bowled slow to them they would thrash the air like demented dervishes or flounder without contact like stranded whales. It was still no good. For them the action had to be like a speeded-up film run wild. At least that was the background before patient coaching, preserving what was best in their whirlwind motions, sifted the wheat from the chaff with gratifying results. But I never did succeed in taming a demon from the interior: the more's the pity.

An item of the greatest interest, which I would take with batteries from Naduruloulou to Vunidawa, was a wireless set. There was not another in the whole province. On it, the inhabitants could hear at the open house, into which I made the resthouse, the war news in the weekly Fijian language programme with its reports of the Fiji Regiment in the Solomons. Young women would float down in the dark 10 or 15 miles, often on the swollen Wainimala River, carried by the current on single bamboo poles under their arms. Having listened in deep silence, punctuated by a few clicking sounds of surprise, they would sleep overnight and walk back cheerfully over the not inconsiderable ruggedness of the routes to their villages. It was an area and time of much rain. Once, on my way back to Naduruloulou, floods marooned my car at Korovou, where I could go neither forwards nor back, and the only accommodation for the night was a police cell, my only experience of one but not at all unwelcome in the circumstances, with police food and drink as sustenance.

There was another memorable expedition from Vunidawa — of a sombre nature. At least it would have been without the accompaniment of NMP Ratu Tevita Mara Latianara. While I was in Vunidawa, news came through, first communicated by messages on *lali*s (hollowed-out wooden drums) beaten from village to village, that Ratu Manasa, the *Taukei ni Waluvu* (Owner of the Floods), highest chief of Waima, Matailobau and Nagonenicolo, had died at Nairukuruku. The day before, he had requested that I visit him at Vunidawa hospital, where he asked for an advance of £5, which I agreed, so as to be able to go to Suva as ordered by the NMP for treatment of a gastric ulcer. Instead, however, he had struggled home up river.

It was the standard belief that, with the death of the holder of the hereditary title, floods would follow for a fortnight. I had to go to the ceremony of *reguregu* and have presented on my behalf by my *matanivanua* a whale's tooth for mourning. It had been fine up to now, but on the day after the news (funerals have to be quick in the tropics) the heavens opened with torrents. The river swept up at a forbidding level and with menacing currents. It was exceedingly slippery on the soapstone and clay paths where the viscosity of the mud was as of the most tenacious glue. I took off my shoes. Native Medical Practitioner Ratu Tevita Mara, of the highest rank in Serua, a coastal province, wanted to come with me.

I never travelled anywhere by horse in Fiji, except, that is, to cross without a saddle and stirrups a river at Namulomulo in the back regions of Nadi, round which the river formed an encircling moat, and it was impossible to ford it except by horse as there were no boats. I found the experience extremely unnerving and could not reconcile myself to the height of the horse, which was up to its stomach in the river. Its surprising width was no comfort as I could only hold on precariously to its neck and mane while it semi-stumbled across. I always preferred on land to trust my own two feet, particularly on precipitous paths with deep ravines where I thought four legs less sure of negotiating the narrowness than two. So, eschewing horses, I squelched through the knee-high clay to the *Taukei ni Waluvu*'s home.

Ratu Tevita Mara weighed 19 stone: not more than five feet five inches tall, he was absolutely square. He had no alternative but to make some sort of progress by horse. It looked a tiny mount for so compendious a human figure. But there it was, up to its thighs in the clay, extricating its four legs with the same, if not greater, difficulty than I was experiencing with my two less heavy legs. Ratu Tevita had a perpetual, rumbling, frame-shaking laugh. It was he who had first told me of the *Taukei ni Waluvu*'s death. Amid his stomach convolutions, he announced it with a broad smile. If his nervous habit were not well known, I would naturally have thought it the height of disrespect: as it was, I knew he was grieving. Walking alongside his half-submerged horse for the whole journey, I found distinctly odd his constant merriment of appearance not in keeping with the sombre nature of his conversation. I wondered how he would be at our destination.

I was ushered through the side door of the chiefly house to a mound of mats, surrounded by women, all in black, wailing, sometimes ululating, nonstop as dictated by custom. They were fanning the anointed, recumbent figure in the centre of the thatched house. As my *matanivanua* presented my *reguregu*, I was obliged to have to look at the corpse — the third dead person,

219

after Grif and Turaga, both in Nadi District, I had seen and, indeed, have ever seen, except for prostrate figures strewn across American expressways while I was being conveyed at breakneck speed by drivers in no way inhibited by the murderous crashes.

Then I was followed by Ratu Tevita Mara who, while his *matanivanua* was solemnly making his presentation of a whale's tooth, guffawed with apparent mirth (as he had during the solemn presentation on my behalf) throughout the ceremony and our stay in the house, which was for the minimum possible decent period before returning to Vunidawa as the torrents continued to fall, filling in our footsteps and horse steps when we retraced them. Ratu Mara's unusual affliction has a medical term which I cannot recall. The symptoms were, of course, known to the subjects of the *Taukei ni Waluvu*. Had I been forced to take a bet, I would have wagered that Ratu Tevita Mara, then about 40, would not have lived another ten years. In fact he survived actively at that weight, with his explosive mirth for all occasions, for another 45 years, dying only recently and admired by all who knew him.

I had barely returned to Naduruloulou when, with Ratu Sukuna, Ratu Edward Cakobau (who was in charge of the firing party), Ratu George Cakobau, Ratu Glanvill Wellington Lalabalavu (Tui Cakau) and Ratu Tiale Wimbledon Thomas Vuiyasawa (Ratu Sukuna's brother), I attended with a *reguregu* the funeral of Ratu Luke, Tui Nakelo, who had been in the labour battalion in France in the First World War. Going to the grave outside the village, we had to squelch in mud almost as deep as on the route to the *Taukei ni Waluvu*'s funeral.

By way of some relief after these melancholy occasions, Anne and I had Ratu Edward and Ratu George together to dinner at Naduruloulou and to play the hilarious game of Pit, which never failed to amuse those to whom we introduced it. Playing it, they submerged their attitudes towards each other, often so apparent otherwise when together. Joviality was shared by them to an extent that I had not seen before and was not to see afterwards. Petrol and mantles were now so short that we had to substitute for one pressure benzine lantern five kerosene lamps with fluted glass as illumination for the game. The open gauze windows attracted up to 30 giant moths and the dogs indulged in frantic hunting, stunning many who lay with resentful, orange, incandescent eyes staring up from the floor until we rescued them.

There was an unusual aspect of an expedition to inspect a village up the Waidina River, on which I was accompanied by the assistant provincial scribe, Ratu Waka Vosailagi, and a provincial constable. It was all proceeding in the usual convivial manner of travelling when with Fijians — one could never be bored with them: there was always more to be learned about their language and customs and, for them, life was meant to be one of extroverted joy. We were some way from Naduruloulou and had stopped at a Naitasiri village where there was a welcoming chiefly ceremony before the inspection. The provincial constable had delivered a few summonses for non-payment of rates. He had shown some reticence about calling at this particular village, but for no clear reason.

As we were getting into the punt to go to the next village, the women descended on him and rubbed mud over his shirt and on to the part that is sacrosanct to every Fijian — his head of fuzzy hair. He made mock protest and, having been pushed into the river, he pulled with much pleasure a woman in with him. Ratu Waka, unmolested, was vastly entertained. I did not know what it was all about until, as we punted off the bank with the constable on board hurling laughing insults at the women who were hurling back as many as they received, Ratu Waka explained it as the custom of *tauvu*.

The constable belonged to a village from an entirely different part of Fiji, which was historically 'twinned' in *tauvu* with the one at which we had called. Because these pairs of villages, scattered at random throughout the archipelago, shared ancestral founders (the meaning of *tauvu*), women were at liberty to assault such visitors almost as hard as they wished, short of physical injury. No researcher has accumulated the pairs of villages in a custom so ancient that Fijians do not understand how it originated, but if they did it is doubtful whether any revelatory pattern would emerge. It is one of the main unsolved mysteries of Fijian custom.

I saw two other instances of *tauvu*. One was at a village on the

Wainimala River just outside Vunidawa where one of my officials, another provincial constable, was suddenly set on by the women in the house in which we were informally drinking *yaqona* at night. He had to flee to another village by swimming across the river in utter blackness, for he could not stay in the one I was in.

The second occurred in my Ford V8 Coupé on the road opposite Navuso village (the highest in status in Naitasiri Province) on the other side of the Rewa River. I was giving a lift into nearby Nausori to a Kasavu woman, who was sitting in the back dicky seat as I had someone in the front with me, when I saw the massive form of Native Stipendiary Magistrate Semi Nate, Fiji's champion heavyweight boxer, on the road side and offered him a lift. Into the back he climbed.

We had not gone far before I heard a commotion at the back and thought, not entirely without disrespect for Semi's bulk, that it was a broken axle. Looking in the rear mirror, I saw the woman beating Semi on top of his sacred head with a basket. I stopped and Semi descended to walk into Nausori. It transpired that he belonged to the village that was *tauvu* with Kasavu. The woman had exercised her duty to belabour the distant, gigantic relation with impunity and good humour.

It was as well to know, particularly in the interior, which shrubs, flowers, birds and insects were totemic and sacred. These could never be plucked, picked or molested by strangers without retribution. Stuart Reay (who had been with me in the near riot on the site of the Nadi aerodrome) once, as DC Colo North, deliberately — to see the outcome of what he had heard — plucked a shrub leaf and let the women of the village see that he had done so. Their response showed no respect for the European as such in these circumstances, or perhaps they realized that in his case it was done out of provocation rather than innocence: they half jokingly pulled him to the ground and pummelled him with their hands.

For me, on a later expedition, there was personal tragedy ahead. I was on *raikoro* up the Waidina River some way from Naduru-loulou (I remember being sunburnt, although there was no sun, by the glare from the river). No sooner had the Tui Waidina (a loyal,

competent man of the highest rank on that river and the only
Fijian I knew to be cross-eyed) concluded the welcoming ceremony
at his chiefly village of Nabukaluka than a provincial constable
dismounted on the edge of the village and tied up his horse. He
came up to me, squatted down as custom dictated, and handed me
a letter from Nott enclosing a telegram from Leicester. It had been
sent by my father: I was shocked to read in it that my mother had
angina pectoris and would live for only a week.

Nott kindly asked in the note if he could do anything and
suggested that I return to Naduruloulou. There was in fact no
point in returning and, in my immediate reply carried on horse-
back, I requested him to send as fast as possible a telegram that I
wrote out. I had not heard from my mother for two or three
months but, because it was so difficult to get mail through on the
sea past German and Japanese submarines, this was not an
unusually long period. When the Japanese war interfered with the
leave Anne and I would normally have taken two years previously,
I had wondered whether her waving to me, with dignity and
bravery, from the Richmond Road, Leicester, window as the taxi
took me off *en route* to London and the docks in 1938 had been
the last sight I would have of her. Being so far away meant no
reduction, but perhaps an increase, in the grief I felt.

I explained to the worried-looking Fijians round me what had
happened, or was going to happen, and they could not have been
more considerate. I retired to the Tui's house, which he had by
custom vacated, and contemplated. When I re-emerged they asked
if I would prefer that the *meke*s (sitting dances by men and women
separately) be cancelled. I said that they were to continue and all
was to proceed normally. Solemnly they agreed. The *meke*s went
on until early morning and helped take my mind off the news a
little. When I expressed tiredness they readily agreed that I should
return to the Tui's house.

I had not been there a quarter of an hour, preparing for sleep
under the mosquito net, when there was a quiet little knock on the
door. It was a girl sent by the Tui to share time with me and
relieve the load of my grief. After about an hour, she retired.
Then, shortly afterwards but before I had gone to sleep, there was

223

another light, polite knock. It was another girl on the same mission. Again, after about an hour, she went. And then there was a third repetition. By the end of this all-night vigil, dawn was imminent. We had made it through the night, as the song goes. I was eternally grateful for such wonderful people.

Two days later, after having inspected some villages with the Tui, I returned to Naduruloulou where Anne had meanwhile received the ultimately expected news. I had received the telegram at Nabukaluka on 25 April: my mother had died on this date aged 73. Of her family of four, all sons, the eldest had died nearly 20 years earlier, Charles was unable through pressing war commitments at a high level to leave London and see her more than rarely, and I, the youngest, was 12,000 untraversable miles away. She had not seen me since I left England as long as six years ago. Only Eric, the third son, in a reserved occupation designing vital heating and ventilating equipment for war use and living in Leicester, was able to see her: he was alone with our father in being able to do so. It was a lonely end.

Given that the chances of an earlier end to the war had much improved, it was so sad that she had been unable to survive the remaining two years until our return. My cursing of the Japanese became even more vehement than before — and that had been pretty fierce: it has never ceased. On 10 January, Anne had written to my mother reporting that we had just had four Americans — two colonels, a major and a captain, to Christmas dinner with crackers and hats and saying: 'The news has improved so much just lately that I believe that we can safely think of coming home in so many months' time instead of so many years.' This was partly wishful thinking and partly to bolster up my mother's hopes. I do not know if she received it before she died.

There was now a chance — and a need in Nott's, as well as my, view when he suggested it — for Anne and me to take a couple of months' local leave. Christopher Legge, of whom more later, could relieve me, not for the only time.

I thought that the medical officer's house in Navua would make as pleasant a change as it would be possible to obtain anywhere. Though it had been unoccupied for years and hardly anyone ever

224

used it, it had been cleaned up for local leave purposes. Set on a hill, it had a view of rice fields and of the large bridge across the Navua River. Below the circuminsular road there was a bank on which to sunbathe (for limited periods in the scorching sun) and to relax. On the side of the river I would chat in Hindi with an Indian girl of about 14 washing clothes on a stone. Her features were classically superb, her poise for her age remarkable. She lived in the poorest shanty a few yards away. I must have been the only European to whom she had talked. I was also writing *Bronze and Clay*, a general book on the Pacific that has never been joined by me to my seven publications, but has been cannibalized in part for at least a couple of them, *Best Stories of the South Seas* (1967) and *The People from the Horizon: An Illustrated History of the Europeans among the South Sea Islanders* (1979), and for these random reminiscences. Anne enjoyed filling in her time typing it as I produced the chapters.

We developed a cosy evening habit of ambling down a cul-de-sac off the circuminsular road and walking alongside the Navua River to the minute Navua township and the Navua Hotel. After dinner we would play the betting card game, Newmarket, with the proprietors. We were the hotel's only visitors. Then we would amble back in the moonlight past the long-abandoned, short-lived, derelict sugar mill to the house on the hill and our two dogs.

The Navua Government Station on the beach at Naitonitoni (where the residential frontier had been drawn between Bill Burrows and Jack Bradley) was only a mile away, at the terminus of the cul-de-sac, and I went there in the middle of my leave to officiate at the Empire Day celebrations. On all government stations these always took the predictable form of girl guides and boy scouts parading before the flagstaff, with the administrative officer making a speech to uncomprehending children explaining the nature of the Empire. The odd adult would turn up more out of a sense of loyalty than curiosity.

Although not residents, we were invited to an Indian wedding near our temporary house — a feast of colour but monotonous, like perhaps all weddings. Indian music never seemed to my ear anything but discordant. We had been to a Tongan wedding in

Sawana, Lau, where the singing was harmonious, but never to a Fijian wedding.

Soon after this, via the Navua Government Station (our temporary house was not on the telephone), I received from the Colonial Secretary a telegram saying that I was to be posted to the Secretariat and should not return to Naduruloulou at the end of my local leave. I was to be Establishment Officer — quite the most pleasant of headquarters jobs for anyone with my limited seniority. It was a previous holder of the post who had advised sealed lips on touching Fiji soil in 1938. I had been luckily somewhat refreshed by the local leave as it was plainly to be hard work ahead under the closest scrutiny from the top. I was exhilarated by this news.

My second period at Naduruloulou had been extremely happy apart from my mother's death, and if I was to move this was the right time, given that leave to England (although due in 1942) still seemed certain to be postponed for years until Japan was defeated. And, in 1944, the likelihood of that happening appeared remote in the extreme. The Japanese would have to be driven back relentlessly and painfully slowly, island by island, to Japan and then, the greatest horror of all, Japan itself would have to be invaded over every square inch and totally suppressed — so time-consuming and annihilating for American and Allied personnel that it was something one dared not even contemplate.

On 22 April 1945, I wrote to Charles from the Secretariat in Suva:

> I'm taking advantage of a bitterly cold temperature of 75 degrees to use a burst of energy on this letter. We have just gone through a very humid, close summer when one is overdue for leave and overworked: little is left but inertia. The humidity has frequently been 99 per cent and it is that which devitalizes. I never thought that there would be a time when I would be nostalgic for grey bleak days in small quantities. ... The Fiji climate is undoubtedly healthy, particularly for its Fiji-born population but for us exiles under wartime stress (which has been largely one of worry for

226

you) it is neurasthenia-making. . . . Did you read Pamela
Hansford Johnson's ecstatic review of *Stranger and Brother*
in *The Windmill*?

The last sentence was a reference to his future wife's reception of
one of Charles's works (later retitled *George Passant*) at the start
of his leviathan *Strangers and Brothers* series.

Our bungalow in the Government Domain of Suva was next
door to the new Chief Justice Sir Claud Seton (1945–9) and his
wife Eleanor, a pleasantly unpresumptuous lady with whom I
would chat over the hibiscus hedge while we were mutually
gardening. Anne and I had engaged the comely part-European,
Wati Witherow, as our housegirl — referred to earlier in connection with *draunikau* (witchcraft).

It was a short car ride to the fine mass of Government Buildings,
now six years old and pristine white. The Secretariat occupied the
place of honour in them next to the lofty clock tower within
which the Colonial Secretary was ensconced at an altitude
considered fitting for his elevated status. But, although having
been held by the town to be at least twice as large as was
necessary, the buildings were now becoming seriously cramped.
The war had brought in special departments, which after it tended
to defy extinction.

My duties as Establishment Officer, steeped almost exclusively in
confidential personal files on subjects of promotion and demotion,
accomplishments and misdemeanours, successes and failures (Anne
was helping the Colonial Secretary with all other non-personnel
confidential files), were demanding, but relieved, however, by interviewing stenographers and other applicants for clerical positions,
which therefore meant being visited by attractive, ambitious young
women. Some of these had gravitated from very isolated parts of
the colony, like Dianne Marie St Aubyn from Buca Bay, a chocolate-
box beauty in a wide-brimmed picture hat, who literally wept on
my shoulder in the hope that she would not have to return to the
plantation. I could not place her in the Secretariat, where the
standard of stenography was very high, but I was able to appoint
her to a department in Suva.

Suva's were the brightest (some would say the only) lights in the colony. There was no competition for it as a capital. Already engaged as stenographers was a galaxy of looks — the statuesque Lesley Miller, whose father was Town Clerk, Suva, later to become a planter on Taveuni; the curvaceous Loloma Viti Witherow, daughter of a Rewa dairy farmer; the minute and mischievous Sheila and Freda McHugh twins; Joan Teulon, granddaughter of a name known in English Victorian architecture; and the two Hopewell daughters of a copra planter on Koro island. I was the first to introduce part-Europeans, including the stately yet irreverent Linda Caine (whose father, a photographer, had been a leper on Makogai island), the effervescent Betty Emberson who became a Hansard reporter and married Kenneth Bain, an administrative officer junior to me, and Betty Whiteside from a fine family so fair as not to look Euronesian. These appointments not only had an effect on the Secretariat (they were in other departments too) but also on the Suva Tennis Club: my introducing them into that European preserve, where there were no Indians (who played well), Chinese or Fijians (who played not at all), did not make me too popular.

No Indians, by unwritten principle of very long standing, not to become a shibboleth until near independence, worked in the Secretariat. The Fijians in it were the *crème de la crème*. Their strength was their disinterest in the secrets with which the Secretariat primarily dealt. They were led by a middle-aged Lauan, Ulaiasi (Ulysses) Vosabalavu, who took off his glasses to peer at the files an inch from his eyes. A diplomatic helper in my controversial foundation of the Suva Cricket Association in 1940, he kept the Fijian staff in top order with his unfailing joviality. The custodian of the archives was a Lauan and entirely the opposite in temperament. Aisea Savou was never known to laugh: gravenfaced, he spent most of his time in the chilly vaults among the archives.

Ratu Penaia Ganilau (the son of a Roko Tui Cakaudrove by a commoner who was not his wife), who had been there from 1937 until 1942, had now left for military service. He later gained the DSO in Malaya and went on to become a colonel, which until the

1980s was the highest rank any Fijian officer had ever attained and, apart from him held only by Ratu Sukuna and Ratu Edward Cakobau. His Secretariat training (which imbued in him a lifelong sense of confidentiality) and unfailing *bonhomie* would have made him less likely to have been overwhelmed by the files and verbal procedure that descended on him as Governor-General in the 1980s. It was he who had given me the cup of *yaqona* on the second of my first two appearances at the Secretariat in the old Government Buildings in 1938 (on the first occasion it had been his predecessor as Governor-General, Ratu Sir George Cakobau), both of them delivering it, as was the custom, squatting down and clapping their hands. It would have seemed incredible then for either them, or me, to imagine that they would reach the highest government position in the land. But in the modesty that Fijian eminence never loses they would recall to me their early days as the bearers of a cup of *kava* to a cadet of one or two days' standing for his first taste.

The Secretariat was no longer dominated by C. W. T. Johnson, who had been exiled to the post of consul in Tonga just before retirement after almost a lifetime in the vortex of administrative manipulation (without passing a single one of the examinations he insisted on all others passing).

The Colonial Secretary was just changing. Newboult, whom I thought full of discernment, was recalled to England to be prepared for posting to Malaya: it will be remembered that he had been on Duff Cooper's staff in Singapore just before the city was captured. In 1944, John Nicoll had come to be Colonial Secretary. Before this he had been a district officer in North Borneo and Tanganyika and Deputy Colonial Secretary, Trinidad, and later went on to become Colonial Secretary, Hong Kong, and (as Sir John) Governor of Singapore. Slim, angular with an extremely large nose that seemed to guide his movements to and from his office in the eyrie directly under the Government Buildings' clock in its tower, he was brisk and decisive in his minuting. Other than my particular duties, including the interviewing, I found that life in the Secretariat revolved almost wholly around drafting dispatches to the Secretary of State for the Colonies for signature

229

by the Governor (I learned to have Roget's *Thesaurus* at hand to relieve the stereotyped jargon), and files coming 'in' for minuting, files going 'out' minuted and files 'pending'.

I was wisely advised by Assistant Colonial Secretary Harold Cooper, a Billy Bunter-looking man who was not otherwise always wise, never to put off into 'pending' the more difficult files simply because they were more difficult. He pointed out correctly that they had to be dealt with sometime: so why not now? On hot long days it was a temptation to let the more intricate files mount up and to deal with the easiest ones first. But he was right, though it took as much energy to face them as to start and write a book (always the most difficult stage, pushing oneself through that pain barrier). It was Cooper who persuaded me at this time to found and edit the *Journal of the Civil Servants' Association for Fiji and the Western Pacific* (I never could resist the lure of print).

The sole user in government of red ink, the Governor, was mild-looking, imperturbable Sir Alexander William George Herder Grantham. He was, however, unique among governors in Fiji's history in that, on dipping his pen in the viceregal red inkwell, he signed his minutes to the Colonial Secretary (who in turn transmitted them to the assistant secretaries) with a regal single G for Grantham and never with the energy-exhausting A. W. G. H. G. Lazlo Biro had yet to invent his pen. The colour conveyed an imperiousness that was out of character in his case.

There were four assistant secretaries. Section A dealt with war matters, Section B (myself under the name of Establishment Officer) with personnel, discipline, protocol, appointments and dismissals, Section C with the other remaining subjects including being clerk to the Executive and Legislative Councils, and Section F with finance. Section D, dealing with leave, came in later when leave really opened up, but I had to deal with the first (and, I must honestly record, the most difficult because of the huge log jam) arrangements for it in Section B.

I wrote to Charles from the Secretariat on 10 October 1945:

It will indeed be a negative epic of the war if it has failed to interrupt seriously the *Strangers and Brothers* series. We

230

look forward greatly to *Charles March* [the book of a Jewish family into which he was drawn, retitled *The Conscience of the Rich*] and *The Masters*. ... It is a sad fact that promotion only comes through being in the Secretariat.

One might as well attend Whitehall offices throughout one's life from 8.00 a.m. to 5.00 p.m. Mine happens to be the only interesting work in the Secretariat — dealing with people, their frailties and strengths. But there is no need to have come out the enormous distance that I have in order to do Establishment work. It is, it's true, a change from the district life — which is, however, the real Fiji with an individuality that is rapidly fading but is still full of interest. I have never really acclimatized myself to a rigid office existence, pushing through in office hours as many files as is possible so as to avoid having to push the remainder through in one's leisured moments. I value my leisure far too much. ... I should perhaps have come into it [the Secretariat] when I would have been fresher — on perhaps return from long leave. ... Jo Sukuna [I addressed him as such to Charles: it was not until 1948 at the time of the New Zealand cricket tour that he asked me to call him Jo] lends me his *Observer* with articles by Robertson-Glasgow which amuse us both considerably. ... Anne sends her love.

And then again, on 2 February 1946:

I shall be glad to leave the Secretariat where it is a tradition that the place should be understaffed even in peace-time. The Governor blandly told us at a dinner to one of us on transfer to Mauritius that a Secretariat officer can earn promotion only by working at least four hours overtime a day beyond the hours of 8.30 to 1.00 and 2.00 to 4.00 when one is expected to work flat out unremittingly and largely on unconstructive, soulless (and, I believe) entirely clerical routine.

Immediately afterwards, I wrote:

Jo Sukuna, CBE, received a K in the New Year's Honours and is now Sir Lala S. He and I form a Robertson-Glasgow style admiration circle and his knowledge of cricketers' temperaments, initials and achievements is the best that I have come across among virtually complete exiles from the first-class game.

The prospect of honours, not in Sukuna's case as he worked at his own dignified, whimsical pace as Secretary for Fijian Affairs (which the post of Adviser on Native Affairs had become), was the carrot urging on the mules overladen with files.

If one put work in a position overriding all other action, even domestic or family obligations, and if one did not blot the copy-book, the ordinary administrative officer, especially with some Secretariat experience, could expect an OBE (widely known as Other Blokes' Efforts) at about 45 and before retirement at 55 a CMG (Call Me God). The earlier MBE (My Bloody Efforts) stage was usually leapfrogged and was the reward for officers generally other than in the administration.

The stages of KCMG and GCMG (dubbed by some anonymous wit in the Colonial Office with time to spare for pondering over such flippancies, one suspects, Kindly Call Me God and God Calls Me God) were reserved for governors. When colonies obtained independence their governors fortuitously incumbent at a particular moment in a colony's history automatically became Governors-General with a GCMG.

Luck was even more noticeable if one's posting to a colony coincided with a sovereign's visit and one was involved in the organization for the monarch. Then there could be expected to be received from him (or her) the MVO, CVO, KCVO (if Governor) and GCVO (if Governor-General). However long-term the prospect of an honour or however far away retirement was, these were (no one could deny without being a liar) considerations for keeping one's nose over the files until one was nearly submerged. 'File stamina' was a special, if not covetable, way of administrative life, next after stamina as in general life.

Because it dealt with personnel and discipline, more confidentiality surrounded my section, with its red files, than any other section (with buff files), although some of Section A's green files dealing with the war were obviously secret. My office was one of the few to be kept locked when I was out. The rest of the vast Government Buildings would remain mostly open overnight, with the empty stone corridors of power ringing sharply under one's shoes on nocturnal visits. Of course, stores and bars in the town (and in districts) would be closed firmly, but not offices in either the districts or the capital, such was public indifference to their contents. Most of them, of course, would have safes for cash and confidential papers but in the total absence of air-conditioning zephyrs were too precious to be locked out.

I had an impressive young Fijian as my confidential clerk. Over several years in the post he was not for a moment indiscreet. Misiwata R. D. Vula (Moon) of handsome, eager features had two gleaming rows of teeth — more than I would have thought possible to crowd into a mouth and widely displayed in his huge, regular smile. It was a delight to have him work for me. Later in the 1950s he joined the Fiji military forces and went into the Malayan emergency as a lieutenant to fight against the terrorist guerrillas, from where he would write to me in England graphic, spirited, happy letters. I was astounded to discover when these stopped that he had gone on leave to his home in Nasigatoka and had died, at barely 30, after having turned his face to the wall.

It was understood that he had been *draunikau*d — this psychological killing has already been described. It was remarkable that a man of his acquaintance with Europeans, and now with the outside world of Malaya opened up to him in the army, should have succumbed. There were rumours that he had been involved with an uncle in a dispute over family land boundaries. Though a commoner, Vula would have made an intelligent, imaginative leader of his people for the years after independence when quality was in demand. I had taught him cricket. He slavishly modelled himself on my style, unconsciously making a caricature of my stepping exaggeratedly far forward or as far back as possible for maximum benefit of time with which to play the ball. With his long legs spread out in doing so, he resembled a giant spider and, from elementary ineptitude, he made himself quite effective — almost reaching state level in Negri Sembilan.

Old Man Vosa, as he was affectionately known in the Secretariat where he presided over the clerks, had joined Ratu George Cakobau, Charles Cheng (a partner in the leading Chinese merchandise firm of Joong Hing Loong), J. F. Grant (the Christian Indian owner of the Lilac Cinema), the portly Harold Cooper and myself in establishing the first all-races social club in Suva. The minute founding it said that 'A number of Suva gentlemen resolved to form a Club which would be known as the Union Club.' As a vice-president, Ratu Sukuna, now knighted, gave it his blessing. I was on its small founding committee, along with Vosa, Cooper and Bramhanand Raghvanand, brother of the charming Nadi sub-accountant, Bhaskaranand Basavanand.

I had taken over from Raghvanand occupation of my first bungalow in Naduruloulou and he had been one of the panel examining my oral Hindi. A genial Brahmin, he was Sukuna's right-hand Indian, his eyes and ears for the other main race in the colony, Raghu, as he was known, and John Amputch, a Catholic, were the only Indians as our co-founders. The club had to triumph against some European sniping. It still survives, having forgotten the traumatic moments of its being founded, for, in a social sense, interracial fluidity (if not harmony) has altered out of all recognition since those days.

The military presence was still paramount in Suva. Just as one's cricket opponents were almost all army or air-force personnel, so too did the trucks and jeeps far outnumber the civilian cars in Suva's streets.

One outstanding occasion, which will never be repeated, was the presentation, on Albert Park in front of serried ranks of troops, of the Victoria Cross, gained posthumously by the Lauan corporal, Sefanaia Sukanaivalu (ironically this means Return from the War). His two aged parents (his father was the expert on coconut crabs whom we have met) had never left their island of Yacata for the capital before; they squatted meekly on the floor of the dais in the middle of the vast park while the Governor, Alexander Grantham, bent over almost double in his tight white colonial governor's uniform (I could not conceal from myself the irreverent belief that his trousers must split) to hand down the award. Ratu Sukuna had previously read the citation on the microphone. The troops marched past in the longest display to be seen in Fiji until very recent times, when the army is reported to have built up to proportions that are questioned.

Grantham had been Colonial Secretary in Bermuda, Jamaica and Nigeria — an unusually varied run of posts at that level — and brought modest, unpompous touches compared with Sir Philip Mitchell's swollen self-importance. Mitchell's stout South African wife had, by contrast, been in the background and was once mistaken for a servant by an American visitor to the GH kitchen, asking: 'Say, cook, could I have a glass of water?' Grantham's American wife may have been petite and very deaf, but she was strong-willed and managed, despite wartime economies, to work wonders in white with the repainting and furnishing of the interior of Government House.

Grantham, partnered by me in a friendly tennis match on the court of the enigmatic Henry Vaskess, Secretary of the Western Pacific High Commission, who was an absolute loner (he lived with a part-European) given only to rare exclusive tennis on his own court, suffered virtually the same fate as had Sir Owen Corrie when playing with me. I served not on to the top of his bald head but hard into the middle of His Excellency's back. Less prominent a serve than to Corrie's head, but more prominent in the sense of striking a Governor compared with a Chief Justice.

This bland man, who managed to secure after Fiji almost the top gubernatorial post ranking after Nigeria and Kenya, that of Hong Kong, whence he had started as a cadet, had a rather rasping voice. It carried at a party. On Fiji Independence Day in 1970 at Marlborough House, London, we re-met for the first time since 1948 and I introduced him to Charles, who was amused (I was embarrassed) by his saying loud and clear, 'Tell me, Snow, who was the man who succeeded me? He wasn't very good, was he?' He was referring to a Governor with whom I had got on as well as I had with Grantham. It was not an accurate assertion and I was aware that, although he had long since died, his widow, whom I liked, might be within earshot of such a penetrating voice.

There were now not many Americans left behind in Fiji. But those who were still present collected successfully many of the most attractive women. For part-Europeans and Europeans alike, it was a promise of paradise. Among those snapped up was the lithesome, pearl-skinned Olga Crooks of mixed blood, perhaps the most alluring woman of that period. She would surely have been Miss Fiji had that title existed. But the locals were not the only ones to be experiencing changes when so much had seemed to stand still in the long years between 1942 and 1945.

No sooner had the announcement of Roosevelt's death been received than there came the incomprehensible news of an atomic bomb on Hiroshima, followed before we could grasp its significance by the second one on Nagasaki. This was the finest news I ever heard. I do not mind how reactionary this statement might appear to some. Largely incomprehensible as it was, it was indubitably the best thing that could have happened. It was arguable that it should have been followed up in the surrender terms with occupation of Tokyo and the execution after trial of Emperor Hirohito, Commander-in-Chief and of course privy to all Japanese plans and codes of behaviour. Of that I personally have not the slightest doubt.

My feelings are reinforced by the growing evidence that the Japanese are aiming covertly and overtly — it is only too apparent if one studies them without paranoia — at domination of the Pacific, including Australia, of which their loss of the war deprived them. Theirs has been a peacetime victory over America and its allies in influence over the Pacific and other parts of the world. I remain uncompromisingly and unapologetically anti-Japanese. As cruel and intrinsically barbaric a nation as that, with of course a few individual exceptions such as the saviour of the Singapore Botanical Gardens and my friend John Corner, described in volume 2, should have been emasculated and denationalized. It is the old lesson of Berlin not having been occupied after the First World War. Had it been, the Second World War might never have started.

There is no doubt too, though I could not agree later with Charles about this, that the two atomic bombs were necessary as urgently as possible. Dropping them not only patently saved the lives of many thousands of European and American prisoners of war who were dying daily at a great, accelerating rate, but also the lives of perhaps millions of the Allied forces who would have had to invade the besieged, fanatical Japanese fighting to the last man in their country. It was clear that advance warning about the first bomb had had no effect. It was equally clear that the actual dropping of one on Hiroshima had not been sufficiently heeded. There had to be at least another dropped.

After Nagasaki there was a case, in the context of saving Allied lives, for similar bombs on two or three more military targets spread through Japan, including one on Tokyo itself and its divine Shinto regime, with necessarily devastating results likely to stop all Japanese mania not then but for decades, if not forever. The case would too have been for avoiding the palace of the Emperor so that he could be captured alive for trial for the same end as the extreme Nazi leaders received at Nuremberg. The unprovoked Japanese anti-racial fanaticism was as unforgivable as the anti-Jewish and anti-Gypsy mania of the Germans. How insensitive could we be to have invited Hirohito to England on a State visit after the war and to have Prince Philip represent Britain at his funeral?

The Netherlands showed more sense, perspective and sympathy with the sufferers to this day by refusing to be represented. No pusillanimity there. We shamefully did not show the same firmness of mind and moral courage. As for Germans supporting Hitler, there can similarly be no forgiveness for Japanese (the odd dissenter always excepted) supporting Hirohito. One cannot say that about the past sufficiently pointedly for the future. There can be no mawkishness here, even, or especially, for those of extra sentimental proclivities like myself. It was heartening to see that, on the new Japanese Emperor's State visit to the Netherlands in 1991, Queen Beatrix ignored the protocol of the State banquet to include in her speech Holland's disgust over the Emperor's lack of apology and compensation for Japanese viciousness and barbarism.

With two bombs dropped, the Japanese were even then not as contrite and subjugated as they should have been. It was not a case of Supreme Allied Commander General MacArthur showing generosity of action, but complete unimaginativeness for which the reckoning has not yet been reached. We did not have this in perspective at the time. There was just immense relief that the world had opened up again. The jubilation of the non-Japanese in the Pacific was even greater than over the earlier defeat of Germany.

Leave always depended on the 'exigencies of the Service', a fine saving phrase. It was never a right, always a privilege. I was high up on the list for it now that ships were slowly beginning to operate between New Zealand, Australia and England, although naturally priority had to be given to returning released prisoners of war, so many in irrecoverably fragile physical and mental conditions, and war-weary troops. But by 1945, three years overdue and at the end of a seven-year period of work with only the two months' break at Navua, I was promised leave next after two of my contemporaries, Collins (still shell-shocked after the episode on Ocean Island) and another (his relations with Fijians and Indians and others were an insurmountable psychological block to him: he should have been retired prematurely or never selected originally), who were thought to be in greater need. The other three of my contemporaries of 1938, like the latter of the two just mentioned, had not been in districts overwhelmed by war pressure. Of the six composing the unprecedentedly large intake of cadets in 1938, only Collins and myself could reasonably be regarded as having been most directly involved. The question of need for leave was only one of fine degree.

I had developed, perhaps as soon as I felt that I could relax a little once the war had ended, a concealed phobia about attending formal functions, such as Government House dinners, which I would never have thought possible because I used to enjoy them greatly, more for what I could observe at them than for any other reason. And, indeed, I had enjoyed actually organizing them as extra ADC six years earlier. I now tended to avoid congregations of people in rooms, a kind of claustrophobia, though not dissimilar to agoraphobia (literally, dislike of crowds as in the Greek marketplace *agora*), which enveloped me suddenly after overworking 20 years later. In earlier days I suppose that tropical neurasthenia would have been the term used but I kept myself away from doctors. Anne was in reasonably good health. Her sojourn had been six years compared with my eight.

She had enjoyed being confidential clerk to Colonial Secretary John Nicoll in the last year and had been to classes in Fijian, following which she took the government examination. She was the only woman ever to pass it — extraordinarily, as she was, of all the candidates sitting for it, not an established civil servant: her job was only a wartime temporary one. Her helping me to pass the examination in 1941 in Lau had been of inestimable value to her.

Our sights were now on England. The Leicestershire County Cricket Club had indicated that it would find me a game or two at a minimum. We were facing up to the problem of having to put our dogs into quarantine for the six months' leave, plus two months for travelling (one month to England and one month return), with the probability of their not recognizing us on our return, when suddenly Bonzo, my favourite, in our Suva bungalow where he revelled in the garden developed an unidentifiable illness.

He lay down on the verandah one night out of breath. I lifted his head and, with a shaking death-rattle, he died in my arms. After the veterinary surgeon had seen him next day and done a post mortem, I buried him in the garden. His heart had been choked by the heart-worm transmitted by the bites of mosquitoes. Then, within a fortnight, his female companion died of a fever equally suddenly and was buried with him: they had had a joyous if very brief life together. It was for us a sadness but we consoled ourselves that having to part with them for eight months and return to them would have been difficult.

One now signed the Governor's Book 'p.p.c.' (*pour prendre congé*), which could, but seldom did, lead to an invitation to hospitality at Government House: it was a useless convention, with an orderly taking in the book from the verandah of the Governor's office nightly. To my knowledge, at least one governor, Harry Luke, never looked at it. Not to sign when going on leave could, in theory, incur a reprimand, but I never knew it to do so. Fijians and Indians never took the taxi up the hill for the purpose, but then they seldom went on overseas leave.

The time came for departure for Auckland on the *Matua* (the Union Steamship Company of New Zealand's 4250-ton banana and copra ship) which normally had one-class accommodation for 70 and had throughout the war (it was built in 1936) been the sole regular communicating link between Fiji, Tonga, Samoa and New Zealand, a praiseworthy record indeed with Japanese craft hovering about. I had had a good few dealings on leave matters with the manager of the company in Suva and he fitted us in. MOF was marked on our tickets. We did not know what this meant, but, on reaching our cabin, we realized that it was a one-berth cabin with a mattress on the floor for the second person. The ship was perforce taking many times more its quota than it normally did. Our voyage to Auckland and journey by train from there to Wellington were comfortable and full of exciting prospects. We left from Wellington after dinner with Nicoll, who was also going on leave to England, but by the Blue Star Line's Cape Horn route.

Our ship was the nearly obsolescent 15,320-ton Shaw, Savill & Albion one-class steamer *Akaroa*, which dated from 1914 and until 1932 had been called the *Euripides* (it lasted until 1954). I had not been in a ship as big. Its normal capacity was 190 passengers: it was crammed with forces personnel returning to England from New Zealand and released prisoners of war of the Japanese who had been recuperating in New Zealand. At our saloon table was an ex-prisoner of war reunited with a pretty daughter, Jean Booth, of about six. His wife had died in New Zealand. To our discomfort, Lieutenant Booth (I forget his first name) had to decline every item on the menu for each meal. The only substance he could possibly eat was rice in its plainest form, which had been his sole diet for the previous three years.

Our great friend, Ernie (Long Jim) Turner, manager of Cable & Wireless, Suva, was happily with us. The ship had few luxuries. It had recently been decommissioned from war duties. We had been advised that, as there were no deckchairs for the month-long voyage, we should buy our own in Wellington. There was therefore the unusual scene of all passengers climbing the gangway with a deckchair under his or her arm as though for a day excursion. The voyage was by way of Pitcairn's Islands, but calling was abandoned because of turbulent weather. Sea hawks came aboard from the Galapagos group, 600 miles away. These and an albatross, immediately seasick on its landing on our swaying deck, were the only fauna seen until green finches reached us about 400 miles away from the vast Gulf of Panama.

At the Panama Canal, we went ashore three times in the day to Panama City opposite Balboa, where we saw a Carib Indian carrying a marmoset on his knee in a bus. As big as a hand with a bushy tail as long as an arm, it chattered shrilly and continuously like a bird. There was a great diversity of racial types — American Indians (Panamanians), Negroes, Spaniards and East Indians, including Sikhs. Spanish was the lingua franca. Going through the Gatun Locks I saw a bright green lizard on the massive gates and black butterflies with iridescent green bands on their wings. Leaving the Panama coast at nightfall, there were violent purple electric storms over the Colombian mountain peaks.

Although we were 20 miles off land, biplane dragonflies with earwig-like nippers at the end of their tails and wild-eyed, agitated moths of Fiji size and colouring, plus some black ones with white chevrons, came aboard with cicadas for the ride. By daylight, Venezuela was seen, then Aruba before we tied up to take on oil in Curaçao. Willemstad, the capital, seemed aflame in a deep red sunset. We had tinned squid, I can't think why, for dinner there.

There was no more land, except the Azores distantly in the Atlantic. At this stage of the voyage, recovering from my run-down, not fully fit condition while in the Pacific, where it was also rough, I won the mixed and men's doubles finals of deck tennis. To my surprise, I had been defeated in the men's singles final by a 55-year-old New Zealand wool buyer, who commuted twice a year from New Zealand to London by ship for the wool auctions. He was quite professional. Somehow, I also managed to be in the finals of the men's doubles of deck quoits, while Anne won with her partner the women's doubles. All the way from Fiji to New Zealand and from New Zealand to within sight of the Lizard, the sea and sky had been cobalt blue (other than the day ahead of Pitcairn). At the Lizard off Cornwall it became grey in sea and sky. I could scarcely wait to see England, and all it meant, again.

10
Turning Turtle and Welcoming Lepers

I was taken aback by Charles's pale, wan, tired face, but he was about to have his first overseas holiday since before the war. He loaned us his flat at 20 Hyde Park Place overlooking the park. But first we had to go to Leicester to see my father and Anne's parents.

My brother Eric whisked me off to the Leicestershire ground at Grace Road. Regrettably, my beloved Aylestone Road venue had been partly built over. The new secretary had little knowledge of cricket, or of the county before the war. It was also abundantly clear that the professionals were not going to relinquish any places to an amateur. Before the war, nothing revitalized a side of jaded pros more than amateurs knocking on the door. As a token of the promise of matches made to me in Fiji before coming on leave, I was fitted into the full county team for a charity match. Though I had not played on pure grass since 1938, I was put in first and, before rain caused abandonment, saw the first four of the regular team (Lester, G., Tompkin, M., Prentice, F. T. and Jackson V. E. — initials after names were *de rigueur* to describe professionals on the score-cards) all out for single figures in the score of 44 for 4, P. A. Snow's share being 11 not out. I was given no other chance.

There was an ironic sequel to Leicestershire's cold shoulder. I had resumed playing for the Gentlemen of Leicestershire (the strongest team outside the county ground) for whom before the

war I never had a failure. For a match with Northamptonshire
2nd XI, they turned up at Northampton, through some mix-up,
with 12, including me, while Northants only had 10. So it was
arranged that I play for Northants. Having made 50 without
blemish or worry as opening bat while others failed to make
double figures, I was watching alone in front of the pavilion when
the secretary, Lieutenant-Colonel Alleyne St George Coldwell,
came and sat with me. He was wearing the purple, green and
black striped tie of the Stragglers of Asia, a club that has elected
me as an honorary member because I met the prerequisite of six
years' residence, or playing, east of Suez.

Immediately, he said that he liked my technique and applic-
ability to the game and offered me terms to play for the Northamptonshire County team. P. E. Murray-Willis had already been
installed as captain. I had played with him before the war when he
was regarded as an eccentric, flopping about in a friendly manner
here and there. Disenchantment about him had by now set in for
Northants who wanted a successor. Coldwell told me that he was
not offering me professional status but that of an amateur with
'expenses' in lieu of a salary. These did not amount to as much as
my government salary and I explained that I was on leave from
Fiji where my career lay. Pressing on, Coldwell stated that I would
be captain as soon as Murray-Willis could be decently discarded.
Murray-Willis had recently made himself conspicuous versus
Surrey by pursuing a ball with his peculiar flailing arms and legs,
making little or no progress on the turf and even less than progress
when he stopped in the demented-looking chase to retrieve his cap
which had fallen off.

When I declined the offer with regret and thanks, A. W. Childs-
Clarke, who had played a little for Middlesex years before, was
appointed captain for 1947 with no effect on Northamptonshire's
melancholy record of scarcely a win for over a decade. Then of
course they got it right with the appointment of the dynamic
Freddie Brown. But Northants had shown me greater consideration than the county of my birth. I had meanwhile narrowly
missed another chance of entering first-class cricket, this time on a
regular basis.

So we returned to London. Marvellous, we thought, as we revelled in the vast number of people. It is a cliché to state that for us there was magic in the air. Every night we would stay out, absorbing the sights, sounds and smells, and returning to the flat's dignified location stimulated to the full.

We visited the Fiji contingent's camp for the Victory Parade and saw Sukuna, and Edward and George Cakobau. As we knew little about London, Edward, who had studied the underground as though it were a map of the Solomon Islands' battle terrain, was our guide. We were invited to play for Sir Pelham Warner's XI. Edward wore his *sulu* and, although it was cold and damp, was barefooted. A Pathé News reel tended to focus on them and we saw ourselves for the first time on film. Sir Pelham Warner, editor of *The Cricketer*, and assistant editor Arthur Langford were charmed by Ted, who in turn found them warm and kind friends. Ted stayed on, with Penaia Ganilau, for a one-year Colonial Administration course at Oxford.

I was invited back to Leicester as the youngest person ever to present the prizes at Newton's speech day. In the course of what I suppose was trying to steer away from giving the type of oration of which I had heard so many, I said that I was more accustomed to speaking in Fijian than in English, sometimes making more than three speeches a day, but admitted that it would be hardly palatable for the audience (of 2000) if I did just that.

Too soon came the date for our return on the New Zealand Shipping Company's *Rakaia* (10,000 tons) from the Royal Albert Docks. We were deprived by two days of a first Christmas in England for over eight years. This trip was again via Curaçao through the Panama Canal, with again a fascinating visit to Panama City. There were only 40 passengers, but a doctor was obliged to be on board when in excess of 12, which was just as well as Anne was now pregnant. Also on board were Kingsley and Jane Roth, good friends since 1940. He was an administrative officer senior to me and most knowledgeable about Fijian custom. A Christ's man, quarter Jewish of Hungarian *émigré* descent, while he was DC Rewa a medical board had forced him out of Fiji after he contracted Weil's disease, which is transmitted by rats.

244

This had been contrived by the jealous C. W. T. Johnson. When Luke became Governor, he secretly manœuvred Roth back to Fiji. I knew this as only Luke and I were privy to the confidential cablegrams I decoded between him and the Secretary of State. Luke told me not to mention a word to anyone, least of all to Johnson, a leading Mason, with Masonry as insidious as elsewhere, who was flabbergasted to see Kingsley again. Such was Service intrigue.

This time there was an unexpected stopoff at the remotest colony in Britain's imperial history — Pitcairn's Islands (this term is carefully stated because more than one island is named after their first European discoverer, a midshipman). It came under the jurisdiction of the Governor of Fiji. As the ship's medical officer had been asked by wireless to look at an injured young girl, we were consequently able to buy pineapples (the best in the world) and wood carvings, and to leave letters with cash for stamps. Their language was practically impossible to follow for two reasons. First, the islanders spoke a mixture of Tahitian and English and used words, such as 'nary' and 'tarry', that dated back in their ultimate isolation to the time of Christian's mutiny on the *Bounty* in 1789. And second, they were virtually toothless. It would be supremely ironical, bearing in mind its mutinous origin, if this were to be the last colony of the most widespread empire in history.

It was then from New Zealand to Suva and a posting to Section F (finance) in the Secretariat and to the Southern District headquarters in Suva superseding Naduruloulou. At our house on Old Hospital Hill (since bulldozed into Walu Bay) we had a memorable visit from a fine stag beetle. As I was out at an evening meeting Anne had a mah-jong four. All was proceeding smoothly in the hot sultry night until a pair of giant mandibles could be seen coming over the open window ledge. Gradually, the whole creature climbed up and over — to fly about wildly inside. Fiji has the largest flying insects in the world: this was one. The giant stag beetle lumbered about while the mah-jong players disintegrated. It was suggested that Anne should get her tennis racquet. A few swipes with it were ineffective.

Our elegant neighbour, Averil Hewitt-Dutton, wife of the

inspector of mines (both were Australians), had that morning been given an elaborate coiffure. It is well known that just as stag beetles stick their mandibles through shirts and have to be made to loosen their grip by a lit match being held near their rears (if not too near the shirts), once they land in hair this has to be cut to force out the beetles. Averil, clutching her hair, asked Anne if she had a tennis racquet cover. This was put over Averil's hairdo. Then all four retreated into the only wholly mosquito-proof room in the house — our bedroom — where they waited until I returned.

I managed to put a large empty jam jar over the beetle and put in some nail polish remover. The acetone would render the creature immobile and I could keep the beetle as a fine specimen. The jar made airtight, the five-inch long, shiny, brown beetle was left in it for three days, which I judged long enough to have knocked it out. When the cap was twisted off the jar, the insect moved from it to the table and then jetted off into the garden. Whether it survived we did not know, but it deserved its liberty. Apparently their carapaces contain air cells to help revive such rude human assaults on them.

I had seen only one before when it had joined in at table tennis after dinner in a Suva resident's house soon after my arrival in Fiji. Then it had tried to help me by flinging itself into the shirt on the back of an opponent who was withstanding my spin rather too well. A lit match held behind its posterior made it release its mandibles, enabling the game to proceed and me to win by a close margin. As a former ally, this representative of the stag beetle species was therefore only half-heartedly dealt with me on this occasion. I was, unlike Humphrey Evans, positively not a pin-sticker of flying or other creatures. One caught by Humphrey remains a supreme example at the Natural History Museum, London.

Being in Suva enabled me to found the Fiji Cricket Association with the support of Ratu Sir Lala Sukuna, Clive Brewster, Ben Marks and Long Jim Turner. This was the first nationwide multi-racial sporting organization in Fiji's history. I was also sufficiently refreshed by my leave to be able to found the Fiji Table Tennis Association in Suva. This was the only game the Chinese joined in:

they contributed a dozen clubs and competition was intense. I observed at the table that unless I attacked immediately after the serve with a smash their tactics would wear me down. As it was, they never managed to devise a defensive reply and I was able to establish myself as the leading player. To my pleasure, the next best, before about a dozen Chinese, was an NMP, Benijamini (Benjamin) Lomaloma, who had adopted a style that lay somewhere between mine and theirs.

We invariably shopped at Chinese stores. With his partner Charles Louis Cheng, consul for China, the ever-smiling owner of Joong Hing Loong's, C. H. Gordon Honson, used to put on 20-course seated banquets at his house for 50 or more guests. So, through them, we arranged for food parcels to be sent to our embattled, rationed families during the ferociously savage winter we had narrowly missed. At this time Charles was having an interesting correspondence with Richard Aldington, referring to a distinguished writer's famous son by a name I cannot reveal. It is a literary secret locked up with me, probably now alone of all people. It would be a minor literary sensation if disclosed.

I was pleased to be able to take my friend, Reg Caten, who was attached to the Southern District office, to Bau: he had deep historical interests, which included looking out for acquisitions on behalf of the Fiji Museum. After a courtesy call on Ranadi Litia Cakobau, we looked at all the graves on the hill reserved for the highest in rank. I am glad that I did this because in the 1980s the hill was flattened and the graves made into a mausoleum. Even in 1947, though, the Bauans were in fact talking of erasing the solitary hill, which was Bau's main landmark.

This was my third time round in the Southern District (it had previously been known as the Rewa District), which I liked for its variety of peoples and terrain. One person I could have done without meeting, however, was Emosi (Amos) Saurara from Tailevu. He was a lunatic in the mental hospital, to which he had been committed after having incited the people of Daku, the village of which he had been head and where he had run a profitable business supplying firewood from the mangrove swamp, to truss up some tribal opponents and deliver them like cannibal victims to the chiefly headquarters on Bau in the pre-Cession manner. He had gone off his head suddenly and with religious overtones. We had known each other when he had been running his enterprising business and, hearing that I was now in the Southern District again, asked from the hospital that I should see him.

Mental hospitals are appalling places: I have the utmost sympathy with those who work there, but I could scarcely forgive the attendant who took me past gibbering idiots and near vegetables to a locked cell and then left me with this demoniac, in no way morose or disconsolate, inmate. The mad glint of triumphant exhilaration in Emosi's eye was new to me. He wanted me to present three crazy, nonsensical, scriptural scrolls crammed with biblical annotations to the highest authorities. After a quarter of an hour of this almost eyeball-to-eyeball meeting, in which I said as little as possible — I had heard of the astounding strength of a provoked madman — I made for the door with the scrolls and was able to attract the attention of the attendant at the end of a long corridor. It took me days to get over the hideousness and smell of the hot, humid place and of the almost macabre religious frenzy of what I could only consider a 'Methodist Mission victim'.

But I did have a more pleasant duty to perform. I had officiated at the civil marriages of many Indians and some Fijians in my office, but when the Governor's ADC, Major Basil Sellars (later to be Superintendent of Prisons), asked me to perform the simple ceremony for him in the office, it was a one-off occasion and, for me, a unique experience.

As my seniority was growing, I began to wonder where I might next be posted. I never let it be known which districts I either preferred (Nasigatoka and Colo West, Ra, Navua or Levuka) or would have liked markedly less. The posting policy seemed to operate to ensure that people's preferences were discounted — plain perverse administration, which one can see a lot of in a life-time. For two reasons I was not expecting a move — Anne was nearly due to have our child and I was preparing the Fiji team's first cricket tour of New Zealand since 1895. This was due to take place in January 1948 and would be extremely difficult to organize from outside Suva. Nicoll either overlooked or ignored these reasons. I heard that we were to go to Taveuni as soon as the birth had taken place.

Stephanie Dale Vivien Vuikaba Snow was born on 11 June 1947 at 4.40 p.m. I had driven Anne to Nurse Morrison's Maternity Home near the Colonial War Memorial Hospital the previous night at the classic time of midnight in the classically torrential rain down the steep hill and up another.

Since people were seen shaking my hand at the King's Birthday garden party the next day on the rear lawn between Government House and the Governor's office, it looked as though I had been included in the King's Birthday honours published that day. While standing next to me in the queue to pass through to the lawn, Ratu Sukuna asked me why I was being congratulated and, on being told, asked me if I had names for her. When I replied 'Stephanie Dale Vivien', he said that, if Anne and I would like it, he could give us for her the name of his favourite sister, Adi Vuikaba. It was a very rare honour for a Fijian chief of Ratu Sukuna's stature to bestow a name on a European and I warmly accepted his offer.

I later learned some details about Adi Kuini (Queenie) Vuikaba's life. Ratu Sukuna was her eldest brother. She became the first Fijian to be trained overseas as a nurse for the new Colonial War Memorial Hospital, founded in 1923, and she was much liked by the Rodwells when they occupied Government House from 1920 to 1924. She later married a man from deepest Colo, Ratu Tomasi (Thomas) Latianara, and their son, Ratu Aseri Latianara Qoro, became Roko Tui Naitasiri. Her granddaughter and namesake, Adi Kuini Teimumu Vuikaba, was to marry a visitor to our house in Angmering, Lieutenant Savenaca Draunidalo, who was ADC to the Governor-General, Ratu Sir George Cakobau, when he paid us a visit. She later married Dr Timoci (Timothy) Bavadra, the last prime minister before the coups of 1987. Fijian visitors to England always address Stephanie as Di Vui, a respectful form of intimate recognition of her being Vuikaba by courtesy of Ratu Sukuna, who himself always referred to her as Adi Vuikaba.

Although I let it be known that a move to Taveuni would be too soon if it were to be within the next three months, Nicoll considered it vital for Collins to be relieved because he was in a state of depression. Further, the venerable Ratu Glanvill Wellington Lalabalavu, Roko Tui Cakaudrove and Tui Cakau, had recently died and could not be replaced quickly by Ratu Sukuna's brother, Ratu Tiale Wimbledon Thomas Vuiyasawa. So Taveuni, the third most important island, was short of administration.

When I heard that the day-and-a-half voyage to Taveuni was to be on the *Adi Beti*, I protested further because I knew that this top-heavy, slight, sail-less vessel was restricted to moving only within the reefs. My objection was overruled and, soon after dawn on 5 August, Anne, Stephanie and I embarked with G. E. Overton, a Maori inspector of schools from the New Zealand Department of Education, who wished to see some outlying schools. The journey through the Rewa delta and tributaries and across to Levuka was in a rising wind. In Levuka we stayed with a close lifelong friend, Christopher Legge, and his American wife in the DO's house on the spot where the first Government House had been sited in Sir Arthur Gordon's time.

We left Levuka the next day in a high wind and by the time we had passed the leper island of Makogai and were heading for the middle of the Koro Sea, far out of sight of land, conditions became intolerable and it was obvious that we could not reach either Nasavusavu or Taveuni before nightfall. The captain had given us his cabin. The shallow ship was rolling and pitching so much that green seas were breaking uninterruptedly over the deck. Everything not secured swung about crushingly. What could stop us from turning turtle?

The captain roped himself to the wheel while the one deckhand stayed below with the engineer. The Maori inspector, belying the nautical prowess of his ancestors, retired to his little cabin after agreeing with me that the captain should be persuaded to turn back. The captain, a part-European, hesitated, pointing out the dangers of capsizing if struck broadside while doing so. Eventually, he chose what he thought was a momentary lessening of the waves ahead, but in turning we were struck by three huge waves, which indeed nearly turned us over. It was estimated that the last roll had been 80 degrees. I later learned that the largest waves in such conditions move in threes. Then we were followed by monstrous waves overtaking the low stern of the ship. I felt so ill and alarmed that I was almost past caring whether I lived or died. Anne, a better sailor, was prostrate. Anne had put Stephanie in the captain's map drawer, but then had to feed her. After an eternity, we reached some protection at the wharf at Makogai, the leprosarium island. With the diminution of most of the motion I recovered the will to survive.

I was much heartened by the welcome of the Catholic sisters, who had devoted their lives to looking after lepers. They brought to the vessel chicken, lettuce, butter, eggs, milk and iced beer (we had taken no food on board as normally our destination would have been reached the same day) and invited the Maori inspector and me to tour the island with them. I had never expected to see this remarkable institution. As Anne had a two-month-old child, they were not permitted to go ashore. It was my thirty-second birthday, which I had reckoned myself lucky to reach.

Taking my time, I sent off a telegram from the wireless station on the island refusing point blank to go further on the *Adi Beti*, reporting incidentally that our valuable china (it was over 100 years old, practically our only family heirloom) was being broken, and asking for a larger vessel to be sent. Back came apologies (remarkable from a Colonial Secretary: it was in fact not now Nicoll who was acting as Governor but, acting as CS, P. D. Macdonald, with whom I never worked happily and for whom I had no liking) and advice to retreat to Levuka where the *Degei*, about four times the size of the *Adi Beti*, would be sent for me.

Dr Cyril Austin, the medical superintendent of the settlement, was away. He lived on the opposite side of the island to the lepers' quarters. The sister in charge, Mother Superior Mary Agnes, had spent 50 years in Fiji, some at Wairiki on Taveuni, but 31 of them on Makogai: she was the soul of hospitality. She arranged a tour for Overton and me. Two nuns, one of them a young Scottish one with an American accent, Sister Kaska, whose sparkling brown eyes I still recall vividly (I had after all just miraculously been given a second life and had sharpened senses, or so it seems to me on reflection), were our escorts: they went ahead of us and young girl patients held open the doors, which we were not allowed to touch.

The lepers in bed looked like any other patients in the many hospitals I had toured. Among them were some beaming smiles of welcome. They were in the preliminary stages and it was hoped that they could be cured. But if they had tuberculosis in addition, then as it receded the leprosy increased and vice versa — an odd and disappointing medical fact as they are caused by a similar bacteria. There were one or two with the characteristic leonine faces, bulbous noses and puffy eye sockets. Fingers, legs and arms or what remained of them were heavily bandaged. Leprosy is in three forms — skin tissue, nerve and bone, the latter two being the most painful, requiring dissection of nerves and amputation of bones. The largest number of patients were Indians, but a number of Gilbertese had just arrived. There were four Europeans, including two Catholic priests.

The disease is said (with what degree of accuracy I do not know) primarily to be associated with dirt: bacteria from it showing on skin and insidiously spreading along nerves. Cleanliness was held to be its biggest deterrent. I never thought Catholic mission settlements or villages under their influence as clean as others: some of the occupants appeared over-clothed and under-washed. Too many Indian habitations, urban as well as rural, were conspicuously dirty. Fijians are a meticulously clean people. We were not shown into the worst ward where we were told that limbs were totally missing and the inmates beyond cure. The new anodyne, chaulmoogra oil, was expected to show dramatic improvements, but it was still too early for prognostication with conviction.

As it happened, in the 1960s, so much progress had been made — I found this spectacular leap forward very moving — that it was possible to close the leprosarium, transferring the few cases to care near Suva. In particular, a new drug, Promin, obliterated the disease within weeks. Now sheep are raised on what were the desolate grass spaces of Makogai. On leaving the soil to return to the boat at the wharf, we had to dip our shoes in formalin as prophylactic. I had also seen the biggest lizard I was ever to see in Fiji, nine inches long, not counting its tail, and an inch wide: I noticed that it was the sole occupant of Makogai School as we were passing it. We were never more appreciative than of the way we were looked after there and we left full of deepest respect and profound thanks. The sea behind us propelled us at a great rate to Levuka, where Christopher and Jane Legge again took us in.

I had first seen Christopher in 1938 looking like Sanders of the River sitting on a deckchair on a little put-put (outboard-engined dinghy). He had come down from Vunidawa to meet me at Naduru-loulou soon after my arrival in Fiji. Legge had been a high-jumping Blue for Cambridge — one of the last to clear six feet with the scissors movement of legs. He established a different sort of record, best reported in these salient points from the *British Medical Journal*:

On January 11th 1934 a man was admitted to the Hospital of Tropical Diseases. Born in England, he had resided in Nigeria since 1928 except for periods of furlough at home. In Nigeria he had five attacks of malaria. He returned to England in November 1933 and on December 9th he had another attack of malaria which developed into blackwater fever and from this he was recovering when admitted into the Hospital of Tropical Diseases. For twelve days after admission he showed some swing of temperature from 97 degrees to 90.4 degrees Fahrenheit: the spleen was palpable but no malarial parasites could be found in the blood. On January 23rd a rigor occurred and the temperature reached 102 degrees. The next day the temperature subsided. On February 7th the temperature again shot up to 101 degrees, but on this occasion the blood showed malignant tertian malaria to be present. This was followed on Friday 9th by another rigour, which commenced at 7.00 p.m. and blood slides taken immediately showed, in addition, parasites and benign tertian malaria. At 8.00 p.m. the temperature had risen to 107 degrees ... so orders were given for it to be recorded every 15 minutes. At 8.30 p.m. the thermometer showed 110 degrees: so another thermometer was at once obtained. At 8.40 p.m. the mercury passed the 110 degree mark, the limit of the calibration on the first thermometer, while on the second thermometer used, which had been selected because it showed some calibration above the 110 degree mark, the mercury reached the top of the instrument level with a mark estimated at 115 degrees. Orders were at once given to sponge the patient but before this was done the temperature showed a fall to 105 degrees. ... During the whole period of the hyperpyrexia the patient's condition was good: he was quite rational, no cerebral symptoms were present and there was no lack of consciousness. Respiration was regular all through the period but at the peak was panting in type, expiration ending with a soft grunt, while the patient complained of a sensation of compression like a weight on his chest. Treatment with atebrin was at once instituted and no subsequent hyperpyrexia occurred. The patient is now convalescent. That the patient sustained a temperature exceeding 110 degrees Fahrenheit is undoubted. He had been accustomed to his temperature being taken and could have had no idea that it was higher than usual during this particular period, so the suspicion of his biting both thermometers can be eliminated. No hot drinks were given and all other sources of error have been investigated.

Christopher's remained one of the most dramatic medical cases of its kind. I thought that his demonstrations of absentmindedness were a residue of this illness, but this was not apparently the case. It is doubtful whether his father, Sir Thomas Legge, Home Office senior medical inspector of factories, or his grandfather, Reverend Professor James Legge, for years a missionary in China and then the first professor of Chinese at Oxford, had the same characteristic, but his sister Sylvia was as hesitant in her speech as Christopher was in his. He had earlier shown symptoms of what seemed to be amnesia, but was actually only slowness of reaction. He had in fact a remarkable memory. This could catch out anyone thinking of taking advantage of him.

He was a fine eccentric in Fiji, to where he had been transferred because it was non-malarial. He became a legend, constantly bemusing Fijians who were unaware of his underlying sharpness. When he retired from Fiji (he and I had often handed over to each other in stations) he became custodian of collections at the Field Museum of Natural History on the delightful shore of Lake Michigan, Chicago, from where his wife came. He made the hustle and bustle of that city adhere to his own pace rather than vice versa and it was diverting to watch Chicago's inhabitants (hustling Negro taxi drivers, coffee-shop attendants, overhead railway staff and the like) adapting to his backwater tempo.

Weakened by the attempted voyage over the Koro Sea, I was taken by him to the Ovalau Club in Levuka — the oldest in Fiji and dating back to the first colonial days in 1879 — for Levuka-type morning drinks. They went to my head. On returning to the Legges' home, I am reported by Anne as having ceaselessly switched on and off the electric lights throughout the house before retiring to the bedroom with the room itself beginning to revolve, its walls rising higher and higher and the floor dropping into abysses. The *Adi Beti* party were not the only ones to be involved in drama. Christopher was always inclined to be top heavy and unsteady looking and, on descending a hill while showing us over the Catholic mission at Cawaci, he fell on his knee. After inspection at the hospital, it was judged wise for him to go into Suva in case it was fractured (which it proved to be). A taxi took him to the wharf from where we wheeled him on a truck along the copra railway lines to the *Island Queen*, a ketch waiting to sail in the comparatively sheltered waters from Levuka to the capital.

The *Degei* arrived three days later and its size was assuring. Even so, this Public Works Department vessel, the largest owned by the government, moved about a good deal on the day-long voyage to Taveuni, which we reached after dark at a wide-open anchorage. Looking back on it, I am astounded by the risk we took in disembarking in the blackness on the steeply rising and falling swell. I remember hair-raisingly handing Stephanie down in a bundle to a Fijian waiting poised with his bare toes hooked on the gunwale of the dinghy, his arms upheld and outstretched. Between us we had to judge precisely (and absolutely precisely) the

255

rise of the dinghy up to the side of the *Degei* so that I could lean over quickly and half-put half-drop her into the Fijian's arms before the dinghy lurched back again into the depths.

We all then switchbacked in the dinghy to the shore where Dennis Sandiford, the English part-owner of Qacavulo estate, was waiting for us in an open-backed copra lorry. He took Anne and Stephanie into the front of the lorry with him while I somehow clung on to the open back, preventing myself from sliding down it as the truck made a precipitous climb — all in Stygian darkness — along a ravine path of large loose gravel to Dennis and Anne Sandiford's plantation house, which they shared with Anne's brother, Jim Krone, and his decorative fair Austrian wife, Olga. Our relief was intense after a delicious meal.

Next morning I took over from Collins, who did not appear to know where we were anyway. The clerk, a chief of the highest rank in Rewa, had absented himself, ostensibly to collect tax revenue across the Somosomo Straits, but in fact, as I realized when he went on local leave after my arrival, he had been away deliberately for the handover from Collins so that he could conceal a receipt book.

The discovery coincided with a planter telling me of rumours that a clerk was gambling heavily and spending lavishly on taxis and a woman. This was an inauspicious start to my time on Taveuni. Just as were settling in, the defalcation business had to be settled. We were visited, on my request, by an auditor (there could have been no kinder and more cooperative man than Harry Stanley, an Australian and the best tennis player in the colony: he gave me immense help and we had a most pleasurable friendship from this first meeting), a police inspector and a magistrate (since I clearly could not take the case). They all stayed in our large house for a fortnight.

Meanwhile, I had been sent a telegram by Ratu Sukuna saying that I was to be captain of the Fiji cricket team to tour New Zealand in January 1948, and asking if I would take Ratu George Cakobau in the side. I have already told of my reaction to this in describing my meeting with George in 1938 when he held out my first cup of *kava*. There were exciting times ahead.

11

The Odd Beachcomber, First-Class Arrival and Departure

Taveuni, the third largest island in Fiji after Viti Levu and Vanua Levu, was a rich district to which to be posted, in the sense that its black volcanic soil is so fertile that, amid much competition, it had become known as the Garden of Fiji. Amid such lushness, the planters had no difficulty providing hospitality: their welcomes to their friends were second to none in the group. There were a dozen plantations of coconut palms constituting the major copra production area in the colony. Most were spacious but palms will not grow on land higher than 1000 feet. A steamy island, 26 miles long and about 7 miles wide, Taveuni slopes up from both ends to Des Voeux Peak (4000 feet) and, from the sea, looks like a gargantuan half-immersed humpback whale. From the air it is predominantly like a vertebra with a slope along one side to the Somosomo Straits and a precipitous drop all along on the other to the very seldom pacific Pacific Ocean.

It was this, the uninhabited side of Taveuni, with waterfalls sheer down to the sea and no beaches, inlets or villages, that had provided my first view of a Fijian island from the *Port Jackson* in 1938. On the inhabited side, a steep rocky road over Irish bridges (concrete depressions over which each year between 200 and 300 inches of rain pour down creeks to the sea) runs parallel to the

257

Somosomo Straits. This often turbulent channel, complex in its currents, separates by five miles at the nearest point Taveuni from the mass of Vanua Levu (much of it relatively unknown). The edge of the road on Taveuni drops down an alarmingly precipitous 750 feet into the straits. A car went over it after my time — the passenger, a planter's daughter, was killed; the driver, the son of another planter, survived.

Taveuni was as near as could be to being feudal, with freehold copra estates lining the coastal road at regular intervals. Bags of sweet-smelling coconut flesh would be transported to the *Yanawai* — owned by Burns Philp (South Sea) Company and by Fijian standards a reasonably comfortable steamer (it was the largest in the whole group) — about every three weeks under the direction of the supercargo, Seth Douglas. As a man of imposing looks, reassuring stature and pleasant demeanour, his visits were keenly looked forward to, not least as a decoration on the otherwise limited horizon, by the European women on the island. The ship was the only link, other than a telegraphic one, with the rest of the world.

The island was unofficially divided between north and south. In the centre was the DO's residence, the most imposing on the island. In a letter to Charles from Waiyevo (the Government Station), Taveuni, dated 1 October 1947, I wrote:

> This is just the place to join us in. The best house of any in all the Districts (that is, Administrative Officers' houses) — the grounds, park-like and colourful with kingfishers, parrots, golden doves (practically extinct and highly handsome), taper off in a sylvan swimming pool and climb up a densely forested range towards a lake in an extinct crater. ... If the tour (by the cricket team to New Zealand) becomes definite in the next month or so it is of course practically certain that I shall be recalled to Suva to arrange it. ... Stephanie is very well. I send a first photograph (taken at one month old). She will probably continue to have auburn/dark brown hair and her eyes remarkable for a Snow appear to be changing from blue to brown.

Our house was set on a large, trim lawn with flagstaff, fountain (which I created) and leaning flame-of-the-forest trees, up which six turkeys would whirl for the night like helicopters, disturbing shrubs and people's hair. It was the only green-roofed house on Taveuni: the rest of the building gleamed in white against the highly forested vertebra of the island rising steeply behind it to the low clouds over the top. (The corrugated iron roof above the white walls looked so much better painted green rather than red, which was in any case often neglected.)

A rare golden dove with a green head stood proudly on a little tree at a corner of the house looking at the sunset over the straits each dusk. The honey eaters and black and white Australian magpies with a most melodious warble retired earlier. A couple of kingfishers, the length of their beaks extending as far as the rest of their bodies, which were as stubby as those of kookaburras, would dive rapidly to the grass for their dinner. As dark descended, about three score giant toads would hop out from under the house (built on low stilts providing storage for anti-hurricane shutters) on to the lawn determinedly seeking food with the lines of their lips sullenly turned down at twenty-five past seven o'clock. Their hunger somewhat appeased, their lips would then set at a quarter-to-three but never more satisfied-looking than with that rather non-committed, neutral expression of their views on life. One or two would swivel round at right angles to hop up the half dozen steps on to our verandah.

In the spacious, elegant grounds between the house and the Country Club I planted two jacaranda, two hydrocarpus, two cashew nuts, two yemene, six royal palms, two mahoganies, two Valencia sweet oranges, two grapefruit, one Mediterranean sweet orange, one lagerstroemia, six flamboyants, six tulip trees, two cassia grandis, four bauhina (butterfly trees) and some dwarf Malaya palms. It was one of my weaknesses to create botanical gardens wherever I could, a fashion that seemed to have lapsed since the beginning of the century. I later added two traveller's palms and single specimens each of teak, rubber, cinnamon, clove, cocoa, rose apple, tamarind and cannonball. I should add that between the mountain-fed pool and our back lawn there were

259

large plantations of bananas and pineapples. They grew with arrogant ease.

It was said that the north and south were always at loggerheads and only came together to oppose the centre. In the early 1940s, when Lindsay Verrier was Medical Officer, this virtually perpetual state of civil war between north and south was suspended and replaced with a north–south alliance against the government. In my three years on Taveuni — my longest period in any district — I managed to keep the peace between the two ends: so much so that they joined together in petitioning for me to remain, an unprecedented piece of Taveuni history. My achievement was due to two factors for which I could not take credit. Traditionally difficult for any administrator was Percy McConnell, whose father had been similarly inclined from Cession of the group in 1874 onwards.

We got on with McConnell all right but it may have helped that he retired from his plantation halfway through my time. In Christopher Legge's time as DO, about three years before, a real dilemma arose. McConnell had been prosecuted for some breach of labour regulations and Legge had no alternative but to fine him £10, in default two weeks' imprisonment. McConnell went back home and returned to the station with a toothbrush, demanding to be put in the gaol. It was the rule that Europeans could only be in prison in Suva gaol where the appropriate diet prevailed. There was no ship to Suva for three weeks. So Legge had McConnell on his hands and met the problem in the only way possible. He told McConnell that the fine he had refused to pay had in fact been paid — by Legge himself, although McConnell did not know but might have guessed.

Taveuni had only one telephone line running the length of the island. The instruments hung on the wall. There was no dialling, only a circular movement with a handle — a full turn for a long ringing sound, half a turn for a short one. Each house had its code. Our house was one long. The range extended to permutations of up to six long, six short, six long for houses at the extreme ends of the island. The telephone was thus ringing everywhere all day. For a person starved of friends or society in general it was a boon: for everyone else, barely sufferable. Once, when in the course of two persons in the south talking to each other, they heard a click and one of them said, 'That would be Mrs McConnell on the line.' A voice along the line said indignantly 'Oh no it isn't. I'm out of the house.' Mrs McConnell lived in the north and in the past: she alone of all the planters' wives made her call on Anne in gloves and hat. We not only got on with the McConnells, we liked them. But perhaps that state might not have lasted without incident for a full three years.

A second reason for the peacekeeping over our three years — and one that characterized Taveuni's administration through the 1930s to the 1950s — was the stalwart presence near the Government Station, on an estate technically just in the south, of Wynter Wallace Warden, a JP. (The north had to have a JP too for balance — William George Mackay, who was an ally of McConnell's. He was a good friend of ours and led the petition for us not to move.) Like all the planters, except one or two in the north who were part-European, Wal Warden was an Australian and a fine example of one. He had fought in France in the First World War and was the epitome of level-headedness, with a wry sense of humour and a diplomatic interest in everything. He had been on the island as a manager — never an owner — for a score of years. He was as near neutral as anyone could be on Taveuni. His advice could be sought. It was he who had tipped me off with the rumour about the Rewan chiefly clerk's excessive spending, which was arousing suspicions about his having fiddled the cash. Wal's family — his wife, Dorothy, two sons, Bill and Ron, and attractive blonde daughter, Margo — were delightful. It was a great comfort having him there to share the isolation of Taveuni or Waiyevo.

In the far south were two cousins in separate, historic homesteads dating back to the cotton days before Cession and the arrival of copra. The senior of these was the pallid Adrian Rood Tarte, whose way with Fijians was as unfortunate as his name would suggest. In fact he was proud of his name and would say with customary acerbity: 'I was born Rood, christened Rood and have remained Rood ever since.' His father had somewhat quixotically or absent-mindedly given him the second name of his plantation partner, James Rood Fry. His wife, known as Aunt Edie, was a dignified figure who tried to confer grace and poise in counterweight to Rood. Reported to be the essence of ineffable rudeness, he never seemed to me to live up to his name.

The younger cousin, James Valentine Tarte, living separately but nearby, whose father was English, was a small, dapper, bronzed man with brilliantined hair, thin black moustache and a general 1920s film-star look. He himself always pronounced 'film' as 'filum'. As small as Douglas Fairbanks senior, he could have been his double. Valen (as he was known) was a model employer and, among other comforts, provided his workers with a cinema (Vuna Hall), which he invited me to open before a capacity audience of 400. He cleared a strip on his plantation in my time for the first plane to land from Suva. He eventually separated from his charming Australian wife, Nell, to consort with the attractive daughter of a Fijian employee.

Valen would have fitted neatly into the antebellum aura of the Deep South of America. It was at his Waimaqera estate that I observed him rescue his Indian houseboy, Mahadeo, from electrocution. We both saw him in agony holding on to a wire from the house's electricity plant. Quicker-witted than me, Valen grabbed a wooden pole and banged the arm free. Mahadeo was prostrate and in convulsions. I rang the hospital for advice (the medical officer was away). Blankets, hot whisky and forcing him to walk restored him. Valen's son Daryl, now secretary of the Copra and Sugar Boards, recently published a splendid biography of Fiji's first President, Taveuni-born Ratu Sir Penaia Ganilau.

Nearest to the government station was a decrepit old planter, J. G. F. Taylor. Known as Hurricane Jack, Taylor was always prognosticating hurricanes. I heard him say with fearful sagacity that 'each year we are past a hurricane we are nearer another'; they were indeed understandably the lurking trauma in planters' lives. We had a severe one on Taveuni in 1948.

My time, as in my Lomaloma but more concentratedly, was often spent as administrator of estates, postmaster and sub-accountant. In addition, I had my court work, police work (I was officer-in-charge with a sergeant major and three constables), gaol work (I was the prison superintendent) and, because the grounds were extensive and well worth improving, spent time with the Sikh warder implementing changes and extensions. I also had to travel regularly on duty to the other side of the straits — to Nasavusavu (I was in charge of both Taveuni and Nasavusavu Districts), Buca Bay, Natewa Bay, Fawn Harbour and to the islands of Kioa and Rabe, all of which, except Rabe, came under my jurisdiction.

As two or three place names are invariably misspelt, I should mention that the ones I use here had the backing of Ratu Sukuna. In a discussion with him about these and others, he told me that from earliest days Europeans corrupted Nasavusavu into Savusavu (to save energy, no doubt), Rabe into Rabi, and Nasigatoka into Sigatoka. I tried to lead a campaign to have these impurities removed, but they were too ingrained and still appear wrongly on official maps. Ratu Sukuna was the indisputable authority and always punctilious in his spelling, which I have followed throughout these observations. He tired of correcting officials who ought to have known better. Very few Europeans knew the language even remotely and many part-Europeans felt it desirable to distance themselves further from their ethnic connections by not speaking Fijian.

I would try to ensure that my visits by car to each end of Taveuni were equally distributed (there were only about 20 vehicles on the single-track road). This meant travelling, if going north, through Somosomo village, the home of the handsome young copper-skinned Tui Cakau. Here the vivaciously pretty Adi Senimili Cakobau (daughter of Ratu Josefa Cakobau, whose branch of the royal dynasty had been exiled from Bau 70 years earlier) would, at the risk of being regarded as forward, wave to me.

Sometimes I would see her returning from having fished in the sea, her blouse and *sulu* wet through, and, to her intense pleasure, would give her a lift. Her elder sister, Adi Loa Cakobau, was also striking looking, with the same brilliant black eyes: she was married to a European plantation overseer in the extreme north, but was in advance of her times for her European proclivities. Their son, Cecil Arthur Cakobau Browne, who had inherited his mother's looks, was the best batsman in the Fiji cricket sides from the 1970s to the 1990s.

On the side of the road to the north (his allegiances were with it) lived a figure out of the 1900s. He had an unpainted, corrugated iron shed in which he would make and repair firearms, which planters used for shooting cattle. His craftsmanship was such that he would mend anything, poring over the object with his steel-rimmed spectacles, bushy white moustache and tousled white hair. Logan H. Morrisby hated Fijians — the feeling was mutual. He regarded them as useless and treacherous in every way. Although well read, he was dogmatic and prejudiced to a totally unacceptable level. He had gone to Australia from England and worked on launches in Australian rivers before, God knows why, settling in a country he loathed. He wore braces, a dirty, striped, flannel shirt with no collar and heavy blue serge trousers, making no concession to either the heat or the fact that he was not working in a craftsman's hovel in the English Midlands. He had a twin brother, John, who was completely hermitical; few people had ever seen him in the tin shack they both inhabited. John was said to hoard newspapers and to spend all day on top of the printed sheets browned by age. He and Logan were said never to talk to each other. One dawn I heard a knocking on my front door which was open. There was Logan, unkempt, dishevelled and distraught. His brother had been missing for three days and he thought that he had better tell me. He would not deign to report to the Fijian sergeant major of police. I sent out a search party. John could have walked into the sea and been devoured by sharks or vanished in the thick mountain bush and been attacked by ferocious wild pigs and dogs. No trace was ever found.

One of Taveuni's main eccentrics in my time was Père Yves Helliet, a Breton in charge of the Catholic mission at Wairiki. Wairiki is a mile from Waiyevo and exactly on the 180° meridian where, in 1949, I put up a signboard proclaiming 'THIS IS THE ONLY MOTOR ROAD IN THE WORLD TO CROSS THIS, THE 180° MERIDIAN. WAIRIKI, TAVEUNI, FIJI.' I had carefully checked the exact location with the New Zealand navy and also with a world map, taking it as unlikely that an uttermost tip of Siberia had a road. The board was, I believe, elaborated a little by an interested governor in the 1950s. Father Helliet was gnomish, no taller than five feet, with a two-foot long white beard trailing from his aquiline face to his waist. He was always cheerful and excitable, gesticulating energetically under my nose, grasping my arms and exclaiming 'By Jiminy'. He would send me weekly notes signed 'For God and Souls ✠ Yves Helliet' (the ✠ being the sign of the Cross) containing minor complaints about how some Fijian's behaviour (Protestant of course) had cast some slight (imagined rather than real) aspersion on his mission. He was dressed always in a long black habit (malodorous from stale incense and sweat in the heat) from neck down to shiny, black, laced-up boots on which he would progress at never less than a trot. And he was a heavy *yaqona* drinker. He was a memorable, harmless, idiosyncratic, if anachronistic, addition to the Taveuni scenery.

Social life for those who liked tennis was focused centrally on the Country Club. This was almost alongside our house and behind our back lawn there was a dark, extremely cold, swimming pool, which was fed directly from the slopes of the extinct volcano, Des Voeux Peak. It was used by people who wanted to experience its Antarctic chill as a change from the sweltering heat of the tennis courts. There were enough people around — planters' daughters and sons, some planters and their wives (almost exclusively from the south), the English medical officer and his wife, and the New Zealander headmaster of the Provincial School and his wife — to make full use of both the pool and the tennis. They were all very congenial and the standard of tennis was good.

On 12 October 1947, I wrote to Charles by air mail (sea from Taveuni to Suva, air from Suva to England) that:

A letter is already on its way to you on the surface ... necessarily so because it contains the first photographs of Stephanie, still somewhat nebulous or amorphous but perhaps markedly Snovian which may not be an advantage in a female. People do describe her however as pretty. What is certain is that she is continuously cheerful. It is very likely that I shall be going into Suva to coach the team during December up to the tour in late January when I shall very likely go as Captain. My only rival is Edward Cakobau who will probably not be quite back from England. He did not get a Blue, more, I think, through health and dietary reasons than any shortcomings in standard ... Sir Lala Sukuna is staying with us for a week; he is writing an abstract work on Philosophy ... I am very sorry about Hardy [he had just died].

Then, on 6 December 1947, I wrote again to say that 'Sir Lala Sukuna is probably going with the team as manager.' Unfortunately, however, Ratu Sukuna was unable to leave Fiji, and this left the team with its only plain weakness. The tour came on faster than I had estimated. There was no doubt that my being so far from Suva was causing plans to be less carefully made than I had hoped.

Before the time came for me to go into Suva, Christopher and Jane Legge had come from Levuka to relieve me for the three months. Anne was helped in looking after Stephanie by Sulueti, the daughter of Peni Vunidilo, one of the constables who had been in Lomaloma with me and who, when under the influence of too much grog (*yaqona*), used to claim that he was the man who had clubbed and killed the headstrong missionary, Reverend Thomas Baker, in the heart of the Colo wilderness. Constable Peni never quite lived this down: he would often appear shamefaced. It had been his grandfather who had committed the act in 1867 at Gagadelavatu near Nabutautau on the Upper Sigatoka River. Evidently the occurrence lay heavily on the family conscience.

To catch the slightest breeze, Stephanie used to be put near the aerial roots of the huge spreading weeping-fig tree, from which a mosquito net was suspended to cover her. One day Sulueti came in to tell me that there was a *mimimata*, a member of the giant praying mantis family, inside the net. We both rushed back to capture it. Its reputation was that it secreted an unpleasant white substance believed to cause blindness if squirted into an eye. From then on, having at last seen one, we were always circumspect about them.

Regrets mixed with complex anticipation, I left on the *Yanawai*

ABOVE. A Guadalcanal hero, District Officer Martin Clemens, with his faithful company, 1942. *(Photo: U.S. Marine Corps)* LEFT. Author in Colonial Service full dress... and very hot too. *(Photo: Noel S. Williams)* BELOW. The Governor, Sir Alexender Grantham, presenting a posthumous V.C. to corporal Sukanaivalu's parents whom Fiji custom required to squat. Suva, 1945. *(Photo: Rob R. Wright)*

ABOVE. Author and wife at Leicester on leave, 1946. *(Photo: Leicester Evening Mail)* RIGHT. Ratu Sir Lala Sukuna in morning dress, Fijian style, 1946. *(Photo: Author)* BELOW. The Fiji cricket team touring New Zealand, 1948. Author, as captain, seated in centre with Ratu Sir George Cakobau, vice-captain, on his right, bare footed. Bula standing third from left. *(Photo: Dominion, Wellington)*

from the bush (which is how the Viti Levu Europeans regarded Taveuni) for the considerable adventure of the first properly representative cricket tour of New Zealand.

At the eleventh hour, cancellation was threatened. A severe epidemic of poliomyelitis was sweeping through New Zealand and children were being kept away from public events. When the question was put to the Inspector-General of the South Pacific Health Service, Dr (later Sir) John Buchanan, in Suva — a man of wide experience and broad outlook who became Chief Medical Officer for the Colonies at the Colonial Office — he decided that the team could go, advising that it should not be in confined spaces, which was unlikely. In the event, notably as we progressed further south, New Zealand relaxed its precautions and, by half-way through the three-month tour, the epidemic had been forgotten. Hordes of children, with autograph books under their arms, used to come and watch us and hold up our departures until all the team's signatures had been collected.

I was at a disadvantage at the outset, compared with the rest of my team, because I had been unable to have any games or practice apart from a few gentle balls on the narrow back lawn between our house and the pineapple and banana grove (and swimming pool) from Harry Stanley (the auditor), Inspector Max Lovell and Bertie Gregg (the magistrate visiting for the case of the chiefly Rewan embezzler). But I knew my team, having played with or against them all for nearly a decade. To my satisfaction, I prevailed on the selectors that an extra batsman, Ilikena Lasarusa (Lazarus) Bula, should be taken at the last minute. This Lauan was to prove the outstanding success in terms of statistics (over 1000 runs in the 17 matches), personality and appeal to the Bula-captivated spectators filling the grounds.

The *Matua* was held up at Suva wharf for four hours. Ratu Sukuna, who had invited me to dinner at his house, Rairaiwaqa, the previous night after I had made a broadcast, most considerately spent the period of delay with me and the vice-captain, Ratu George Cakobau, walking the decks and giving the team much heart. The wharf was crowded and I was deluged with telegrams of good wishes constantly coming aboard.

267

At the first dinner on board, CID Sergeant Aisea Turuva (Turaga's brother) gave the less sophisticated Fijians tuition in the use of knives and forks. But some of them did not put the skills into practice until the voyage was ending when the least sophisticated of the team, Semi Ravouvou, from the inland Nadi village of Saunaka and having no English, but a voracious appetite on recovering from *mal de mer*, looked at the menu card and ordered by pointing to the steward everything on it including the date. He was never allowed by his fellow tourists to forget that aberration.

After passing close enough to Kadavu island to see all the villages facing the liner route, it became so rough that most of us retired to lie down. A hurricane was nearby — it was the season. The weather conditions were too bad for all but the four or five coastal Fijians; the rest of us spent all but one of the four days below decks in an awful communal hold with about 40 bunks of recumbent figures. Not until we were safely within Auckland harbour on the last day did Mosese (Moses) Bogisa, from the non-maritime province of Nadi, appear. I was needlessly concerned for him and the youngest player, Harry Apted, a 23-year-old part-European who had also been unable to eat anything for three days. I had forgotten that recovery can be almost instantaneous once the ship's movement had ceased. Apted was, after Bula, the most successful batsman in the team, with little short of 1000 runs.

Seeing the imposing skyline of Auckland's buildings, the sprawl of the city and the bustle of its teeming inhabitants (intimidating for me after Taveuni's solitariness, as I believe it was also for Fijians in the team viewing an urban scene for the first time) gave me cold feet. The risk was enormous, particularly for me. After all, the mere idea, the concept of the tour, had been solely mine. I had had to raise the finance, or at least the guarantees for it: such stalwarts as Robert Crompton, Sir Henry Scott, Ben Marks and Ken Stuart were among influential guarantors. But the crucial factor was Ratu Sir Lala Sukuna volunteering to persuade every Fijian province to help subsidize the venture. (In the event, no guarantor was needed for a rescue.) He had been the unshakeable believer in the success of the tour in all its aspects.

Although by the time of my transfer to Taveuni I thought that I had done all that was necessary, I had been upset by Nicoll nearly sabotaging my last stages of preparation in posting me away from Suva and, I confess, in those last five months, I was worried about my lack of grip. Anyone who has been in charge of Fiji cricket administration, nationally or in districts, would recognize my misgivings. Had the tour been a failure, the obloquy would have been mine and mine alone, all too neatly pinned down in a small country with no one to whom to pass the buck. Sukuna's faith in me to this point was what kept me buoyant before the tour got under way. But what had I let myself in for? Here I was with ten Fijians (Edward Cakobau still to come) and four part-Europeans (Apted, Raddock, Fenn and Wendt — the last named was of German Samoan descent) whose only testing had been playing internally in Fiji with practically no standard against which to measure them. We could lose every match, some — possibly all of them — by huge margins. None except Edward, George and I had played on grass wickets. Perhaps we wouldn't attract any spectators at all. It had every potential for disaster and when the press came on board to interview me I had to put a brave face on my inner feelings.

The proper line to take from the start, it occurred to me, was to say that we had come to learn. My greatest gratification was when the press, which gave us marvellous coverage, at the end of the three months, stated: 'They came to learn. They stayed to teach.' They were referring to the quite magnificent fielding (I had expected that, at least, to be good), the terrific hitting, notably by Bula, the skilful bowling, markedly by Viliame Mataika (noble-headed constable who, for slumbering in the Government House sentry box, had been demoted from corporal), Maurice Fenn (a part-Fijian, part-European) and Isoa (Esau) Logavatu, in whose features you could see that the tour was a dream of paradise come true, the elegant batting styles of Apted and Ratu George Cakobau, the almost professional all-round competence of Ratu Edward Cakobau, the spirit in which the matches were played and the number of times we defeated the New Zealand opposition.

Also favourably commented on was our uniquely (in the cricket scene) taking the field in single file almost to the pitch — an idea of Ernie Turner's, now strategically placed for us as manager of Cable & Wireless in Auckland. Long Jim (as he liked to be called by me) was full of worldly wisdom, ethnic tolerance and technical cricket sagacity. I owed much to this modest, outstanding Australian Anglophile. Bringing up the end of the file was the smallest player, Pat Raddock, a part-European: at five feet tall he was almost obscured by his pads and gloves. This fine wicketkeeper/batsman was happy to contribute this solemn/comic touch to round off the dignified procession. He did go in first to bat.

The first of many civic receptions took place in Auckland City Hall. The wonderment shown by the people of this city in seeing in their main streets these powerful, tall, barefooted Fijians with tremendous heads of black fuzzy hair (trimmed like hedges) wearing cream, calf-length *sulu*s and black blazers (with crests of the colony's ornamental coat-of-arms) was equalled only by the bewilderment of the Fijians themselves. They confessed, through me (speaking at the City Hall reception), to being surprised by the unceasing flow of white people along both sides of the vast streets.

It was important to get off to a good start on the field. And that is what happened, with Fiji having much the better of the first two-day match against Northland (where I surprised myself by immediately being among the runs) and a win in the second match, against Waikato. In our first three-day match, against Auckland, the performance came down to earth against some Test-match players. But we did learn from that. And from then on we had the better of the matches up to meeting the major provincial team of Wellington over three days. That was the real turning point. If there was one phase of the tour that was pronouncedly more exciting than any other, it was at Wellington: 19 runs were needed when Viliame, the last man (the policeman readily given to sleep not only on sentry duty but also on trains when, as mentioned later, he was injured and was now accompanied by a runner) joined Fenn. The frenzied scrambling between the wickets by Fenn and the runner cannot be described. Fiji beat Wellington by one wicket. It was Fiji's initial first-class win.

Good performances followed throughout from almost everyone and we closed the tour with a resounding win in a second match of three days' duration against the relative might of Auckland, which included its Test players such as Bert Sutcliffe, then the outstanding left-hand batsman in the world.

I had asked for first-class status for the five three-day matches when we started holding our own in them or even winning. Mean-spiritedly, and in defiance of all logic (less relevantly, we were increasing their gate money and general interest in the game), New Zealand declined to give such status until I had fought for it relentlessly right up to 1987, when a last-ditch appeal was made to the International Cricket Conference and a big majority vote by the countries led by Pakistan, the West Indies and India at last gave justice. I am a patient man (and was mostly a heavily defensive patient batsman: despite a pronounced one-eyed stance, with 90 per cent of my scoring shots on the leg side — a real imbalance that inevitably cramped my statistics, which would take on a different look only if they represented hours spent at the crease), but this fight for 39 years from 1948 for proper recognition of the team's successes nearly exhausted me.

It had always been warming to receive throughout (from 1948) the knowledgeable support, based on his playing against us coupled with his perceptive judgement, of Walter Hadlee, New Zealand's distinguished captain and most eminent administrator. That my 1948 team was given first-class status in 1987 can be regarded as a fair example to anyone of reward for pertinacity. It had the *Guinness Book of Records* effect of making the senior survivor, Ratu George Cakobau (at 75) and myself (at 72) the oldest cricketers ever to be graded first-class. (An Indian prince had once actually played at that level aged 70: I cannot imagine how.) It was a record to have waited 39 years for first-class status. In the meanwhile, the majority of the team had died.

In my case, so close to it for Leicestershire in 1938, I had made it virtually 50 years later. At age 72 I could scarcely credit that I was an acknowledged first-class player with five matches and nine innings. I was only sorry that my batting average was 17.73 and my bowling average 25.25: there were so many irresistible distractions. But the unusual nature of the justice of the decision was more than rewarding. After the conference voting I was touched by the New Zealand number two representative, Graham Dowling, the former New Zealand captain and then its chief administrator, being the first to congratulate me.

· The Fijians had attracted large crowds by their sportsmanship and their élan, with white knee-length skirts flying in the air as they fielded. They bowled as fast as they could. Isoa and Viliame were the quickest, but not as fast as, for instance, Turaga (what an impact he would have made). Fijians were convinced that slow bowling indicated possession of feeble arms. But paradoxically for them, the robust Fenn was far and away the most dangerous bowler in the side, with his placid floaters taking, astonishingly, 100 wickets in the mere 17 matches. Less paradoxically for them, the gentle trundlers, Apted and I, fell into that category, requiring them to field spectacularly when he and I bowled. Apted was himself quite the most brilliant, if not flamboyant, fielder in the team. Turuva's movements in the field managed to be both stately and electric, while Petero, with his bare simian feet clawing into the grass and his *sulu* flying apart, was aggressiveness itself. These three, with Bula always impressively in the picture, were outstanding in the field. I was interested that, on return to his Lauan village after the tour, Bula taught his sturdy younger brother to abandon speed and imitate Fenn's style and method uniquely among indigenous Fijians in his career tragically cut off as we shall see.

The team, apart from their cricketing feats, were also a tremendous social success, their dignified, pleasant bearing being commented on constantly by spectators, officials and the press. They always obliged the crowds and, by means of broadcasts, those unable to visit the grounds (including children prevented from attending at some centres by the poliomyelitis restrictions), with South Sea Island songs. Petero, whose less than handsome features went with a fine husky voice, excelled in the solos that Fijians so rarely give. We never left a ground or an assembly without singing, invariably on request, the always affecting farewell lament, *Isa Lei*. After the dramatic victory over Wellington, a large crowd on the quay saw off our ferry across the Cook Straits for Lyttelton in South Island.

It was our turn to be sung to, the assembly rendering extempore the wonderfully melodious Maori farewell *Haere mai*, as we steamed off towards further thrilling encounters on the other island. All the players on this historic tour have been mentioned except Aria (about to be referred to), and the left-hand pace bowlers Alf Wendt (who was a little past his all-round prime, which had indeed been very good in Fiji on concrete, but his steady head as a batsman was useful in an adventurous team) and Tevita Uate. Tevita's effectiveness as a fast bowler on turf as opposed to concrete was indissolubly weak, but he remained a cheerful *kava*-mixing comptroller. He died young in his Lauan village not long after the tour. We had less baggage than any team touring New Zealand previously and subsequently, but Warwick Watts, a New Zealander, who had been scorer with the Australian tourists under W. A. Brown two years earlier, couldn't resist attaching himself to our modest luggage and score book.

The spectators were always pro-Fijian, even to the extent of barracking their own home teams. Many grounds returned record attendances and it was said that the Fijians were the most popular side to visit the Dominion, after being at the outset virtually unknown. An excerpt from *The Press*, Christchurch's morning paper, was typical of journalists' and crowds' reactions:

THE FIJIANS. A POPULAR VISITING TEAM. APPRECIATIVE
CROWD AT LANCASTER PARK

Since G. Parr's All-England Eleven played 22 of Canterbury at Hagley Park in February, 1864, Christchurch cricket enthusiasts have seen many overseas teams in action, but few of them could have been received with the warmth which greeted the Fijians at Lancaster Park on Saturday. The crowd, officially estimated at 11,000, was one of the largest which has gathered at a cricket match locally, and for six sunny hours it was delighted with the play of the visitors. Cricket crowds often show a rather partisan outlook, and this one was no exception; its hopes and fears, however, were all directed towards the progress of the Fijians.

The visiting team showed an obvious enjoyment in its cricket, and the spectators could not help but share the feeling. The Fijians gave cricket lovers every reason to remember them. Early in the morning play, the opening batsmen, P. T. Raddock and H. J. Apted, gave an exhibition of stroke play worthy of the connoisseur, while their quick running between the wickets had the crowd shouting with excitement. Later, Bula gave one of the most satisfying exhibitions of hitting ever seen at a ground, while P. A. Snow played a captain's innings which might have come from a boy's story book.

At the end of the innings there was some straight comedy, with the last two batsmen roaring instructions to each other, running almost impossible singles, beginning others and scrambling back, and playing some of the worst but most captivating strokes the ground has known.

In yet another mood, the Fijians, at the tea interval, entertained the crowd with their singing in harmony of two sentimental songs of their homeland.

It was at this ground that Mosese was lost. A six was hit by a Canterbury player out of the ground. Mosese, in the outfield, jumped over two fences, threw the ball back and play was about to resume when it was noticed that Mosese had not returned. Another fielder was sent to the back of the large grandstand to find him but came back with gestures of defeat, which amused the crowd. Mosese simply could not be found, so the game proceeded.

With ten men, Fiji ran out a Canterbury batsman. After an over, Mosese appeared from quite the other side of the ground to discover a fresh batsman in the middle and the fieldsmen in different positions. It transpired that he could not jump back over the fence as the ground was much lower outside. Mosese eventually came in through the main Memorial gates, the gatekeepers not a little reluctant to let anyone in without money or a pass as well as astonished by the belated appearance of a fuzzy-haired Fijian in a cream skirt. And Mosese's English was not good enough to explain the position. The crowd was highly entertained by this diverting incident.

Inevitably, we had our camp followers. New Zealand is, or was, starved of visitors and women found the team (in some cases the first cricketers whom they had watched) alluring, with ourselves not a little allured. It would be remiss of me not to report that some attention came my way as the captain and sole European player. Some of the load on the field was lifted delectably when off it. There had been a story spread that the team consisted entirely of bachelors. Whether or not this was believed, there could not have been a greater warmth of reception.

No stage fright was experienced when we were asked to appear from behind the stage curtain in the interval at His Majesty's Theatre, Dunedin, of a Maori performance to mark the Otago Centenary. Before a packed house, the team gave a superb rendering of songs, followed by less euphonic speeches by Gosling, the unpersonable manager, and myself. We were later given a Maori chiefly reception at Ohinemutu when Ratu George Cakobau, as the paramount chief of Fiji, was chief guest, speaking, as custom dictated in Maori–Fijian relationship, in Fijian which, not being understood by Maoris, had to be translated into English by me. We had been welcomed by touching of foreheads followed by a most melodic *poi* dance. This involved the rhythmic twisting of suspended balls of flax by women in flax skirts, some of them part-European (the classically beautiful Marjorie Jenkins was the leader and, as custom dictated, she adopted me for the night) and markedly attractive. They helped us to make ourselves less aware of the sulphurous fumes of the geysers (which took me right back to my earliest Leicester days within range of gasworks).

All experience was fresh to most of us. Invited to climb the quite splendid, symmetrical cone of Mount Egmont, we set off with every intention of reaching the snow — the first that all but Edward, George and I had seen — until we realized that such steep climbing would have disastrous effects on unaccustomed muscles for the next day's play. Regretfully, it had to be called off at 1000 feet, 5000 feet below the snow line.

Fijians' lack of sophistication was a great draw for onlookers. The more worldly members of the team were also amused by it, especially when Kaminieli Aria, a police corporal from Nadi and the largest member of the team at 18 stone, asked a waitress to pass him the milk and she absentmindedly gave him a silver jug resembling that used for milk but now full of mayonnaise. Aria poured it in his tea, drank it and was heard to warn us that New Zealand milk could be a shade sour. He saw fun in everything, including himself. Broadcasting from Suva on his return, he proudly declared with his sunburst of a laugh, 'My friend, Auckland zoo's biggest elephant, couldn't carry my weight.'

Semi, who had bought his first pipe from which he was inseparable, also caused amusement when he broke it by falling out of bed in his sleep (he was accustomed to sleeping at home on mats on the floor) with the extinguished pipe still in his mouth. Bowl and mouthpiece, to his distress, now lay permanently separated. We had to buy a replacement of the beloved new appurtenance for him first thing in the morning.

It was a long time before the team ceased exclaiming with half shock, half fun whenever a train plunged through a tunnel. Trains were a pleasurable novelty, except to six-foot-three-inch Viliame who, lying asleep on a seat with his bare foot stretched forward, had it trapped in a door by a guard passing through. There was that other injury alluded to earlier. Ratu George, towards the end of the tour, was to let a fast ball hit and break a bare toe. This was one of the rare instances in Fiji's cricket history of a barefooted player coming unstuck on the field. Despite these two foot casualties, there was much gain in not wearing shoes, particularly for fielders, who were so much faster in movement.

The barefooted Fijians could not master European dancing: they would stand back in admiration at even my amateur performances in the early hours with Coral, the sinuous, attention-holding singer of Martin Winiata's Maori cabaret band in Christchurch.

From Whangarei in the extreme, almost subtropical north to Invercargill in the deepest south (the nearest town on the globe to the Antarctic) an immense fuss was made of the team without affecting heads in the slightest. Off the field, the tour was one long (without seeming to me long in the least) diplomatic and stimulating success. On the field, aided by the fact that it only rained one afternoon, in Nelson (ironically holding the highest annual sunshine figures in the country), the tour of 17 three- and two-day matches was no less a triumph than the off-the-field excellence they had achieved among such marvellously attractive people in a wonderfully receptive country linked closely to Fiji, not least through its being a mutual front line of defence in the war. The bigger the crowd, the better the team played. Having suffered from agoraphobia (dislike of crowds on wide hard surfaces) since 1967, I find this astonishing to reflect on personally. I could not now appear on a ground even in a walking capacity. I loved crowds in 1948: nearly 50 years on I detest them.

As captain, I met some distinctive figures in New Zealand's cricket history. When I was not batting, they would come and chat with me, to my enjoyment. Douglas Hay, who lived to be 91, had played for Auckland against the Fijians in 1895. Only two-day matches had been played on that Fijian tour, but they had been given first-class status, which made the withholding of that status from the 1948 team until 1987 all the more illogical, as did the fact that the subsequent team (in 1954) was given first-class status in advance, purely on the strength of the 1948 team's performance, despite their record being less good (against opponents lacking Test players then on tour in South Africa) and their appearance less picturesque — footwear had replaced bare feet and trousers had taken the place of *sulu*s.

Douglas Hay had played for New Zealand against England in 1903 and had been the manager of the New Zealand tour of England in 1927. An old friend, Stewart Dempster, who had played for Sir Julien Cahn's XI and been captain of Leicestershire before the war while I was captain of the Leicestershire Second XI, gave the team some useful fielding tips. He was probably New Zealand's greatest batsman ever.

M. L. Page (the only part-Maori, I think, to play for his country) and Ian Cromb, both former New Zealand captains, went out of their way to compliment and advise. Like Hay, two others of a different vintage sought me out to my special pleasure — S. G.

Smith, the Northants, Trinidad and Auckland player, and F. W. Gilligan, the eldest of the three Gilligan county cricketers (of whom two had played for England) and headmaster of Wanganui Collegiate School. I knew of Smith's eminent all-round performances for the West Indies and Northants, but had not realized that he had eventually become a distinguished player in New Zealand. Frank Gilligan shared his brother Arthur's charm — I was only to meet briefly the third brother, Harold.

Walter Hadlee, captain of Canterbury, which defeated us in a close finish to a high-scoring match with Wal and Bula making centuries, asked for my impressions of Fiji's opponents to help him select the New Zealand team he was about to captain for what turned out to be a most successful tour of England in 1949: he became a lifelong friend and frequent visitor to us in England. Wal was always the essence of balance and composure. Three of his sons (to whom he once introduced me) played for New Zealand, their fame culminating in one, Sir Richard.

As he was in Dunedin at the time for the six months' celebration of the Otago Centenary, that human legend, General Sir Bernard (later Lord) Freyberg, VC, GCMG, KCB, KBE, DSO (three bars), Governor-General from 1946 to 1952, and his wife invited us to the temporary Government House where, guided by his comptroller, Neville (later Lord) Wigram, I presented the team. He later came to see us play and, when the teams were lined up in front of the pavilion, I led him down the row reintroducing the Fiji side. A Pathé News film of this was seen by audiences in cinemas throughout New Zealand. The newsreel in the programme also showed excerpts of the practice before the game and some of the game itself. This was the first time I had seen motion pictures of myself actually playing (as opposed to standing with Edward Cakobau at Sir Pelham Warner's side in London in 1946), just as it was for the Fijians, who were delighted but not overwhelmed. The red carpet had certainly been rolled out for us.

Freyberg was of German–Russian origin and his bankrupt father had emigrated from England with him and four other members of his family. Bernard was the youngest. He became New Zealand's champion swimmer, much later failing twice by a few yards to swim the English Channel, and set up as a dentist. He was taking part in the Mexican civil war when the First World War started and at that point he returned to England. He had reason to regard himself as lucky. Wounded nine times (and a further three times in the Second World War), he was awarded the DSO for a brazen swimming exploit to Turkish positions in the Dardanelles. He was then awarded the VC in France and gained a second DSO a few minutes before the armistice.

Extraordinarily, a third DSO came at the eleventh hour of the Second World War, throughout which he was commander of the New Zealand Expeditionary Force, including a period as commander-in-chief in the impossible circumstances of the Crete disaster. He was a friend of Churchill, who asked to see his scars. What goes in has to come out and, on meeting him in Dunedin, I noticed the wounds on his throat where a bullet had entered on one side and emerged on the other. A tall, heavy figure, I was struck, as were so many, by his humility and gentleness. I would have found it hard to convey to the Fijians his quite outstanding distinction had he not greeted us all so modestly and quietly: this impressed the Fijians, who saw it as an indication that he was a man of real depths, a veritable high chief.

Less good for the ego had been an assassination threat, which I or the team (it was never clear which) received by telephone in Wellington before we won that vital match. At lunch in the hotel on Sunday (the second day) I was told that there was a telephone call for me. It turned out to be an anonymous caller in a rough voice threatening me (and also implying the team or members of it) with: 'I am out to get you. I don't forget Fiji and it'll be the end for you.' The tone was ugly enough for me to report it to the police, who judged it prudent for me to leave the hotel inconspicuously for the day (I took a cheerful little train to Silverstream in the Hutt Valley to renew my friendship with Ian Salmond, referred to earlier as second-in-command of the RNZAF at Nadi six years previously) and for the team to keep together, but away from the hotel as much as possible. They said they would provide us with escorts to and from the pavilion for the remaining two days at the ground and at the hotel. We were vulnerable targets. The caller seemed semi-drunk, but no more than that: he had found out where we were staying. I have always assumed that he had fallen foul of authority, either as a soldier or, more likely, as a CCU man, in some Fijian village in Nadi. It was the only sour incident on the sweetest of tours.

By the end of the tour the Fijians were either a little tired or homesick; although, as I pointed out, a tour of England would have been months longer. The fact that we played every day but Sundays (with only that one interruption for rain) contributed to the intensity of the tour. But personally, despite a thigh severely strained early on and persisting to the end, I could have gone on for twice as long with such a splendid team. Ratu George Cakobau (whose name a spectator at the remarkable Pukekura Park ground, New Plymouth, could not get closer to than a shouted 'Kooka-burra') and Ratu Edward Cakobau (joining us from Oxford half-way through) had given me every encouragement, so important as coming from their rank. There was not a dissentient or long face, even among those periodically not selected for matches.

Only J. W. Gosling, the manager (a Fiji-born clerk in commerce who had become a major in the local army — a hostile bowler on matting but unvicious on turf) had been a poor choice. He spoke no Fijian and did not know the colony outside Suva. His speech-making was pathetic and gauche (totally out of tune with the effect of the team in New Zealand) and his lack of social graces and brusqueness made him a marked misfit with the team. It was agreed after the tour that he would not go abroad with a Fiji team again. Sukuna had heard from some New Zealand source how deficient Gosling was and he was emphatic on this ruling. The speech-making was quite important: New Zealanders love it. They were not content, understandably, with Gosling.

I was occasionally called on to speak twice a day (at the lunch interval and at a night function), or sometimes even three times a day when there was a prior mayoral reception. I would sometimes start off with a gambit used by W. G. Grace, as captain on a lengthy tour of Canada, in which he would say 'Never have I seen such a beautiful ground as here at —,' or 'Never have I played on such a superb pitch as here at —,' or 'Never have I seen such beautiful women as here at —.' Then he would sit down, having added merely 'I congratulate you.' I could not get away with just that in New Zealand, but it was a little wearing to think up different felicitous speeches on top of concentrating on captaincy and personal play. And of course the New Zealanders wanted to hear Ratu George's English, which was naturally excellent but was sometimes reticently forthcoming. The late reinforcement of Ratu Edward, with his ever-ready panache for wit and style, was a great bonus.

Never having flown before, and perhaps with more imagination than the Fijians who also had not been in an aeroplane, I was more than displeased when a dockers' strike obstructed the *Matua*: this meant that we had to return by air. Here again, there were holdups as the aircraft was not functioning properly. It was a New Zealand Airways Corporation Short Sunderland flying boat, *Mata'atua*, from Mechanics' Bay, Auckland. Take-off was all right, even with green sea splashing over the fuselage cabin windows, and I did not greatly dislike the smooth progress until, near Kadavu and the end of the journey, we encountered a tropical storm. The aircraft slewed sideways, dipped and rose with the turbulence and generally advanced (I hoped — it was hard to tell) with a side-on crab-like motion until we reached Laucala Bay in Suva where there had been a huge rainstorm, rather dispiriting for those waiting for us. When we came down in the lagoon and the green seas this time completely submerged the windows, I had wondered whether we had not gone down altogether. My first flight had sadly not been confidence-inspiring.

We were received at the landing stage by the Governor's ADC and Nixie Caldwell and Kingsley Roth, both representing Ratu Sir Lala Sukuna who had to be away from Viti Levu. Suva Town Council wanted to give us a civic reception, but I declined. Led by a naturally not over-magnanimous mayor, Alport Barker (who was also editor of the *Fiji Times* which reported the tour adequately), they had been less than lukewarm when we left to go on the tour as an unknown quantity. The Roths put me up, although I was on call for broadcasts and by hostesses whose parties wanted to hear of the tour first hand. The Governor and Lady

Freeston received the team at GH. There was about a week to wait before the *Yanawai* was due to go to Taveuni. This stay with the Roths further strengthened our friendship.

Once back in Fiji I could hardly wait to return to Taveuni to see Anne and Stephanie. At nine months she was of course nicely larger and entertaining. It was impossible to know if she remembered me for the missing three months that had been so full for me. Certainly it took her a few minutes before I seemed familiar to her. Anne had of course received letters and radio summaries of scores with one or two local papers carrying some news. Wal Warden, the judicious planter, and George Kemp, the ebullient New Zealand headmaster of the Provincial School, had helped to keep her informed. Anne had kept Charles as much as possible in the picture as I had simply never had a free moment. His pleasure over the reception of *The Light and the Dark*, out just before the tour, could scarcely have exceeded mine over it. I thought that it gave him a permanent place in English literature.

Settling down again to the Taveuni routine after the Legges had returned to Levuka was not easy. The Roko Tui Cakaudrove, Ratu Tiale Wimbledon Thomas Vuiyasawa, and his staff welcomed me back with an official ceremony. Ratu Sukuna's brother (seven years younger) had many of the fraternal features, including a long upper lip and rather pursed mouth with deep lines on either side. He was taller than Ratu Sir Lala and did not have anything approaching his vocabulary (he had been to an Australian school) or intellect and, perhaps not unnaturally, had an inferiority complex about his brother. Judged quite separately from his brother, he was an impressive chief in his own right. I always enjoyed his picturesque phrases thoughtfully uttered. 'Crocodile tears' was an example and Christopher Legge used to tell the story against himself that one day he (Legge) was a little short-tempered, unusually so from my knowledge of him, and Ratu Tiale solemnly said 'Keep your wool on, Legge' — but Legge was totally bald. Ratu Tiale was a sturdy, ponderous friend in our joint administration of Cakaudrove Province from 1947 to 1950.

On first returning to Taveuni, I most of all missed the daily exercise the tour had involved — and the excited and exciting crowds. I had to launch myself, in my leisure, straight away on to finishing *Cricket in the Fiji Islands*, which the New Zealand publishers, Whitcombe & Tombs of Christchurch and Dunedin, wanted as soon as I had added (and Anne could conclude typing) the story of the recent tour. Fortunately, all research for earlier parts of the history had been previously — if arduously — compiled.

From writing about being captain of a touring team in the lime-light to sitting under a hanging paraffin lantern in the Taveuni hospital taking a dying declaration from a young Indian woman was a return to stark reality, if not quite to everyday existence. In the Scutari-like gloom (which Florence Nightingale had endured in the Crimea) I had to take a deposition at midnight at a bedside. If anyone has been nearly murdered and is almost certain to die, a magistrate, should he be available, rather than a police officer is expected to take down in writing whatever the victim can say.

Valen Tarte had telephoned to say that he was bringing in his car, if he could get over the Irish bridges in the torrential rain, an Indian woman of about 18 who had been assaulted with a cane knife. She had appealed to the driver of a station wagon for help and he had rushed to intercept, but was himself attacked and obliged to flee. She had then fainted through loss of blood. Nearly amputated, each arm had compound fractures and a finger had been severed.

Once the medical officer who attended to her on her arrival had made the necessary sworn statement that the victim was unlikely to recover, the police sergeant major brought in a large dark Indian of Dravidian appearance, handcuffed because any state-ment has to be taken, if possible, in the presence of the accused. He was kept behind a screen so as not to multiply the shock (her pulse and temperature were worrying). With the utmost difficulty and the help of an Indian clerk because she was a Madrasi (normally dark-skinned people but her skin was now parchment-coloured: her sensitive cast of face looked almost Burmese), I managed to get down a few utterances after she had lucidly taken the oath. Illiterate but in any case in too desperate a state, she was unable to put her inked thumb marks at the bottom of the paper on which I had recorded her account.

It was a sombre occasion with wailing relatives, the medical officer and nurses looking on anxiously, the handcuffed accused interpolating wildly and the hurricane lamp flickering. It was, as I heard the case months later, a *crime passionnel*, strangely enough in the relationship of respondent and co-respondent. The young woman survived with her arms just successfully stitched on after having been airlifted to Suva by an RNZAF Catalina for which the open sea off Waiyevo was fortunately calm enough to land. Dying declarations were rare. I never came across another magistrate who had to take one.

After this the open air was appealing and, with the Governor's approval (as required by the ordinance governing archaeological work), I made an unusual expedition. In the 1930s a European copra planter from the Nasavusavu area had first reported seeing in a little enclave in the Vanua Levu forest behind the village of Dakuniba on the opposite side of the Somosomo Straits a jumbled collection of boulders with deep incisions in almost geometrical patterns. There was also another high inscribed boulder in a nearby stream. The villagers knew nothing of their history. An American expedition off a circumnavigatory yacht led by the Fahnestock brothers shortly before the war had been told of them: its members whitewashed and photographed the markings.

Four police constables and the sergeant major, together with six prisoners and a warder, the medical officer and myself tried to lift the boulders with ropes and tackle to see if there were any marks underneath. If there had been, the likelihood was that the whole had formed an inscribed arch or vertical monument. Three days' excavation round a large long stone and then lifting it up with massive effort just sufficiently to venture to look underneath revealed nothing but a curved pig's tooth, which was indeed unusual. A full report was sent, as required, to the Governor who had given permission for this supervised and limited manœuvre, which did not amount to a rearrangement of the stones: I later gave a lecture to the Fiji Society, which was published in its *Transactions*. The keeper of the Department of Oriental Antiquities and Ethnography at the British Museum, H. J. Braunholz, had given it as his opinion that:

A few of the carvings are somewhat suggestive of Kharosthi characters ... which, of the two earliest decipherable inscriptions in India in two different kinds of alphabet, Brahmi and Kharosthi, was the earlier. It was introduced into the Punjab during Persian domination in the fifth century BC and prevailed until the fourth century AD when it was supplemented by Brahmi. It was written from right to left.

Were they so, could they have been pointers through the jungle to a path leading to something of importance? Could they have been landmarks from the sea not far below? These were hypothetical questions raised and perhaps never likely to be answered.

Ours became officially known as the Snow Expedition to Dakuniba. Lectures given to the Fiji Society by later visitors have come no nearer to establishing rhyme or reason for the inscriptions. One or two more incised stones are on Vanua Levu, far from Dakuniba, and some similar ones in the Yasawa Group on the other side of Fiji. There are in addition some undated and unidentified rock paintings on Vatulele Island lying to the west of Viti Levu. And, in all the above instances mentioned, Fijians know nothing of their history.

The expedition had needed to make a special visit across the Somosomo Straits. I had to pay another special one when, as registration officer for Taveuni and Nasavusavu, I had to collect votes for the Legislative Council elections. Elections were for individuals — there were no political parties, which in some ways was an improvement on the British constitutional system — and only Europeans, part-Europeans and Indians voted in them. The Fijians had their own Great Council of Chiefs. I had to go over the straits in my very inadequate, 60-year-old, 30-foot, two-crew yacht, the *Kapaiwai* (the engine of which, when owned by Gus Hennings, had to be forfeited by him in the First World War) to collect a ballot paper at Fawn Harbour from the solitary qualified voter for a European candidate.

A Fijian carried the heavy iron ballot box into which the single voting paper was solemnly inserted after a 14-mile trek along a fine coralline, sandy beach. My call there was on H. M. ('Dad')

Ledger, who led a kind of gentlemanly beachcomber existence at Fawn Harbour, a mere desolate inlet, halfway between Dakuniba and Buca Bay. He had a few coconut trees on two acres and, at an advanced age, eked out an existence on copra, being postmaster and on £12 a year salary as road foreman on a virtually non-existent road with no staff over which to be foreman. For him the visit was one of unconcealed delight in being able to talk to a European — no other lived within miles and then was separated decisively by thickest bush. He was born in Surrey and, apart from the period of the First World War, which was when he had last visited England, he had lived in Fiji since 1907. He reflected unhappier shades of Milton Craig of Lodoni.

On another day I had to cross the straits to collect the votes of the Buca Bay denizens — A. P. Ward, the postmaster, a Seventh Day Adventist and something of a philatelic specialist, was one of half a dozen. Another was Anthony Rupert Patrick St Aubyn, a kinsman of Lord St Levan and the family of St Aubyns of St Michael's Mount, Cornwall. Tony St Aubyn led a quiet copra planter's life at Kubulau with his part-Samoan wife. They had three of the most glamorous daughters imaginable. Dianne was one: she has been met already as applying to me at the Secretariat for a job in the bright lights of Suva in 1945. The youngest, Barbara, had the smooth olive skin of that fine genetic mixture: I could not help seeing much of this when I collided with her on my way to a shower in the cubicle outside the house. She had not heard my bare feet approaching as she emerged, also barefooted and only half covered.

I used to have to pass through Buca Bay on my way down the length of Natewa Bay to the Government Station of Nasavusavu where once a month I would hold court and generally inspect the station. Alfred Small was Officer-in-Charge, a mostly clerical position (he had held it at Navua on my local leave in 1944), but he was unlikely to set the backwater on fire before his impending retirement. With the shortage of staff during the war and until halfway through my time, the administration of Nasavusavu was combined with that of Taveuni in the person of the DO. This imposed too heavy and geographically awkward a burden on the

DO and I pressed successfully for a separation. I would stay for about a week each time at the Hot Springs Hotel, named after the Rotorua-like hot springs, in the centre of Nasavusavu Township.

Major W. E. Willoughby-Tottenham, the veteran president of Fiji's St John's Ambulance Association, of unsteady gait and inevitably known as Wobbly-Tottering, was the absentee owner. I little thought that the day would arrive when huge corn-coloured P & O liners would glide majestically into Nasavusavu Bay, as they did in the 1950s and 1960s, although in the 1870s, when Levuka was obviously too hill-bound to remain the capital for long, Nasavusavu had been considered as a possible site for the premier settlement in Fiji, along with Suva (which was of course selected) and Galoa Bay, Kadavu. The Government Station at Valeci, Nasavusavu, belonged to the last century: it was not one in which to be located for too long. Nevertheless, had I been there I would have made a botanical garden, which would have suited the atmosphere well.

Halfway back up Natewa Bay on my return to Taveuni, I called on Wilfred W. Wright who lived on Nukudrau, a tiny island joined by a mud flat to the mainland and to the Fijian village of Viani. He loathed Fijians, who apparently scarcely ever used his store. He knew where my sympathies lay when I told him that I would be staying the night with them. He insisted on giving me a drink in his tiny shanty-cum-store. No Europeans were near him or called on him. Wright, who had been born in Yorkshire, had left England in 1895 and had not returned home after fighting in the Boer War. His existence was rather different from Tom Stockwell's at Lomaloma. For a start, there was no woman in evidence. Also, he was mad keen on cricket and wanted to know all about my recent tour of New Zealand.

Groping into the cobwebbed recesses of his hut, he drew out a bottle of South African claret in honour of his first outside visitor for more years than he could remember. Had it been uncorked I would have had misgivings about joining him in his drink, but as it was it was not too bad. In England he had been in the wine trade. He spoke of trams with affection as though they still existed and he had used them yesterday. He was Maughamesque all right.

His cast of face was quite distinguished — Edwardian moustache, hair tinged with a little colour (although he was 75), his nose hooked. It was apparent that he changed his singlet and blue short dungarees (they would be called jeans today) seldom. Cauldrons of home-brewed beer were simmering in the kitchen where we drank as contrasted with his ramshackle store.

He was reasonably well-off and held a Bank of New Zealand account. For all his self-imposed remoteness he was a man of no rustic or uncultured mind. The Agriculture Department, he said, received from him constant streams of what he hoped were helpful communications. His hobby was international affairs, a strange pastime for one with no wireless and only weeks-old issues of the *Fiji Times and Herald*. There was no apparent loss in his English, which he had scarcely spoken in years; his mind was as alert as it would be if he were living in the heart of a metropolis. My last sight of him was his seeing me over the mud flat in the light of his hurricane lantern, shaking his head with incredulity that I should spend the evening dining with the Fijians. I pondered whether I was guilty of dereliction but felt reasonably certain that there was little melancholia in him after such passage of time. When he died he left his island to the RSPCA as a final rebuff to Fijians whom he considered, sometimes with an element of accuracy, to be not always well disposed to all animals.

Right over the other side across the considerable width of Natewa Bay in the village of Vuinadi (to hold court jointly with an NSM — cases limited entirely to Fijians), I recall the moonlight etching with absolute verisimilitude the superb crenellated leaves of the breadfruit trees between the *bures* on the soft white sand. They were exact stencils. It was a warm seductive night: the effect of the moon was as if the village were floodlit. I never knew so many moons in Fiji of remarkable intensity surpassing this one.

From the moon to the sun. The *Kapaiwai* was so small that there was no shelter, but in fact my skin was especially badly burnt, so it seemed, when there was no sun and on what seemed to be dull days. So close to the sea there was, I suppose, always a glare and, although I would cover my face in a lot of Nivea cream, in which I then believed, I would be nearly fried. The agony would inevitably come two or three days later when the entire skin would peel off, exposing a tender redness. I must have lost 99 layers of skin in my time in Fiji, not least when I played cricket for a whole day, for I could not bat in a cap or hat and never felt happy wearing one. Ironically, one of my worst bouts of sunburn was from batting for a few hours on the 1948 tour of New Zealand in the opening match at Whangarei in the extreme north of New Zealand in a not very strong sun. After that I had to field throughout the tour in a Cambridge Crusader's cap (there was no team cap), to my distaste.

Returning from Vuinadi involved a most unusual experience. The sea was unsettled in Natewa Bay that morning, noticeably choppy. The sky was threatening. Crossing the bay, the *Kapaiwai* was broadside to the current coming from the vast opening at the top of the bay. Suddenly, the one-eyed veteran captain, Samu (Sam) Ibo, and the bright-eyed engineer, Akeai, who composed the whole crew, pointed to the wide entrance. There seemed to be a mass of angry furrows towering, fuming and dropping ahead. Samu turned the yacht bow straight into it and advised me to hold on tight while Akeai went to the engine. Very quickly the first of the furrows pounded our boat: it lifted the craft up uncomfortably. Then three vast wide waves rolled fast towards us. I hung on like grim death while Samu held both arms on the rudder.

The first wave lifted us up vertically. Then down we plunged into the vortex, only for the second wave to raise us even higher and drop us even lower. It was the third that represented touch and go. The frail craft's nose now jerkily pointed up to the grey sky and we just as suddenly switched back down into the vacuum that it left. With a series of judders, we eventually settled from these tidal waves at sea into predictably rough water, but as it turned out the worst was over and we edged nearer the coast and made for Rabe Island, where Major Francis George Leopold Holland, GM, was DO. I learnt from him that there had been a considerable earthquake below Japan, the sequence of which was expected to affect seas for a substantial distance in two or three days' time. This was what the *Kapaiwai* had encountered in the middle of the bay.

From Natewa Bay — on a different occasion — I saw a water-spout near the ocean's horizon. I asked Samu what action would be taken if it approached. His reply that he would steer away from it was hardly assuring, given the relative speeds of the *Kapaiwai* and waterspouts. The truth was that if the phenomenon came one's way, in all but the fastest of craft one would be hurtled into the air up the spout of churning water and descend in pieces. This accounts for the total disappearance without trace of some craft.

Rabe island was bought by the Ocean Islanders after the war. These Micronesian Banabans (from part of the Gilbert Islands) had amassed royalties from their island having been ravaged by the British Phosphate Commission's excavations of guano and, after being exiled by the Japanese during the war, they had sagely been advised to move to the lushness of Rabe, formerly a copra plantation owned by Lever Brothers. Accustomed as they were to a virtually coralline existence, it took them some time to settle in to a hilly one. Their Fijian neighbours were tolerant of the depredations on their own fishing in the Buca Bay area.

Led by a Methodist pastor, Tito Rotan, they became rapacious and litigious, alleging that their royalties on Ocean Island had been inadequate for 50 years. Their civil action was the longest ever to be held in the British courts. Journalists and those not understanding Ocean Island, Rabe island and the islanders became publicity-minded and emotive. Reason was conspicious by its absence. They did not prove their case. Ocean Islanders always had the reputation of being largely sea lawyers — or bush lawyers as that species were known in Fiji.

It was Ocean Island to which I had been invited to go by Sir Harry Luke in 1941 just before the bombing that followed Pearl Harbor. Major Holland, helping others to escape, was a fugitive from the Gilberts where he had been Director of Education when the Japanese threatened invasion: he was awarded the GM for his organization and maintaining hazardous communications with the WPHC's Suva headquarters.

Another example of island transmigration, which added interest to being District Officer Taveuni, was a happier one, partly because of the difference between Micronesian and Polynesian temperaments. It was my duty to board at Waiyevo a ship, the *Awahou*, carrying a load of Ellice Islanders — Polynesians, unlike the Micronesian Gilbertese — from overcrowded Vaitupu Island to Kioa island, which was directly opposite Taveuni on the approach to Buca Bay. These people were most attractive; the women had quite huge, really liquid black eyes and absolutely straight hair. They faced a tremendous contrast in life from their over-crowded, six-foot-high atolls to craggy, hilly Kioa. Their relationship with Fijians over matters like fishing boundaries (they were better, as were Gilbertese, in fishing technique than Fijians) was more tactful than that of the Rabe Banabans.

The first migration had been brought to Kioa from Vaitupu by Major Donald Kennedy, a strong character who after 20 years' administration in the Gilbert and Ellice Islands had been courage itself as a district officer in the Solomon Islands during the Japanese invasions and had been awarded the DSO. He had a predilection for native women, drinking and, sadly, a degree of sadism, practically unknown in the history of British administrators in the Pacific and, it is hoped, elsewhere. Larger than life, Kennedy died solitarily on Kadavu in Fiji. It was the second Ellice Island migration that I had watched over from Taveuni. Kioa is still Tuvaluan (as Ellice Islanders have been renamed) in its people: they have retained their identity and some solitariness from their own kind following the example of Kennedy.

I was periodically missing that wonderful social whirligig of the cricket tour of New Zealand and finding Taveuni life inevitably an anticlimax. Whether it was for that reason or for the lack of the strict physical regimen the daily cricket had represented — now I only had tennis once a week — I was suddenly infected with a plague of carbuncles. I thought the first to be a boil or a mere septic sore until it turned into a crater containing seven boils on my waistline. Then I developed seven more carbuncles, each with its craters, three more in a cluster on my waistline, one on my shoulder, one on my back, one on my jawbone and one on my knee — this latter the most painful, preventing my being able to walk the few yards to the office.

Work was brought to me at the house and, to cap it all, proofs from New Zealand of *Cricket in the Fiji Islands*, which had to be checked while the *Yanawai* turned round on its three to four days in Buca Bay, Rabe and Rotuma. Wal Warden was kind enough to help me with them. I could only wear a loose dressing gown in public and, in private, nothing. It is only in such circumstances that one realizes how dependent one's body is on a waist for wearing clothes. The carbuncles lasted for about a month, boiling and bursting over like volcanoes and making me feel as hot as an erupting one. In those pre-penicillin days there seemed to be no cure. Then some blessed person, whom I cannot remember, suggested a diet of stout. Within half a week I began to feel cool and the eruptions ceased as rapidly as they had appeared.

I had been conscious all along of the fate of William Pakenham-Walsh, the malnourished cadet stationed before the war on Kadavu, who had a carbuncle stung by a hornet — with fatal effects. When the Prince of Wales recently compared a protruding architectural monstrosity proposed for London with a carbuncle, I could understand and warmly agree with his wish to use an unpleasant-sounding description, but doubted whether he had ever seen a carbuncle, which does not protrude so much as represent a crater. I was clearly very run-down physically. Mentally, Taveuni was too small for me. I felt the claustrophobia as much as the sweltering heat from the island's volcanic soil. Fiji was oppressing me too, partly because of my long sojourn on the island, but more generally because of its prospects. I wrote to Charles on 8 May 1949:

> Our total savings are about £250 and by the time we come on leave at the beginning of 1951 they are unlikely to be more than £350. During our last leave we got through about £200 savings in addition to salary paid during leave. It would have been very much more expensive had we not been able to stay with Eric of course and it is not certain whether we will do the same on our next leave. . . . You were kind enough to say that you would look after Stephanie's education, which at this distance would be an almost impoverishing burden for us. This type of job has

considerable unseen snags — some of them being (a) having to send children away to school and find a change of climate, entailing also a heavy bill for passages; (b) after four-year tours in wearing climates and a narrow circle of pleasures, a lot must be crammed into one's infrequent leaves; (c) the fact that we now have to pay for quarters without being properly compensated in increased salary; (d) that the type of qualities receiving quickest promotion in the Service are not individuality and initiative.

Although it is true that Income Tax is less heavy here there are of course far fewer benefits to be derived here for this very reason — practically no public services.

It was at this time that Pamela Hansford Johnson, his future wife, first addressed Percy as 'Charles dear' in a letter of 4 July 1949.

Humphrey Evans was on the same *Yanawai* on his way up to Rotuma as District Officer/Medical Officer, Rotuma, with his new Swiss wife Hélène, whom we thought charming and who has been previously mentioned. The *Yanawai* returned and the proofs were just in time put in the mail for New Zealand via Suva. The chance to photograph me scrutinizing them on their arrival had not eluded Humphrey.

We were saddened a few months later to hear of Hélène's suicide on Rotuma, as referred to earlier. Wherever Humphrey went he devoted himself to his work and research: the change for Hélène from Geneva and not knowing any of the admittedly difficult language at Rotuma had no doubt contributed to the tragedy.

As usual, we welcomed every moment of a stay with us by Ratu Sir Lala Sukuna. He would delight in reading my copy of the 1907 *Cyclopaedia of Fiji*, its biographies compiled with the exercise of much inventiveness, seen through by Sukuna who would chuckle over their flights of fancy, of the subscribers who paid for insertion of their entries.

An eccentric visitor to us about this time was Captain Hugh Moreton Frewen, spade-bearded, nautically capped in his yacht *Viking Ahoy*. He had loaned it to makers of the film *Blue Lagoon* in the Yasawa Group. Jean Simmons, the leading female in the film, not surprisingly appreciated its tiled bathroom after the primitiveness of work on land in the group. Frewen wanted to sell the vessel and buy a copra estate. He claimed, we all thought unconvincingly, to be closely related to Churchill. Later, we discovered that a Moreton Frewen had married a sister of Jenny Jerome, the wife of Lord Randolph Churchill and mother of Winston. But we never did find out whether his claim was genuine.

I had been determined to improve the Government Station staff, which during Collins's time (perhaps before) had somehow become tainted by corruption, no doubt affected by the Rewan chiefly clerk's embezzlement. Also, with so much travelling across to Vanua Levu (I was in charge of about a third of that island, almost as large as Viti Levu), a financial rearrangement was required. Not only did I succeed in convincing Suva headquarters that I should be relieved of sub-accountant duties but to my delight I found that my trusted old friend, Hindi tutor and ludo opponent from Naduruloulou days, Gajadhar Singh, was to take the position.

He was worthy of a higher status and, while never totally happy in the European-dominated society of Taveuni, he got on with the work and was always an agreeable and efficient companion. I had obtained too a sergeant major of police far superior to his none too bright predecessor. Indeed, Jaoji (George) Suguturaga should have gone far in the police but after I left Fiji he gave it up at inspector rank, married Ratu George Cakobau's ex-wife, and tried commerce unsuccessfully. He was to visit us in England dressed as an inspector in white scallop-edged *sulu*, scarlet cummerbund over dark blue tunic and in brightly polished sandals. His huge head of hair was trimmed like the neatest bush. Fiji-style hair was to be imitated not long after by what was erroneously called Afro-style. The West Indians had cribbed the Fijian (or Ethiopian, pre-Rastafarian) style.

Having recovered from the carbuncle visitation, I was fit enough to organize the visit to Taveuni and Nasavusavu (Holland arranged for the call to Rabe) of the Governor Sir Brian Freeston and his family. They came on the cruiser *Bellona*, whose captain,

Douglas Hammersly Johnston, was a most distinguished-looking and pleasant individual. As the superbly streamlined warship, lent to New Zealand from the Royal Navy, steamed in to anchor off Somosomo village it looked enormous yet sleek.

I took aboard it the *cavuikelekele* party of Fijians for the whale's tooth presentation for the weighing of the anchor. The Tui Cakau (the markedly imperious Ratu Josefa Lalabalavu) made the presentation on bended knees and the Governor's squatting *matanivanua* accepted it after he (the Governor) had taken it in both hands as he sat next to the captain and me. Then I went back in the cruiser's launch with the crew ceremonially holding boat hooks at right angles. The official party walked behind the Governor to the *vakatunaloa* (temporary structure of palm leaves ornamented with hibiscus and crotons) and its row of chairs for the gamut of presentations of further whales' teeth representing offerings of *yaqona* and crops and the mixing of the chiefly *yaqona* drink.

The six-foot-six-inch Governor looked gaunt. His career had been in the Colonial Office except for a short time in Tanganyika and the governorship before Fiji of the Leeward Islands. In his official white uniform and plumed helmet he did not look the proconsular type. Bespectacled and stork-like, he was a man of gentle nature, approachability and humanity, helped considerably by his wife who had been a doctor and was fascinated by Fijian customs, about which she asked me to correspond with her directly. At Waiyevo we put on a garden party under the huge weeping fig tree on the lawn beside the house to which the ship's officers were also invited.

This was the last occasion of its kind on Taveuni: no vessel as large as a cruiser ever subsequently visited the island and no vessel anywhere near its size carried a governor there. Freeston was interested, and I was flattered, that some of the officers knew of me as captain of the recent touring cricket team representing Fiji. New Zealand is small enough for names once heard not to be easily forgotten.

From Taveuni I embarked on the *Bellona* as part of the viceregal party. It was the sheerest luxury to cross the Somosomo Straits, at last without being thrown about on a frail craft, and pass through Buca Bay on the supremely elegant length of the cruiser, standing on the bridge with the captain and listening to his quiet orders through the glistening brass instruments and pipelines to various parts of the ship. At a meal in the capacious saloon with the Captain, the Governor and his family, I had my first experience of drinking the toast to the King sitting down in accordance with naval custom.

To my eyes, the Rabe ceremony for the Governor looked (and perhaps was) artificial compared with the Fijian custom on Taveuni. Then, the rapier-like shape swiftly glided through the straits to tower over Nasavusavu wharf where, having introduced Freeston to the Nasavusavu worthies and to a Fijian welcome, I had to return to Taveuni on the humble *Kapaiwai*, which had been waiting for me — truly anticlimatic and uncomfortable as usual, scarcely visible below the wharf.

But before then, on the voyage from Rabe to Nasavusavu, by pure chance while they were walking round the deck past the porthole of my cabin, I overheard Lady Freeston say to her daughter Stella (who was only about 19 at the time) 'Yes, Mr Snow should be transferred to Suva. He is one to go far.' I was much heartened to hear this and was struck by the extraordinary coincidence of the remark being made outside my porthole: they could not have known that I was in that cabin. I believe that Ratu Sukuna, who had said when I was transferred to Taveuni that it should not be for long as there was so much that I could do in Suva, must have spoken to Freeston before he sailed to Taveuni.

Sukuna, I knew, minded very much that none of the administrative officers were playing any public games with the Fijians when, from every consideration, it was important that they should. Collins had done so once or twice. Before him, Islay McOwan, Baker, Pennefather, Howard and a few others of their vintage had been active in this respect, as had some predecessors, but currently there was no one. Sukuna felt administrators had a duty to use their position of leadership to foster, or preferably (if they could or had any ball sense) participate in, interracial public games. Tennis was insufficiently multiracial; hockey very little so;

rugby and association football and golf not at all. I myself was disappointed that no administrative officer in either the districts or the capital encouraged interracial cricket and that very few of them engaged in any form of social contact between the races. As it was, it was too easy for me to be outstanding in this respect. This is said with no sanctimoniousness. It was a simple fact. For Sukuna it took on real significance and he worked for me to be where I could be most effective in this respect. But I was not transferred to Suva for another year.

When invited to stay at Government House in return for our hospitality in Taveuni, Anne and I were rather taken aback by Freeston saying to Lady Mabel after dinner, 'Now, Mother,' (he always called her this — rather ungubernatorial, I thought) 'let's get the table out.' This was in the small annexe off the drawing room and was the signal, we realized, for the bridge that he played nightly, frenetically and — I was told — unskilfully. We had to confess that we never played it. In truth, we avoided learning it as it was so regularly a source of dissent amid the postmortems that too often followed in Fiji. We played almost every other game, notably poker and *vingt-et-un* (pontoon) as they involved no partnership embarrassment. The Freestons must have heard that we were card players and assumed that this could only be bridge.

So Freeston, with a sigh that he could not suppress, said 'Well, Mother, I expect that the Snows after their long journey [from Taveuni] would like an early night.' This viceregal command was the order of the day or rather the night. We were ushered off to bed: it was only nine o'clock. He never really immersed himself in things Fijian. Nevertheless, Lady Freeston did. We had not lost too many marks over the bridge deficiency for Lady Freeston later invited me frequently to be her partner on the tennis court in its beautiful setting in front of Government House.

When the traditional length of stay at Government House expired, we moved to the Grand Pacific Hotel to await a vessel for return to Taveuni. The tranquil Maughamesque atmosphere (Willie did actually stay there but described it inaccurately) was broken one evening when our Somosomo housegirl, Bale, tripped on a dark concrete step while carrying Stephanie's meal on a tray, the crashing of which sounded like a premature dinner gong. She was knocked out by the contact with the concrete and was taken through the hotel on a stretcher. We were immensely relieved that what was suspected to be a fractured skull turned out to have been avoided, probably by the large, fuzzy, resilient mass of hair on her head softening the blow. It was not, however, for that safety factor that, with only the rarest interlude forced on us by necessity when we had to have Indian cooks, we employed exclusively Fijian or part-Fijian household staff. It was because they created the kind of atmosphere in which Anne and I felt most comfortable.

While still on Taveuni, it was not long before we were visited by another New Zealand warship. This time it was a frigate a fraction of the size of *Bellona*, HMNZS *Pukaki* under Commander L. E. Herricks, but it made an entertaining change in the now dull routine of Taveuni life. Again there were ceremonies and a garden party, as well as a buffet dinner for 45 with the garden fountain illuminated.

Soon afterwards, 1000 residents assembled on our front lawn (an indication of its size) to celebrate Cession Day on 10 October, the seventy-fifth anniversary. I had invited the descendant of a signatory of the Deed of Cession, Tui Cakau, to help me distribute 1600 ornamental boxes of sweets to children. On this day annually I reflected privately on the special amicable relationship between the administration, chiefs and people when so much of the Empire had been acquired by conquest. It put me at ease for my presence and the chiefly status bestowed on me as a colonial administrator, obliterating any feeling of intrusion. Remarkably, King Cakobau and disparate high chiefs after several attempts to cede their islands (for payment of an American debt) finally had the magnanimous gift to Queen Victoria and her heirs accepted. Her Cabinet wanted to change the 'barbaric' name of Fiji (Tongans pronounced Viti this way) as savouring too ferociously of the cannibalism for which it was uniquely notorious. Characteristically, Prime Minister Disraeli suggested Windsor Islands, but the Queen held out for the distinctive Fiji.

The lawn was that night put to further original use by the Fiji Regiment Band, which paraded lit by car headlights. Villagers travelled miles for this show, prepared to endure the downpour

ABOVE. The author presenting the Fiji cricket team touring New Zealand, 1948, later granted first-class status, to the Governor-General of New Zealand, General Sir Bernard Freyberg, V.C., 1948. *(Photo: N.Z. Pathé News)* BELOW. The team always took the field in single file behind the author, as captain, and Ratu Sir George Cakobau, vice-captain. Bula, fifth in line from front, scored 120 in the second innings of this first-class match v. Canterbury, 1948. *(Photo: Star-Sun, Christchurch)*

ABOVE LEFT. Ratu Sir Edward Cakobau joined the Fiji team half way through the New Zealand tour on his return from Oxford, 1948. *(Photo: Rob R. Wright)* ABOVE CENTRE. A Chieftainess, Adi Senimili Cakobau, in costume on Taveuni Island for a *meke* for the Governor and the New Zealand cruiser, Bellona, 1948. *(Photo: H.M.N.Z.S. Bellona)* ABOVE RIGHT. Cherie Wright, grandaughter of a District Commissioner, Fiji, and a Samoan lady of rank, 1950. *(Photo: Rob R. Wright)* BELOW. Sir Leonard Hutton drinking *kava* at a ceremoy at Nadi Airport for the England cricket team returning from Australia, 1950. Denis Compton in centre with author on his left, next to Cyril Washbrook. *(Photo: Fiji Cricket Association)*

(part of Taveuni's 300-inch annual rainfall), which cascaded like the combined widths of the American and Canadian Niagara Falls and with the same intensity.

Not long afterwards there was an earthquake. I was talking to the doctor in the middle of the road leading to the hospital when we found ourselves swaying away from each other. We both commented on it. There were two tremors, one for two seconds, the next for about the same time length of time five seconds after the first. I had heard them at night before but not noticed one so obviously. They were rare in Fiji: the worst, which occurred shortly after we left the country, helped seriously to damage our possessions.

The final visitor in our lengthy list of callers during our three years on Taveuni was the new Colonial Secretary, Richard Stoddart, on a small yacht, *Royal Flight*. Though extremely reserved, he turned out to be a most amiable person and, I felt certain, was more observant than he appeared. Colonial Secretary Fiji from 1949 to 1957, he had come from being Chief Assistant Secretary, Sierra Leone. This was his first trip away from Suva.

Before his arrival, however, the exhilarating news had come through that I was to be transferred to Suva and on promotion — to the post of Assistant Colonial Secretary (Development). This was an unexpected first-class move. Jim Coode was to come from being District Officer Rabe, where after the Governor's visit there he had succeeded Holland and was, it was considered, underemployed on that small island and even smaller settlement, to take over from me — as he had done in Lautoka in 1943.

I took Stoddart and his party on journeys to both the south and north of Taveuni, leaving Anne to complete the packing up — indeed the house was full of crates, not the setting we would have chosen for receiving the Colonial Secretary (who was Acting Governor for this visit).

My heart sank when at the north end Bill Mackay, inveterate opponent or critic of most preceding district officers, pleaded with Stoddart for me to stay on Taveuni, saying that he had a petition to this effect. Stoddart, showing a blend of tact and firmness that I was to see on later occasions while I was Assistant Colonial Secretary, thanked him for his thoughtful suggestion and the expression of goodwill towards the government, but stated that he knew that Mackay would recognize that I could continue to do good for Taveuni and the country while in charge of the new (and the first) Development Plan for the Colony. Mackay wryly agreed. I made sure that we followed Stoddart's departure from Taveuni as promptly as possible. Three days later, after the Roko (Ratu Tiale) had presented me with an inscribed whale's tooth commemorating our three years' harmonious association, we left on the Public Works Department's steamer, *Degei*.

And so the 1950s started with me in the Secretariat learning to take over from P. Nightingale, whom I had known well when he was in Levuka and I in Lomaloma.

Cricket in the Fiji Islands had come out at the end of 1949. Sukuna had written the Foreword, describing it as 'an undoubted success' and Sir Pelham Warner the generous Introduction. It was quickly and enthusiastically reviewed by people from all over the world, including Neville (later Sir) Cardus and John Arlott. As Eric's *History of Leicestershire Cricket* and Charles's *Time of Hope* had been published simultaneously, it was almost certainly a record for three brothers to have books out in the same year. With a print-run of only 500 copies selling at £1 each, it has now become a rarity worth £100. I had given all the proceeds to the Fiji Cricket Association and all copies were quickly sold out. One was sent to Prince Philip as president of the MCC. Anne Griffiths, a former secretary of his and widow of a Fiji district officer after my time — both she and her husband became friends of mine — came across it recently while cataloguing Prince Philip's library at Windsor Castle. I often wonder whether Prince Philip read it: perhaps he at least looked at its illustrations.

My Secretariat posting was interrupted by my having to help as DO Southern in Suva for a brief while. This involved taking charge of Levuka and staying at the Royal Hotel, which belonged to the beachcomber era. It did not surprise me to see a figure come to breakfast in striped pyjamas. He was a remittance man named Howley living on the Lomaiviti island of Gau who had come to

Levuka's post office to collect his payoff. We were alone in the dining room. Now waiting for a ketch to go to his island, he returned to his chair on the upper verandah to sleep the day away with a bottle at his side. My visits to Levuka (it could no longer boast a resident administrative officer) were never longer than a few days at a time, but I did manage to get to know the singularities of the old capital. It did not take long to get round Levuka or the rest of Ovalau. After holding court there, making myself familiar with its historical relics, human and material, and soaking in the Royal Hotel's *fin-de-siècle* aura, I was ready to return to Viti Levu.

I had been appointed Deputy Sheriff in 1940 when I was in Lau and it was a long time before I found out what the duties of this post involved (apart from perhaps once in a lifetime reading the Riot Act). These were, it seemed, principally (or solely) attending, with a doctor and the Superintendent of Prisons, at Suva gaol any executions in the absence of the Sheriff who was also the registrar of the Supreme Court. I had forgotten all about this office of mine until I was shocked to be told that the Sheriff was ill and an execution was due to take place in two days' time. The couple who were to accompany me to witness justice being done by hanging said that the thing to do was to close one's eyes: they always did. I was still trying to summon up the strength for what was clearly and not surprisingly an ordeal for all concerned — except perhaps the hangman — when the Sheriff announced, the day after he had been taken ill and the day before the due date, that he was again fit and would carry out his duty. This was an experience I was most relieved to have escaped, albeit narrowly.

Mindful of Ratu Sukuna's consciousness of what I could do for cricket, I let myself be re-elected secretary of the Fiji Cricket Association, of which he had remained president. It was not long before I heard the old cry from Australians and more sophisticated part-Europeans, 'Good on yer, Phil'. I always took this to mean that I had been accepted, as few English people were, as one of them — which was for me a comforting achievement.

I also found that Australians, in particular, accorded respect to those who could beat them, although they did not like losing and did not readily or even gracefully acknowledge being beaten. This used to make me think of Douglas Jardine, especially when I first went to Fiji in 1938 and more than held my own as an English cricketer among razor-keen Australians not too far removed in time from what between 1932 and 1933 the Australians had pejoratively termed the 'body-line series'. There was no doubt that they respected, however grudgingly, Jardine's capacity to win, but I don't think they would have gone so far as to call out 'Good on yer, Doug'. By the time I knew Jardine personally and saw him with Australians, it was so long after 1932/3 that any feeling as such could not be discerned.

On Taveuni I had managed to play a little cricket on a small ground at the Provincial School but managed to score two hundreds, helped by the short boundary and the grass well mown by the boys. In Suva it was still hard work for me to get beyond 70 runs. The grass was so thick (the ground was owned without pride by the Suva Town Council) and the boundaries long. My method of defensive play exhausted me in the heat and in the skin-removing sun (no oils or protective creams were available other than Nivea: in later years, on the French Riviera, I discovered the bronzing Ambre Solaire oil, just right for me). But my bowling had become relatively more efficient.

With tennis at the Country Club in Taveuni and coaching from Suva's number one player Harry Stanley, when I was not playing cricket I was making advances in a game I dearly liked. Had there been enough light after cricket ended at 6.00 p.m., even in Fiji's heat I would happily have gone on to play sets of tennis. But dusk came along so fast that it was always dark at 6.30 p.m. and I mostly had to confine tennis to the non-cricket season, May to September (when, incidentally, it was markedly cooler and often grey-skied). I was very gratified when Harry Stanley and the number two player, Hamilton Huntley, the sole announcer and major-domo of Radio ZJV (Suva), selected me to play for Suva versus Ba — not in the singles but as a doubles partner for Stanley, and we won. This selection gave me as much sporting pleasure as anything outside my cricket.

When at this time I gave my lecture on the rock carvings at Dakuniba and elsewhere in Fiji to the Fiji Society, of which I had been made a vice-president (the president was Bay Parham, my colleague of early days as Agriculture Officer in Naduruloulou, now assistant director of agriculture), I was flattered that there was the largest attendance for many a session and that the discussion afterwards was the liveliest that the denizens of the society could recall.

There was a further unexpected delay in my taking over as Assistant Colonial Secretary from Nightingale, who was going to act as financial secretary. L. A. H. de B. Secchi, a recently appointed administrative officer from Gibraltar, went down suddenly with tuberculosis while he was clerk to the Executive and Legislative Councils and Assistant Secretary A (Section C of my previous time in the Secretariat). This happened just two days before a meeting of the Legislative Council.

This body of officials comprising the Colonial Secretary, Financial Secretary, Director of Agriculture, Director of Education, Director of Medical Services, Director of Public Works, Commissioner of Labour, Senior District Commissioner and elected individuals representing Fijian chiefs, Indians and Europeans in equal quantities met under the chairmanship of the Governor in the impressive Legislative Council Chamber. It had a semi-parliamentary procedure which, never having been at a session, I did not know and had two days in which to learn. This meant being allowed to visit Secchi in the tuberculosis hospital, though in my own interest the medical authorities only reluctantly granted their permission. Since the disease was regarded at that time in Fiji as highly infectious, my time with him was strictly rationed to half an hour. I worked throughout the two nights committing to memory the procedure.

Somehow I got through the three-day sitting without a fault and was congratulated by almost everyone, including veteran Indian and Fijian members. It had involved reading the long, convoluted warrants under the King's signature of awards and decorations to five recipients, one of them shaking visibly at the knees — I tried to speed up my reading for him. Besides that, running the Executive Council, consisting only of the Governor, CS, FS, DMS and a trio of Fijian, Indian and European unofficial members, was plain sailing. As was Section A work in the Secretariat after my experience in the more demanding Sections B and F.

But it was a relief to take over at last from Nightingale. The post largely involved implementing the first Seven-Year Development Plan about which I was enthusiastic except for preliminary work to inaugurate local air services. My first and only experience of flying had not convinced me that it was a delectable alternative to the rough handling one received from inter-island sailing craft. I had three flying experts with whom to work. One was Harold Gatty, the Tasmanian. As mentioned early on, he had been navigator in the first flight round the world (in 1930 with Wiley Post as pilot: in that capacity Post was later killed with Will Rogers, the American film actor).

Now owning the Lau island of Katafaga where Count von Lückner had called during the First World War, Gatty took a deep interest in Fiji and, through our common Lau interest, we had become friends. From his exploits as a navigator, the taciturn Gatty had strong theories about telltale signs being able to guide shipwrecked (or air-wrecked) individuals. He wrote *Nature is Your Guide: How to Find Your Way on Land and Sea* (1958). From this arose a violent controversy with Alain Bombard, a French sailor who decided to test his theories the hard way by drifting across the Atlantic. Bombard refuted Gatty's claims.

Gatty was keen to start an air service between islands in Fiji. He was strongly supported in this by Maurice Scott, who was later to marry Gatty's Dutch widow. It was Maurice who had attempted to create havoc while I was holding court in the Naduruloulou courthouse when he became bored by a fellow lawyer, Said Hassan, who while defending his clients could without fail be relied upon to say to a witness: 'I put it to you that your story is a whole tissue of lies.'

John Briscoe came out from the London Air Ministry to advise. It was not long before he succeeded his father as baronet. There was a controversy over whether the aeroplanes should be land- or sea-based. He and I tended towards the latter while Gatty and Scott opted for land planes, which were to gain the day. Rather to my dismay, even the remotest, most beautiful islands have been given airstrips, but obviously one cannot deny their usefulness in an emergency. I would simply sooner have seen them use lagoons, which nearly all the islands have, although admittedly even they can be absurdly rough. It was wise to defer to the more professional judgements of Scott and Gatty in my case, although Briscoe had had much flying experience and, like Scott, had gained the DFC.

There are, however, Pacific islands that do not have a lagoon of any kind. One is Easter Island and I was invited to visit it by none other than the redoubtable Captain Patrick Gordon (later Sir Gordon) Taylor, pioneer of so many flights with Sir Charles Kingsford-Smith and Charles Ulm, who were the first to fly into Fiji across the Pacific (together) and who both disappeared flying (separately). Taylor gained the George Cross by walking out on a wing to extinguish a fire on an engine, thereby saving the aircraft, *Southern Cross*, and the crew. No one could match his reputation for intrepidity. It inspired confidence in everyone and almost in me. He had come on an experimental flight from Australia via Fiji, whence he intended to go on to Tahiti, Mangareva, Easter Island and Chile.

I met him on behalf of the Governor at Laucala Bay in Suva. His Consolidated PBY Catalina looked no stronger than any of the many I had seen there during the war. He confounded me by declaring that one of his passengers from Australia was leaving his plane in Suva. Would I take the empty space? He was equally confounded when I promptly declined. It had occurred to me that while landing in Tahiti's lagoons might have its attractions, venturing forth into the wild vastness of the Pacific to do something that no one had previously attempted — to land in the totally unprotected sea round Easter Island — was not for me. What if the sea were too rough to come down? There would be no fuel to return — no alternative but to descend on the sea and hope to survive. He simply *had* to pick up fuel there for any further flying. There could be no landing on the island itself with a Catalina. I did not tell him of the thoughts going through my mind but, to his surprise, simply demurred that I would not be able to get leave.

He did set off again the next day with his attractive female companion and three others — but with an empty place, which in reality probably helped him by lightening the Catalina. I heard later that when he reached Easter Island it was decidedly rough as there was nothing but unprotected coast and open sea — as I well knew — but he was just able to stay long enough to fill up with aviation spirit. He had reached Easter Island and proved his point — hazardously. He did not go ashore. If I had been on the flight I would have been mortified to have gone so far and been deprived of seeing the dolicocephalic statues and the islanders themselves.

But then pioneer sea and air travellers tended to be all the same — nonstop round the world, passing over or near all those countries and seeing none or nothing of them. That is a type of individuality I cannot understand, but it does not detract from Robin Knox-Johnston's circumnavigation without stopping anywhere at all. It was unique, but by some quirk did not attract a spontaneous knighthood like Chichester's and Rose's for the same feats but with stops — Chichester once and Rose twice.

More mundane work as Assistant Colonial Secretary was implementing my suggestion that streets in Suva bearing no names should be given them. Enlisting Ratu Sukuna's aid, I drew up a list of unidentifiable roads and uncommemorated governors, colonial secretaries, chief justices, chiefs, prominent individuals, birds and islands. Sukuna and I, looking at a map, noticed a street in a serpentine shape. He was amused that we should whimsically name it 'Pikeu', Lauan for zigzag, and so it has remained, although hardly anyone knows its origin and is baffled by it — and will be more baffled by it when someone straightens the road.

Similarly, a square, practically so if not quite, of new houses (in one of which lived the Nightingales, both well-known and accomplished singers) awaited a label. Accordingly, it was named by me and my committee, *nem con*, Berkeley Square, after Chief Justice Sir Henry Berkeley, mentioned earlier. Of course, long after the Nightingales had left Fiji, later civic busybodies missed the whole point and confused history by altering the name to Berkeley Crescent, compounding the interference by misspelling it Berkley and of course mispronouncing it, both out of local ignorance which could on occasion be lamentable. Of course, *And a Nightingale Sang in Berkeley Square* is one of the immortal tunes, but plainly failed to make its mark in Fiji.

We ourselves lived in a superb double-storeyed balconied, concrete house. This type, of which there were only six, was built by W. F. Hedges, the architect for the new Government Buildings when they were being constructed. It was the apex of our or anyone's housing ambitions in Fiji. No better houses have been built in Fiji in the last 50 years.

To relieve John Gittins so that he could have two months' local leave in New Zealand and meet his wife returning from England, I held the post of Assistant Colonial Secretary (Administration) jointly with that of Assistant Colonial Secretary (Development). This gave me the office next door and three steps up to that of the Colonial Secretary in his tower. Dick Stoddart was slow, indecisive but kindly and an extremely good listener. Had he been a little stronger and more independent, he would have made an outstanding Colonial Secretary. He was to retire from the position without promotion to a governorship: possibly he was too nice.

The post of ACS (Administration) was the one that I most enjoyed and felt suited my experience best. I had after all been Assistant Secretary A Section (formerly C), B Section and F Section (D had faded out after a short duration: E never existed). I had too been in all the districts, Southern (three times), Eastern (twice), Western (twice) and Northern (for a long spell). Only Nasigatoka, Ra, and Ba on Vitu Levu, Kadavu outside it, and Macuata and Bua on Vanua Levu were relatively unknown to me (only the last two totally: I never felt any deprivation about them). Few, if any, of my contemporaries matched my fortuitous range of postings.

Had I thought that I would be appointed ACS (A) for a three-year tour of duty, Fiji would tempt me back, with the realization that I would after that, unless I blotted my copybook, have to be transferred to another colony for promotion as a Colonial Secretary (a post I would not have enjoyed except in Fiji). Knowing the languages, I would have loved that, but no CS in recent times had spent his previous career in Fiji. I had satiated my interest and completed my research in the districts — except for covetable Nasigatoka and Ra, but my seniority had now taken me above the likelihood of ever being posted to those delectable areas.

In the Secretariat hierarchy, I had reached the number three general position in the administration of the colony, descending in order from the Governor and the Colonial Secretary to ACS (sometimes the Financial Secretary, who was more specialized, intervened in cases of acting appointments when the Governor or CS were away). In descending order of minuting files and dispatches, these were: (4) Section secretaries A, B, C to (3) ACS to (2) CS to (1) HE the Governor (replying of course in his red ink). It was certainly a pleasure to have draft dispatches to the Secretary of State for the Colonies and minutes all prepared for one merely to initial and propel 'upstairs' or to amend slightly without the drudgery of the original drafting.

What I did find less than satisfactory was that some of the section secretaries had not served in districts and did not know the intrinsic, fundamental Fiji, compared with my background before being Assistant Secretary B (1944–5), Assistant Secretary A (1950) (and Assistant Secretary F — directly responsible to the Financial Secretary in 1947) when the two above me were also unfamiliar with country existence. This was an essential frailty of the administration shared, I believe, with India and other colonies besides Fiji. Apart from this common weakness, there was little or nothing in the quintessential Fiji official or unofficial life to be compared with any other part outside the South Seas. Non-Pacific areas of imperial administration, such as India, Ceylon, Malaya, Africa, Hong Kong, involved totally different experiences, making it important that one's life in the Colony of Fiji should be recorded now to encapsulate the individuality of the South Seas fragment of Empire before it is too late to recall unhazily.

About this time I saw something that has remained indelibly in my memory. At the South Pacific Conference at Nasinu, the back of a very small taxi was boarded first by the Crown Prince of Tonga weighing 22 stone, whereupon the vehicle sagged noticeably, and then by the Prime Minister (the Crown Prince's younger brother) weighing 20 stone. Now the rear of the taxi touched the ground and the nose pointed upwards at 45°. In that way it proceeded, fortunately downhill and then along the flat, to Suva about seven miles away and presumably disembarked the royal load there without incident. I had never before and have never since seen a vehicle move along in that manner, uplifted and at the same time depressed.

Sukuna gave a lunch at his (Jimmy Borron's) house for the Crown Prince of Tonga, who was to succeed his mother, Queen Salote, as King Taufa'hau Tupou IV in 1966. Only half a dozen men were invited — the Colonial and Financial Secretaries, the Deputy Secretary for Fijian Affairs, the Director of Lands and myself. Maraia did not join us. The Crown Prince expressed interest when Sukuna told him that I had written *Cricket in the Fiji Islands*, but I doubt if he ever read it. There was little encouragement of the game in Tonga where there was latent natural skill. No one ever found it easy to talk to the Crown Prince — he was less expansive in words than in girth — but Sukuna made a gracious host. He had, however, never had much contact with Salote as, unlike Ted Cakobau, he had few Tongan connections.

On our return to Suva from Taveuni we attended many parties in repayment of our hospitality on that island, but these gatherings were nearly always of the same people. The Colonial Secretary, the Financial Secretary, the Commissioner of Police, the Conservator of Forests, the Comptroller of Customs, the Attorney General, the Director of Lands, the Commander of the Military Forces, the Adjutant, the Postmaster General, the Director of Public Works, the Accountant General and the Superintendent of Prisons were steady party goers and givers, along with the heads of the two banks and of the two leading commercial firms. No Europeans with Fijian or Euronesian wives and no part-Europeans (who never advanced beyond a certain point either in government or the big mercantile concerns) would be present.

It was shameful that such fine citizens as part-Europeans were never on the social rounds. They could only be fraternized with on cricket grounds to which — and because of which — I directed so much of my leisure energy. The Euronesians would excel also at hockey, shared with a few Indians but no Fijians, but did not play tennis until I made myself unpopular with European players by manœuvring them into the Suva Tennis Club. As for soccer, only Indians played it, despite there being 230,000 Fijians to 250,000 Indians. Difference in physique largely accounted for rugby being the preserve of Fijians. Just as there were 5000 Europeans and 5000 part-Europeans so were there about as many Chinese.

When I had founded the Fiji Table Tennis Association in 1947, to my surprise its leading exponents turned out to be taut-reflexed Chinese with their machine-gun-like style played close to the table. This was before Chinese hegemony in the world: their staccato technique has seriously retarded the game. (One can only feel nostalgic about the flashing, dramatic brilliance of the Czech, Hungarian and Austrian players of half a century ago such as Barna, Vana, Szabados, Bellak and Bergmann.) The Chinese had had to be lambasted and confounded by my heavy artillery and mortar tactics — smashing, slicing from a distance and drop shots — before I could take the Fiji singles championship. The Fijian, NMP (a clumsy prefix later replaced by Dr although without the requisite degree) Benijamini Lomaloma was coached by me in doubles to adopt my up-and-away-from-the-table strategy and we managed to retain that title together against the limpet-like Chinese defence.

As players only of individual card games like poker and pontoon, Anne and I eschewed bridge parties not simply for their aggressive postmortems but also because they were composed entirely of Europeans. Anne played mah-jong. It was in a different form from that played in the exclusively Chinese saloons in the town: quick-fire, slap-dash style was the spectacle and pizzicato the sound. Both stakes and resonance were high. Anne's circle was European with a couple of charming women so pale that unless you knew your Fiji history and studied Euronesian genealogy, which I found fascinating, you would never have known them to be part-Europeans. We were pleased to be part of, if often alone in, breaching what were incontrovertible colour bars.

That they were largely inconspicuous was principally because, as a class, part-Europeans almost never obtruded. Not only would there be no part-Europeans at Suva's high-echelon drinks parties on Sunday mornings (Saturday mornings were part of the working week), but no Indians or Fijians — except very rarely the cosmopolitan man about town Ratu Edward. Ratu Sir Lala Sukuna was very occasionally invited but, he told me, he never went to them.

When we gave a large party to repay all those we owed, it was a coup to have Sukuna's presence and, also unusually, he brought Maraia, of whom we were especially fond. I could inveigle him only by having whisky and a regular service of *yaqona* offered to him by a squatting Fijian. As Edward and George Cakobau were there with my Indian friend, John Amputch, two or three Euronesians and the Chinese Gordon Honson and Charles Cheng, whose hospitality we had so much enjoyed, in addition to the Colonial Secretary and the heads of the government departments and commercial firms mentioned above, it was unusual in composition — edging towards a cross-section with Suva's top-level people. I had wished to bring in other strata for I longed to break up the rarefied air, but as this was to be our final party there was no time.

For me, two extra appointments were beginning to take effect — as a trustee of the Fiji Museum and a member of the Legislative Council, the latter entitling me to carry the prefix 'Hon.' before my name. But I was now feeling in real need of another leave to England. Much had happened in the four-year term. I was restless when there was no cricket or tennis on wet Saturday afternoons. A symptom of this was that I would take Stephanie in the car to the wharf and sit in it looking at the lagoon. On the way we would pass the end of the botanical gardens and park under the rows of weeping fig trees on Cakobau Road hill to watch the women's netball. It was virtually all Euronesian.

I had long learnt that there were distinct and delicate grades of part-European and that the lighter their skin the closer they came to being accepted as Europeans. These gradients were probably just as marked in the Caribbean countries with their castes of mulattos, quadroons and creoles, terms which were unknown in the South Seas but which nevertheless in the background ruled their place in society according to their own reckoning. The question did not arise with Indians, who aimed for purity of caste, and there were no untouchables in Fiji. The darker-bronzed part-Europeans were not far removed from familiarity with Fijians, using their language from which the paler-skinned Euronesians kept well away and uninhibitedly declined to learn.

Of the many fine part-European families, the Wrights, resident in Suva, were among the most outstanding. The light-olive limbs and startling South Seas' loveliness of Cherie Wright gracefully moving up and down the netball court, bouncing elegantly, held one's attention. Aged 19, she was to become the colony's leading fashion designer. Her uncle Rob Wright, the Public Relations Office photographer, was the best photographer Fiji could possibly have produced. His work could not be excelled. Some of his studies were masterpieces. He was the son of Georgius Wright, one of the colony's earliest English district commissioners after they had been known as stipendiary magistrates. Georgius Wright had married Mary Eliza, whose master mariner American father, Captain Benjamin Hughes, became a planter in Fiji after marrying a high-ranking Samoan, Melia Anai. One does not have to look far for the splendid genes produced in their descendants: the beautiful part-Samoan mixture was in Rob's mother and Cherie.

Other part-European family names for female pulchritude, male handsomeness, skill in sport, occupations and professions included Whiteside, Rounds, St Aubyn, Caine, Crooks, Bentley, Wendt, Gibson, Raddock, Witherow, Apted, Hopewell, Fenn, Browne, Evans, Ah Koy, Emberson, Williams, A'Costa, Hennings and Whippy. Two Whiteside brothers married two sisters of a Snow family originally from England (no relations of mine) settling in Fiji. The families would contain skin tones of cream in coffee ranging through the coppers and bronzes so determinedly sought on beaches and in gardens by Caucasians. Their European ancestry would be English, Australian, New Zealander, seldom American, and the admixture would be Samoan, Tongan, Fijian, Rotuman and Chinese, but virtually never Indian.

The Matson Line's *Monterey* and *Mariposa* (18,563 tons) had not been alongside the wharf since they had been used as troop-ships during the war. The Union Steamship Company of New

The Odd Beachcomber, First-Class Arrival and Departure

Zealand's *Aorangi* (17,481 tons) was resuming its Vancouver–Sydney voyages, but of course that company's *Niagara* (13,415 tons) was still at the bottom of the ocean with a lot of gold to be recovered. Once, when Stephanie and I were on the wharf, the then last word in streamlined majesty arrived — Cunard's *Caronia* (34,183 tons). Of a much greater size than any ship I had seen up to that stage, its huge funnel raked back almost arrogantly. From its various shades of green paint, it disgorged masses of opulent-looking, ageing American or Australian tourists in Panama hats, sporting shirts and shorts. They radiated freedom, leisure, the outside world. Although competing with the special South Seas' charm like that of the Wrights, this made me strongly nostalgic. It made me want to be off the islands again and to sail away, simply for a change.

My feelings were reinforced in 1951 by seeing the England cricket team come from New Zealand and then go off again. Although their travel was by air, I could have endured even that method. When I had heard that MCC were likely to return from Australia to England via New Zealand, Fiji, Hawaii and the USA, I had invited the manager in Australia, Brigadier Michael Green, to make arrangements for their brief stay. He was himself returning by the Asia route, as was F. R. Brown, the captain whom I was later to come to know well. With the assistance of Aisea Turuva, who had become assistant Roko Tui Ba, I organized a ceremonial reception for the party at Nadi airport, where they would be spending five hours from midnight to 5.00 a.m. while changing planes for Hawaii.

Denis Compton, in the absence of Green and Brown, was in charge. When he introduced me to Leonard (later Sir) Hutton, Cyril Washbrook, Alec (later Sir) Bedser, J. J. Warr (later president of the MCC), John Dewes (later a master at Rugby) — I was to see a lot of the last two — and the others, I was surprised by his voice. I had only known prewar professionals and the professionals of Leicestershire just after the war, and it was only the exception who spoke well, free of dialect. Compton had to make the response after the elaborate, splendidly performed *yaqona* ceremony. His quiet intonation, his demeanour and his choice of words were

313

absolutely right for the occasion. He had been given no briefing. No aristocratic captain could have done better. It was incredible that he had been a scorecard seller at Lord's.

A similar surprise occurred years later when meeting Herbert Sutcliffe, who had played for Yorkshire and England most of his professional life and could have been the seventh Lord Hawke himself as one waited in vain for the slightest lapse into a Yorkshire accent. After all, he had, as an orphan, left school at 13 to learn how to fasten boot uppers to soles. His friendships with amateurs on tours had rubbed away his dialect: he became an affluent businessman on retirement, living in a mansion with servants but, unlike Compton, this paragon absurdly failed to be given an honour.

Just at the end of the Fiji season, in April, I was selected to captain the Suva team on a visit to Levuka, but as it was very near my departure on leave, I did not go. On the team's return, the launch *Jubilee* collided with another in Levuka's harbour and two Suva players sitting on the front of the launch were thrown into the lagoon. Pat Raddock was rescued. The other was never found. Bula, the hero of our 1948 team in New Zealand, was one of the party. It was his brother, at this date the most promising of all-rounders, who was drowned. Bula was never the same person after the tragedy. At the last match of the season on Albert Park in Suva, as president of the Suva Cricket Association, I called all the players of five matches on the ground to the flagstaff and, with the Suva flag at half mast, paid tribute to the Fijian, Bula grieving publicly. It was a melancholy end to what might turn out to be my last cricket in Fiji and on my much-cherished Albert Park. After a good all-round performance against Bau that Saturday, I didn't know if I would set foot on it again.

We had arranged to take the *Matua* from Suva to Auckland, a train from Auckland to Wellington, the *Wanganella* from Wellington to Sydney and then the Orient Line's *Orcades* (28,472 tons), the largest ship I would have sailed in, from Sydney via Ceylon and Suez to England. The trauma of travelling — strikes by dockside labour — maddeningly chose to put the *Matua* out of action (as it had at the end of the 1948 cricket tour of New

Zealand), leaving no alternative but for us to have to fly the 2000 miles from Nadi to Sydney nonstop in eight hours. My fond idea of sailing slowly off from Suva wharf and my having explained this to Stephanie in our frequent visits to the wharf to watch departures, among which ours would be one, was thwarted.

With our effects packed into sturdy crates and deposited in the Government Stores at Walu Bay — this was the practice on leaving but nothing could be insured — we spent our penultimate evening as guests at dinner of Ian (an administrative officer junior to me who was later knighted) and Nancy (one of the remarkable quintet of Kearsley sisters) Thomson and left the Grand Pacific Hotel by taxi next day for Nadi Hotel.

The admirable Aisea Turuva, so dignified a member of my team on the 1948 cricket tour of New Zealand and brother of Turagu, the eminent Nadi player who had accidentally electrocuted himself nine years earlier, surprised me by having organized, in his new post as assistant Roko Tui Ba, a leaving ceremony in the fine provincial compound *bure* next to the house in which we had lived at Nadi Government Station in 1941 and 1942 (where Sir Cyril Newall's petrol lamps had been sabotaged). It was excellently performed and I was very touched. We spent our last night at Nadi Hotel (on the site of the house of the police inspector, who now lived in our former house as there was no DO, Nadi) where I remet Mara Hennings, Gus's elegant youngest daughter whom we had last seen on Naitauba in Lau a decade earlier. Next morning a taxi called to take us to the airport manager's house at Namaka. I had worked with him and he laid on VIP treatment for me.

The facilities on the RMA *Adventurer*, a four-propellered British Commonwealth Pacific Airlines DC6, looked reassuringly first-class compared with those of the Sunderland, my only previous experience of a plane. As we were boarding it, on the scorching tarmac we were astonished to see Wati Witherow and Maria, our housegirls to whom we had said farewell in Suva three days earlier. They had given no indication that they would be following us. We were very touched by their making the long and expensive journey from Suva to Nadi. I had no Fiji currency. So, I gave some Australian cash to the airport manager, which I asked him to

315

exchange to pay for their return bus fares after we had said goodbye to them for the second time with deep feelings of affection.

It seemed an eternity before we realized that the *Adventurer* had finally taken off from the runway (with the construction of which I had been vitally connected in Fiji's blackest war days). It seemed to us as though the lovely country and lovely people and ourselves were loth to part. Stephanie was too young to participate, but with nothing else to do on the plane and to soften our thoughts Anne and I played a form of 'consequences' for two persons. The name of the game was to have a certain appropriateness. What would follow?

Bibliography

Aldington, Richard (1959) *Portrait of a Rebel: The Life and Work of Robert Louis Stevenson*, London, Evans

Allen, Percy S. (ed.) (1907) *The Cyclopaedia of Fiji*, Sydney, The Cyclopaedia Company

Attenborough, Sir David Frederick (1960) *Quest in Paradise*, London, Butterworth

Berwick, Samuel Lawrence (ed.) (1990) *Who's Who in Fiji*, Suva, Berwick Publishing House

Braddon, Russell (1952) *The Naked Island*, London, Werner Laurie

Brewster, Adolph Brewster (Joske) (1922) *The Hill Tribes of Fiji*, London, Seeley Service

— (1937) *King of the Cannibal Isles*, London, Robert Hale

British Medical Journal (1934) 'An Unusual Case of Hyperpyrexian Malaria', London, 5 May, pp. 801–2

Carmichael, Peter and June Knox-Mawer (1968) *A World of Islands*, London, Collins

Caten, Reginald Robert Cecil (1997) *Vosalevu: Memories of Life in Fiji during Four Decades 1924–1953*, Carlisle, Western Australia, Hesperian Press

Chamberlain, Walter and Herbert Chamberlain (n.d.) 'Journal of Travel from January 1875 to July 1879', unpublished manuscript

Clunie, Fergus Gourlay Anderson Urquhart and Philip Albert Snow (1986) 'Notes on Travels in the Interior of the Island of Viti Levu by Eduard Graeffe, translated by Stefanie Vuikaba Snow Waine', *Domodomo: Fiji Museum Journal*, vol. 4, no. 3, pp. 98–140

Corner, Edred John Henry (1981) *The Marquis*, Singapore, Heinemann

Corney, Bolton Glanvill, James Stewart and Basil Home Thomson (1896) *Report of the Commission Appointed to Inquire into the Decrease of Native Population*, Suva, Government Printer

Des Voeux, Sir George William (1903) *My Colonial Service*, London, John Murray

Bibliography

Forrestel, Vice Admiral E. P. (1966) *Admiral Raymond A. Spruance, USN: A Study in Command*, Washington, Director of Naval History

Freyberg, Paul Richard (1991) *Bernard Freyberg, VC: Soldier of Two Nations*, London, Hodder & Stoughton

Frost, Richard (1992) *Enigmatic Proconsul: Sir Philip Mitchell and the Twilight of Empire*, London and New York, Radcliffe Press

Garvey, Sir Ronald Herbert (1983) *Gentleman Pauper*, Bognor Regis, New Horizon

Gatty, Harold Charles (1958) *Nature is Your Guide: How to Find your Way on Land and Sea*, London, Collins

Geraghty, Paul Alban Christopher Vincent (1983) *The History of the Fijian Languages*, Honolulu, University of Hawaii Press

Gillion, Kenneth R. (1977) *The Fiji Indians*, Canberra, Australian National University

Gittins, (Josephine Amy) Anne (1991) *Tales of the Fiji Islands*, Salisbury, Lavenham Press

Gorman, G. E. and J. J. Mills (1994) *Fiji*, volume 173, World Bibliographical Series, Oxford, Clio Press

Grantham, Sir Alexander William George Herder (1965) *Via Ports: From Hong Kong to Hong Kong*, Hong Kong, Hong Kong University Press

Haddon, Alfred Cort (1901) *Head-Hunters: Black, White and Brown*, London, Methuen

Hadlee, Walter Arnold (1993) *The Innings of a Lifetime*, Auckland, David Bateman

Heald, Tim (1994) *Denis Compton*, London, Pavilion

Heyerdahl, Thor (1950) *The Kon-Tiki Expedition*, London, George Allen & Unwin

Hignell, Andrew (1995) *The Skipper: A Biography of Wilf Wooller*, Royston, Limlow Books

Hill, Alan (1990) *Herbert Sutcliffe: Cricket Maestro*, London, Simon & Schuster

— (1994) *Bill Edrich: A Biography*, London, André Deutsch

Holmes, Lowell D. (1984) *Samoan Islands Bibliography*, Kansas, Wichita, Poly Concepts

Iremonger, Lucille d'Oyen (1948) *It's a Bigger Life*, London, Hutchinson

Johnson, Pamela Hansford (1974) *Important to Me: Personalia*, London, Macmillan

Journal de la Société des Océanistes, Paris

Kay, John (ed.) (1959) *Cricket Heroes*, London, Phoenix

Knox-Mawer, June (1965) *A Gift of Islands*, London, John Murray

— (1986) *Tales from Paradise: Memories of the British in the South Pacific*, London, BBC Ariel

— (1995) *The Shadow of Wings*, London, Weidenfeld & Nicolson

Bibliography

Lewis, Patricia K. G. (1984) *Charles Allberry: A Portrait*, Cambridge, E. & E. Plumridge

Lukach, Harry Charles (1910) *Bibliography of Sierra Leone*, Oxford, Oxford University Press

Luke, Sir Harry Charles (1952) *From a South Seas Diary 1938–1942*, London, Nicolson & Watson

— (1953) *Cities and Men: An Autobiography*, London, Geoffrey Bles

Maddocks, Sir Kenneth Phipson (1988) *Of No Fixed Abode*, Ipswich, Wolsey Press

Marquand, David (1977) *Ramsay MacDonald*, London, Jonathan Cape

Martin-Jenkins, Christopher (1996) *World Cricketers: A Biographical Dictionary*, Oxford, Oxford University Press

May, Hal and James G. Lesniak (eds) (1990) *Contemporary Authors*, Detroit, Gale Research

Mayer, Adrian Curtius (1961) *Peasants of the Pacific: A Study of Fiji Indian Rural Society*, London, Routledge & Kegan Paul

Milner, George Bertram (1972) *Fijian Grammar*, Suva, Government Press

Native Medical Practitioner, The: Journal of the Central Medical School, Suva, for the Native Medical Practitioners in Fiji and the Neighbouring Island Groups, Suva, Government Printer

N'Yeurt, Antoine De Ramon, Will C. McClatchey and Hans Schmidt (1996) *A Bibliography of Rotuma*, Suva, University of South Pacific

O'Reilly, Père Patrick Georges Farell and Edouard Reitman (1967) *Bibliographie de Tahiti et de la Polynésie française*, Paris, Musée de l'Homme

Peel, Richard (n.d.) *Old Sinister: A Memoir of Sir Arthur Richards, GCMG, First Baron Milverton of Lagos and Clifton 1885–1975*, Cambridge, F. & P. Piggott

Robertson-Glasgow, Raymond Charles (1943) *Cricket Prints: Some Batsmen and Bowlers 1920–1940*, London, T. Werner Laurie

Rose, Kenneth Vivian (1983) *King George V*, London, Weidenfeld & Nicolson

Roth, George Kingsley (1973) *Fijian Way of Life* (second edition, with introduction by G. B. Milner), Melbourne, Oxford University Press

Roth, Jane F. Violet and Steven Hooper (eds) (1990) *The Fiji Journals of Baron Anatole von Hügel 1875–1877*, Suva, Fiji Museum

Scarr, Deryck (ed.) (1983) *Fiji: The Three Legged Stool. Selected Writings of Ratu Sir Lala Sukuna*, London, Macmillan Educational

Schütz, Albert James (1978) *Suva: A History and Guide*, Sydney, Pacific Publications

Snow, Charles Percy (1932) *Death under Sail*, London, Heinemann

— (1933) *New Lives for Old*, London, Gollancz (anonymously)

— (1934) *The Search*, London, Gollancz

— (1938) *Richard Aldington: An Appreciation*, London: Heinemann

319

Bibliography

— (1940) *Strangers and Brothers* (retitled *George Passant*), London, Faber & Faber

— (1947) *The Light and the Dark*, London, Faber & Faber

— (1948) 'The Mathematician on Cricket', *The Saturday Book*, 8th Year, pp. 65–73

— (1949) *Time of Hope*, London, Faber & Faber

— (1951) *The Masters*, London, Macmillan

Snow, Edward Eric (1949) *A History of Leicestershire Cricket*, Leicester, Backus

— (1964) *Sir Julien Cahn's XI*, Leicester, E. E. Snow

Snow, Philip Albert (1940–50) 'Diaries and Annual Reports of District Commissioner, Lau 1940–1941, Nadi 1941–1943, Lautoka 1943–1944 and Taveuni and Nasavusavu 1947–1950', typescript in National Archives of Fiji

— (1943) *Civil Defence Services, Lautoka*, Suva, Government Printer

— (1943) *Important Notice: Air Raids*, Lautoka, Lautoka Print

— (1943) *Mo Ni Kila: Na Kaba ni Meca mai Macawa*, Lautoka, Lautoka Print

— (1945) *Bronze and Clay* or *The Thin Edge of the World*, typescript

— (1946) *The Journal of the European Civil Servants' Association: Fiji and Western Pacific*, Suva, Government Printer

— (1946–51) 'Diaries of Ocean Voyages 1946, 1947, 1951', manuscript

— (1948) 'Diary of Fiji Cricket Team's New Zealand Tour, 1948', manuscript

— (1949) *Cricket in the Fiji Islands*, Christchurch and Dunedin, Whitcombe & Tombs

— (1951) 'Cricket in Fiji', *Go*, October/November, pp. 49–51, 95

— (1952) 'Cricket op de Zuidzee-eilanden', *Cricket*, Leiden, 23 May, pp. 8–10

— (1953) 'Rock Carvings in Fiji', *Fiji Society Transactions for 1950*, New Plymouth, New Zealand, Avery Press

— (1953) 'The Friendly Isles', *Go*, September/October, pp. 56–8

— (1954) 'The Nature of Fiji and Tonga', *Discovery*, February, pp. 67–9

— (1969) *Bibliography of Fiji, Tonga and Rotuma, Volume 1*, Canberra, Australian National University Press and Coral Gables, Miami University Press

— (1971) 'Introduction' to George Palmer, *Kidnapping in the South Seas*, London, Dawsons of Pall Mall

— (1973) 'Introduction' to Berthold Seeman, *Viti: An Account of a Government Mission to the Vitian or Fijian Islands 1860–1861*, London, Dawsons of Pall Mall

— (1974) 'A Century in the Fiji Islands', *Wisden Cricketers' Almanack*, London, Sporting Handbooks, pp. 123–9

Bibliography

— (1982) *Stranger and Brother: A Portrait of C. P. Snow*, London, Macmillan and New York, Scribner (reprint 1983)

— (1988) 'The Rarest Printed Work on the Pacific? A Bibliographer's Proposition', *Domodomo: Fiji Museum Journal*, vol. 1, no. 4, pp. 30–43

— (1991) 'Introduction' to Anne Gittins, *Tales of the Fiji Islands*, Salisbury, Lavenham Press

— (1997) Preface to Reginald Robert Cecil Caten, *Vosalevu: Memories of Life in Fiji During Four Decades 1924–1953*, Carlisle, Western Australia, Hesperian Press

Snow, Philip Albert and Stefanie Vuikaba Snow Waine (1979) *The People from the Horizon: An Illustrated History of the Europeans among the South Sea Islanders*, Oxford, Phaidon and New York, E. P. Dutton (London, McLaren, 1986)

Stanmore, Lord (Sir Arthur Charles Hamilton-Gordon) (1897–1912) *Fiji: Records of Public and Private Life 1875–1880*, Edinburgh, R. & R. Clark

Sukuna, Ratu Sir Josefa Lalabalavu Vanaaliali (1932–40) 'Diaries and Annual Reports of District Commissioner, Lau', typescript in National Archives of Fiji

— (1939) *The Fijian's View of the European*, Suva, Defence Club

— (1940) 'Notes on Handing-over to P. A. Snow as District Commissioner, Lau', typescript in National Archives of Fiji

— (1951) *Reports of the Secretary for Fijian Affairs 1948–51*, Suva, Government Printer

Swanton, Ernest William (ed.) (1966) *The World of Cricket*, London, Michael Joseph

— (1977) *Follow On*, London, Collins

Swanton, Ernest William and John Woodcock (eds) (1980) *Barclays World of Cricket*, London, Collins

Swanton, Ernest William, George Plumptre and John Woodcock (eds) (1986) *Barclays World of Cricket*, London, Willow

Tarte, Daryl (1993) *Turaga: The Life and Times and Chiefly Authority of Ratu Sir Penaia Ganilau, GCMG, KCVO, KBE, DSO*, Suva, Fiji Times

Thomson, Sir Basil Home (1888) 'New Guinea 1888', manuscript

— (1894) *South Sea Yarns*, London, William Blackwood

— (1894) *The Diversions of a Prime Minister*, London, William Blackwood

— (1900) 'Journal (Tonga and Niue) 1900', manuscript

— (1902) *Savage Island*, London, John Murray

— (1908) *The Fijians: A Study of the Decay of Custom*, London, William Heinemann

— (1939) *The Scene Changes*, London, Collins

Tudor, Judy (ed.) (1968) *Pacific Islands Year Book and Who's Who*, Sydney, Pacific Publications (tenth edition)

Bibliography

Waine, Stefanie Vuikaba Snow (trans.) (1984) 'Theodor Kleinschmidt's Notes on the Hill Tribes of Viti Levu 1877–1878', *Domodomo: Fiji Museum Journal*, vol. 2, no. 4, pp. 138–96

Ziegler, Philip (1985) *Mountbatten: The Official Biography*, London, Collins

Index

Index

Australian magpies, 259
Australians, 5, 36, 44, 77, 84–6, 95, 151, 157, 162, 180–1, 196, 206, 209, 246, 256, 261–2, 270, 273, 301–2, 313
Austria, 67
avocado pears, 29, 130
Avea, 97
Awahou, 291
Aylestone Park, 1
Aylestone Road, Leicester, 5, 21–2, 196, 235
Azores, 241

Ba, 184–6, 302, 307
Ba, Roko Tui, 313, 315
Bahamas, 86, 126
Bain, Kenneth Ross, OBE (1923–), 228
Baker, Ernest Laidlaw (1880–1955), 36–7, 39, 43, 51, 54, 63, 83, 180–1, 296
Baker, Revd Thomas (?–1867), 266
Balboa, 26, 241
Baldwin of Bewdley, 1st Earl, Stanley, KG, PC, FRS, MP (1867–1947), 73
Bale, Frank (1891–1969), 5–6
Balekiwai, Filikesa, 81
Baluchistan, 131
bamboo, 50, 58, 89, 120, 215, 218
Banaba(ns), 160, 290; *see also* Ocean Island(ers)
Bank of New South Wales, 86
Bank of New Zealand, 86, 288
Barbados, 199
Bari, 114
Barker, Sir Thomas William Alport, CBE, JP, 182, 281
Barna, Victor, 310
barracuda, 150
Barton, Cecil James Juxon Talbot, CMG, OBE (1891–1980), 35, 65–7, 71, 85–6, 95, 110, 198
Basavanand, Bhaskaranand (1906–?), 157, 234
Batiki, 46, 56, 59, 205
Bau, 32–5, 42, 45, 49, 62, 81–3, 85, 96, 98, 104, 116, 247, 248, 263, 314
Bau, Vunivalu of, 32, 205
bauhina (butterfly tree), 259
Bavadra, Timoci Uluivuda (1934–89), 249
Bay of Biscay, 25, 108
Beaconsfield, 1st Earl of, Benjamin Disraeli (1808–81), 298

Beatrix, Queen, 237
Beaumanor School, 2
Beaumanor Villas, 2
Bechu, 80–1, 84
Bedser, Sir Alec Victor, CBE (1918–), 313
Beightler, Major General R. S., 193
Belgium, 4, 109, 124
Bell Airacobras, 163–4, 174, 186
Bellak, Lazlo, 310
Bellona, HMNZS, 294–5, 298
Bergmann, Richard, 310
Berkeley, Sir Henry Spencer, KC, JP (1851–1918), 194, 306
Berkeley, Captain Reginald Cheyne, MC, MP (1890–1935), 194
Berlin, 236
Bermuda, 235
Bernal, John Desmond, FRS (1901–71), 68
Best Stories of the South Seas, 225
Bevan, Aneurin, PC, MP (1897–1960), 16
Bevin, Ernest, PC, MP (1881–1951), 140
Berridge, William (1892–1968), 6
Birdwood of Anzac and Totnes, Field Marshal, 1st Baron, William Riddell, GCB, GCSI, GCMG, GCVO, CIE, DSO (1865–1951), 15
Birmingham, 115, 127
Biro, Lazlo, 230
Bligh Water, 180
Blitz, 24, 87, 123, 177
Blue Star Line, 240
Blunt, Anthony Frederick (1902–83), 16
Board of Visitors for Hospitals, 138, 146
Boeing B17, 169
Boer War, 185, 287
Bogisa, Mosese (1922–?), 268, 274–5
Bombard, Alain, 304
Bombay, 85
Booth, Jean, 240
Booth, Lieutenant, 240
Borge, Victor (1908–), 48
Borron, James Sawyers Kidston Bradock, 129–31, 154, 309
Borron, Zena, 129
Bose, Subha Chandra, 161
botanical gardens, 125–6, 259, 287, 311; *see also* Singapore Botanical Gardens
Bougainville, 206
Bounty, HMS, 245

324

Index

Index

Colo East, 37, 89, 91, 204, 209–11
Colo North, 89, 212, 222
Colo West, 89, 171, 248
Colombia, 25, 241
Colonial Office, 19–20, 23, 69, 232, 267, 295
Colonial Secretary, 30, 35, 65–6, 84, 95, 99–101, 110, 119, 140, 154, 174, 198–9, 226–7, 229–30, 235, 239, 251, 299–300, 303, 306–8, 311
Colonial Secretary' Office, 77
Colonial Service, 19–20, 22, 44, 69, 182, 185, 189, 191, 195, 200
Colonial Sugar Refining Company, 37, 42, 44, 77, 79–80, 157–8, 183–4, 195, 204, 206, 208
Colonial War Memorial Hospital, 77, 249
Colorado, 189
Commander-in-Chief, 236, 279
 Fiji and Western Pacific, 90
 Task Force, 191
 US Fleet, 169, 201
Commissioner for Native Land Reserves, 116, 135
Commissioner of Police, 42, 75, 153, 197, 309
Communist Club, 16
Communist Party, 16
Compton, Denis Charles Scott, CBE (1918–97), 313–14
Coode, Edward James, OBE (1918–), 201, 299
Cook, Captain James, FRS (1728–79), 140
Cook Straits, 272
Cooper, Alfred Duff; *see* Norwich of Aldwick, 1st Viscount
Cooper, Harold (1908–), 230, 234
copra, 28, 97, 123, 129–30, 139, 152, 206, 228, 240, 255–6, 258, 261–2, 284, 286, 290, 294
Coral Sea, 191
Corner, Edred John Henry, CBE, FRS (1906–96), 236
Cornwall, 241, 286
Corrie, Sir Owen Cecil Kirkpatrick, MC (1882–1965), 110, 194, 235
Coventry, 123
Cowan, Gilbert Connolly (1911–), 29
Craig, John (1884–?), 95
Craig, Matilda, 208

Craig, Milton, JP, 207–8, 286
Craig, William, 207
Crete, 279
Crewe, 207
Crewe, 1st Marquess of, Robert Offley Ashburton Crewe-Milnes, KG, PC, Royal Victorian Chain (1858–1945), 93
cricket, 2, 5, 7–9, 11–12, 16, 18, 31–2, 35, 36, 56, 72–5, 76, 79–80, 83–6, 88, 93, 98, 101, 104, 106, 129, 132–3, 136, 153, 158–9, 163–5, 173, 195–6, 207–9, 211–12, 216–17, 231–4, 242–3, 248, 256, 258, 263, 265–7, 269–78, 287, 291, 295, 297, 301–2, 309, 311, 313–15; *see also* Fiji Cricket Association; International Cricket Conference; Lautoka Cricket Association; Leicestershire; Northamptonshire; Nadi Cricket Association; Rewa Cricket Association; Suva Cricket Association; Suva Cricket Club; United Cricket Association
Cricket in the Fiji Islands, 209, 283, 292, 300, 309
Cricketer, The, 244
Crisp, Robert James, DSO, MC (1911–94), 72
Cromb, Ian Burns (1905–84), 277
Crompton, Robert, CBE, KC, JP, 268
Crooks, Olga, 236, 312
croton, 49, 126, 214, 295
Crusaders, 8
Culebra Cut, 26
culex mosquito, 142
Curaçao, 25, 241, 244
Cyprus, 19

Daku, 247
Dakuniba, 284–6, 303
Dardanelles, 279
Darwin, Sir Charles Galton, KBE, MC, FRS (1887–1962), 13–14, 16
Darwin, Charles Robert (1809–82), 7, 13
Davidson, W. L., 39
Dawkes, George Owen (1920–), 6
DDT, 47, 142
deck tennis, 18, 25, 49, 116, 241
Defence Club, 66, 106

327

Index

Index

Index

Hughes, Captain Benjamin (1832–99), 312

Hughes, Melia Anai (?–1920), 312

Humber, 44, 110

Huntingfield, 5th Baron, William Charles Arcedeckne Vanneck, KCMG, JP (1883–1969), 92

Huntley, Hamilton, 302

hurricane(s), 82–3, 144–5, 147, 262, 268

Hutson, Lady, 215

Hutson, Sir Eyre, KCMG (1864–1936), 71

Hutt Valley, 279

Hutton, John Henry, CIE, PRAI (1885–1968), 20, 25

Hutton, Sir Leonard (1916–90), 313

Huxley, Sir Julian Sorell, FRS (1887–1975), 79

Hyde Park Place, London, 242

hydrocarpus, 259

hyperpyrexia malaria, 254

I am a Camera, 79

i luva ni tawake, 104

I Sosomi ni Kovana, 119

Ibo, Samu, 289–90

illegitimacy, 33, 62, 66–7

im Thurn, Sir Everard Ferdinand, KCMG, KBE, CB (1852–1932), 69, 71, 93, 99–101

Inayt, 51, 59, 90

independence, 33, 45–6, 173, 206, 228, 232–3, 235

India, 15, 36, 55, 71, 113, 161, 167, 170, 173, 215, 271, 285, 308

Indian Army, 9

Indian Ocean, 109

Indian(s), 36–40, 42–4, 46, 48–9, 55, 57, 59, 62, 71, 80–2, 84, 86, 98, 107–8, 121, 132, 135, 155–7, 161, 168, 170, 172–4, 178–9, 184, 187, 195, 199, 209–10, 225, 228, 234, 238–9, 248, 252, 283, 285, 298, 303–4, 310, 312

Indochina, 162

inspector(s) of police, 46, 51, 81, 85, 129, 137, 151, 157, 162, 173, 205, 256, 267, 294, 315

International Brigade, 11

International Cricket Conference, 271

Invercargill, 276

iodine, 143

Iremonger, Thomas Lascelles Isa Shandon Valiant, MP (1916–), 171, 180

Island Queen, 255

Isle of Man, 160

Italy, 114

Iwojima, 201

jacaranda, 259

Jackson, Sir Henry Moore, KCMG (1849–1908), 71

Jackson, Victor Edward (1916–65), 242

Jamaica, 235

Japan, 160, 162, 170, 188–9, 226, 237, 289

Japanese, 10, 114, 148, 159–63, 165–7, 169–70, 180, 182, 184–5, 188–91, 193, 195, 201–2, 223–4, 226, 236–8, 240, 290–1

Jardine, Douglas Robert (1900–58), 86, 302

Java, 10

Jays & Campbells, 72

Jellicoe, 1st Earl, John Rushworth Jellicoe, GCB, OM, GCVO (1859–1935), 189

Jellicoe Road, Leicester, 108–9

Jellicoe Road, Suva, 109

Jenkins, Marjorie, 275

Jessop, Gilbert Laird (1874–1955), 11

Jessop, Revd Gilbert Laird Osborne (1906–90), 11

Johnson, Amy, CBE (1903–41), 129

Johnson, Charles Walter Trevor (1893–?), 30, 84, 95, 181, 229, 245

Johnson, Pamela Hansford; *see* Snow, Lady

Johnston, Douglas Hammersly, CVO, 295

Joong Hing Loong, 234, 247

Joske, Adolph Brewster; *see* Brewster, Adolph Brewster

Joske, Paul, 84

Joske's Thumb, 90, 110

Jubilee, 314

justice(s) of the peace, 10, 34, 123, 171–2, 207–8, 261

Kabara, 152

332

Index

Index

missionary/missionaries, 41, 62, 64–5,
   88, 119, 141, 161, 245, 254, 266
Mitchell, Sir Charles Bullen Hugh,
   GCMG (–1899), 71
Mitchell, Major General Sir Philip Euen,
   GCMG, MC (1890–1964), 182–3,
   198–9, 235
Moala, 152
Monckton, Hugh Claud (1881–?), 181
mongoose, 165, 216
monogamy, 62
Monroe, Marilyn (1926–62), 196
Monroe, Vice Admiral, 191
Monterey, 74–5, 90, 107, 312
Mopelia, 128
Morkel, Denijs Paul Beck (1906–80), 72
Morris Cowley, 12, 17
Morris Hedstrom, 77, 130, 182
Morris Minor, 37
Morrisby, John, 264
Morrisby, Logan H., 264
Mosley, Sir Oswald Ernald, 6th Baronet,
   MP (1896–1980), 16
mosquito(es), 41, 51–3, 55, 57, 142–4,
   147, 215, 223, 239, 266
moth(s), 60, 70, 221, 241
Mountbatten of Burma, Admiral of the
   Fleet, 1st Earl, Louis Francis Albert
   Victor Nicholas Mountbatten, KG, PC,
   GCB, OM, GCSI, GCIE, GCVO, DSO, FRS,
   (1900–79), 15–16
Munia, 97, 138
Munro, Sir Robert Lindsay, CBE
   (1907–95), 39
Murray-Willis, Peter Earnshaw (1910–),
   243
Muslim(s), 20, 40–1, 43, 157, 173
Mussolini, Benito (1883–1945), 19
mynah bird, 118

Nabavatu, 127, 130, 134
Nabukaluka, 223, 224
Nabutautau, 266
Nadaravakawalu, 216
Nadarivatu, 89, 200
Nadi, 154, 155–6, 158, 160, 163, 165,
   167, 169–71, 173–5, 178, 180, 182,
   185–8, 191–2, 196, 209–10, 213, 219–
   20, 222, 234, 268, 276, 279–80, 313,
   315
Nadi Cricket Association, 173

Nadi Hotel, 315
Nadi River, 168
Nadi-Vuda Bay, 188
Nadroga, 205
Nadroga and Navosa, Roko Tui, 171
Naduruloulou, 28, 35, 37, 41, 45, 47,
   50, 52, 55–6, 60, 65, 74–7, 79–80, 83–
   5, 87, 89–90, 109, 151, 203, 205, 209,
   212, 218, 220–4, 226, 234, 245, 253,
   294, 303–4
Naga Hills, 20
Nagasaki, 236–7
Nagonenicolo, 218
Nagumo, Admiral Chuichi, 162, 174
Nailatikau, Adi Vasemaca Koila
   (1953–), 82
Nailatikau, Brigadier Ratu Epeli, CBE,
   LVO (1941–), 82
Naiqaqi, 80
Nairukuruku, 218
Naitasiri, 35, 204, 209, 221–2
Naitasiri, Roko Tui, 249
Naitauba, 127, 129, 315
Naitonitoni, 225
Naivucini, 216
Nakavu, 175
Nakelo, Tui, 220
Namaka, 163–4, 167–8, 177, 315
Namalata, 97, 152
Namoli, 192
Namosi, 213
Namotomoto, 163–4, 175
Namulomulo, 219
Nanise, 56
Naomi; *see* Popplewell, Naomi
Napier, 207
Narewa, 175
Narokorokoyawa, 213–16
Nasavusavu, 93, 250, 263, 284–7, 294,
   296
Nasigatoka, 89, 155, 186, 203, 205,
   233, 248, 263, 307–8
Nasinu, 308
Natabua, 135, 181, 192–3, 197, 200, 204
Natabua School, 195
Nate, Semi, 222
Natewa Bay, 263, 286–90
Native Department, 30, 32, 34, 102,
   170
Native Medical Practitioner (NMP),
   115, 118, 212, 218–19, 247, 310

Index

Index

Ohinemutu, 275
Ohio, 193
Okinawa, 201
Old Hospital Hill, Suva, 245
Oneata, 140
Ono-i-Lau, 138
Orcades, 314
Orient Line, 314
Orion, 115
Ormsby-Gore, W. G. A.; *see* Harlech, 4th Baron
Otago Centenary, 275, 278
Otago University, 132
Ovalau, 207, 301
Ovalau Club, 255
Overton, G. E., 250–1
Oxford, 10, 17, 21, 97, 100–1, 132, 135, 151, 244, 254, 280
oysters, 130

P & O, 108, 287
Pacific, 20, 26–7, 51, 59, 62, 69, 93, 112, 118, 133, 141, 156, 159, 165–6, 169, 179–81, 188–9, 191, 201–2, 225, 236, 238, 241, 257, 291, 305, 308; *see also* South Pacific; Western Pacific
Page, Milford Laurenson (1902–87), 277
Pakenham-Walsh, William, 51, 292
Pakistan, 6, 271
Palestine, 67, 109
Pan American Airways, 156
Panama Canal, 25–6, 143, 241, 244
Panama City, 26, 241, 244
Panama, Gulf of, 241
Papiamento, 25
Papua, 21
Papua New Guinea, 44
Parham, Bayard Eugene Vincent, OBE (1902–), 56, 205, 303
Paris, 101, 139
Parr, George (1826–91), 273
part-European(s), 16, 31, 48, 77, 80–1, 84–5, 87, 97, 121, 124, 193, 206, 208–9, 227–8, 235–6, 250, 261, 263, 268–70, 285, 301, 309–10
Part-Europeans' Sports Club, 79–80
Passant, George, 13
Patel, Ambalal Dahyabhai (1905–69), 161, 173
Patel, Shiwabhai Bhailalbhai (1894–1986), 135, 173, 197

Pattern of Islands, A, 21
Patton, General George Smith, CB (1885–1945), 193
pawpaw/papaya, 29, 49, 110, 137
Pearl Harbor, 91, 114, 159–64, 169, 183, 189, 191, 201, 290
Peebles, Ian Alexander Ross (1908–80), 72
Pemberton, Sir Max, JP (1863–1950), 128
Pennefather, Charles Edward de Fonblanque (1885–1949), 115, 150–1, 180–1, 191, 296
penny notes, 178–9
People from the Horizon, The, 225
pepper, 30
Perham, Dame Margery, DCMG, CBE (1895–1982), 21
Persian lilacs, 126
persimmon, 126
Peterhouse, 15
Petty Cury, Cambridge, 13–14
Philip, Prince, Duke of Edinburgh, KG, KT, OM, GBE, FRS (1921–), 237, 300
Philippines, 165, 183
Phoenix islands, 51
pidgin English, 20, 44
pigeon, 55
pineapple, 137, 245, 260, 267
Pitcairn's Islands, 26, 240–1, 245
Players, 12
Plumb, Sir John Harold (1911–), 16–17
Pollitt, Harry (1890–1960), 16
Polynesia, 68, 70, 80, 87, 128, 134, 155, 210, 290–1
Popplewell, Naomi, 2, 4
population, 62, 94, 130, 184, 226
Port Jackson, 24, 257
Port Said, 109
Post, Wiley, 41, 304
Potter, Brigadier Leslie, CBE, DSO, 168
Prentice, Francis Thomas (1912–78), 242
President of Fiji, 34, 84, 103, 132, 153, 205, 262
Prime Minister of Fiji, 206, 249, 308
Prince of Wales, 162
Probert, Jack (1892–?), 85, 162
Promin, 252
pronunciation in Fijian, 31, 33, 97, 121, 132, 307, 178n

338

Index

provincial commissioner(s), 20, 78, 113, 132, 137–8, 141, 145–7, 180, 186, 191–3, 199, 201–2, 210
provincial constable, 48, 57, 221–3
Provincial Council, 150, 210
Provincial School, 265, 282, 302
Puamau, Adi Veniana, 132–3
Public Works Department, 77, 137, 170, 255, 300
Pukaki, HMNZS, 298
Punjab, 285
Pushtu, 173

Qacavulo, 256
qaloqalovi, 104
Qolikoro, Lusiana, 132
Qoro, Ratu Aseri Latianara, OBE (1924–), 249
Queen's Road, Viti Levu, 155
Queen Victoria School, 77
Queensland, 54, 131, 199

Ra, 98, 155, 157, 199, 203, 248, 307–8
Ra, Roko Tui, 98
Rabe, 160, 263, 289–90, 292, 294, 296, 299
Rabi, Isador Isaac (1898–1988), 68
Rabukawaqa, Sir Josua Rasilau, KBE, MVO (1917–91), 209
Raddock, Patrick Tasman, MBE (1920–77), 269–70, 274, 312, 314
Radio ZJV (Suva), 302
Raghvanand, Bramhanand (1898–?), 234
rain trees, 58
Rairaiwaqa, 130, 267
Raitilawa, Josua, 121, 144
Rakaia, 244
Raman, Choy (1914–), 42, 48
Ramayan, 173
Random Harvest, 13
Rankine, Sir John Dalzell, KCMG, KCVO (1907–87), 198–9
Rankine, Sir Richard Sims Donkin, KCMG (?–1961), 198
rats, 52, 124, 165, 215, 244
Ravouvou, Semi, 268, 273, 276
Reay, Charles Stuart de Cairos, CBE (1895–?), 171–2, 180, 222
Receiver of Wrecks, 138
Red Sea, 109
Repulse, 162

Resident Commissioner, 160
Resident Magistrate, 174, 181–2, 188, 193
Rewa, 34–5, 37, 44, 55, 57, 143, 205, 209, 228, 244, 247, 256, 267, 294
Rewa Cricket Association, 208–9
Rewa River, 28, 41, 49, 63, 65, 77, 83–4, 89, 121, 203, 222, 250
Rhodes, Wilfred (1877–1973), 6
Ribbentrop–Molotov non-aggression pact, 89
Richards, Sir Arthur; *see* Milverton of Lagos and Clifton, 1st Baron
Richardson, H. R. W., 195
Richmond, Admiral Sir Herbert W., KCB (1871–1946), 15
Richmond Road, Leicester, 1–2, 7, 24, 114, 223
Riot Act, 171–2, 301
robber crab, 148–9
Robertson-Glasgow, Raymond Charles (1901–65), 106, 231–2
Robins, Robert Walter Vivian (1906–68), 72
Rodwell, Sir Cecil Hunter-, GCMG, JP (1874–1953), 71, 249
Rogers, William Penn Adair (1879–1935), 304
Roko Tui, 42, 82, 98, 122, 131–2, 171, 192, 205, 228, 249–50, 282, 313, 315
Ronaldson, Captain H., 200
Roosevelt, President Franklin Delano (1882–1945), 236
roqo tabakau, 100
Rose, John Holland (1855–1942), 14, 306
Rose, Kenneth Vivian, CBE (1924–), 73
Rose, Sir Alec Richard (1908–?), 306
rose apple, 259
Rotan, Tito, 290
Roth, George Kingsley, CMG, OBE (1903–60), 108–10, 244–5, 281–2
Roth, Jane F. Violet, 108, 110, 244, 281–2
Rotuma, 78–9, 292–3, 312
Rought-Rought, Basil William (1904–), 11
Rought-Rought, Desmond Charles (1912–70), 11–12
Rought-Rought, Rodney Charles (1808–1979), 11
Rounds, Jessie, 208, 312

339

Index

Index

Index

Sukuna, Ratu Sir Josefa Lalabalavu Vanaaliali, KCMG, KBE (1888–1958), 31–2, 41–2, 45, 66, 92–107, 110, 112, 116–19, 122, 126, 129–33, 135, 137, 142, 144, 147–8, 157, 159, 183, 197–8, 209–11, 220, 229, 231–2, 234–5, 244, 246, 249–50, 256, 263, 266–9, 280–2, 293, 296–7, 300–1, 306, 309, 311
Sunday Times, 202
superintendent of police, 46, 137, 181, 187
superintendent of prisons, 248, 301, 309
Supreme Allied Commander, 238
Supreme Court, 34, 194, 197, 301
Surrey, 243, 286
Sussex, 66, 211
Susui, 97, 152
Sutcliffe, Bert, MBE (1923–), 271,
Sutcliffe, Herbert (1894–1978), 314
Sutherland, William (1857–?), 99–100
Suva, 25, 28–30, 35, 39, 44, 46, 53, 56, 60, 65–6, 74–5, 79–80, 83–6, 90–1, 93, 96, 98, 102, 105, 107–10, 112, 115–16, 123–5, 129–31, 133, 135, 139, 143, 151–6, 159, 166–7, 170, 176–7, 180, 183–7, 194–5, 197–8, 203–4, 206, 209, 218, 226–8, 234, 239–40, 245–6, 248, 252, 255, 258, 260, 262, 265–7, 269, 276, 280–1, 284, 286–7, 293–4, 296–7, 299–300, 302, 304–6, 309–12, 314–15; street names in, 195, 306–7; wharf, 28, 74, 109, 163, 311, 315
Suva Bay, 27, 90, 109
Suva Cricket Association, 84, 108, 158, 209, 228, 314
Suva Cricket Club, 84
Suva Tennis Club, 228, 310
Suva Town Council, 85, 281, 302
Sweden, 124
Sweet-Escott, Sir Ernest Bickham, KCMG (1857–1941), 71
Sydney, 109, 156, 313–15
Szabados, Mike, 310

table tennis, 17, 18, 79–80, 86, 121, 246, 310; *see also* Fiji Table Tennis Association
taboo, 134
Tahiti, 130, 245, 305

Tailevu, 35, 207, 247
Tailevu, Roko Tui, 82
Taj Mahal Hotel, Bombay, 85
Takiveikata, Ratu Inoke M. (–1997), 205, 209
tamarind, 259
Tamil(s), 42, 44, 48, 173
Tana, Ratu Jovesa, 192
Tanganyika, 229, 295
tapa, 104, 147
taralala, 64, 216
Tarawa, 160–1, 201
Tareguci, Livai, 115–16
taro, 142, 208
Tarte, Adrian Rood, 261–2
Tarte, Daryl, 262
Tarte, Edith, 261
Tarte, James Valentine (1904–?), 262, 283
Tarte, Nell, 262
Tasmania(n), 51, 109, 126, 190, 304
Tassaforonga, 188
Tatler, The, 15
Taufa'ahau Tupou IV, King of Tonga, GCMG, GCVO, KBE (1918), 308–9; *see also* Tonga, Crown Prince of
Taukei ni Waluvu, 218–20
Taulevu, 212
tauvu, 221–2
Taveuni, 26, 28, 52, 78, 143, 148–9, 197, 206, 228, 249, 250–1, 255–65, 267–8, 282–3, 285–7, 290–2, 294–300, 302, 309
Tawake, Ratu Isireli (1889–?), 82
Taylor, J. G. F., 262
Taylor, Captain Sir Patrick Gordon, GC, MC (?–1966), 305
teak, 259
Tedder of Glenguin, Marshal of the RAF, 1st Baron, Arthur William Tedder, GCB (1890–1967), 213
Telegu, 173
tennis, 17, 36, 41, 48, 79, 166, 192, 194–6, 204, 206, 228, 235, 256, 265, 291, 296–7, 302, 310–11; *see also* Suva Tennis Club
Teulon, Joan, 224
Thames, River, 28
Thatcher, Baroness, Margaret Hilda Thatcher, FRS, MP (1925–), 120
Theodore, Edward George, 199–200